People of Pascua

People of Pascua

Edward H. Spicer

Edited by
Kathleen M. Sands and
Rosamond B. Spicer

The University of Arizona Press, Tucson

The University of Arizona Press
Copyright © 1988
The Arizona Board of Regents
All Rights Reserved

This book was set in 10/13 Linotron 202 Galliard.
Manufactured in the U.S.A.
The maps and diagrams in this book were prepared by
Nora Voutas from data provided by Rosamond B. Spicer.

98 96 94 93 92 91 90 88   5 4 3 2 1

Library of Congress Cataloging in Publication Data

Spicer, Edward Holland, 1906–
    People of Pascua / Edward H. Spicer ; edited by Kathleen M. Sands,
Rosamond B. Spicer.
        p. cm.
    Bibliography: p.
    Includes index.
    ISBN 0-8165-1069-5 (alk. paper)
        1. Yaqui Indians—Social life and customs.   2. Yaqui Indians—
Biography.   3. Indians of North America—Arizona—Social life and
customs.   4. Pascua Village (Ariz.)—Social life and customs.
5. Indians of North America—Arizona—Biography.   6. Pascua Village
(Ariz.)—Biography.   I. Sands, Kathleen M.   II. Spicer, Rosamond B.
III. Title.
E99.Y3S615   1988
979.1'77—dc 19   88-20802
                                                                        CIP

British Library Cataloguing in Publication data are available.

With love
to the people of Pascua Village without whose
patience and understanding this book
could never have been written.
Lios em chiokoebu ute'sia.

CONTENTS

ILLUSTRATIONS

Photographs

PREFACE

It was during the spring and summer of 1941 that Edward H. Spicer wrote the first draft of *People of Pascua*, as a report on fieldwork carried out in Tucson, Arizona, from July 1936 to July 1937, and from early 1940 through the summer of 1941. Somewhat later, he prepared a second draft of the report, with yet a third and final draft written in 1952 after he had returned to a teaching position in the Department of Anthropology at the University of Arizona.

Although the drafts were similar, each one contained changes in organization and new ideas garnered from colleagues' comments and suggestions and from his own experience and thinking in the intervening years. Other outlines with ideas for still different organizations of the material are in his files in the Arizona State Museum.

After a good deal of soul-searching and discussion, Spicer rather regretfully deposited all these drafts in the Arizona State Museum archives. He and others had come to the conclusion that although the material was of considerable importance as a study of Yaqui culture and of the varieties of Yaqui personalities and their contact with the surrounding ethnic groups, the descriptions of the individuals were too personal and might not be well received by the individuals involved or their families. The pictures of these persons are honest and sensitive, the analysis impartial, but the whole was not always entirely complimentary. The details of the lives were well known to most Yaquis, but putting them in published form was another matter. The book, Spicer felt, should wait; thus he sacrificed the professional recognition he would have gained from publishing the manuscript in order to protect the people who had entrusted him with their life histories.

Over the years, Spicer continued to talk about the manuscript and about his wish that it be published at some point. But *People of Pascua* was but one of many works with which he was concerned, and even after his retirement from teaching in 1978, other obligations prevented further work on the manuscript. *The Yaquis: A Cultural History* (1980) was being prepared for publication. His writing on persistent cultural systems throughout the world was underway; and he was editing Muriel Thayer Painter's *With Good Heart* (1986). Travel, correspondence, community involvement, presentations, meetings, short writing projects, and failing health all prevented the realization of publication of that early manuscript for which he felt affection, but more importantly, commitment.

In 1984, forty-three years after the first writing, and after the death of the author and most of those about whom he had written, we carefully evaluated the manuscript, decided that its time had come, and, with the encouragement of the University of Arizona Press, began to prepare it for publication. We have edited the volume with great care and a light hand. One of our primary concerns was that the author's ideas should come through clearly, never, of course, tampering with his concepts. We first worked separately, each reading the manuscript and making our own corrections and marking questions, and then together we discussed our suggestions and agreed on all changes.

During the three years we worked on this manuscript, we examined previous drafts and field notes for dates, verifications of spelling, and additional information. We also contacted Yaqui scholars who are Yaqui to clarify data, such as meanings of certain Yaqui names mentioned in the text, and to get their reaction to the content of the text, which was favorable. At the same time, we struggled with ways to remind the reader of the period of the study so that it might not be misinterpreted as being a contemporary work. In some cases we changed tenses, only to change them back again because the result was confusing. Most often we settled for opportunities to inject a date, or we excised a contemporary reference that would mislead the reader. Words like "now," phrases like "last year," or "in the last decade" were deleted or replaced with a specific date. Throughout, we edited for stylistic consistency, and occasionally we made rhetorical changes to clarify meaning or correct an error. At the request of the University of Arizona Press editors, we deleted repetitious material and, as a result, consolidated two chapters. The completed manuscript went through five editings, each one more refined. The point was not to change or improve the existing text, but to clean up the minor errors always present in a draft, to clarify ambiguous statements, to add information which would minimize difficulties for readers in approaching a work completed four decades before publication, and to provide updates on certain aspects of Yaqui culture and other cultures through the inclusion of editors' notes.

People of Pascua, as it stands now, is a description of Yaqui culture at a definite time and place—1936 through 1941 in Pascua Village, Tucson, Arizona, and surrounding environs. Updating it to a contemporary work would not only have been impossible and would have required enormous amounts of research that inevitably would have duplicated other works Spicer had written, but it would have violated his intentions of examining a particular period in the history of Pascua Village. *People of Pascua* is an early phase of Edward H. Spicer's forty-six years of study and writing about Yaqui people (over thirty published essays and four book-length studies) both in Arizona and Sonora, Mexico. It is a study now severely out of sequence in the chronology of his work. Had it been published in the early 1940s when it was completed, it would have been a useful companion volume to *Pascua, A Yaqui Village in Arizona* (1940), which is a comprehensive ethnographic study of the cultural patterns and institutions of the Yaquis of Pascua. The fact that *Pascua* was reissued in 1984 suggests its importance in the analysis of Yaqui culture and also provided impetus for publication of this book. With both volumes now available, Spicer's Yaqui studies are more complete and greatly enriched, and a record of the dynamics of Yaqui culture is readily accessible to a broad readership, including Yaquis who have come to acknowledge Spicer's work as an important contribution to the published record of their history and culture.

It is important to recognize that *People of Pascua* represents a time in Yaqui history that is past. Changes in Yaqui culture have been well documented by Spicer over the years, culminating in his comprehensive work, *The Yaquis: A Cultural History* (1980). This book treats of the dynamic and enduring nature of Yaqui culture—ideas that first germinated in his Pascua fieldwork in the late 1930s and early 1940s; it also describes many of the changes affecting Yaquis, and hence Pascuans, that have taken place since Yaquis entered the United States. In it, Spicer points out that significant changes in Arizona society in the late 1950s have had a major impact on the individual and collective lives of residents of Pascua. Post World War II growth of the Tucson urban area engulfed the village that in 1941 was on the edge of the city, making Pascua an enclave of ethnic culture within a modern southwestern city. Of great importance were economic developments in areas Arizona Yaquis had relied on for employment. For instance, a surplus of cotton led to cutbacks in production in the period following World War II, causing a serious reduction in labor forces. Introduction of cotton-picking machines by the mid-1950s led to further labor cutbacks, and the farm labor Spicer describes in *People of Pascua* all but ceased. With regular, family oriented agricultural work at an end, Yaquis were left to search out odd jobs, take temporary employment, or, with adequate training, make their way into service and production industries of various sorts, breaking ties with traditional, land-oriented work. Many were forced to seek economic assistance, at least until they could adapt to new job requirements. Other changes of a different nature were also taking place, especially through government programs that targeted the economically deprived for financial support. Housing improvements became a major community goal, and eventually support was gained so that modern housing became common in the village in the 1980s. But this same desire for better housing led to even more drastic changes when a group of Pascuans, assisted by a committee of local Tucsonans, in 1964, persuaded the government to grant to the Yaquis 202 acres of federal land fifteen miles southwest of Tucson for resettlement of Pascua residents who chose to move there. The Office of Economic Opportunity helped with this program. A significant number moved to the new village, and in 1978, through the efforts of the groups that founded the new village, Pascua Pueblo, the Yaqui people were recognized by the United States government as an American Indian tribe. By 1979 the new village was one of the largest Yaqui settlements outside of Mexico (Spicer 1980). These changes were not without problems for the people who remained in Old Pascua. Their population was seriously eroded as some two hundred residents moved to the new village, causing strain in fulfilling ceremonial work and resentment within the village toward former residents. The relationship set up with the government came fully loaded with bureaucratic complexities, delays, and demands that forced members of the village to adapt to new ways of approaching and solving problems. While further details of cultural change could be included here, they would simply duplicate Spicer's thorough analysis in *The Yaquis*; thus it is perhaps sufficient simply to point out that the intricate system of Yaqui contacts with the Anglo world intensified considerably after the writing of *People of Pascua* and continued to change each day, offering a rich area for further exploration of the issues and patterns revealed in this book. A sequel to *People of Pascua* might well provide a useful longitudinal study of a community under pressures which have brought far-reaching changes.[1] Certainly it would be useful to follow the lives of the younger individuals whose life histories make up a portion of the *People of Pascua* text in order to test the accuracy of Spicer's interpretations and the effectiveness of his methods.

The Use of the Narrative

As we worked toward the preparation of *People of Pascua* for publication, we came to hope that this book would not only take its proper place in the sequence of Spicer's work, but that it might demonstrate many of the advances made in the study of ethnicity and personality over the past four decades. We wanted it both ways—a historical piece and a contemporary work, too. We deliberately attempted, therefore, to incorporate certain things into our contributions to this book. In light of recent trends toward more humanistic writing in anthropology, and particularly the growing awareness and analysis of the impact of the anthropologist in a culture, and of the even greater effect of the anthropologist on individuals from whom he or she elicits information, we thought it important that a brief life history of Edward H. Spicer be a part of this volume. We agreed that since Roz Spicer was also collecting data with her husband during the 1936–37 and 1940–41 field periods, some sense of her life history seemed important, too. As David G. Mandelbaum (1973) says, "turning points" are extremely important for the understanding of life passage and life history studies. We expanded his statement to include not only the individuals chosen as subjects for life histories, but the collectors' as well. Hence, Roz describes the experience of living in Pascua as a turning point in the road of their work and life together, and she also charts the "turns" that brought them to Pascua. Her narrative style of recording their backgrounds and life in Pascua is also in harmony with new insights into anthropological writing. Vincent Crapanzano has recently demonstrated that Kluckhohn knew his business when he called for more information on methodology. In both *The Fourth World of Foster Bennett* (1972) and *Tuhami: Portrait of a Moroccan* (1980), Crapanzano makes explicit the collaborative nature of the life history method by narrating his view of his experiences in the field as well as presenting and analyzing the narratives he collected. Jean Paul DuMont uses the same strategy in his book *The Head Man and I* (1978), and Renato Rosaldo supports this approach in his work with Ilongot headhunters (1980) when he says that the first person narrative "can be a consciously chosen analytical method, not merely a literary device."

Though we have added elements of narration to this volume, it is Spicer's narration of Yaqui life histories that allows the possibility of the addition of narrative analysis of his methods and interpretations. Though Spicer never intended his portraits of Pascuans to be portraits in the literary sense—his eye was always on these individuals in relationship to cultural processes and forces—and reading them as biographies would be unsatisfactory, perhaps even for Yaqui descendants searching for life histories of their forebearers, Spicer's interwoven narration and interpretation is warmly human. The ambiguous nature of man—comic and tragic, flawed yet worthy of respect—is Spicer's concern. Nowhere in this book does he call any of the people about whom he writes a "subject." They represent types, but they are not simply objects of scrutiny. They are living people who affected and were affected by him. The lives of these sixteen people would be unknown outside of their own community if they had not entered into Spicer's project, and hence, into the pages of this book.

In using life history, Edward H. Spicer has not only contributed to the field of anthropology, but he has caught the drama of Yaqui history at a level of intimacy rarely found in nonliterary text. He has created a drama with compelling events, revealing dialogue, tense conflicts, characters who are believable and changing, a setting that is at once familiar and exotic, enduring themes, recognizable symbols and images, and perhaps most importantly, a viewpoint that is consistent and penetrating.

Names

We know that in *People of Pascua* Spicer was describing real individuals with whom he was well acquainted. He wrote the first drafts using the names by which they were called. In the third draft Spicer adopted some use of pseudonyms, though not consistently throughout. He did this, of course, to protect the identity of individuals. To the editors, this seemed unnecessary and ineffective, since, whatever device to obscure actual identity might be used, the Yaquis themselves would undoubtedly be able to identify the individuals. Furthermore, we knew from reading the field notes that the fieldworkers had frequently informed the Yaquis with whom they talked that the material might be used in a future publication and none had objected. Therefore, after much discussion, we decided to employ actual names in this book.

Interestingly, Yaquis, particularly in the period when they were persecuted and hunted down by the Mexican government to be either shot or deported, were in the habit of constantly taking on different names to escape detention or death. They are not averse to doing so even to this day. Perhaps in the light of this, the use of pseudonyms would have seemed to the Yaquis not totally inappropriate.

Ethnic Terminology

Many designations for ethnic groups have changed since the time when this work was written. At that time the term "Black" was not in common use. "Negro" was then the proper term. "Mexican American" or "Spanish American" was used for those who had come across the border from Mexico or whose antecedents had either been born in the United States or had crossed the border at some time. Various experimental names have been assayed, but "Mexican American" was the most accepted at the time of the writing of this book.

Orthography

In the field, Yaqui words were recorded in a modified International Phonetic Alphabet and they are so spelled here..The vowels in Yaqui are pronounced much as in Spanish, as are also the I.P.A. vowels. The glottal stop in Yaqui words is indicated by an apostrophe ('). During the mid-1980s there has been a definite effort on the part of a group of Yaqui scholars, working with both tribal elders and linguists, to systematize the writing of the Yaqui language and to publish a dictionary.

Photographs and Illustrations

The Spicer collection of photographs of Yaqui locales, events, and individuals, taken by Roz Spicer and David J. Jones, Jr., is the source of the photos in the book. They were selected by Roz Spicer because of her knowledge of the period and people of the study.

Yaqui Cooperation

The Yaqui tribe is among the first in the nation to develop and implement an official language and research policy requiring approval of all scholarship on Yaqui topics. This policy, enacted in the mid-1980s, postdates Spicer's field research and writing by four decades, but because of his concern for the personal nature of some of the material he collected and the use of biography in the *People of Pascua* text, and because we support the concept of Yaqui influence on the public dissemination of information concerning their traditions and history, we have made every effort, as we are sure Spicer would have, to cooperate with the Yaqui tribe and participate in the implementation of the policy that protects their villages from undue intrusion and gives them a measure of control over material published about their culture.

Our first step, even before beginning to edit, was to contact the one Yaqui whom we knew to be still living, Refugio Savala, the author of *Autobiography of a Yaqui Poet* (1980). Having cooperated with Kay Sands in preparing that book for publication, he readily gave his assent to the use of his biography in the Spicer text.

As well as consulting Yaqui experts during the preparation of the manuscript, in the spring of 1986 we placed a near-final draft of the text in the Pascua Village community center office for perusal by village residents, particularly subjects or descendants of those portrayed in the text. Realizing that it would be impossible to track down every descendant of those individuals portrayed in the biographies, we hoped to elicit a general approval from the San Ignacio Yaqui Council, which represents the village of Old Pascua. To that end, in the early spring of 1986, we went before that Council at an open meeting and requested response from Council members and any tribal members who wished to comment. During the ensuing discussion, tribal members requested that the manuscript be made available again, until May 1987, for further study. At the May meeting, the Council determined that it was not their role to confer an official approval and advised tribal members who had comments or objections to make them directly to the editors. As of June 1987, no objections had been raised, which we take to be tacit approval of the text and compliance with the spirit of the Yaqui language and research policy. Edward H. Spicer intended this work to contribute toward a fuller understanding of the Yaquis' experience in Arizona and their ethnic survival in an alien and rapidly changing setting. It is presented in his memory and in gratitude to those Yaquis who so generously offered their life stories for *People of Pascua*.

K.M.S.

R.B.S.

Looking Back Fifty Years

Rosamond B. Spicer

The experience of living in Pascua for a year really seems, as I think back, to have set the course of all the following years for my husband Ned and myself. One way to think of life is as a road, straight or meandering, with continual branchings. One follows the road, sometimes slowly, sometimes in great haste, and when the branches appear, one may stumble into one or another, hardly knowing there is a choice. Or sometimes one stands and with careful consideration chooses a certain branch, not really knowing where it may lead, selecting it just because it looks the most interesting or challenging, the most likely to lead to some satisfaction of a limitless curiosity, toward some understanding and ordering of the strange world in which we find ourselves. So it is was in the latter way that we chose the road which led to Pascua Village and the Yaquis.

Two Roads

It might be useful before proceeding with the description of our life in Pascua to say a little about our lives before that time. Ned was born to a family which practiced the way of life of the Society of Friends, or Quakers, and had lived a happy childhood in the single-tax community of Arden, Delaware.[1] He did not go to formal school until the seventh grade.

His experiences were rich in learning about the woods, about chores in a village without running water or electricity, in Shakespearean plays, in copying for his father long lists of words and phrases in the language of the Delaware Indians, and in hearing discussions of such subjects as political theory and philosophy. The Quaker way of life emphasized concern and respect for human beings; it had little in it of music or ritual.

His father died when Ned was sixteen and there followed, after graduation from high school, a period of wandering and working, interspersed with college or university. There was Commonwealth College, in Leesville, Louisiana, where the students raised their own food and sometimes had just molasses and peanut butter for every meal and where professors strongly affirmed the rights of *every* human being—including women. Then there was a stint as cook's helper and Ordinary Seaman on "banana boats" in the Caribbean, ore boats on the Great Lakes, and then on a freighter on the Atlantic to Germany. At the University of Delaware from 1925 to 1927, he gave up the study of chemistry and all desire to become a DuPont chemist and turned to English literature, writing, and drama. For a year at the Johns Hopkins University in Baltimore, Maryland, he became deeply absorbed in economics and wrote an outstanding paper on the labor movement in England; but here his work was sharply cut off by a stay in the Maryland State Sanatorium to control tuberculosis, probably contracted during his seafaring days. While at the sanatorium, he studied astronomy and contributed to astronomical knowledge by plotting the meteor showers of August and November.

After leaving the Sanatorium in 1929, he chose the road west, on a Greyhound bus, with but a few dollars in his pocket. He first became an orange picker in the Salt River Valley of Arizona, then washed windows at the Arizona Biltmore until they wanted to promote him to working indoors as "hall boy," at which point by fortuitous circumstance he joined the Arizona fruit inspection service and was stationed at Yuma and at Salome.

Inspecting cars, catching smallpox, exploring the desert, and reading widely, he studied Morgan's *Ancient Society* and Kroeber's *Anthropology*. After two years, by 1931, he finally had saved enough money to come to the University of Arizona, to the Department of Archaeology headed by Dean Byron F. Cummings. Although Ned's B.A. was in economics, it was mainly digging and potsherds that occupied him as he tried to associate the ancient cultures with what he had read in Morgan and to relate the prehistoric cultures to each other and to the life that emerged from those prehistoric diggings. A report on King's Ruin in northwestern Arizona constituted his M.A. thesis under Cummings.

During this period, Dr. John H. Provinse, a social anthropologist interested in primitive law, arrived from the University of Chicago to teach in Arizona's Department of Archaeology. He brought a broadened vision that led Ned in 1934 to take the road which led to the University of Chicago, where social and cultural anthropology, as well as linguistics, physical anthropology, and more studies in archaeology opened out new horizons for the serious student.

But again tuberculosis—or perhaps it was something more akin to valley fever—forced a stay of many months in Billings Hospital on the University of Chicago campus. Finally released, the road again led to Tucson, Arizona, and the renewal of the friendship with John Provinse. John, ever of the exploring mind and on the lookout for intriguing problems to study, had become aware of the little-known village of Yaqui Indians on the northwest corner of town and dedicated to San Ygnacio. He wondered why and how the Yaquis had revived their Easter ceremonies on the new economic base, so different from the agricultural one from which they had come. John had already arranged for two anthropology students, Philip Welles ("Felipe" to all his friends) and David J. Jones, Jr., to live there in the village in the nonfunctioning hospital building, and he suggested that Ned join them. Dave and Phil had stayed there while they attended classes at the university during the academic year 1935–36. Ned joined them in April 1936.

The "hospital" was an adobe building of eight rooms, with a tin gable roof and rather rough cement floors that were very hard to sweep. Miss Thamar Richey, a maiden lady and down-to-earth retired schoolteacher from Kansas, had seen the need of the Yaquis settled there in Pascua and in 1924 had prevailed upon the school district to build a one-room schoolhouse where she taught kindergarten and 1-C (pre–first grade). Two years later she had also somehow encouraged the construction of this hospital building, hoping it would serve to alleviate some of the medical problems in the village. I suppose funds were not forthcoming for the hoped for nurse and supplies, so she was allowing students who might "help the Yaqui Indians" to use it, rent free.

In the front three rooms of the "hospital" lived an old man who said he was a Mayo Indian. Felipe, Dave, and Ned had the four rooms in the back —two bedrooms, a kitchen, and a living room. The living room became a gathering place for a number of neighboring Yaqui boys and their friends and sometimes their sisters; they were attracted by Felipe's charm and his mastery of the guitar, his knowledge of Mexican songs and *corridos,* and his perfect facility in Spanish. They were also intrigued by his chosen footwear —Yaqui sandals. Dave managed some Spanish and was cheery and friendly. Ned had never studied Spanish, the language which he was most to use for the remainder of his life, though he knew some Latin, French, German, and Russian. He soon began to pick up Spanish and to study it with Alicia Aguirre, a friend of Felipe's. He also began to write down some of the Yaqui words and phrases which the boys gave him. They talked mostly in Spanish, though one of the sisters spoke good English.

Felipe and Dave and Ned, on their way back and forth to the university, saw that various kinds of ceremonies were sometimes in progress but did not attend any except those at Easter. Nor did the visiting Yaqui boys shed much light on the ceremonies. One ceremony, the funeral for a baby, they could see out the window. Others were at the church directly to the east of the "hospital"; there were ceremonies at other homes as well.

In June, Ned left for Chicago, to return on July 3, 1936, with his bride. We had met the day we both walked into the Department of Anthropology at the University of Chicago, even though we had been born within three miles of each other just north of Philadelphia, Pennsylvania. My road had been somewhat more standard. The community where I grew up, Bryn Athyn, was founded for the sake of a religion, Swedenborgianism, or the Church of the New Jerusalem. The religion was based on a new enlightenment, and the community was one which stayed much to itself, with its own schools, community life, and church. The ritual was somewhat like that of the Episcopal or the Catholic church; the education "classical." Along with the usual subjects, we studied Hebrew, Latin, Greek, and French; I heard many languages and accents—Spanish only once. My father was a scholar, like Ned's, with a deep interest in all people and an ability to be at home in a hut or a palace—which indeed he had been. On a memorable trip in 1929 he had taken the family to the West Coast and up to Canada and down to Mexico, the same year that Ned had arrived in Phoenix. Other summers I had spent in primitive cabins on lakes or at the seashore, and two at the University of Pennsylvania Museum working on ancient Egyptian pottery—at the same time rehearsing with a modern dance group for performance with the Philadelphia Orchestra.

My thirst for knowledge and "acceptable" (to my family) adventure took the road to Northwestern University where my "field of concentration" (a new concept at the time) was archaeology, of which cultural anthropology under Melville Herskovits was a large part. And then on to the University of Chicago in 1934 for further awakening there. A new road for me, a new awareness, came with the studies under Robert Redfield, A. R. Radcliffe-Brown, Fay Cooper-Cole, W. Lloyd Warner, and the others of that stimulating period. The study of Near Eastern history and hieroglyphics at Chicago's Oriental Institute, esoteric as it may seem, gave visions of another people and another culture. At the conclusion of my course work at Chicago, Ned arrived from Tucson and thenceforth our two roads led in the same direction.

The Road Together: to Pascua

The first road we took was toward Tucson and the village of Pascua, for the University of Chicago had seen fit to fund Ned's proposal for a year in the field to study the adjustment that this group of Yaqui Indians had made in their adopted home in the United States, how they had managed to remain distinct from the Mexican population, and how the elaborate set of ceremonies, particularly those at Easter, was maintained despite apparent assimilation into American economic life—the problem which John Provinse had outlined.

Our mothers, though saying nothing, doubtless wondered if we might be scalped. My father probably would have liked to join us, for he had done such things as spending six weeks on a University of Chicago geological expedition at the bottom of the Grand Canyon in 1906 and had visited the Hopi villages and taken offerings of watermelons down into the kivas.

For our trip west, "Rocinante," our Model A, was packed to the gills. On the running boards were strapped bedrolls (blankets rolled up in canvas and pinned with horse blanket pins—*not* sleeping bags). Suitcases and boxes of books made it necessary to tie down the cover over the rear baggage compartment with a rope. I cannot remember what they were, but the rest of our meager worldly possessions were tied to the front and rear bumpers. I do not recall any trouble with that hardy robin's-egg blue Model A coupe, other than the probability of a few flat tires. We both worked on those—before I could get my driver's license I had, at the insistence of my brothers, learned to mend and change a tire. Ned was attached to Model As because, he said, all you needed to fix them was a piece of baling wire.

Rocinante served us long and true. More than once we transported twelve to fifteen Yaqui youngsters and adults in it, and very frequently four or five. I do not remember the exact price of gas, but it was close to ten cents a gallon; a night's lodging was about $2.00. At the end of our honeymoon trip from Chicago, we arrived in Pascua on a hot Friday afternoon, July 3, 1936. I was a slender twenty-two, Ned a handsome twenty-nine. My first diary entrance was as follows:

Friday, July 3, 1936. We arrived in Tucson about 5:30 and went right to Doc's [John Provinse's]. After a pleasant supper and evening there, we finally headed for the village we would call home for the next year. It was a dismal enough feeling to arrive late in the evening with everything in the state that only two boys can keep it. Our welcome came from El Viejo, a blind old Yaqui who lives in the front four rooms of our house. He seemed glad to see us in a very reserved way . . .

This seemed a rather dreary and discouraging entrance into Pascua . . . and it seemed that it would be impossible to get to know anyone enough to be able to talk to him . . . The only encouraging thought was that every ethnologist must have been in the same position at the first try and that after all the Yaquis were just as human as we were.

The "Hospital"

I suppose it was hot, for the temperatures in the summer in Tucson go up to well over 100 degrees Fahrenheit, sometimes to 110. My previous experience with this kind of hot, dry heat had been on the 1929 trip when all I could think of was that we were driving through a blast furnace. But I do not really remember the heat at Pascua, only that a cooling shower could be taken in the heavy summer rains in the evening. Nor did we really mind the cold nights in the winter when we stayed at fiestas— we just added more warm clothes. I did not realize it then, but I have since learned that temperatures can reach well below freezing just before dawn in Tucson. We did not mind, I guess, because the Yaquis seldom complained and we were absorbed in our work.

Ned and I moved our belongings into the back four rooms and started to settle in. For a few months Dave occupied a fifth; when he left, it became a storeroom. A trunk was waiting for us which contained wedding presents—the fancy tablecloths and linens stayed therein! I quickly adapted to a more or less primitive way of living.

There were several wells in the village and our water supply was a thirty-five foot well, supplied with a bucket and pulley. Every so often the well had to be deepened. Our well was situated between the hospital and an adobe three-holer—with hot gravel and many puncture vine thorns precluding a quick run with bare feet. We did not use water from the irrigation ditch to the west of the village as many of the people did, but carried five-gallon cans from friends' homes, or from the Ye Olde Green Lantern across "Miracle Mile," the newly developing entrance into Tucson, for our drinking water. I quickly found out how efficient Aladdin lamps with their glowing mantles were—and also the nuisance of washing the chimneys every day. For a shower we rigged up a frame covered with burlap at the end of the wide hall. One stood in the square washtub and poured the water from a counter-weighted watering can. As a desert cooler for our food we made another burlap-covered frame above which hung a Papago *olla*. From a faucet, which we had inserted in the bottom of the olla, water slowly dripped onto the burlap. That olla and a couple of canvas desert water bags supplied cool drinking water. I washed clothes in the square washtub with water drawn from the well and warmed in the sun.

The kitchen had a three-burner kerosene stove that worked pretty well, a table and three chairs, various cupboards and orange crates for storage of food and a miscellaneous assortment of dishes and pots and pans. A study soon became a necessity, supplied with two tables, typewriters, and the ubiquitous orange crates. The bedroom had two narrow, folding metal cots, and again, the orange crates.

But probably the most important room in the house was the living room on the southeast corner, for there we had a bed which served double duty as a couch, two or three quite comfortable chairs, a rug, and a round table with a small supply of various types of magazines. There was also a hand-cranked phonograph and a small supply of records, and Felipe and Dave's guitars hung on the walls. I think, in proper housekeeping fashion, we put up homemade or borrowed curtains. In short, we had a home.

Village Activities

The hospital was on the north edge of the village, with a considerable expanse of desert between it and that dirt road then called DeMoss Petrie, now Grant Road, and there was desert as far as the eye could see to the north. To the east of the hospital was the religious plaza with the church of San Ygnacio made of railroad ties placed upright, the *Pascola ramada* of adobe, the fiesta kitchen enclosed in pieces of tin, and the much-used

The Plaza of Pascua Village, February 1937. Church of San Ygnacio, *center,* the "hospital," *right,* behind the pumphouse; the Pascola dance ramada, *left. Photograph by David J. Jones, Jr.*

Calle Matus, Pascua Village, March 1937. To the right is Pancha's store. *Photograph by David J. Jones, Jr.*

outhouse in the southwest corner. The plaza was enclosed with a wire fence. A gasoline pump had once supplied water for the kitchen and the now bedraggled tamarisk trees along the fence.

To the west and south of us were our neighbors. Their homes were made of sundry materials such as could be collected, most often from the city dump. We found through the year, however, that the people were continually adding to and improving their houses, building on new adobe brick rooms and changing the ramadas and houses as the need arose, needs such as a new composition of the household or a household fiesta with its special requirements.

It was obvious from the moment we arrived that the children and teenagers from the surrounding households were accustomed to visiting our house. From Ned's notes:

The . . . [neighbor family] women and children all came over in a body to see Roz while Mrs. Brown was here. They stayed around and disconcerted Roz because they didn't say much of anything.

But they did smile shyly. Many of our first visitors—and throughout the year—were the very young children of our neighbors, from age three and up. We tried to keep a supply of crackers on hand for them. The slightly older ones liked the Mexican records and the magazines, or just to visit and sit and chat, or to use our paper and crayons. The teenagers often brought their friends, who most often turned out to be *Matachin* dancers. English was out of the question, except with a few. I found that I would have to learn Spanish at once; from our visitors we had our first words of Yaqui. I bought a Spanish grammar and studied assiduously, and Ned and I together took a course at the "Y." Slowly, through trial and error, we became more and more proficient in both Spanish and Yaqui, until at the end of the year we were doing fairly well, though still lacking in complete comprehension. How we admired those young people who could speak two or three languages with ease, passing from one tongue to another at will! With most the preference was for Yaqui. There is no doubt that we could have learned more details and nuances had we started out with an ability to speak and understand Spanish and Yaqui, but because of our careful method of checking, observation, and participation, I do not believe that we made errors in understanding the people and the culture.

We welcomed all to our house, but we were at first as shy in visiting their homes as most of the Yaquis were in coming to ours. They had no reason to trust us and we discovered later that some of them thought we

Our frequent visitors,
affectionately called José
"Galleta" (cookie) Valencia,
left, and Feliz "Vichi" (hairless)
Valencia, November 1936.
*Photograph by Rosamond B.
Spicer.*

might be working with the immigration service to report on whether they
were in the United States illegally and should be deported. It just took
time to dispel that notion.

An early acquaintance was with the Mexican storekeepers, Joe and Pancha, who maintained a tiny store in the middle of the village. Joe was
friendly and anxious to talk about the state of the world, about religion
and philosophy, and about his neighbors and their activities.

At first there were, of course, many people whose names we did not
know when we went to the ceremonies. We had to refer to them in some
way so we used our own descriptive nicknames, such as "Bullet Head,"
"Mrs. Buck Teeth," or "Little White Pants," later learning and, of course,
using their real names. Yaquis also used nicknames, and we found out
eventually that Ned was known as "Tomato Face" because of his ruddy
complexion. I do not remember ever knowing what nickname they used
for me.

Ned and Dave and Felipe had had the opportunity to attend the Easter
ceremonies the previous spring (1936), had seen that there were other

activities around the plaza and various fiestas at households; they had learned the names of some of the ceremonial groups—but to me it was all completely new. My introduction to ceremony really came in mid-July when on Sunday there was an infant baptism with couple dancing; a few days later a baby funeral at which the Matachinis danced; a practice dance or vespers for the Matachinis on Thursday; what was probably a catechism class at the Santa Rosa church on Saturday; a name-day party with a *piñata* the same evening; on Sunday morning a service at the Yaqui church followed in the evening by a Matachin pole dance. On Wednesday there had also been a funeral in Barrio Libre which we hunted for but did not find. There were many weeks when ceremonies were this frequent, others when they were fewer.

Many Yaqui ceremonies last all night and into the next morning. We could not attend all, but a great many we did attend, with one or the other of us staying the night, for we learned that only when spending the night was a person fully participating and helping in the ceremony, even if he was not an actual ceremonial participant. It was also at these ceremonies that we became acquainted with and talked to the variety of people who attended them. A few words around a fire on a cold night, close attention to what took place at the ceremony—all of this led to our growing understanding and appreciation of the Yaqui life and culture. A ceremony also provided a time to learn the names of people, their place in the structure of the village, and about the various ceremonial organizations and their duties.

Neither Ned nor I had any knowledge of Catholic ritual from our previous backgrounds or experience. Perhaps it was just as well that we did not, though such knowledge might have been helpful in more quickly sorting out Yaqui practices from standard Catholic procedures. As it was, however, it was as much an ethnographic task to learn about Catholic ritual as used by the Yaquis as it was to learn about any other part of the Yaqui ceremonies. We recorded in detail what we saw at the ceremonies, including the *Maestro* service. We purchased a Missal and at times tried to follow the services with that, although the prayers and *alabanzas* were just as likely to be said or sung in Spanish or Yaqui as in Latin. The Maestros each had their own notebooks in which the various prayers were handwritten in any or all of the three languages. During the year we learned a good deal about what, in the ceremonies, was standard Mexican-type Catholic, and what was the Yaqui usage.

An older Yaqui man, Lucas Chavez, who is one of the people described later in the book, became much interested in our efforts to learn the Yaqui language and Yaqui history and one day came to our house and volunteered to tell us about what he knew. His stated reason for doing this was that students who are not "ashamed" to learn the Yaqui language could learn all about the Yaquis through their language and thus learn about the suffering of the Yaquis and could then help them in the light of this knowledge. In a letter of introduction to one of his relatives, Lucas said that Ned was "a student of all the languages of the universe" and that he, Lucas, was teaching Ned Yaqui.

The two men developed a respect and affection for each other. Lucas talked of Yaqui history from far in the past up to the most recent, about the Río Yaqui, and about the ceremonies and their meanings. He criticized or praised other Yaquis according to how well they practiced Yaqui values, the values which were those he knew from the Yaqui River. He was very clear about which Yaquis were of "good family." He himself was very devout and proper. His eyes would shine when reading certain passages from a Catholic prayer book. There were also many occasions which brought tears to his eyes, sometimes in sorrow that Yaquis were no longer doing things properly, sometimes when he felt that he did not have sufficient knowledge of some particular subject which he felt that he as a Yaqui should possess—such as kinship terms—and sometimes he was deeply affected by a death.

Using a borrowed trailer often Ned went out with various men to cut wood for the fiestas. When Lucas went along, he showed that he knew the desert and its plants and was an efficient woodcutter. When we had jobs to do, such as cleaning out our well, he often volunteered his help.

I speak of Lucas as some length since he was the first Yaqui who presented us with an organized view of his culture; during many hours of talk and throughout our stay, he was always ready to discuss Yaqui subjects with us.

Lucas was not paid any set sum, but we did always see that he had food to eat and wood to burn, and there were other exchanges. The interviews with him were the only formal, regular interviews that we held. All other talks were on an informal, irregular basis, while visiting at homes, at fiestas, or while being together in other activities.

Slowly our friends and acquaintances in the village widened as we attended the many ceremonies and strolled through the village. More and more people came to visit us, young and old, male and female. In November a man came to ask what to do about a drunk who had awakened his household the night before, trying to bother his wife, he said. Ned's method that time, and throughout, was to try and understand what had happened, to take the discussion to a Yaqui official, to try and reach a consensus of opinion about what should be done, and to discourage precipitous action—such as calling the sheriff—unless the Yaquis insisted upon it. In this particular case it was finally decided that the worried man would knock on our window if the drunk should bother them again during the night. We heard nothing further about it.

In late November and through the cotton-picking season, the village was almost deserted as the people went to live and work on the cotton ranches. Since we had been told where those ranches were, and where throughout the southern part of the state there were other villages where Yaquis lived the year round, we decided to visit those places. Carrying two or three letters of introduction, and having been given names of relatives of Pascuans in the various places, we spent two weeks making a tour, camping all the way. We were gratified to find a uniformly warm welcome everywhere we went. It was also a pleasure when we returned to Pascua to find a real welcome and to be told that we had been missed.

From that time on we became more and more involved in village life. We were informed of every fiesta, and indeed attended almost all, many through the whole night. They asked us to apply our skills to help out. Ned was asked to assist the *Fariseos* in making lists of the food needed for the various fiestas during Lent; many times he went out to cut loads of wood; he went to the *oficinas* to obtain permits for the fiestas from the sheriff so that they would know to send someone out to keep order— always a concern. Always a Yaqui accompanied him.

During the Matachin season they observed Ned's interest in the Matachin dance and, half seriously, asked if he would not dance Matachin. Our house came to be included in the village *limosnas* (the collection of food or money offerings by a ceremonial society), to which we always contributed what we could for a fiesta. Having been trained in a church choir, I naturally began to sing with the *Cantoras* (church singers) and was asked to do so frequently. Sometimes I helped with the altar decorations or with the cooking at a fiesta. Yaqui tortillas are characteristically at least eighteen inches across and take practice and skill to make; the Yaqui women could hardly control their mirth with my first holey and lumpy attempts. I felt highly honored when I was asked to don the kerchief and crown of a carrier of the Virgin.

We were often called upon to participate in another way that year. There was a measles epidemic and a great many babies and young children died. We were asked time and again to call the county doctor to ask that busy man to come out and then to conduct him to the households in need of his services. Often there was not much he could do—it was before the time of the "miracle drugs." There was pneumonia and tuberculosis, as well. Few villagers would go to the hospital, it was too lonely and too strange and the treatment too far from their experience. There were many deaths. A death meant gathering *padrinos* and *madrinas* (godfathers and godmothers) together, notifying the undertaker who was assigned the care of the county cases for that month, arranging with the Father at the church of the Holy Family for the funeral service, often going to other villages for a limosna, and many other errands. Our car was on call for all such occasions. We tried to fill in the gaps that our friends and neighbors could not. Our car and our English made it a little easier for them in these times of real need at the height of the Great Depression.

There were many times, too, when my interest and lay skill at nursing were of use, like in treating bad cases of impetigo, or cuts, and taking people to the clinic. All such things we did only when asked; we never interfered otherwise. Rather, we were interested in their way of treating illness.

Often family disputes were referred to us for mediation. Ned's gentle and nonauthoritarian way usually led to discussion and an attempt to get those involved to settle the problem themselves, rather than resort either to the courts or to blows, as sometimes happened. When requested, however, we did accompany people to lawyers or to court, making attempts to explain the procedures—and ourselves learning at the same time.

One day someone came over and said that there was a "bum" sleeping on the altar in the church and would Ned get him off. Ned went over and had a conversation with the man and got him to agree to sleep on the rug on the floor and not on the altar. That was agreeable to everyone.

Money was very scarce. Few families had a worker with a steady job. Wages, for anyone with any kind of a job, were very low. To give exact amounts would have little meaning in inflation dollars. Some people were actually without food at times. We sometimes helped to distribute food and clothing, and also frequently loaned a few dollars here and there, although our funds were often low, too, particularly toward the end of the month. I doubt if we had a great deal more than some of the Yaquis ($100.00 a month as a grant from the University of Chicago), but at least it was regular. I cannot remember that we left being owed anything by any

Yaqui. That they always paid back what they borrowed was their reputation with everyone.

We bought an inexpensive ($12.95, I believe) 35mm Argus camera shortly after we arrived in Pascua; Davie Jones had a good Voitlander, lent to him by Tad Nichols. All the pictures that we took were with permission, whether of ceremonies, houses, or people. Many were by request. We always kept a set of the pictures handy for people to look at. If anyone requested copies, we always had them made and took them over to the family. For most, those were their only pictures of the period. I do not know of anyone else who owned a working camera or had money to buy film. I wish I had had the camera handy when Ned acted as Santa Claus at Miss Richey's school Christmas party.

Miss Richey did a great deal for the people. She was unremitting in her efforts to collect food and clothes for those in need. Every day in her almost-uniform of starched white skirt and shirtwaist she visited the homes in the village to see who was sick or lacking in food. The welfare department knew her for her referral of cases to them. She loved the little ones in her school room and did her best to make them "good citizens" and send them on to regular school with the ability to speak English. With her sturdy sense of justice she defended the Yaquis' right to practice their own religion, probably as sturdily as she would have defended her own right to be a Presbyterian. We heard her more than once scolding a missionary for interfering with village ceremonies by playing gospel hymns and preaching at them—in English—over his car's loudspeaker. She could not stand the thought of the Yaquis being "condemned to hell," as some of the missionaries said, because they were not of that particular missionary's persuasion.

A duty which fell on us with some frequency were requests by employers to find workers in such occupations as making adobes, farming and ranching jobs, or gardening. We would always try to fill their needs and spread the word that such and such a job was available. Usually, one of the village leaders would then take over the task of actually trying to find the requested workers.

From the various kinds of assistance which we were able to give grew remarks that Ned should be *Kobanao* (governor) of the village. On the Yaqui River there were Kobanaos who handled the affairs of the villages; in Pascua there had been a Yaqui "chief," Juan Pistola, and several only partially recognized "chiefs" following after Pistola. There was indeed a need for someone in that role. Ned felt complimented, as we certainly were when we were called *Yoemem* (the Yaqui term for themselves), but of course he never presumed or wished to take that role. He only tried to help where he could. Perhaps our place in the society was more practically expressed by this statement by a villager: "We need an American in the village. They [the Yaquis] don't know where to go to get things done." In any case, we were at times kept very busy.

But it was by no means a one-way street. There were many times when Yaquis would come to our aid, as when we had to fix the roof after it had been blown off by a dust devil, or when we had to deepen our well. We also borrowed things, like the trailer to haul wood, for we had to have wood for our little heating stove, as the villagers had to have wood for their households and their fiestas. Someone had a crowbar we sometimes had to borrow, and there were other items which they willingly shared with us, as they also shared their food, both at fiestas and in their homes. Perhaps what they gave most, however, was their friendship, their trust, their understanding of our needs, and their knowledge of their culture.

Ned Spicer with his *ahijado* (godson) of the rosary, Feliz Valencia, and Feliz's mother, Manuela, March 1937. *Photograph by Rosamond B. Spicer.*

Roz Spicer with Luis Alvarez on the porch of the "hospital," February 1937. *Photograph by David J. Jones, Jr.*

The trust and friendship was made apparent when Ned was asked to become *padrino del rosario* for a little neighbor boy. That happened at Eastertime, and it was to us a very meaningful occasion, as it was to be addressed thereafter as *nino* and *nina, compai* and *comai* (godfather, godmother, co-father, co-mother) by many who had heretofore been just friends. We were then actually a part of the social structure and realized that we had taken on ceremonial and social responsibilities. I was asked to be a madrina by one of the Fariseos, but it turned out that that year he served as Fariseo in Barrio Libre instead of in Pascua. He later said that he was sorry that it had turned out that way.

A trait which often delighted us was that of a keen sense of humor. We were aware of it in the ceremonial context of the *Pascola* banter and their seemingly ridiculous and imaginative stories. We saw the play of the *Chapayekas* where in superb fashion they mimicked such things as Americans taking pictures or playing a game of golf, making people laugh delightedly. The humor was in everyday life, too. There was an old man, a hard worker, who sometimes got drunk and in that state seemed very happy.

He would come home and sing to his mesquite tree or have a conversation with an imaginary horse. One day as he was approaching us in such a mood, one of the young men with us remarked quietly, "Here comes the radio again." One never knew when some such humorous remark might be forthcoming. And all such manifestations were much appreciated by those who heard. In teaching us the language there were many jokes and plays on words in which they instructed us.

There were numerous Yaquis who showed great musical and artistic ability. Most of them obviously loved music. Our guitar was often borrowed and, in walking through the village, it was usually possible to hear someone playing or practicing a guitar, a violin, a harp, a flute, or a drum. Some could play all of those instruments, picking up the skill entirely by ear. Ned's one tune on the mandolin and my feeble struggle with the guitar were certainly no match for these able musicians. They also seemed to conquer complicated rhythms and dance steps with ease. One day we had as a guest Anna Mae Sharp, a fine violinist who taught at the University of Arizona. A Matachin violinist came to listen to her playing and the complete absorption reflected in his face was wonderful to see. She played European classical music and he, on her violin, played the European-derived folk tunes which the Matachinis dance to. It was a remarkable exchange.

All through the year our Spanish and Yaqui had been improving. We had come to understand and speak Spanish fairly well. In fact I find a note which says, in connection with a visit with a woman three times my age with whom I was speaking Spanish, "I felt we were just two friends gossiping." In Yaqui we could get the gist of what was being said and carry on simple conversations, and we were continually trying to learn more. However, after some ten months of learning, when Ned and I were sitting with several people while they were talking Yaqui, Ned comments in his diary: "Roz and I sat there like poor stolid Indians with nothing whatever to say." But we could and did teach several to write Yaqui.

Our Friends

Though we were actively involved with many people in the village, it is largely with the people of whom Ned writes that we were most involved, whom we knew the best. They willingly shared with us their thoughts, their doubts and fears, the happenings in their lives. On the surface his writing about them may appear detached and analytical, but back of it is a depth of feeling and a warmth of understanding. Had Ned written this as a novel, there would be more of a development of characters. What he has done is another way to delineate character and, even more than character, to describe where each person fit into Yaqui culture, what each contributed to it, what each derived from it, as well as their relationship with the other surrounding cultures.

So far what I have sketched has been in rather general terms. I would like to say a few words about our association with each of the people about whom Ned writes. Lucas Chavez I have already mentioned. Tomás Alvarez, the Matachin Kobanao, we began to know soon after our arrival in Pascua. It was the young Matachin dancers who so often came to our house, and after seeing us at a few ceremonies Tom came also, though at first rather shyly. He was warm and friendly. Ned at one point described him as debonair. He encouraged our interest in the steps and patterns of the dance and before long he was inviting us to eat at the table with the Matachinis and their musicians and would have had me dancing Matachin had I been a boy. He had no car and was much in need of our help in transportation. Though criticized for his lack of knowledge, he was, nevertheless, one of the leaders of the village, and he sought our help in various ways.

Although not himself an active ceremonial participant, Rosario Escalante was the husband of the head altar woman, and other members of his family were much involved in ceremonial affairs. The whole family was knowledgeable, hospitable, and friendly, and we found ourselves welcome and easy in visiting their home. Josefina remembers when we were Cantoras together.

Cayetano Lopez lived near us. For many years he had had considerable dealings with "gringos," and he early came to find out what we were up to and also how we might be of use to him. His life had not been too happy or satisfying, but he had intellectual curiosity and did a good deal of reading in English, trying to gain a knowledge in law and history. He rather liked to expound his beliefs to Ned, who found his ideas, as well as his values, often somewhat confused. Nevertheless, throughout the year he was most helpful, enjoying telling us what he knew and how he interpreted things. He was deeply concerned that Yaquis might be deported or unwisely, he felt, influenced to return to the Río Yaqui.

Though Refugio Savala came to Pascua only briefly, we talked with him several times while he was in town. Earlier he had been in contact with John Provinse at the University of Arizona, and had taken John some of his poetry and other writings. A deeper acquaintance came in 1939–40 when Ned was teaching at the university. We came to appreciate the depth of his thinking and the poetry of his soul.

Jesús García we came to know during the course of ceremonial events. He still occasionally danced Matachin and was one to the leading Chapa-yekas. He seemed to feel that we were acceptable and even allowed me to nurse his badly cut foot.

We saw and talked to Juan Silvas at many ceremonies. Perhaps we had the closest contact with him over a family affair where we were brought in as mediators by both parties. At times I thought he would have made a tough Yaqui warrior (though I was recently told that he was part Mayo).

Guadalupe Balthazar was referred to by almost all Pascuans as being the reservoir of knowledge about Yaqui culture, especially about the meanings of Yaqui ceremony. He was the head *Temasti*. We saw him methodically going about his duties in the church and at household fiestas, quiet but friendly, always dignified. Later on in the year we called on him at his home and received a courteous welcome. Had we been fluent in his language, I think he would have given us more of the benefit of his acknowledged wisdom, though in Spanish he did tell us many things.

With the harpist, José María Casillas, and his whole household, we had a free and easy contact, although they only occasionally visited our house. He was a musician and a craftsman, making harps for his own use, for other harpists, or for collectors; he also carved Pascola masks. At the wedding of his daughter, I steadfastly refused a glass of whiskey which he proffered, until I finally got the signal that it was the expected thing to do.

Partly as a carryover from our Anglo culture, and partly being sensitive to what seemed to be expected in Yaqui culture, Ned more freely associated with the men and I with the women. There certainly was no strict dichotomy, but under ordinary circumstances it was just easier that way.

Juana Amarillas was a woman of great inner dignity who always showed devotion to her family and to her duty as Cantora. Though we saw her constantly at ceremonies, for a long time we did not know her name. Eventually, however, she became one of my closest friends. At one point she held her arm next to mine, saying, "The skin is of different color but the blood inside is the same." It was also of her that the well-known portrait artist, Eben F. Comins, said, "She reminds me of my New England grandmother."

One always remembers Josefa Araiza, whom we called Chepa, as wearing a broad grin on her round and powerful face. As the head *kiosti,* we saw her at most ceremonies. She certainly was not loquacious, but she was accustomed to quiet command. She spoke Yaqui by preference, as did most of the older people, but was quite conversant in Spanish. She seemed a woman of action and had to consider the question carefully if asked about the meaning of those actions. To drop in at her house was always a pleasant experience.

Joaquina Martínez, Chepa's daughter, was seldom at ceremonies, though she was sometimes in the kitchen and helped to teach me how to make tortillas. She was visibly distraught when her husband was found dead. We attended the whole of the funeral service and the burial and gave some small assistance. Joaquina and the whole family rather accepted us after that.

Two of the young people whom Ned describes were members of this same family. Dolores Richey Martínez we had taken on a number of Matachin limosna trips to Marana and other places. I can still see him squeezing into the little compartment behind the seat of Rocinante. Watching him dance as *Malinche* was to be aware that at age twelve he was an accomplished dancer in those complicated steps and patterns. He sometimes did not stay all night at a ceremony because he had to go to school in the morning. He was a handsome lad, a good student, always polite, rather serious but appreciative of a good joke. Josefina Escalante, somewhat older than Richey, was a Cantora. With her regular features and pleasant look she seemed one of the most attractive young girls in the village. Both spoke quite good English, as well as Yaqui and Spanish.

Joe D. Romero was a rather constant companion of Tomás Alvarez, and we saw a good deal of him. He enjoyed coming to our house and looking at our magazines and pictures. He appeared really to enjoy dancing Matachin and was becoming one of the leaders in the dance formation. He seemed to like to draw us into the village life just because he enjoyed his life and he liked us. He asked little in return.

Young Presillano Valenzuela, about eleven, and Salamina, his older sister who was in her early twenties, were among the first who visited "the boys" in our house. "Presie" came often with his somewhat older brother, Dolores, who danced Matachin just because he wanted to. They belonged to a family which ran the gamut in the ways of viewing Yaqui life, from the grandparents' complete adherence to old Yaqui ways to the young people's experimentation with the ways of the culture that surrounded them. They had what seemed more than their share of sickness, death, and other troubles. We were called upon to bring the doctor, arrange funerals, and even to intervene in family quarrels.

To the best of my memory of that time, now some fifty years ago, and with reminders from various notes, these are thumbnail sketches of our relationships with the people whom Ned describes in Part II of this book. Each was different in life view and experience from all the others. We were friends with all and liked them each for their own special qualities. I guess they liked us for their own reasons. A young woman made a more general kind of statement to me one day:

The Yaquis think that you are very curious about Yaqui things. But the Yaquis like you very much because you help the people who are sick, you help in funerals, and you stay up all night at fiestas.

The relationships and happenings which I have been describing took place over the span of the year, 1936 to 1937. In this time we learned to know these people and they became our friends. We learned what remarkable people they are; we learned their strengths and their frailties. We learned how they contributed to the culture of which they were a part, and we learned what "being Yaqui" meant to them. We indeed came to share their lives, and we felt their generosity in allowing us to do so. We were involved, almost totally. I hope I have indicated how much and in what ways. We were involved, yet both we and they knew that we were "gringos" and they Yaquis—Yoemem. A few days before we left we were discussing with the Captain of the Fariseos, who was also a Maestro, what should be done about a very ill Fariseo, and the Maestro commented:

You ought to stay here longer because you do not know nearly all about our religion; there are many things that you have not seen so far. Everything does not happen inside of one year and if it does not happen you cannot see it.

He spoke the truth. In the years since 1937 we have continued to learn more—and there is still more to learn. In the fall of 1939, after a year and a half at Dillard University, a Black university in New Orleans, we returned for two years to Tucson where Ned was instructor in the Department of Anthropology. A grant-in-aid from the Social Science Research Council in the spring of 1940 allowed us to work again with the people of Pascua. Since we could not at this time reciprocate in helping out at the village to the extent that we had when we lived there, we either visited in the village or Ned brought in to the university the various persons about whom he wished to write. Lucas Chavez proudly delivered a lecture in one of Ned's classes. The interviewees were given recompense for their time. The same amount was paid to various students in anthropology who helped to organize and file the large amounts of material. We both talked with the various people and always explained the purpose of the project, finding them most willing to cooperate.

During the federally required alien registration in the summer of 1940, Ned assisted many Yaquis in filling out the government forms, both at the downtown post office and in the Pascola ramada at Pascua. Some of the Yaqui leaders had suggested that this would be helpful. He tried to explain to the worried Yaquis what was required and to assuage their fears. He even gave the requisite oath, in Yaqui, to one old man who had become confused in Spanish.

During part of the summer and fall of 1941, we once again went and lived in the hospital at Pascua while we were waiting for permission from the Mexican government to go to live and study on the Yaqui River in Sonora. The Yaqui River was the homeland of the Yaquis and from whence, over many years, they had come to the United States. We lived in the town of Potam on the Yaqui River during part of 1941–1942 and returned after the war years in the summer of 1947 and again briefly in 1970 and 1979.

After returning to the University of Arizona in 1946, we began working again with the Yaquis around Tucson on various problems and projects, visiting them and attending their ceremonies. During the years we have been aware of many changes.

There is always more to learn.

Ned and I together chose the branching of the road of life that led us to involvement with the Yaqui people. The choice of this path has had a profound influence on our lives; perhaps there has been some small measure of influence on them, as individuals and as a group.

Being absorbed in the workings of Yaqui culture gave us insight into, and help in understanding, the many other national, ethnic, and minority groups with whom we have since worked or had contact—Papagos, Seris, Apaches, Hopis, Navajos, Cherokees, Blacks, Mexicans, Japanese, Catalans, Basques, Irish, and Welsh. Branching out to all these groups from a Yaqui base led to theoretical formulations about culture and society, and to recognized scholarly contributions to anthropological theory. Thus

Ned's career, by the chance that our road led to the Yaquis, could be said to be firmly based on a Yaqui foundation. Of direct financial gain from work with the Yaquis, through writing or any other sources, there was little. The gain was rather in the direction of a career in teaching and research; in other words, in an enhanced ability to pass on to students, to colleagues, to the public, to other groups, the wisdom derived, at least in part, from the remarkable year at Pascua Village, S.Y.

People of Pascua

Yaqui Indians in Arizona, 1880 to 1941

Scattered across Arizona, along the line of the Southern Pacific Railroad from Nogales to Yuma, live some 3,000 Yaqui Indians. They are very much a part of the conglomerate, mobile society of the rapidly growing southwestern state in which they have lived for more than fifty years. Like the Spanish-speaking Mexican Americans and the English-speaking Anglo Americans of the region, they have shifted residence from town to town, moved from town to cotton ranch and back again, worked where work was available, gone on relief, and helped to build the railroad, the highways, and the irrigation systems. The Yaquis say that their forebearers had roamed the country even before the coming of the Spanish.

Some have lived among and intermarried with the relatively secluded Papago Indians on and off their reservations; some have lived briefly on the less secluded Pima Indian reservation; a few have known and intermarried with Negroes; many more have lived among and intermarried with Mexican Americans; and all the younger ones have mingled intimately with all the varieties of children in the Anglo-American dominated schools.

Yet with all this shuffling about and intermingling with a variety of peoples the Yaquis have remained distinct. Their distinctness is something which not only they feel, but something of which the peoples among whom they live are very much aware.

That this small group of immigrant Indians, for a large part refugees from Mexico, should have retained its identity in the welter of races and traditions in southern Arizona is not necessarily cause for surprise. There are other equally small groups of Indians in various parts of the United States, isolated on reservations, who have not been swallowed up in the dominant culture of their regions.

Indeed, if we extend our view to include others besides Indians, it is apparent that one of the striking features of the society of the United States is the existence within it of groups who for generations have been regarded by others as diverging from some supposed norm of common culture. Every region of the United States contains some such groups, both rural and urban. The Iroquois of New York state, the Acadian French of Louisiana, the rural Spanish Americans of New Mexico, the Polish ethnic enclave in Chicago, the Chinatowns of many of our metropolises, the Amish of Pennsylvania, and a great many others are products of this persistent process of the encysting of peoples in the society of the United States. It is of such common occurrence that it is surprising to find, as widespread as it is, the assumption that the normal, expectable course for immigrants and for enclaved native groups is assimilation.

It is true, of course, that an equally striking feature of life in the United States has been an assimilation of immigrant groups to certain aspects of the dominant culture that have become widespread over the country. Second- and third-generation immigrants and portions of the Indian population have been intensively subjected to a form of directed culture change through a fairly uniform school system which has spread widely among them certain patterns of social behavior and certain traditions. Most of the distinct cultural groups in the United States may be explained largely in terms of isolation from the school system, or in terms of the influence of a parallel, but different, system of education. The prominence of assimilation, so closely bound up with this special feature of the culture of the United States, has tended to focus attention away from the cases in which assimilation has not taken place and even to influence scientific opinion in the direction of assuming assimilation as the usual result of immigrant minorities coming into contact with an established larger society.

The obvious fact is, however, that small immigrant groups, even in the United States with its highly developed and specialized instrument for assimilation, behave in different ways. Under certain conditions successive generations become more and more assimilated; under other conditions there is not a regular and progressive assimilation from generation to generation; and under still other conditions, rare in the United States, the changes in the culture of the immigrant groups cannot be described in terms of assimilation.

The instance of the Yaqui Indians in Arizona is one among many in the United States in which it is possible to examine the conditions under which men and women persist in maintaining customs and beliefs which are quite dissimilar from those of their neighbors. It is an especially interesting case because it cannot be explained in terms of such simple factors as geographical isolation, or racial differences giving rise to social distance, or even of economic specialization establishing for the group a unique role in the total economic system. The Yaquis, as we have indicated, intermingle and intermarry with the heterogeneous population of southern Arizona; they do not live apart like many of the other Indians on relatively isolated reservations. In racial characteristics they differ from a majority of the Anglo Americans, but they are not racially distinct from other Indians, nor from a majority of the Mexican Americans, from all of whom they maintain an identity quite apart. In adapting to life in Arizona they have taken up ways of making a living which do not differentiate them from Anglo or Mexican Americans or others in the region; hence their distinctness is not bound up with any unique economic specialty.

It is to other factors that we must turn in our effort to understand the place they have assumed in Arizona society. These other influences lie rooted in the events of Mexican history during the nineteenth century and in the specific type of institutions and ideas which Yaquis have developed through several centuries. In Arizona, as refugees from a tribe defeated and dispersed in the late 1800s by Mexican military action, Yaquis' experiences have differed sharply from those of the people .among whom they have settled. These experiences have produced a particular set of attitudes and goals in Yaquis, and knowledge of Yaqui history has also affected Anglo Americans and Mexican Americans and produced a special set of attitudes toward Yaquis. Moreover, the cultural traditions which Yaquis have carried with them from the state of Sonora, Mexico, into Arizona are of a kind, as we shall see, which have been especially effective for the transmission of behaviors and viewpoints from one generation to another. As we examine this historical and cultural background of the Arizona Yaquis, we begin to understand the conditions which have brought about the preservation through three generations of their identity as Yaquis. We gain some understanding also of the manner in which they have balanced the acceptance of many features of the culture of the United States with adherence to their own traditional ways. We shall, in other words, gain insight into processes of assimilation as they work in conjunction with processes of cultural conservatism under conditions of culture contact.

The method chosen for this study of acculturation is that of the analysis of the life stories of individual Yaqui men, women, and children. The persons whose experiences are presented span in their lives one of the three most important periods in the history of the Yaqui people.

Three times since 1600, events have taken place in the Yaqui homeland in Sonora which have resulted in profound changes in the way of life of Yaquis. The first of these occurred during the first quarter of the seventeenth century. It was marked by battles with Spanish soldiers in which the Yaquis were victorious and yet after which they invited missionaries to come into their territory. Jesuit missionaries, including the vigorous Antonio Pérez de Ribas, arrived in the Yaqui country in 1617. Rapidly, they baptized hundreds of children, built churches, introduced European wheat and cattle, and turned Yaquis toward the acceptance of many Christian ideas and rituals. Within twenty-five years after the arrival of the Jesuits, their influence had extended widely throughout the estimated 30,000 Yaquis. The effects were deep-going. During the next century Yaqui society was reorganized along the lines of the European Christian villages of the 1500s. Jesuit religious ideas and Spanish military and political ideas fused with aboriginal Yaqui traditions. As the former slowly gained dominance during more than a century of peaceful contact, the distinctive Yaqui culture crystallized, a culture which was neither wholly Indian nor wholly Spanish, but something new. It is this culture which persists in main outline even down to 1941 in Arizona.

The second period of change and new influence came some two hundred years after the arrival of the Jesuits, in the second quarter of the nineteenth century. As before, the new era was ushered in by warfare. Mexico's War for Independence in 1820 resulted in social upheaval and political confusion in northwestern Mexico. As Spanish control disintegrated and the Mexican government falteringly attempted new controls, a Yaqui leader called Juan Bandera, inspired by a vision of the Virgin of Guadalupe, conceived the idea of Indian independence from Mexico. His plan included the Opatas, the Lower Pimas, and the Mayos as well as the Yaquis. Working with leaders of the other Indians, he formed an effective military organization and for several years seemed close to gaining the goal of independence. Defeated in battle in 1832, his vision and his military-political organization nevertheless became the source of a new era for Yaquis. For the next sixty years, sporadic fighting and smoldering rebellion characterized the relations of Yaquis with the Mexicans in Sonora. The Yaqui villages adapted the Jesuit-inspired ceremonial organization to purposes of warfare, and each village became a closely integrated unit with a highly distinctive government of church, civil, and military officials. The nineteenth century form of Yaqui culture was again something new, based solidly on the Spanish-Indian forms of the preceding century but adapted to conditions of almost constant warfare.

The third period of rapid change began in the 1880s and extended into the early twentieth century. Its beginning was marked by decisive military defeats of the Yaquis in the later 1880s and early 1890s. The defeats were followed by the flight of thousands of Yaquis from their homeland and the deportation by the Mexican government of thousands more to various parts of Mexico. The defeats temporarily destroyed Yaqui organization, except for small groups of guerrillas remaining in the mountains, but they did not destroy the symbols or the memory of the old institutions in terms of which Yaqui culture had been integrated during the nineteenth century. The widely dispersed Yaquis came into contact, all over Mexico and the southwestern United States, with other peoples and with technology and political institutions of Western civilization. However, wherever they settled they began to some extent to revive the old forms of Yaqui culture in the new settings, leading to redevelopment, or revival, of much of the old culture, but in forms which of necessity have had to be adapted to a new set of social and economic relations.

As Yaquis have settled down again after the dispersal, three varieties of Yaqui culture have developed, one in the old homeland on the Yaqui River, another in the Sonora cities, and the third in the settlements in southern Arizona.

The older people whom we shall consider in this study are men and women who have lived through this third period of social upheaval and culture change. As we review their lives, we see what it meant to live in a Yaqui village prepared for war; we live through battles with them and follow them in flight for their freedom or for their lives. We gain some idea of what the break-up of families meant, of how children were forced to take up new lives far from relatives, alone among strange people. We see how Yaquis came together again in Arizona and, as we see them trying to rebuild a society, we begin to have some understanding of what they gain from the revival of Yaqui symbols of solidarity and Yaqui institutions. We see the influences on the new version of Yaqui culture of peace, hard times,

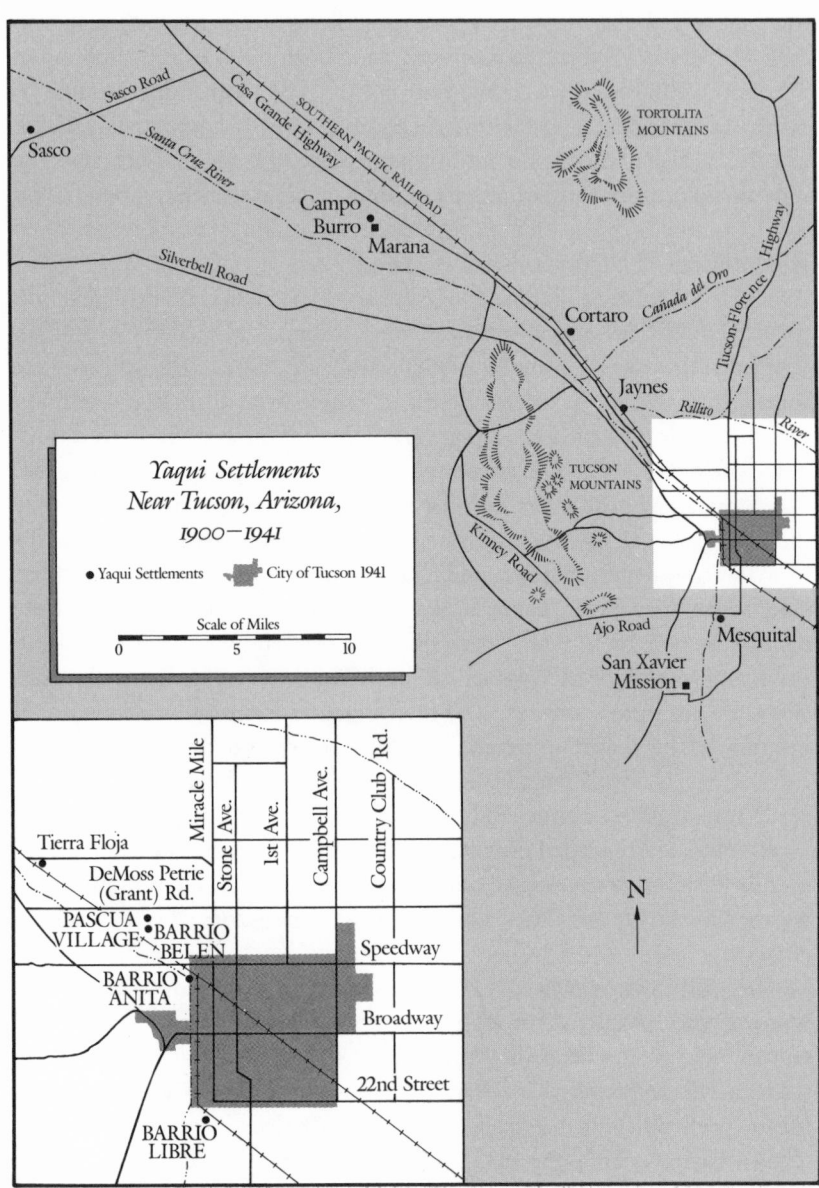

Yaqui Settlements
Near Tucson, Arizona,
1900–1941

● Yaqui Settlements   City of Tucson 1941

Scale of Miles
0   5   10

increasing job opportunities, the sense of being strangers in a new land —influences that work always through the complex channels of individual men and women.

The younger people are the children and the children's children of the men and women who lived through war and the dispersal. Part of the cultural environment that they have grown up in has been established for them by their parents, but they are experiencing other ways of life through school and friends and jobs. They clearly have the problem of reconciling what their parents have re-established as the right and proper way to live with other customs and other standards. Their needs in the new situation and their awareness of other points of view are inevitably influencing the Yaqui culture which their parents are teaching them to participate in. There are conflicts and there are surprisingly easy adjustments. These are the themes of this study.

PART I

The Cultural Environment of Arizona Yaquis

CHAPTER I
Yaqui Culture Patterns

The people who call themselves Yaquis in Arizona are in greater or lesser degree familiar with a number of customs which no one else in the region practices. All of the adults, and even the children from the age of about six or seven upward, are quite aware that some of their relatives, friends, and other associates are to be differentiated from others on the basis of whether or not they practice these customs. They make distinctions not only in this general way, but also more specifically, in terms of the number of distinctively Yaqui ways of behavior that characterize various individuals. Thus a common characterization of certain middle-aged or older men and women is that they are "very Yaqui." This evidently means that they practice Yaqui customs more consistently than do others or that they practice more of them than others do. Whole family groups, as well as individuals, may be spoken of in this way. It is clear that within the category of Yaqui, degrees of being Yaqui are widely recognized.

The behavior on which such distinctions rest range from ways of eating to ways of worshipping. For someone to be regarded as Yaqui by other Yaquis, it is by no means necessary that he practice the whole range of Yaqui customs. His behavior may be characterized by only the use of the Yaqui language, while his family and religious life show none of the other distinctively Yaqui behaviors, and yet he will be characterized as Yaqui.

The stock of Yaqui customs finds expression in very different combinations in the activities of individuals in the communities of Yaquis. Hence what we shall now discuss as the distinctively Yaqui customs must not be regarded as descriptions of what all those who call themselves Yaquis actually practice. Some of those which we shall describe are apparent in the behavior of only a small number of Yaquis in Arizona; others are practiced by many more, and still others by a large majority. The list that follows is by no means, therefore, an attempt to describe the model behavior of Arizona Yaquis; it is rather a catalog of behaviors which Yaquis have been observed to practice and which have not been observed for other peoples in Arizona.

Distinctive Yaqui Customs

Language

Perhaps the ultimate test applied by any Yaqui to determine whether or not another person is Yaqui is the test of language. An individual may not currently use the Yaqui language, but if he is known ever to have used it regularly and idiomatically, he is classified by others as Yaqui. Knowing and using the language means that an individual is aware of innumerable terms and ways of speaking that no one else in the Arizona milieu knows. Only if he knows the language does one know the term by which Yaquis designate themselves. This term is *Yoemem,* which has the connotation of "the people." Yaquis do not, except when talking with others who are not Yaquis, use the term *Yaqui* for themselves. To know and use Yoemem and its derivatives, like *yoemnooka* (the Yaqui language), is to be privy to a whole point of view about Yaquis as a sort of pivot of the social world. Similarly, only if one knows the Yaqui language can Yaqui institutions and village officials be spoken of with understanding and without ambiguity. To use *chief* or *jefe* to designate a village official is to brand oneself as an outsider, but to use *Kobanao* is an immediate sign that one understands the village as a Yaqui does. Then there are the many little expressions which have not been translated from or into Spanish or English, such as "as easy as killing lizards," use of which indicates acquaintance in an intimate way with a whole idiom of thought. Use of the language thus, even if it is not accompanied by any other participation in Yaqui customs, indicates an intimate awareness of most of them. It is probably the only completely common denominator of those who call themselves Yaqui in Arizona.

Knowledge of the Eight Pueblos and the Dispersal

For all generations of Yaquis in the United States, there is an "old country" which consists of the area of the lower Yaqui River drainage (some three hundred miles to the south of the Mexican–United States border) in southern Sonora. The central feature of this "old country" is the *wohnaiki pweplum,* or Eight Pueblos—Cocorit, Bacum, Torim, Vicam, Potam, Rahum, Huirivis, and Belem, which were the principal Yaqui settlements. Almost every formal public oration includes a mention of them and points out that although "the people" may no longer be there, they still remember them. For the oldest immigrant generation, the Eight Pueblos constitute a point of cultural reference. The ultimate standard of behavior is their memory of the way things were done on the "river" and in the Eight Pueblos. Every adult can name the Pueblos and for many of them the old life in them, of the period of their childhood, has become a sort of "Golden Age" to which they look backward constantly.

The history of Yaquis since the breakup of the society after defeats in the 1880s is a further point of common understanding. Loss of relatives and friends and the fighting with the Mexicans and flights for their own lives are bitter memories for most of the older persons. "To have suffered as we did is to know what it is to be a Yaqui," says an old man. There is a feeling among the older people that no one should attempt leadership among them in Arizona unless he has suffered in this way, because only one with that experience can "understand the people." This consciousness of suffering and of a lost Golden Age on Yaqui land in Yaqui country carries with it a hatred, of greater or lesser degree, of Mexicans who are regarded as having caused the suffering and brought about the dispersal of Yaquis from their homeland. Among younger Yaquis there is a great deal of difference in the way that they regard this history of flight and suffering, but whether they regard it as something better forgotten or as a continuing source of grievance against Mexicans, they share with their elders an acute awareness of it. Thus history, as well as language, is a basis of common understanding which sets Yaquis of whatever generation off from other people in Arizona.

Food

Yaquis have preserved a number of food customs which differ greatly from those of the Anglo Americans, although they are closely similar in most instances to those of the Mexican Americans. For example, stew of beef, chick-peas, and sometimes other vegetables, called *wakabaki* when used as a fiesta food, is a characteristic combination peculiar to Yaquis and regarded by them as a sort of national dish.

There is a cultural pattern for eating. The techniques employ bowls, cups, spoons, and tortillas, not knives, forks, and plates. Different stews, meats, and *atole* (a drink of cornmeal) are served and eaten as separate courses, and the same bowls, cleaned between servings, are used by individuals for each course. Food is served at tables and is never eaten from the containers in which it was cooked; tortillas are stacked in one or more piles directly on a cloth lying on the table. It is improper to eat rapidly or to show much interest in food; Yaquis pick delicately at their food and appear to be little interested in it. It is, however, improper to leave any food on the table at a fiesta. Individuals may bring buckets and send back the surplus to their families or to anyone whom they care to. A prayer of thanksgiving is always said at the close of a fiesta meal and a few families observe this custom in their private households.

Food is an important interest at the time of a fiesta. It is regarded as the compensation that a household group or the village as a whole gives to ceremonial performers and their families. The ceremonial society members often talk about the amount and quality of food which they had at a certain fiesta. Givers of a fiesta worry about getting sufficient food and about whether it is enjoyed or not. It is, however, never proper for them to suggest that there has been enough food or that it has been good food.

All important relationships between groups of Yaquis within a village involve ceremonial exchanges of food. Not only must the ceremonial societies be given food for the ritual and other work they perform, but also two families whose children marry engage in an exchange of feasts, and a significant and indispensable part of the ceremony is the presentation of a basket of corn tamales or other food by the bride's family to the women of the groom's family. The basis of the establishment of the more important godparent relationships is an exchange of feasts. A village as a whole cooperates with the private *Fiestero* by presenting food, in return for which the houses are blessed by the ceremonial society that makes the collection. In this manner food serves as a medium of exchange and as an instrument for the establishment and fulfillment of social obligations within any Yaqui village. It has a high ritual value since it is indispensable in all the important ceremonies. Its importance in this connection is one of the features that distinguishes Yaqui religious life from that of the surrounding peoples.

Clothing

Yaquis in Arizona dressed in various ways, some in accordance with fashions of the turn of the century in Sonora and some more in the manner of Anglo Americans. Considering the older fashions, there is a much greater contrast between the clothes of the women and those of the surrounding people than is the case of the clothes of the men. The older women generally wear full, ankle-length skirts—the Mother Hubbard skirts common among Papago, Apache, and other reservation Indian women, with a short-sleeved, brightly embroidered underwaist covered by a full, sleeved blouse of print material. This garment fully covers the upper body and fits loosely. The older women wear their hair long, often done into tight little braids, and keep it covered with a cloth. Usually, while working around the house, they use a Turkish towel to cover the hair; when leaving the house a white or black cloth is worn. This is the *rebozo*, or simple shawl, used by older Mexican-American women in Arizona as well as by Yaquis. Yaqui women go barefoot around the house, although they always wear shoes when they leave the house to go anywhere.

The men present little contrast with others of low-income groups. Only a few Yaqui men possess suits of the Anglo-American type with matching coat and pants, and they never wear neckties, although a colored handkerchief is sometimes worn about the neck. The hair is cut short and parted or combed straight back. The clothes and hairdress of the men are regarded as being essentially the same now as they were formerly in Sonora, except for the substitution of leather shoes for hide sandals, and felt hats for straw sombreros. Sandals are now worn only on ceremonial occasions by members of the *Fariseo* society.

Dress has no status association within Yaqui society. Type of clothing does not indicate social position in the group, such as leadership in a ceremonial society. Furthermore, there is no consistent difference in the dress of families which are generally accorded different social ratings in a village. Status is indicated only by means of special paraphernalia used at the time of a public function and usually worn in addition to the ordinary daily garb.

Clothing of women is regarded as having the important use of keeping

the body thoroughly covered, and hence newer fashions which reveal the
bodies of younger women are regarded negatively by older women and
men. This high value of keeping the body covered seems to have a different
basis from among Anglo Americans. It is connected with the Yaqui belief
that other "Indians" (and Yaquis in an earlier state) wore too little clothing
and were, therefore, "wild people."

Land

Yaquis have become urbanized in Arizona in the sense that they do not
entertain ideas of possessing land on which they could pursue agriculture,
yet older Yaquis maintain an intense interest in land. One of the well-
known traditions is that in Sonora Yaquis had title from the King of Spain
to a definitely bounded area along the Yaqui River. This title is supposed
to have been lost, and its loss is thought to have given rise to the troubles
with the Mexicans over land which resulted in the gradual encroachment
of the latter on Yaqui territory. Thus the loss of the tribal lands is regarded
as the source of the dependent condition of Yaquis everywhere at present.
The idea is often expressed that Yaquis in Arizona, as well as elsewhere,
really own land in Sonora and that they are suffering a great injustice in
being denied it. This idea lies back of two important attitudes: (1) that of
dislike for Mexicans who are regarded as responsible for the injustice; and
(2) gratitude to Americans for permitting Yaquis to occupy land in the
United States.

The concept of communal management of village lands devoted to
churches or adobe-supply appears in the Arizona communities. Such land
is controlled by the ceremonial societies which make up the church organization.

Work

There are two kinds of work recognized by Yaquis, both of which go
by the name of *tekipanoa*. This term is applied to work for wages as well
as to ceremonial work, which includes both ritual activity and the labor of
preparing dance grounds, gathering wood for fiesta fires, and organizing
ceremonial activities. The valuations which are placed on the two kinds of
work are somewhat complex.[1] In brief, it may be said that work for wages,
or ordinary economic production, is highly valued, and individuals who
are steady producers for their households are respected for that activity.

However, ceremonial work is also highly important. Young men are urged not to neglect it. Members of ceremonial societies regard their work as of great significance and, moreover, say that they enjoy it and derive from it very definite satisfaction, akin to spiritual renewal. They refer to it frequently as hard and exacting, but that very quality is regarded as indicating its importance and necessity.

The result of this high valuation of the two kinds of work and the feeling that they are of at least equal importance is that individuals find themselves frequently in conflict as to which to engage in. The universal dilemma is: "Shall I quit my job to participate in this ceremony or shall I not?" Or looked at in another way: "Shall I take this job and miss my work at the ceremony?" The conflict is significant for the culture and indicates a fundamental inconsistency in the economic and ceremonial patterns.

Work is an important focus of interest, whichever type is being considered. The particular type of economic work, however, is not connected with the Yaqui prestige system. Railroad labor, ranch labor, adobe-making, and other forms of employment are all of equal status within a Yaqui community.

On the other hand, grades of status within a Yaqui village do depend on the extent and nature of ceremonial work. Regularity in the latter is highly valued and publicly praised and gives an individual status in the community. Prominence is also attainable through efficiency and high ability in the performance of ceremonial labor. Thus we may see an important difference in the social meanings of the two kinds of labor. The character of performance of ceremonial labor is connected with social status, while that of economic labor is not.

Money

Yaqui interest in money has not developed to the point where there is concern with it apart from what it will bring in immediate values. In the years up to 1941, the only forms of saving which the writer has been able to discover are the installment buying of lots and automobiles and the occasional saving of small amounts by a woman of a household to tide her family over a ceremonial season during which she knows no one will be working for its support. The accumulations of money for future utilization is recognized by Yaquis as a trait of other people and generally remains outside the range of Yaqui culture. The current saying that "a Yaqui never saves a cent" indicates the awareness of the saving principle and at the same time the lack of adherence to it by Yaquis. Money is thus a direct value for Yaquis and lacks the complications attendant on its utilization in such activities as saving, investment, and interest.

The place of money in Yaqui culture is not easy to make clear. All non-ceremonial labor is work for wages. Economic relations with the world of non-Yaquis, particularly Anglo Americans, are maintained through the money nexus. Yet in the fundamental relations within a Yaqui community, as we have seen, the nexus between groups and individuals in their formal dealings with each other is not money. Inter-Yaqui relationships are for the most part based on food exchanges which are thoroughly ritualized. This may be brought home very vividly in connection with the production of ritual musical instruments and other ceremonial paraphernalia by Yaquis. These goods are produced by specialists in small numbers as needed with no reference to a money valuation whatever. Makers who have not been accustomed to selling their products to Anglo Americans as curios are entirely unable to quote a price; a relationship between the object and money is nonexistent. If it is given to a Yaqui in need of it, there is often no formal return payment of any kind, but sometimes a purely arbitrary price, which, it is admitted, has no relationship to time or labor expended, is placed on the object. This price is always extremely low by any Anglo-American standard for time, labor, and materials. A Yaqui specialist who makes such things recognizes this himself because he has been working for employers and receiving wages all his life. Yet he persists in saying that "among ourselves in these things there is no price."

Money has no relation to status in a Yaqui village. Size of income or the amount and kind of property may be envied but have not yet been recognized as having any relationship to status within the village. Status depends rather on ceremonial tekipanoa (together with a number of other factors which will be mentioned below), and individuals who carry this out in superior fashion are very likely to have less money income than others, although there is no absolute correlation here. Again it must be emphasized that money is highly valued. It is merely not connected with the most worthwhile activities and hence not with social prestige or rank.

Names and Titles

It requires a good deal of exposure to Yaqui ways before one understands the place of an individual's name in Yaqui thinking. To understand the cultural significance of the indefiniteness of the Yaqui personal name requires still greater intimacy with the people. Yaquis do not think in terms of surnames of the Anglo- or Mexican-American type so much as in terms of the Christian name. This is true despite the fact that almost every individual has both a surname and a Christian name assigned to him. In conversation Yaquis habitually speak of "that man" or "this woman" or perhaps of "that man who lives over there." The listener is expected to understand who is meant from the context. Moreover, the listener, if he is a Yaqui, usually does understand to whom reference is made and rarely has to ask for more specific identification if the person referred to is a Yaqui. He knows because he is familiar with everyone in the village and because a conversation ordinarily deals with village affairs.

Moreover, little importance is attached to precise identifications in, for example, discussion of ceremonial events which are going to take place. It is enough to know that someone is going to serve as Maestro and that someone else is going to be the Fiestero.

The process of making a positive identification, as let us say for an inquiring Anglo American who is not familiar with the world of village life, is a difficult one for a Yaqui. To indicate what is involved, let us take a hypothetical example. A Yaqui man may identify a person about whom he is talking by making reference to the fact that he has a godparent relationship with him. To a Yaqui the identification as *kompai* of the speaker would immediately reduce the possibilities and he could often guess who was meant. However, a man's *compadres* are usually numerous and this in some cases might be insufficient; in such cases resort is often made to the Christian name, so that he would be described as Kompai Juan. But again there are many Juans, and anyone is likely to have many compadres named Juan. If conceivably the identity were still not understood by the listener, the speaker would proceed to identify Juan by reference to his ceremonial office during Lent, as for example, Juan Pilato. This in any ordinary case would clinch the matter and all doubts would be removed, but it happens that there are individuals who have no village office. In such cases there is always a nickname to fall back on. Thus a Juan might be described as Juan Molonko (shorty). It will be noted that in none of these instances has a surname of the European type been used, and this is typical of Yaqui practice.

The surname is not a clear identification among Yaquis for several reasons: (1) they do not habitually think in terms of surnames and hence it requires a special effort to make associations with them when they are used; (2) there is a rather limited stock of surnames in use among Arizona Yaquis, and hence there are many Juan Valenzuelas and many José Floreses, and so forth; (3) the surnames have not until recently become established within any of the families, because men have for various reasons changed them and because there are no definitely established patterns of handing them down to children, or even of transferring them from husbands to wives, or vice versa. Thus the one type of terminology, the binomial personal name, which would make identification possible in the mind of an outsider, has no such utility to a Yaqui.

In what manner then do Yaquis make use of names? They make most use of personal names which have reference to village office and to personal characteristics. Examples of these would be the following: *kahe'eme* (does not drink), *molonko* (shorty), *ili maihto* (little maestro), *maihto lo'i* (lame maestro), *bue'u koparia* (tall singer), *katomim* (never has any money), *katekiak* (not chosen, meaning has no village office), and *panocha* (brown sugar, referring to a man who worked for a number of years in a sugar manufactory). Every Yaqui is referred to by others by means of such terms. The most respected and distinguished individuals in a village are known widely by these descriptive terms and are referred to by them whenever necessary. But a descriptive term is not used to a person's face, for obviously such identification is not necessary if the person is present, and also because the ones indicating physical characteristics are not thought to be quite complimentary. In addition, every Yaqui has a definite Christian name with which he is baptized and which he retains throughout life. These are used as vocatives to one's face.

There are, however, surnames. Although there is confusion due to the practice of name-changing, and a given individual may have used three or more during the course of his life, every Yaqui in Arizona does have a surname of some sort. There are two kinds, Yaqui and Spanish. The Yaqui ones are ordinarily occupational, such as Buikamea (singer), Kuchaleo (fisher), Buanamea (crier), and Husakamea (brown). The Spanish ones are the common Mexican surnames, such as Martínez, Valenzuela, García, Vasquez, Valencia, Escalante, Alvarez, Chavez, or Flores.

The true Yaqui personal name has never been a term of address. The introduction of the Christian given name provided a personal name which could be used as a term of address, but in a sense this is an impersonal name because it indicates nothing about that particular person or the relationship between individuals using it. The Yaqui terms of address described above were of a kind which indicated such relationship. They are still used widely among Yaquis, but it is apparent that they are slowly going out of use. Reference is made to kinship terms and to certain traditional terms of respect. Within a family, insofar as the old Yaqui words are still used, kinship terms are used between members in the intercourse of daily life. Certain of these are also made use of in a wider sense. The terms *achai* (father), *mala* (mother), *sai* and *saila* (older and younger brother), and *ako* and *wai* (older and younger sister) are used between persons not related by blood to indicate the nature of the relationship. In addition, there are respect terms which are not part of the kinship terminology, such as *nuhmea* (young man) and *naaka* (young woman) which are widely used. Yaquis feel that it is important to use these because they establish at once the relative ages and therefore the relative social status of individuals in relation to each other. All of the above terms have meaning in connection with the whole social structure. These are the titles of Yaqui custom, for the village office terms are not used in face to face relationships. The system of titles is based rather on kinship and relative age. The village office term is descriptive, while the title is relational in its meaning.

This discussion of names and titles indicates an important character of Yaqui society. It is intimately personal and greatly concerned with the maintenance of status relations. It is, moreover, unitary, having a single system of status rather than several systems within which several distinct sets of status terms or titles are used, as is the case in Anglo- or Mexican-American society.

Authority

There is a strong sense among Yaquis of age as conferring authority. This is indicated in many ways. A grandfather or grandmother in a household assumes authority over a father or mother as well as over the other members of the household. An eldest sibling is recognized as dominant over his or her younger siblings not only during the growing-up period, but also in later adult life. Several larger Yaqui households are organized on this basis of the dominance of an adult older sibling. The oldest rather than necessarily the most able member of a ceremonial society is regarded as the normal head of the group, although among Arizona Yaquis the unequal knowledge of ritual on the part of individuals and the interference of the Anglo-American economic pattern frequently result in breaches of this rule to produce greater efficiency in the organization. The Yaqui kinship terminology, but not the mixed Spanish-Yaqui, emphasizes relative age in each generation. The oldest *Pascola* Dancer receives precedence and dominates the younger Pascolas at a fiesta. The term *yo'owe,* or elder, has definite connotations of authority and of something to be deferred to. This term, when used in sermons applying to ancestors, has connotations also of mystic infallibility and an absolute standard of authority.

Authority deriving from age is without relevance to the sex of an individual. There is no general belief that males are or should be dominant over females or vice versa. Dominance in any social group depends first on relative age, secondly on personality. The manner in which this principle of Yaqui culture has been affected by circumstances in Arizona will become clear later on.

Education

The methods by which the younger people are taught proper behavior differs in different societies. The relationships between younger and older people in any society are characterized by the assumption on the part of those older that the younger must learn to behave as their elders do. Yaqui treatment of children illustrates a basic point of view in the culture. Because authority is distributed among a considerable number of people, not confined to the mother or father in the elementary family, in a large household all the older members of the kin group are constantly concerned to direct the child's behavior. No single person is the ultimate source of conditioning. Moreover, other persons outside the household and kin circle are called on as godparents to take an interest in the behavior of the child. Three of four sets of godparents are established early in the child's life, within the first four or five years, and these become the object of strong respect attitudes immediately, attitudes which the family is at great pains to make clear to the child. Thus, there is a large, intimate group of elders who early become a conditioning milieu. They take their responsibilities quite seriously and impress this seriousness on the child. In general, the attitude of this group toward the child may be described as grave and kindly interest backed by a stern inexorability. Voices are not raised in telling a child how to behave. The more aberrant or annoying the behavior is, to the adult, the more likely he is to speak in a low voice. Physical punishment is occasionally resorted to, but the more usual method is denial of privileges. Thus, confinement and denial of food are methods of coercion which are in general use. Even these methods seem to be used rather rarely. Anglo

Americans are constantly impressed by the use of little more than the simple sanction of quiet disapproval on the part of almost any adult man or woman.

A fundamental characteristic of Yaqui society, which is being much affected by Anglo-American customs, is that children are not formally excluded from seeing or hearing any of the domestic activities of their elders. The life and the talk of the household are open to them almost from the time of their birth. There is a similar situation in regard to public affairs. Children of all ages attend the community ceremonies, behaving very much as they please during them, that is, sitting quietly and watching them intently or running about among the participants or participating. It is an important fact that Yaqui children have as many formal means of participation in the community life as do the adults; there is more opportunity in this respect for children, in fact, than for adult women. Children take part with adults as full-fledged participants, and their work is regarded as equally important to themselves and to the society as is that of the adults.

It must be pointed out, however, that there are two influences at work in Yaqui society which are in direct opposition to the essential nature of Yaqui education. The first is that of wage labor. Young boys cannot go out with their fathers to learn productive labor techniques until they are large enough to command a regular wage. Thus, economic labor is placed in a compartment outside the life of the community, and boys do not have the opportunity to adjust to it until they are fully grown. Secondly, there is the Anglo-American-administered school. Except during cotton-picking season, Yaqui children are sent to school by their parents, and the school is regarded by the parents as giving valuable training. But in sending them to school, Yaqui parents are establishing their children in a realm of authority outside their own culture, and they are admitting the importance of certain techniques which they themselves do not often possess and consequently cannot give to their children. The children become oriented, therefore, in a dual tradition.

The education of children in a Yaqui village is not taken care of entirely through kin and compadre circles and participation in ceremony. There are also public sermons which are regarded as extremely important. Maestros, Pascolas, and heads of ceremonial societies all deliver sermons which are designed both to emphasize desirable moral patterns and to point out the source of Yaqui beliefs. The importance of ceremonial tekipanoa is repeatedly stressed in them. Young men are enjoined not to get drunk when participating in ceremonies.[2] The elders, both dead and living, are pointed out as the natural source of authority and moral sanction. In addition, there is always an effort in a good sermon to explain the meaning of ceremonials in terms of Yaqui tradition.

Sexual Life

Yaquis appear very matter-of-fact on the subject of sex. There is no avoidance of the subject, and it provides the basis for a humorous tradition, but there seems to be less interest among adult men and women in the details of sex relations and the genitals than is the case of Anglo Americans generally.

Men and women keep their bodies well covered in the intimacy of domestic life as well as in public and are careful, in the case of both sexes, not to be seen dressing or undressing even by members of their own family. There is a well-developed sense of modesty concerning the sexual act and the sexual organs, but it does not enjoin complete privacy, and there is no strong verbal taboo on them.

This set of attitudes is quite apparent in connection with Pascola clowns who discuss sexual matters in public at fiestas as freely as they discuss anything else. The bashfulness of young men and women about sexual relations, the incongruity physically or socially of sexual partners, the sexual behavior of animals are all utilized in making jokes and funny stories. There is reference not only verbally but also by pantomime to the genitals and to the sexual act in the by-play of the Pascolas during ceremonies. But this is not the exclusive or the central interest of Pascola humor. It is a source of humor merely on a par with many others, and in this it reflects the general trend of Yaqui culture.

Yaquis attach little inherent value to virginity. Young boys and girls have rather free relations during adolescence, but they are expected not to associate with each other publicly. It is recognized that they frequently make use of the all-night fiesta for meeting each other, because they must carry out their relations clandestinely, far secluded from the fiesta or home, and this they do, even to the extent that other boys and girls of their own ages have to guess at the degree of intimacy. There are no formal patterns in Yaqui culture for the public association of young men and women in intimate fashion, such as the dances of Anglo Americans. Such public intimacy appears indecent to Yaquis.

Children are not infrequently born as a result of the early relationships.

Such results are regarded as undesirable, but the children born are not considered to bear any social stigma, and the family into which they are born has no feeling of shame. The feeling is rather one of bad luck. Gossip is always rife as to the fathers of the children, but it is not thought that having a child in this way is reason for marriage between the boy and girl, although parents in arranging marriages for their sons are inclined to reject girls with such a history.

Marriage is regarded as a very serious obligation, and the ideal that it should be stable and enduring is strongly held. The arrangements should be made by parents. Neither of these ideals is actually realized among Arizona Yaquis. Indissolubility of union is maintained by permitting an individual to go through a marriage ceremony only once. After that, if the mate dies, it is recognized that economic necessity requires the reestablishment of a household and hence the taking of a new mate. Thus, there seems to be a disharmony in Yaqui culture as a result of thinking of marriage in two categories, the economic and the ritual. In any given situation, an individual Yaqui may regard marriage according to either one of these categories. It makes for inconsistency in attitudes.

The Dead

It is proper to be frightened of certain ghostly aspects of the dead and to perform rites of exorcism. The funeral *novena* within nine days of the death of a person has the function of removing these last dangerous presences. However, the dead are primarily the ancestors, and as such they are still members of the household who must be offered food each year on All Souls' Day when they come back to the village. They are not powerful spirits and have no direct control of the interests of the living, but there is a behavior toward them which it is highly important to observe. They will be unhappy if their names are not entered in the family's Books of the Dead and recited at fiestas. Thus, a family must get the Maestro to speak of them frequently so that they will know they are not being forgotten. There is a certain idea that the dead need the help of the living if they have gone to purgatory, but the belief in this seems not to be general. There is rather stronger feeling that the dead are helpful to the living, that they have manifestations as "angel guardians" and may "intercede" with deities on behalf of the living.

One cannot escape the feeling that essentially the belief in the dead as living beings is a belief in the continuity of the household as a social structure operating through all the past generations as well as in the present to perpetuate Yaqui culture. They are mentioned in every ceremony and in every sermon as a timeless assemblage from which the present people sprang and to whom the present ones owe everything and with whose attitudes they must conform. The appeal to their authority is not vague and spasmodic; it is constant and very definite. The *animam* (souls) are the *yo'oria,* or elders, and as such are the final arbiters of Yaqui culture.

The various symbols of the dead—the Books of the Dead in which their names are written; the *wikosam,* or breech-clout strings by which they mount to the sky; the tables with their food which appear on All Souls' Day; and the parts of the Mass for the Dead taken from the Roman Missal and read at almost every ceremony are of primary significance in the social solidarity of Yaquis. Eliminate the interest in the dead and the kin groups would lack a central symbol, the basis of godparent obligations would be destroyed, and the meaning of a large proportion of the ritual would be lost.

The Deities

The deities of Yaqui belief are Jesus, Mary, God, certain saints of the Roman Catholic pantheon, and probably a few animals such as the water serpent, the deer, and the horned toad. Of the animals, there is doubt because their role in the culture has altered profoundly in recent times. The other deities are superficially the ones of Christianity. They were introduced to the Yaquis sometime after 1617 by the Jesuits and have gone through a process of adjustment to Yaqui ways of thought during the past three hundred years. They go by Spanish names, such as María Santísima, Dios, San José, and San Francisco Xavier, but the two major ones are also called by Yaqui terms. Mary is "Our Mother" (*itom ai*) and Jesus is "Our Father" (*itom achai*). Mary has manifestations which would not usually be recognized in a Catholic church. She is the Holy Cross honored with flowers and a fiesta in May, and she is even sometimes identified with the simple wooden crosses which stand in the houseyards and the church plaza and are admitted to ward off evil things like lightning. Jesus, too, is thought of as a household cross sometimes. These identifications may hark back to an earlier time before the Jesuits, but they have been thoroughly integrated into the primarily Christian dogma by means of myths which say that Mary turned her body into a tree on which Jesus was crucified.

What could be more natural than to think of Mary, Jesus, and the Cross all as one?

The essential feature of the worship of Jesus and Mary is an interest in curing. Through this interest the various ceremonial societies are created and maintained, and through them, the whole community possesses a working unity. Jesus and Mary are both curers to whom one may appeal through the *manda*. One makes a manda by promising himself or a member of his family to serve Jesus or Mary in return for a cure. The manda is usually operative for the whole of a person's life and requires that the service be rendered in formal ways in the company of others who have made similar vows. This service consists essentially of singing and dancing, but also of the incidental labors attendant on the carrying out of any ceremony. The deities' interest in singing and dancing gives these activities a special meaning, which is largely absent or vestigial in the religious life of surrounding peoples. Both a dance and a song, in Yaqui thought, are offerings of devotion to a god; they are not diversions. It must always be recalled that they are work, that is, ceremonial tekipanoa.

The deities are effective curers, but they are also something else. Mary and Jesus are definitely "our Father" and "our Mother," and there may be other associations and survivals from pre-Christian times. Mary is the Virgin who scatters blessings through the feather wands of her *Matachin* dancers; these blessings spread over houses and villages and bring happiness and good luck. Then Mary is the lady of flowers. Her rites usher in the month of May, which older people still call the "mother of months." Flowers are, above all, her symbol, and they mean youth, newness, and freshness, renewal. She is a joy-bringing deity and her devotees make all the use they can of the color red. Jesus has a very different character. His colors are black and purple. His major festival is Lent and Easter, just before the burst of the new year in Mary's month of May, in other words, at the end of the old year. Certainly, his festival of Easter is the most complex and important of all during the year, and this is largely because it demands so much more than Mary's month. The whole Easter season is a season of penitence. This concept of penitence is one of the clearest and most widely agreed upon among Arizona Yaquis. The labor of being a Fariseo (and it is very hard and exacting labor) is penitence. The village as a whole purifies itself through serving Jesus in the long round of Easter ceremonies. His crucifixes are symbols of a stern but merciful judge to whom one must do penance periodically for the good of one's soul.

The Natural World

The various survivals in ritual, in concept, and in attitude, indicate the great importance of the natural world in Yaqui supernaturalism.[3] To Yaquis the natural world is a source of power. Their supernatural world includes the deer, the horned toad, or water snakes and other such beings invested with special powers that may be bestowed upon humans. Each species of animal has a certain "virtue" or power peculiar to itself. There is a language of the deer and a language of the ants, each having a special wisdom. This world of knowledge and power apart from the human world may be approached through dreams and one may receive inspiration from it. The ancients obtained the dances and the songs and the ritual of, certainly, the Pascolas, the Deer Dancers, and probably other performers from this source. The power of these—rituals and dances as acts of prayer to influence the Christian deities—derives ultimately, therefore, from the natural world. Contemporary Yaquis still participate in this power.

Yaquis in Arizona beat on pans and chant Christian alabanzas to save "mother moon" when she is undergoing an eclipse. They sing songs to which the Deer Dancer dances, which speak of a land "underneath the dawn" where a little supernatural deer lived. In the morning after a fiesta, the Deer Dancer throws water—which has derived power through the night as a result of being sung to—over the crowd and this assures fertility to the women on whom it falls. The Pascolas call on the power of the horned toad and the frog and the turtle to keep evil spirits away from a fiesta. Flowers are an important symbol of beneficial power. Hence they appear on the headdresses of the dancers and scatter blessings over the village. Hence also, they are used to break the evil power of the masked *Chapayekas* (the pursuers of Christ) who attack the church on Holy Saturday morning. All of these aspects of the natural world are still vital elements in the religious symbolism of Yaquis.

It is chiefly in the ritual and lore of the Pascolas and Deer Dancers that the old interest in the natural world is still preserved. The flowers of the Matachinis and the Virgin have become highly ritualized, and only a historian can point out their relation to the natural world. But the Pascolas still address the smaller animals in their ritual, imitate them in their dances, and are definitely believed to have learned their skills from them. Moreover, it is the Pascolas whom many Yaquis describe at present as the most distinctively Yaqui of all ceremonial performers. Admitting that other peoples, including Mexicans in Mexico, have Matachinis and even Fariseos, they say that only Yaquis have Pascolas, or that at least other Indians learned about Pascolas from the Yaquis. The Pascolas along with the Deer Dancer are thus symbols of the distinctiveness of the Yaqui people, as well as the primary preservers of the old relationship with the natural world. Eliminate them and Yaquis would lack an important symbol of their identity.

Curing and Witchcraft

In the Yaqui view there are two orders of disease. One is the result of natural causes and may be cured either by the herbal remedies of ordinary Yaqui medical practitioners or by dealing with the benevolent deities, Mary, Jesus, and the saints. The other type of disease is caused by malevolent living human beings who are called *moria'akame*, or witches. There is an elaborate lore about these evildoers with which almost everyone is familiar. The methods of causing illness—by using the hair of an Apache's head, by making a sort of bomb which is cast into the air and may affect a whole village, by the evil eye, and so on—are well known and generally believed in. The witches may be discovered through dreams, particularly through the dreams of curers who know how to combat the witch-caused diseases. It is only through the latter or through the efforts of the witch himself that the diseases may be successfully combated. The benevolent supernaturals seem to be powerless in such cases.

The Interrelations of Yaqui Customs

The distinctive Yaqui customs which have been discussed have not been presented in order of importance, either quantitatively in the general Arizona Yaqui community or qualitatively in the lives of individual Yaquis.[4] They do include the most obvious customs, which may be used in making a differentiation of Yaqui individuals from others.

These customs, it has been pointed out, are practiced in different combinations by different Yaqui individuals. Some idea of the variety of combinations and of the individual variations will become apparent in the biographical sketches which are presented below. It is necessary here, however, to consider some of the customs and beliefs as they appear to focus or orient the activities of individuals.

Certain beliefs and ways of behaving are closely associated; others are not. That is to say, an individual who is observed to practice a certain distinctive Yaqui behavior will be found on further observation to practice certain other behaviors. Ceremonial dancing, for example, is found to be associated in an individual's behavior with a large number of other distinctive customs. On the other hand, the Yaqui forms of witchcraft may be believed in by an individual who exhibits very few of the other distinctive behaviors.

It is these constellations of behaviors, rather than the analyzed elements just presented, that make it possible to speak of a Yaqui culture in Arizona and that give the culture its distinctive qualities. The beliefs in Mary and Jesus, in guardian angels, and in ancestral spirits returning in the months of October and November may be readily matched among peoples in the surrounding societies, and yet it is on these beliefs that a whole system of ideas and social relations has been built by Yaquis. This system consistently requires actions by Yaquis which are sharply different from those of any of the people among whom they are living. These behaviors come to periodic focus in public actions which make Yaquis highly conspicuous as different from their neighbors. Thus, groups of customs are interrelated in such ways that, on the one hand, acceptance of one orients individual Yaquis to the acceptance of many more, and, on the other hand, focuses activities into group actions of which others besides Yaquis become aware.

The custom spoken of above as the manda (promise) is one which may be regarded as linking a great number of the Yaqui customs just discussed, although by no means all of those customs. It is a technique for curing a great variety of illnesses. As a curing technique, its value is solidly related to basic biological needs. It may be turned to on impulse in the privacy of the household, or it may be deliberated on carefully by a group of parents and godparents. The latter may influence a parent to promise the sick child to a ceremonial society, even though the parent may not be convinced of its necessity, or even efficacy. It is thus a technique which is employed by Yaqui families in places where no Yaqui medical specialists are present, where, in fact, the Yaqui family may be completely isolated from any other Yaquis.

Yet, once brought into play, it carries with it a long train of cultural consequences. The child who is regarded as having been cured by the promise to serve a deity must be given every opportunity to fulfill the obligation; only in that way does the cure remain effective. This requires that the parents get in touch—if they have not already—with other Yaquis who are practicing the customs of the ceremony through which the promise may be fulfilled. If, for example, the manda has been made to the Virgin, they must take the child to a Yaqui settlement where ceremonies are held at which Matachinis dance, turn him over to the Matachin Kobanao, and allow him to learn the dance by participating in it. The announcement to the Kobanao of the child's promise immediately establishes an additional authority to that of the parents and compadres over the child; he may be called on to dance at any ceremony whether it suits the convenience of the parents or not. Thus instruction in the specific requirements of the manda proceeds.

But this involves repeated contact with music, ritual, and religious symbols—the tunes not to be heard outside of Yaqui villages in Arizona, the feathered plume wands of the dance society, the headdresses called "flowers" in Yaqui, the church organization of which the Matachinis are only a part, and the altar images and the explanations of their origins and powers. As a Matachin Dancer, the child grows up hearing regularly the sermons of the Maestros who use the old traditional phrases about the Eight Pueblos, "our poor inheritance of land" on the Yaqui River; which emphasize the high importance of ceremonial work; and which open and close with the Yaqui kinship-respect terms. The supernatural sanction, as well as the social sanction, for continuing to dance is impressed again and again on the child as he becomes more proficient in the dance and, usually, grows to like the activity. As he continues to be well, the whole idea of the efficacy of the manda as a curing technique is demonstrated to him.

In this way the manda leads (and we have barely sketched the chief connections here) to the learning of a whole system of beliefs and behaviors that are distinctively Yaqui. We may speak of this constellation as the ceremonial work focus or orientation in Yaqui culture. It is an organization of Yaqui customs which embraces not all, but a great number of those that Yaquis in Arizona practice.

The Yaqui custom of keeping the Books of the Dead is another custom which may carry with it in association a number of other distinctive behaviors. It must be said that it *may* do so, not that it always does. The supernatural sanction supporting the custom is not so strong as the supporting ceremonial labor. Failure to fulfill the various behaviors connected with the Books of the Dead seems in Arizona to be thought to result only in feelings of sadness and discomfort for the dead spirits and a consequent unhappiness for the individual who fails to carry out all the customs. This may be a very strong sanction for some individuals, but it may also obviously be quite weak for others. We do not find this constellation of customs and belief, therefore, so vigorous among Arizona Yaquis as the ceremonial work constellation, but it is, nevertheless, probably the second most important of the major constellations in Yaqui culture.

A Book of the Dead is passed from mother or father to children down either the male or female line, or both. It is a list of the names of dead ancestors and the book is called "the spirits" (understood to be ancestral spirits). It is regarded as obligating the person in whose care it is, to place it as frequently as possible on an altar, that is, on a Yaqui ceremonial altar, for the purpose of having sacred chants and prayers said over it all night during a ceremony. This helps the ancestors and shows them that they are being thought of by the living. The more frequently it is taken out for a ceremony, the better off the whole family, living and dead, will be.

This custom, then, brings at least one member of a family to every ceremony, whether at the church or in a private household. It motivates families to put out tables of food for the ancestors on All Souls' night and to have a Maestro read the names of the dead in the book, together with the village offices they have held, at a ceremony over the household table on All Souls' Day and at the family graves on All Saints' Day at the cemetery. The books are invested with meaning in the recitation of the names at other ceremonies during the year when the books are on the altar, through the sermons which mention the ancestors of all Yaquis in a general standard reference, and in the routine portions of rituals at all ceremonies that include parts of the Mass for the Dead.

The interest in the dead symbolized in the family book and expressed in all rituals is thus interlocked with the ceremonial activities based on the manda and ceremonial work. We may speak of an ancestral dead focus of Yaqui culture and a constellation of beliefs and behaviors which make it up. We might also list three other areas of focus: Pascola arts, ceremonial work, and witchcraft beliefs. All four of the interrelated foci are the source of distinctive Yaqui behaviors, and the four constitute groups of customs and beliefs that are interconnected in different degrees. Yaqui culture in Arizona is expressed through the behavior of individuals as a number of systems of custom and belief, all of which or only some of which may be participated in by various individuals. Participation in the system involving the manda does not necessarily involve beliefs or activities connected with witchcraft, nor with Pascola dancing, though it is rarely to be found completely out of association with the beliefs and customs involving the ancestral dead. There are, in other words, subsystems within the culture that are in greater or lesser degree connected with one another.

This conception of Yaqui culture as it is manifested in Arizona may serve as a basis for considering the relations of Yaqui individuals to other sets of culture patterns in Arizona.

CHAPTER 2

Contacts Between Anglo Americans and Yaquis in Arizona

Yaquis in Arizona live in a social world that includes people of all the major racial stocks and with cultural characteristics that range from the Western and Oriental civilizations to various of the American-Indian cultures. The network of social relations links Yaquis with Papagos, Pimas, Mexicans, Chinese, Negroes, and Anglo Americans. The relations with each of these different ethnic groups are not the same, and consequently, Yaquis distinguish all of these groups one from the other. They have learned to expect certain characteristic attitudes and behaviors from each of them. Some they have learned to know only as employers, others as sellers of goods, others as fellow laborers. Growing up in a Yaqui community means not only learning the distinctive Yaqui ways of behavior, but also the ways of these other peoples. It is only through an understanding of the place of Yaquis within this whole complex social structure that we can gain insight into what has happened and is happening to the traditional ways of Yaqui behavior.

Relations with Anglo Americans

While every Yaqui is constantly aware of the English-speaking people who dominate the social life of southern Arizona as hirers of labor, as wielders of political authority, and as teachers in the schools, only various segments of the culturally dominant group are aware of Yaquis. Some Anglo Americans are interested in Yaquis as men and women who will work for them, some are interested in them as buyers of the goods they have to sell, some see them as public charges to be cared for, some are interested in saving their souls, and some are interested in them as having a special and different culture. Among those who have these various special interests in Yaquis there are a few who have come to know Yaquis as whole persons and have become interested in them as such. But the Anglo American who knows any Yaqui in the way that he knows members of his own family or close friends is an exception. For the most part, the relations with Anglo Americans are of the partial and instrumental sort as dictated by the specialized interest involved. We shall consider the nature of these relations in an effort to map out in a general way the web of social relations within which Arizona Yaquis live.

Economic Relations

Certain occupations, between the 1800s and 1941, have been traditional among Yaquis in Arizona.[1] These are adobe making, pick-and-shovel labor on railroad gangs, and ranch work including cotton picking and irrigation. Adobe making is an occupation which has permitted the men who work at it to live continuously in a Yaqui concentration of population, going out daily to their jobs. There are relatively few Yaquis who have engaged in it. The railroad work may carry individuals or families far away into other states for long periods of time. It has been a mainstay in Yaqui life in the past and a source of some of the most influential contacts with Anglo-American culture, but it has become decreasingly attractive as Yaqui settlements have increased in Arizona and railroad maintenance is becoming mechanized.

The occupation which has maintained the largest and steadiest demand for Yaquis is ranching. When there was no building and when railroads were laying off men, as for example in the period from 1929 to 1937, the agricultural industry of southern Arizona was hiring men to work on the great acreages of irrigated land devoted to citrus, truck, and cotton. In the first forty years of the twentieth century, the great majority of Yaqui men have been employed intermittently at cultivating cotton, irrigating various crops, and other miscellaneous ranch work. This means that they usually live in one of the Yaqui centers, going out with gangs daily to work for one of the large irrigation or "water-users" cooperatives, or to take jobs with private employers for longer or shorter periods, living on the ranch away from the Yaqui center. The former is characteristic of the Yaquis who live in the "company-town" areas in Salt River Valley in the vicinity of Phoenix and Scottsdale. The latter is more characteristic of the Yaquis in the vicinity of Tucson.

Cotton picking in the autumn months has been a feature of the agricultural rhythm which affects almost all Yaquis.[2] Each large irrigation company and nearly every privately owned ranch maintains its own labor camp to take care of its cotton pickers during the September to January season. With very few exceptions, by 1941 every Yaqui in Arizona had at one time or another spent the cotton-picking season in one of these camps. A conservative estimate would be that ninety percent of all Yaquis in the state planned as a regular part of their existence to take up residence in the cotton camps during three to four months each year. This reliance of Yaquis on cotton picking and acceptance of it as a desirable and traditional way of living developed after 1920 and became strongly entrenched in Yaqui economic life. It is regarded as the one sure and definite feature of the annual round of economic activities. The year, as it were, revolves around and climaxes in the intensification of labor in the cotton-picking season.

The cotton-picking activity thus causes periodic depopulation of the Tucson Yaqui centers. Pascua may have as few as five families in residence during the season and perhaps all but one of these would be picking cotton at nearby ranches. There is a similar depopulation of Guadalupe, but the population of the company-town Yaqui centers, such as Scottsdale, Marana, and Eloy increases for the season, and not only are the houses all occupied to capacity, but tents are usually also set up and Yaquis take up residence in these.

Each of the company camps—Scottsdale, Eloy, and Marana—has an established policy of segregation of its laborers' families. In the Scottsdale Yaqui village the plot of land has been set aside by the Salt River Valley Water Users' Association exclusively for Yaquis, and the Yaquis of the village are proud of the fact that "here we don't have any Mexicans, just Yaquis." Similarly, at Eloy a small plot of land has been set aside for Yaquis, and they have built their wattle-and-daub houses there and excluded Mexicans and others. As the Eloy village has grown and assumed the name of Bacatete, the land has become extremely crowded, but still the Yaquis entering the Eloy district prefer to stay there rather than move out into the other camps. In 1941 there is no Anglo camp at Eloy nearer than two miles, and it is five miles to the Negro camp. At Marana, the segregation policy is quite evident. A large strip of land has been set aside for the residence of laborers' families. A series of tents with wooden floors and platforms has been put up; there is running water and well-made latrines.

The houses are placed along streets and each of the streets has a sign posted on it; thus there is Oklahoma Street, Texas Street, Sonora Street, Nogales Street, and finally Papago Street. The name of the street indicates the origin of the people who live on it. When there are not enough Papagos to fill Papago Street, Negroes are assigned to it. At the south end of these rows of tent houses is a small patch of ground with some tamarisk trees on it. Beneath the trees are scattered wattle-and-daub houses and in these live the Yaquis. Here again, there is running water, and elaborate well-made latrines have recently been put up so that there are the same facilities as in the rest of the camp, but the character of the Yaqui section is extremely different, maintaining a strong resemblance to the traditional centers of Yaqui population. It is spoken of as "Campo Burro."

There is also on the private ranches scattered in the vicinity of Chandler, Mesa, Coolidge, and Casa Grande a tendency toward segregation. Each ranch rarely has more than three or four families at the height of its cotton-picking season and, during the rest of the year, perhaps only one or no families. Yaquis go back year after year to the same ranch and thus certain ranches get the name of "Yaqui ranches," while others are "Papago ranches" or "Mexican ranches." This holds for ranches who employ not more than seven or eight families. If the number goes beyond that then there might be some of each, but again segregation appears in the grouping of families of the same kind together with short distances between the Yaqui group, the Mexican group, and the Papagos.

Thus during the periods of ranch work Yaquis remain together, but are segregated from others. The larger the labor camp, the less the contact with Anglo Americans; the smaller the labor camp, the greater the contact. In a large camp such as Marana, the Yaqui section is self-sufficient. The Anglo-American end of the camp is at the extreme opposite end of the dwelling area, fully a half mile away. Contacts with foremen and bosses are most impersonal, and the work gangs tend to be made up of Yaquis and Mexicans or exclusively of Anglo Americans. Mixed groups do appear during cotton-picking season, but the work is highly individual and there is a minimum of contact.

However, on the small ranches there is a rather close relationship between Anglo-American employers and Yaqui laborers. These relationships always show characteristic features. It seems possible to consider them in terms of an older generation group and a newer. For example, we might take the attitudes of a rancher in the Yuma Valley, about sixty years old in 1941, as representative of the first group and those of a couple in their early thirties at a ranch six miles north of Tucson as representative of the second group. The Yuma rancher believes the following things about Yaquis with whom he has had personal contact at the village of Sibakowi over a twenty-year period:

The Yaquis are good workers and they are good people, but they are not good citizens, because they are just Indians and always will be. I was the first one around here to recruit them. It was good to be able to go to the village and get twenty men when you wanted them or just one if you wanted just one. It was easier to have cotton pickers close by than to have to go off around the valley looking for them. The first ones that came in were first class workers, better than any Mexicans. They worked good. But now they aren't so good anymore. The young ones drink a lot. They're getting too Americanized. . . . They didn't used to have cars at first. Now they all have cars and go around working everywhere. . . . The Yaquis have good home training, just as good as ours and that makes them different from the Mexicans. . . . The Yaquis aren't as much like niggers as the Mexicans, because they haven't been peons and had to act that way. They don't attach themselves to you like a dog. . . . They never cheat you or any other Yaqui. If you cheat them, they don't say anything but after that they freeze towards you. . . . They're different from the Mexicans because they never ask any questions about weights or anything; they accept what you put down. . . . The Mexicans rubber at the scales when they weigh in and sometimes they figure a little and come and tell you your record is wrong. When you show them it isn't, they never apologize at all. . . . The Yaquis never steal anything. . . . I wanted to find out something about their religion, but we never went over to see even an Easter dance, because they never invited us.[3]

The other example of the attitudes of ranchers who are thrown into close personal contact with Yaqui employees comes from a couple named Moss who at different times employed a single Yaqui family from Pascua on their ranch:

Mr. Moss said that Juan is a very, very slow worker. For instance, he will never take water into the field with him, but will always come back to the well to get a drink. But he is a good worker and they always find that when they leave him alone with a job to do he gets it done. "We don't know what we would do without him."

They pay Juan $1.50 a day and $2.00 when he is irrigating [the standard wages in the Tucson district in 1937]; they pay Josefina [Juan's wife] nothing, but she washes and irons for Mrs. Moss. They also give them milk, butter, and eggs. . . . Mr. Moss thinks it a good policy to pay Juan whatever is coming to him whenever it is due. . . . "The way the railroad always does it, they say that if they pay a man off and he is broke the night he gets paid, then he will come back to work on Monday and work better. . . ." Both the Mosses are amazed at how little they can live on. Mrs. Moss said that they cook up a great many beans and maybe that accounts for their cheap living. . . .

Mrs. Moss said that they treat Juan and his wife very well, but they let them know that they are Indians. Mrs. Moss has been doing a lot of educating of Josefina in the proper way to live. She came down to Pascua once and saw how the family lived, e.g., lying on the floor in dirty old rags. When she saw that she said she wouldn't let Josefina come down here to have her baby. When they first came to work for them, the only possessions they had were a few old pans in a gunny sack. Mrs. Moss took Josefina into her house and showed her her dishes and other things and now whenever Josefina goes to town on Saturday she buys a few dishes in the ten cent store. Mrs. Moss showed her how to put a cover on her table and Juan made her a little dressing table with shelves which she now uses. The Mosses bought them a stove to cook on after she was shocked when she first went out and saw the mess of ashes that Josefina had around. She showed her how to keep it clean and now thinks that Josefina is gradually learning how to live decently. . . .

Mrs. Moss said she had talked to Josefina (about the baby she was going to have), but Josefina said she had to be down at Pascua with the midwife and would not accept Mrs. Moss' offer of help, and she had to be there [Pascua] where the godmother was, and the family.

Throughout the interviews with ranchers who have employed Yaquis steadily or for short periods in the fall, there appears this same set of attitudes and relationships. The Yaquis are admired and valued as workers and they are always contrasted in this respect with Mexicans and other laborers. It is recognized that they have certain characteristic faults such as occasional drinking or absences from work, but these are always compensated for by the high quality of their work and their honesty. There is also always the insistence that they are different from Anglo Americans or others, that they are Indians and will necessarily remain so, and that this must be kept clearly before them. There is, further, the assumption universally that the Anglo-American employer is superior and that the Yaqui always has marks of his lower status in his ordinary domestic behavior. The younger employers are more often than not, like the couple described above, engaged in a constant effort to "improve" the working and living habits of their Yaqui employees. There goes along with this a considerable but rather casual interest in those customs which mark the Yaquis off from others, namely, their ceremonies and religious concepts.

The necessity under which all Yaquis in Arizona find themselves for securing their means of subsistence through money exchange brings them into almost daily contact with Anglo Americans, Mexican Americans, and

Chinese. Contact with Anglo Americans through these buyer-seller relationships, however, is extremely limited. Most of the buying is carried out with Chinese and, to some extent, with Mexican Americans, members of these groups providing most of the hucksters who cater to Yaqui trade and owning most of the low-price small stores at which Yaquis buy their groceries.[4] The buyer-seller relations of Yaquis with Anglo Americans take two forms; those connected with the buying of clothing and small household gadgets in the large business centers of the southern Arizona towns, and those connected with the buying of all the major necessities of life in company controlled stores in the company towns such as Marana. The first, involving the exchange of money for clothes and household items, are entirely impersonal relations with clerks who are not known to the Yaquis. This trade may be and is often carried on without even the necessity for the persons involved to speak the same language. Often Spanish is made use of in such transactions, but just as frequently no words are exchanged at all. This silent trade perhaps reaches its highest development in the five-and-ten-cent stores, where prices are definitely fixed. The relationship remains impersonal and instrumental in the extreme, but necessitates the complete acceptance on the part of the Yaqui of the Anglo-American evaluation of things and the Anglo-American way of doing business.

The relationship between a company storekeeper and Yaqui workers on company-irrigated lands is considerably more personal. Thus, the storekeeper at Marana, after some ten years experience there, knows and calls all the Yaquis by their first names, knows their paying habits well, and converses with them in Spanish. For all that, the relationship remains largely impersonal, for it seems to be purely their buying habits that he maintains an interest in. He knows only vague odds and ends about their ceremonial life and domestic customs and has no association with them outside the store.

It is a rare Yaqui who has the sort of stake in his community that goes with the ownership of immovable property. Yaquis ordinarily do not own the land they live on, nor do they have even the well-established connection with it that comes from paying rent. The typical Yaqui is a squatter. The village at Yuma called Sibakowi was built at the edge of the irrigated valley against a sandy mesa on land which had no value to any Anglo-American or other residents of the region. They have been permitted to remain there because they are a valuable labor supply. The village of "Eskatel" near Scottsdale was established on a piece of land owned by the Salt River Valley Water Users' Association and Yaquis live there on sufferance.

None may buy any piece of the land, and rent is not charged for its use. The village of Guadalupe consists of forty acres of tax-free land. It was established in 1910 under a federal law and Yaquis settled on it with the understanding that they would buy it as lots. They never paid for the land and it is being held in trust by a superior court judge "for benefit of the Yaqui." The conditions under which they may continue to live there are not clearly defined by law. The Yaqui settlements of Eloy and Marana are on "company" land and Yaquis are subject to removal at any time the company may see fit. In both areas the Yaqui villages have been moved at least once when the company wished to put the land under cultivation. The village of Pascua was established in much the same manner as Guadalupe, but not as tax-free property.[5] It was privately owned by a real-estate company and was to be bought by the Yaquis in the form of house lots. The Yaquis defaulted for the most part; nevertheless, as at Guadalupe, they continue to live on the land. Their status is definitely that of squatters. In the Barrio Libre center of Yaqui settlement in south Tucson, there are also many squatting Yaquis along the banks of the Santa Cruz River and on unused property here and there in the general area.

However, not every Yaqui in Arizona is a squatter or user of land for which he has not paid. Four or five families in Pascua have paid for their lots. A dozen more have moved into Barrio Belen south of Pascua and paid for their lots. Others here and there in Tucson have paid or are paying for land. Similarly, in other southern Arizona towns there are Yaquis who possess small pieces of real estate and maintain ownership through regular payment of taxes. One of the steps in moving out of Yaqui society is the buying of a lot, although this does not necessarily mean that the buyer will cease to be a Yaqui.[6]

The aspects of landownership which are relevant to our analysis are the following. Before the early 1920s the Yaquis had no tradition of owning land in the United States, nor did they have a reservation; they are marked off thus from other Indians in their own and in Anglo-American eyes.[7] Anglo Americans who live in the vicinity of Pascua frequently express themselves as follows: "Those damn Indians are just squatting there. They haven't got any reservation. What right have they got to be here?" Yaquis, in turn, feel extremely insecure and at the same time speak of themselves as grateful to Americans for letting them remain on the latter's land. Yaquis have a strong sense of dependence on the companies which set aside land for them to build villages. The companies, such as those at Eloy and Marana, are free to move the Yaquis about whenever they choose. When such a relocation takes place, they furnish transportation for the wall and roof materials of the houses and help the Yaquis to set them up again in the new place. There is thus more sense of security for the company-town Yaquis than for those who live in areas of doubtful status like Pascua and Guadalupe, but also a greater sense of direct dependence on specific Anglo-American owners whose interests they understand. Also the ties with a specific locality are much weaker than in the case of long-established villages like Pascua and Guadalupe.

For at least twenty years, the city of Tucson has recognized Yaquis as a distinctly needy group. During the minor depression of 1921–22, all the Yaqui families in the Pascua area were on the Red Cross relief rolls at the same time for several months. All but two or three of the families were on the Pima County Welfare Board's rolls at different times from 1922 to 1930, when again the whole Pascua community went on relief. In April 1935, during the Great Depression, a Welfare Board report stated that their records showed a registration of 275 Yaqui Indian families for the whole of Pima County. The report went on to say:

The average load per month for a period of one year is 182 due to the fact that these families pick cotton and work for various farmers during the spring and fall and are not on relief while so employed. (The) average number of persons per family (is) 5. (The) average cost includes food, milk, clothing, and medical supplies. A great many of the Yaqui men have from two to eight days regular work per month caring for lawns, gardens, etc. so that the relief granted in a majority of the cases is supplemental and not the entire living.

During the period 1936–37 (July to July) there were six out of the sixty Yaqui families in Pascua on the Pima County Welfare Board rolls. Of these two were widows with children or grandchildren, one was an old widower pronounced unfit to work by the Board, and three were able-bodied men who had reported themselves as unable to find work. The latter were given jobs on W.P.A. or put to work on the Charities Farms. From 1937 to 1941 the average Welfare Board load of Yaqui families has varied between five and twelve per month. The average outlay per family continued in the neighborhood of $12.00 per month.

Unfortunately, no data are available on aid to Yaquis in Guadalupe and Scottsdale and the other Yaqui centers. It may be said that when work becomes scarce at any of the company villages, there is a return to the old centers such as Pascua, Barrio Libre, and Guadalupe where efforts are made to get on the city or county relief rolls. There is clearly a correlation between general economic conditions and the extent of relief to Yaquis.

The high figures for Yaqui relief correspond with the periods of general national economic depression, 1921–23, and 1930–35. When economic conditions improved, Yaquis were absorbed along with the rest of the population into the wage-earning group.

There are numerous other sources of aid distribution, and in the case of most of these, the Yaquis are singled out from Mexican Americans and others as a specially needy group. These miscellaneous gifts on the part of Anglo-American agencies of various kinds frequently are given special mention in the newspapers when they are directed to Yaquis. Thus, Christmas parties by university sororities and by church groups and needlework guilds are given each year for Yaqui children or adults and they are generally noticed in the paper, sometimes with pictures showing perhaps a group of sorority girls presenting toys and gifts to a group of Yaqui children. The Big Brothers, a group of businessmen in Tucson, each year stages a campaign for funds to give to the poor about Christmastime. They recognize the Yaquis as a distinct group in the population and insist that the food, clothes, and gifts which are to be distributed at Pascua Village go only to Yaquis and not to the Mexican-American families living in or near Pascua. It is an interesting fact in this connection that all the Yaqui population of Barrio Libre is never singled out as a distinct group. Similarly, it is the Pascua school that is thought to contain all the Yaqui schoolchildren and that, therefore, receives all the aid for children that is given out to Yaquis. Tucsonans are not generally aware of the fact that there are many Yaquis of south Tucson in other schools, nor are they aware that nearly half of the registration at the Pascua school is made up of Mexican Americans with no Yaqui blood. The general concept in Tucson is that Pascua is the Yaqui village. There is a similar tendency in the Phoenix area to single out Guadalupe as the Yaqui village there and to ignore in popular thinking the other centers of Yaqui population.

In addition to the miscellaneous groups dispensing aid, which we have just considered, most of the churches are also active. Free bread is often given out by Catholic groups, and Pascua is one chief outlet for second-hand clothing in Tucson. The Pascua school has become, through its teachers, the distributing agency for such frequent gifts by Tucson groups, with the exception of the Catholic church which works through the leader of the Matachin society.

To a number of thoughtful people the Yaquis appear, as a result of their prominence on relief rolls, as a grave social problem. A state senator expressed himself as follows: "I have watched the Yaqui problem for a number of years with terror. . . . We have made efforts to send them back to their wild hill-life in Mexico, but without success." The attitude as expressed by the senator has periodic revival in the form of movements to deport all Yaquis back to Sonora. These recur every three or four years and are generally taken up by some of the more prominent public figures, who, aware of the economic status of the Yaquis, consider such a deportation desirable. Contrary to the views of the employers who consistently maintain a preference for Yaqui to other laborers, these public administrators see only the relief problems and conclude that the elimination of Yaquis from the state would eliminate an important group of such problems. The peculiar concentration of interest and charitable action on less than fifty percent of the resident Yaquis in Tucson indicates the ignorance of the real nature of the Yaqui place in the economic life of southern Arizona.

Political Relations

The political status of Yaquis in Arizona is wrapped up in misconception, neither Yaquis nor the majority of Anglo Americans understanding clearly what that status is. The characterization of them as "men without a country" creeps into almost every written account of Yaquis, whether in newspapers, periodicals, or state papers. This phrase represents a fundamental misconception about their citizenship status and is responsible for a great many attitudes and policies which color their relations with Anglo Americans. To define adequately their true political status, it is not enough to cite laws and statutes concerning their federal or state citizenship. It is necessary also to discuss their actual political relations as they have been maintained between 1900 and 1940 in Arizona.[8] In this section we shall consider, therefore, not only what is on the statute books concerning their status, but also their dealings with the various federal, state, county, and city agencies. In this way we may arrive at an understanding of their political status based on custom and usage rather than wholly on legal pronouncement, for Yaquis do have and have had for some time a political life involving participation in the various political institutions of the state of Arizona.

The usual estimate by welfare boards, the Alien Registry Bureau, and other governmental institutions has been that 90 percent of the heads of Yaqui families are not citizens of the United States. This means that this proportion has been born in Mexico and has not become or signified intention of becoming citizens. A count of those Yaquis in Pascua who presented themselves for alien registration in the autumn of 1940 shows that 82 out of the 450 residents of the village were born in Sonora. Of these 82, 30 were born in Hermosillo, 16 in the vicinity of Guaymas, 8 in the vicinity of Magdalena or Altar, 3 in Ures, 2 in Nogales, Sonora, 14 in Yaqui River towns, and 9 did not know where they were born. Of the 82 who were born in Sonora, the majority knew the exact year in which they crossed the line into the United States. Two came across between 1880 and 1885, 21 between 1900 and 1904, the majority of these in 1903 to 1904. There were 17 who came across between 1907 and 1910, the majority coming in 1907; 26 who crossed over between 1914 and 1918, the majority coming in 1916 and 1917; and only one who crossed as late as 1920. These figures probably stand as a sample of the composition of the Arizona Yaqui population in regard to places of origin and times of arrival in the United States. If we accept them as such, they would indicate that, at a conservative estimate, perhaps one-fourth of the total 1940 Yaqui population was Mexican born, that all of these persons entered the United States prior to 1920, and that 50 percent entered prior to 1907. The dates at which they entered the United States are important in establishing their legal position here.

What is the legal status of this one-fourth of the Yaqui population of Arizona? The United States immigration regulations as enforced in Arizona are as follows: all persons who entered from Mexico prior to 1924 and who possess no papers concerning their entry are not in the United States legally; nevertheless, they cannot be deported because there is no legal provision for starting deportation charges; persons who entered the United States between 1917 and 1924 can be deported only if they can be classified as criminals; all persons who entered after July 1, 1906, are ineligible for citizenship unless they return to Mexico and reenter the United States legally; those who entered prior to that date may register with an immigration official and become eligible for citizenship. Thus the majority of the Mexican-born Yaquis were ineligible in 1940 for citizenship unless they returned to Mexico and reentered the United States; this constitutes about 75 percent of the alien Yaquis. Still accepting the Pascua figures as typical, then, we may calculate that about 19 percent of the total Yaqui population of Arizona in 1940 were actually "men without a country," that is, persons who were not and may not become citizens of the United States. All the persons of this status in Pascua fall into the age group forty to eighty years. Of the remaining 81 percent of Yaquis, 75 percent are citizens of the United States by virtue of having been born in this country.

However, the legal status of this immigrant group of Yaquis remains doubtful. For example, a young man who entered the United States as a child in 1903 applied for citizenship papers in 1937. He was legally entitled to do so since he had entered prior to 1906. In his application he stated that he was "a real Yaqui Indian." His letter of application was returned from the immigration office in El Paso with the statement that he was ineligible to citizenship because he had declared himself to be a Yaqui Indian; only Caucasians and persons of African descent were admitted to citizenship. If he had stated that he was a Mexican, as he was entitled to do since he had been born in Mexico, he could have been eligible for citizenship because Mexicans are classified as Caucasians under federal immigration regulations.

No tests of a similar kind have been made in regard to the approximately 2,400 Yaquis who have been born in the United States. So long as they classify themselves as Indians are they ineligible to citizenship in the United States? This much is certain: if they are legally classified as Indians in the state of Arizona, they are denied certain rights, namely, the right to vote and to marry any but their own race.[9] But this perhaps depends again on whether or not they are classified as wards of the government, rather than as Indians.

Up to 1940 there had been no record of a Yaqui attempting to register for the purpose of voting in an election, at least a Yaqui who called himself a Yaqui in his registration. There seem as yet no evident advantages as recognized by Yaquis in citizenship except that of freedom from fear of deportation, which is one of the ever-recurrent fears among Arizona Yaquis. Every few years this fear is fanned, as has been pointed out above, by government officials of either Arizona or Sonora. As an example, the visit of Governor Roman Yocupicio of Sonora to Arizona in February 1937. He visited the Yaqui settlement of Guadalupe and extended an invitation to all Arizona Yaquis to return to Sonora where they would be settled on the land. The newspapers of Tucson and Phoenix gave some publicity to the proposal, speaking of it favorably, and for some weeks Yaquis remained fearful that there would be a wholesale deportation of them back to Sonora.

The federal government had twice required a general registration of aliens, once in 1918 and once in 1940. At the beginning of the 1940 registration, the director of alien registration gave out the following announcement to the newspapers.

At least two classes of aliens must register who have no opportunity to become citizens, one, Chinese, and the other Yaqui Indians who are in this country as political refugees from Mexico. Many of the latter have lived in this country for years after fleeing from Mexico, and are actually a people without a country, no longer being citizens of Mexico, and unable to become citizens of the United States.[10]

Although this status applied only to a small minority of Arizona Yaquis in 1940, it was generally understood in Arizona as applying to all Yaquis.

The fact that Yaquis have either definite alien status or the borderline status of "men without a country" results in their being constantly under the surveillance of immigration inspectors of the border patrol. Every center of Yaqui population is visited regularly by immigration men for the purpose of checking up on new arrivals from Sonora who have not reported at the border. These officers frequently become trusted friends of Yaquis, if they can speak Spanish, and often help them in various ways in their relations with state and city agencies.[11] It may be said in this connection that it is only the border patrolmen who fully understand the citizenship status of the Yaquis.

Parallel with the general tendency of Anglo Americans to think of all Arizona Yaquis as a non-citizen group, there is a general belief abroad, which is apparent in nearly every newspaper article dealing with Yaquis, that they are somehow constituted as a distinct political unit which has its own separate existence within the general Arizona polity. This belief influences Anglo Americans to speak of Yaqui "chiefs" and of the "Yaqui tribe."[12] This is a deep-rooted conception, having been well developed at least among Tucsonans since about 1915. The effects of this preconception on the relations between Yaquis and Anglo Americans have been manifold and have resulted as much in the disruption of Yaqui communities as in their integration.

The attempt on the part of Anglo Americans to set up a Yaqui political entity with which they might deal in all legal matters, and particularly in the matter of deportation and immigration, began in the Phoenix area about 1912 and in the Tucson area about 1918.[13] In both areas the lack of citizenship status of Yaquis was recognized, and they were established as wards of the government at Guadalupe and as without property rights at Pascua unless they should become citizens. In other words, their status was considered as being something like that of reservation Indians in the United States. Similarly, Anglos sought to set up Yaquis who might represent their various groups as a whole and who were designated as "chiefs." In Tucson the first "chief" recognized by Anglos was Juan Pistola. He was thought in Tucson to be the leader of "all the Yaquis in Arizona." He was backed mainly by a U.S. attorney, Kirk Moore, who used to have frequent conferences with him and his assistants in which Yaqui policies were determined. Through Moore, Pistola was able to make contact with many Anglos. He was instrumental in placing Yaquis on relief rolls in the 1921–22 depression, in freeing the "army of liberation"[14] in 1918, in securing jobs for Yaquis from 1917 to 1922, and finally in getting the real-estate man A. M. Franklin to establish the village of Pascua. During the period of Pistola's ascendancy, the Yaquis were by no means united under his leadership, although the Anglos associated with him continued to act as if they were. The Guadalupe Yaquis were entirely outside his sphere of influence and only a minority of Tucson Yaquis recognized him by even the title which he himself assumed—comandante-general. The Anglos expected him to maintain order at ceremonies in both south Tucson and Pascua. This resulted in his being blamed for a killing which took place in south Tucson, and as a result a large group of Yaquis became disaffected. He further took the position, under Moore's guidance, of opposition to the sending of arms into Mexico. This enterprise was carried on under the auspices of a group of south Tucson Yaquis who called themselves the Society of Little Jesus. Pistola's position in regard to their activity placed them at odds with him. Further friction had arisen between Tucson Yaquis when those from the south side attempted to bring Papagos to patrol a Pascua Easter ceremony. By the time of Pistola's death in 1922, there was absolutely no unity among Tucson Yaquis, and what was left of his leadership was merely a title applied to him by Anglos such as Kirk Moore, Franklin, and others.

Since Pistola's death, the title of chief has been applied to a number of different Yaquis by a number of Anglo-American groups and individuals in Tucson. When Pistola died, it was announced in the newspapers that the new "chief of all the Yaquis" would be Francisco Matus of south Tucson. He was unsuccessful in creating a following anywhere, but continued to be spoken of as "Yaqui chief" until his death in 1928. At about that time, a Yaqui named Guadelupe Flores entered the United States as a political refugee after the 1927 Yaqui "insurrection." He styled himself as "chief of the Arizona Yaquis" and received some recognition as such by newspapers and by certain lawyers in Tucson. At the same time Tomás Alvarez, who had been an assistant to Francisco Matus, was attempting to achieve Anglo recognition as "chief." His strongest influence was with one of the Catholic churches in Tucson, and through the latter he was publicly spoken of in some news items as Yaqui "chief." Meanwhile, Flores had persuaded the people of Pascua to hold an election at which they were instructed to

elect him chief. The election resulted, however, in the complete ignoring
of Flores and the elevation of Lauro Martínez to the doubtful office of
"captain of Pascua Village."

The Yaqui communities in both Tucson and Guadalupe became much
concerned about political leadership as a result of the evident confusion
among Tucson Yaquis and of the suspected activities of Guadalupe Flores
to have all Arizona Yaquis sent back to Sonora. In 1930, a *junta* at Guadalupe appointed Cayetano Lopez as "chief of all the Yaqui Nation in Arizona." Lopez made contact with a Tucson lawyer and had a document
drawn up which stated that a "council on Yaqui Indian Affairs" had been
created and that Lopez with his assistants, Henry Savala, Francisco Valencia, José María Flores, and José Alipas were heading the council. This
new organization received no recognition in the newspapers and represented, rather, a legitimate Yaqui reaction against the activities of Guadalupe Flores rather than an Anglo inspired "chieftainship." The Lopez organization became active in presenting the Yaqui case for wishing to remain
in Arizona to the governor and other officials of the state. Gradually,
Guadalupe Flores began to be recognized by both Anglos and Yaquis as
a charlatan, so that by the time he was deported in 1936, he was without influence even among Anglo-American lawyers in Tucson. The Lopez
organization, which apparently never had any important Yaqui following,
declined, the staff of the chieftainship descended to Savala and finally to
Valencia, and ended with the latter's death in 1936.

Meanwhile, in 1941, the Anglos still believe in a "chief" of the Yaquis.
Thus Tomás Alvarez receives most frequent newspaper recognition as
such, although the head of the Fariseo society is given that title during the
Easter ceremonial season. On the other hand, another individual who also
happens to have the name of Tomás Alvarez is regarded by official Tucson
as the Yaqui "chief" and so designates himself to the sheriff's office, the
Chamber of Commerce, the Alien Registry Bureau, and other organizations. This individual, whom we shall call Tomás Alvarez II, is the type
of person who gives rise to the Anglo conception in regard to chieftainship. He is of part Yaqui blood, but knows very little of the language.
Formerly resident of Pascua, he has lived in a Mexican-American area of
Tucson for about twelve years. He appears in Pascua during the Easter
ceremonies which are attended by many Anglos. Speaking English with
some ability, he tells spectators indiscriminately that he is "chief of all the
Yaquis in Arizona." In similar fashion, he also lets it be known at the sheriff's office and in other government offices in Tucson that he is a "chief."

Consequently, he is called on by official Tucson whenever dealings with Yaquis are necessary. Thus he secured alien registry blanks in the autumn of 1940 when there was general alien registration and distributed them among Pascua Yaquis; he also assisted as interpreter in the office during registration. He was spoken of and treated as "Yaqui chief" by the officials in charge of registration. Again, he was prominent during the Chamber of Commerce activities to promote the Pascua Easter ceremonies in 1941. The members of the committee from the Highway Patrol and the sheriff's office addressed him as chief and relayed messages through him to Pascua Yaquis. No official seemed aware of the fact that he was without standing in the village except as a Spanish-speaking go-between, that he was not resident in the village, and that he was not regarded as a Yaqui by any of the Yaquis.

The political interests of Yaquis and Anglo Americans meet on at least one count, however, and that is in the matter of maintenance of law and order among Yaquis. The Yaquis of Pascua Village have at various times in the past sought to institute their own methods of maintaining law and order. Thus accounts have been obtained from Yaquis and one or two whites describing an effort to control drunks at a fiesta in which a drunk was staked out on the ground until he should sober up. This created a vigorous protest on the part of Anglos, and the practice was ordered discontinued by the sheriff. It has never been repeated since. Again the Yaquis of Pascua instituted their own court in the middle twenties and attempted to settle a dispute between Yaquis involving a case of simple assault. The Yaqui against whom the verdict was rendered disregarded the Yaqui court and took the case to a Tucson court where it was dismissed. The failure of Yaqui efforts to set up their own legal institutions has resulted in a feeling of dependence on the legal institutions of Anglos. The Arizona Yaquis have thus been discouraged from developing any kind of court system or even a policing force.[15] Thus, whether or not disputes or criminal actions involve Anglo Americans, penal sanctions come into operation in Yaqui communities through the Anglo governmental institutions.

Anglo Americans, whether ordinary citizens or officials concerned with the law, do not think of Yaquis as constituting a disorderly group. Although Yaquis appear in newspaper items a dozen or more times a year in Tucson, as breakers of the law for drunken driving, disorderly conduct, or assault and battery, it is rarely reported that they are Yaquis. Consequently, the police court items in the paper are not recognizable as pertaining to Yaquis unless the reader knows the individuals. As a result, Yaqui law-breaking is not given special publicity, and the majority of Anglo Americans do not hold the view that they are disorderly.

Yaquis attempt to make use of the police force and of the courts of the Anglo Americans. One of their major concerns in the Tucson area is in the maintenance of order at fiestas, which typically involves nothing more than the suppression of a few drunken disturbers, both Yaqui and persons of other groups. It is a traditional preliminary of every large ceremony to go into the sheriff's office in Tucson and secure a "permit." In the Yaqui view this is an important and necessary proceeding and gives the essential official sanction for the occasion. To the sheriff it is not considered necessary. To the Yaqui it is thought of as a guarantee that the sheriff will send a deputy out several times during the night to see that order is maintained. To the sheriff it is thought of as a guarantee that the Yaquis themselves will see to keeping order and not that he is under obligation to maintain it, unless specially called to do so. In other words, except for the tradition of the "permit," Yaqui celebrations are not dealt with by the sheriff's office in any way different from that in which it deals with Anglo-American celebrations. The only Yaqui ceremony which is given a special sheriff's force is that at Easter, which is recognized as important for Anglos as well as for Yaquis because of the large crowds which attend it. Since the late 1920s this ceremony has had one or more representatives from the sheriff's office.

Since at least 1918, the Yaquis of Tucson have been accustomed to bringing certain of their legal problems before Anglo courts or peace officials. Those of which there is record include matters concerning the adoption of children, cases of assault and battery, adultery, bootlegging, and witchcraft. Many of those cases have involved the securing of lawyers by Yaquis and the formal trial or hearing of the evidence. There have been from time to time lawyers of Tucson who have for various reasons become especially identified with Yaqui litigation, and they have been sought out consistently by Yaquis to handle their cases. Many of the actions, however, in connection with which Yaquis have called in the law have been settled outside of court by sheriff's men or police officers.

One such was a witchcraft case which took place in Tucson in July 1937. The newspaper account of the incident illustrates the nature of relations between Yaquis and the sheriff's officer who is regarded by both Yaquis and the sheriff's office as a "specialist in Yaqui cases." It also indicates the nature of the difference between Anglo American and Yaquis in fundamental concepts which have to do both with law and with witchcraft. Excerpts from the account follow:

Using a little psychology and the help of "an old woman" sheriff's men aided in the curing of an alleged bewitched Yaqui girl at Pascua village last night. Early last evening a Yaqui came in to the sheriff's office and said that his 15 year old daughter was bewitched and he was afraid that she would die if something was not done at once to relieve her agony. He said she had been suffering for nearly 24 hours. Deputies Al Franco and Ora Shinn went to Pascua and found the girl hysterical and apparently suffering great pain. She was unable to speak but sobbed and moaned continually. The girl's mother told officers that Sunday night her daughter was not feeling well and she sent the girl to the other side of the village to an old lady to get some "home remedy" for her ailment. On the way home the girl passed the home of another woman, who is also known to prepare similar remedies. The parents said that this second woman stopped the girl and asked where she had been. The girl told her. The woman then said, "Why didn't you come to me instead of that other woman?" As the girl was replying, the father said, the old woman touched her and said words to her that cast a spell over her. He said when his daughter returned to her home she was under this spell and suffered fits and convulsions. He said she moaned and suffered through the night and all of yesterday. . . . Franco asked the father what he suggested be done. The father said that since the child had obviously been bewitched the only thing to do was to go to the woman that cast the spell and make her release the child from her coma. The Yaquis named the woman, who they believed bewitched the girl. Franco and Shinn went into the hut in which the woman lives, and found her to be a "kindly intelligent old lady about 70 years of age." She told the officers that she was not a witch but would see if she could help the little girl. Her son handed officers a written statement in which she denounced as "gossips" those who said she was a witch merely because she tries to help her friends who are in need.

Franco said he explained that he didn't wish to take her to jail but merely wanted her to talk to the girl and see if she could do anything for her. She readily consented and went to the girl's house with the officers. Franco said she spoke to the girl for a few minutes and the girl became quiet. After a little bit the girl spoke a few words. The parents were satisfied that she was out of the spell and recovering and the old lady walked to the car to leave. As she did so the girl called out to her and said she had pain in her heart and stomach. The old lady returned, Franco said, and rubbed the child's chest and stomach a little. The girl said she felt much better.[16]

This story was headlined "Case of Witchcraft Closed" but it went on for another week, and again the sheriff's Yaqui "specialist" played a prominent part in the incidents. The newspaper account continues four days later:

At 6:30 o'clock, Antonio Elenes, brother of Francisca [the bewitched girl], rushed into the sheriff's office saying that his sister was dying again. He had run all the

way from Pascua. The officers called Dr. F. W. Allen, county physician, who went
to the village with the brother. . . . Allen said that upon his arrival he had found
that the girl had fainted. He said he treated her and she was all right when he
left her. Dr. Allen said that the girl was at an age when there are natural changes
in her life. He said that she had apparently become worried about her physical
condition and had talked with some of the old women of the village. He said that
these persons had talked witchcraft to her, and she, believing this, was affected by
it. He said other things such as the intense heat, contributed to her hysteria. But
he said she is probably more scared than anything else.

At 8:30 last night, Al Franco, making his regular evening rounds, found that
the girl had again become ill. She was first hysterical, then unconscious. . . . Franco
took charge of the situation. He ordered everyone except those with the girl from
the sultry room. There had been 23 persons crowded into the tiny bedroom. . . .
The group appealed to Franco to go bring Senora Matus to make the girl well
again. [Sra. Matus was the woman named earlier in the week by neighbors as "una
Bruja" (a witch) capable of curing the girl and who did bring the girl out of her fit
the previous Monday night.] As Franco was about to leave for Sra. Matus, several
Yaquis entered the yard and said that they had already been to her little casa and she
was not at home. They said she had gone to the matachinas dance at Holy Family
church in Tucson. . . . Then Francisco Elenes, the father, drove up in his car. He
told Franco, "I am worried for the safety of my little girl, if she is bewitched and
the law does not take a hand, she will die. My sister will be next and I will follow."
He shrugged his shoulders and said, "Es con Dios."

Franco suggested that they get a doctor again. To this they replied, "Why
should we get a doctor? He will just say that she is not sick and there is nothing
the matter with her. We want the old lady," they pleaded.

Franco started for the Holy Family church but on the way met Sra. Matus returning. As she entered the Elenes yard with Franco the eyes of 60 to 70 Yaquis
were upon her. They were gathered in a semi-circle around the Elenes house in
front of which the girl lay. . . . She walked over to the bed and talking in Yaqui began rubbing the girl about the throat, chest and stomach. . . . For 15 or 20 minutes
the old lady rubbed the girl. . . . Finally she said that all this would be unnecessary
were it not for the father calling her "una Bruja" at the sheriff's office and starting
all the commotion. With these words the father said, "No, Senora—no es verdad."
He said he sent only to have the officers seek her aid and not to condemn her.
Franco substantiated Elenes' claim and said he had not named her as one casting
the spell over the girl. With a complete explanation of the situation both Elenes
and Senora Matus were convinced that there had been an understanding.

The witch continued to rub the girl who eventually professed to feel better, and so the incident ended. It had been the final one in a series which
had begun a few months before, all of which involved Francisca Matus
as witch. It was not only the injured persons, like the Elenes family, who
called the sheriff. During the week of the incident described Señora Matus had herself sworn out a charge of disturbing the peace against Fran-

cisco Elenes, the bewitched girl's father, and José Alipas, who had earlier charged that his son had been bewitched by Francisca Matus. As a result of Franco's activities in reestablishing good relations between Elenes and Sra. Matus, the latter's complaint was withdrawn. The activity of Franco in this case is typical of the helpful attitude of sheriff's men in the Tucson region toward Yaquis.

Perhaps a majority of serious troubles in Yaqui villages are settled in the above manner when the law is called in from outside, but there has been, nevertheless, ever since Pistola's time, a constant, if thin, stream of Yaqui cases that were settled in Anglo-American courts in Tucson. Practically all of these may be classified under four heads: (1) the federal government versus Yaquis on charges of illegal distilling of alcohol during the prohibition period; (2) charges of the state against Yaquis for misdemeanors (there is record of only one felony); (3) Yaquis versus Yaquis on charges of adultery, incompetent custody of children, and assault and battery; (4) Yaquis against Anglo-American individuals to obtain title to land for which they have paid contracts. By far, the majority of cases during 1920 to 1930 had to do with illegal distilling. Since 1930 cases of drunkenness and Yaqui suits against land-selling agencies have been dominant.

Such disputes have thrown Yaquis into close contact with certain lawyers. Ever since the days of Juan Pistola, who traced his rise to prominence in Tucson as a result of this wide acquaintance with officers of the peace and lawyers, it has been a notable characteristic of Yaqui leaders that they have many such legal connections. The nature of some of these contacts may be suggested by a quotation from an interview with one lawyer who at one time had a good deal to do with Yaqui cases, not because he solicited them but rather because for some obscure reason he got the name of being effective in their interests:

During the period [1925 to 1930] I had dealings with Cayetano who was associated with Matus. . . . Cayetano took quite some time one day to explain that Matus was "sort of chief" of the Yaquis. I never understood the relationship between Cayetano and Matus—and the other Yaquis. I had the feeling that Matus was simpler and honest, and Cayetano was deriving some benefit from his association with Matus. However, I never could find that Cayetano derived any financial benefit from the business he brought me. I never paid him. Even when I used him independently as an interpreter for Yaqui he refused pay for his services. He must have made arrangements with those whom he brought in to me for clients. It might have been that he was doing it entirely for political reasons. . . . Federal prohibition violations made up the majority of the cases. When the countryside . . . began filling up with . . . pot-bellied Yaquis—it meant the Prohis had picked up another bootlegger. Cayetano never brought in anyone singly. There would always be several men, squaws in gingham—the whole damned family. They would all come into the office and Cayetano would start out with something like "Pedro, they gottum over there in jail, Mr. Allen." He would not introduce them all to me, usually just one—usually the one who would pay the bill afterwards. I would have to sit behind the desk and find out who each one was and finally would suggest that all clear out except Cayetano and one other. Then I could do business. I am allergic to stench, and it was just too much. I got so that I kept a box of cheap cigars or cigarettes on hand and would pass them out. The rest would go outside and sit on the curb or stand against the building. I did not solicit this type of business, and it tended to keep my other clients away. The cigar smoke helped a little—acted as a fumigating agent. I don't know why Cayetano ever selected me. . . . I never made an effort to keep the business, charged my usual fees for Federal Court work. Sometimes it was as high as $100 or $150. There was never any talk of not paying the bill, and it was always paid down to the last dollar or dollar and a half. I would not have done anything if they had not paid at all, but they always paid liberally and cheerfully. Usually it was a big fat squaw who would amble in and bring out a wad of greasy bills from her ample bosom. . . . Some of my work was in connection with land purchases. . . . They never came to me with domestic trouble. I was surprised at that but realized later that it was probably settled at home. . . .

I often had the feeling when the Yaquis were in the office that I was dealing with Mexicans. Once or twice I spoke directly to some of them in Spanish and got an answer. Usually, however, they refused to talk and let Cayetano do all the talking. Probably prearranged. I was surprised that the Mexican element had not touched. If he were acting like a regular Mexican he would have approached me with a proposition to split the fee, but he never asked me for compensation. . . . Another funny thing about these Yaquis. I would spend hours with them sometimes in the office and then would meet them on the street fifteen minutes later and there would never be a sign of recognition. . . . These Yaquis are an expressionless lot. Have you ever noticed it? Or rather, they have two facial expressions—one when they are laughing, and one for every other occasion. . . . Their sense of humor is keen, I would judge. . . . They seem very stupid—in some ways, but not in all. They are very philosophical and have the ability to understand things when explained to them. Certain things seem to come easy. They knew court procedure and learned it easily. They professed, at least, to understand the complicated realty situations in which they became involved. They are superior to some of my white women clients in that respect. With ordinary business affairs though they seem very stupid. They are not adjusted to living in the United States.

This interview illustrates, more clearly than any generalized statement could, how Yaquis appear to the intelligent, ordinary legal-minded Anglo Americans who must have dealings with them, and it indicates also in detail the chief characteristics of Yaqui contacts with such persons which include: choosing a middle-man or go-between, presenting the case as a body and specifically as a kin group, the presentation and handling of the case remaining partially, at least, unintelligible to the Anglo, personal habits which are offensive to an Anglo American and force him to limit his contact still further, strict living up to financial obligations, creation of the view in Anglo Americans that they are clear-minded and intelligent in regard to such things as legal procedure. In general, perhaps, the Yaquis must appear to such a man as country people, but nevertheless strange and slightly mystifying country people, for he cannot understand them even when they do talk, and their ways cannot be explained unless some means of communication is established—and communication remains uniformly faulty.

In the 1930s it was not uncommon in middle-class circles in Tucson to hear the Yaquis spoken of as a "health menace." The state senator who viewed "the Yaqui problem" with horror regarded the "health situation in Pascua as menacing." Attention is called to the fact that all Pascuans have open wells, that they bathe in an open irrigation ditch that flows along the west edge of the village,[17] that they resist efforts of the county doctor and other county officials to give them good medical care when they need it, and that they have a lot of dogs constantly around which constitute an ever-present danger. These are all real facts, but they do not all serve to mark Pascuans off from other inhabitants of Tucson. For example, the first two facts in regard to open water supply are also true of all the Mexican-American section for a mile south of the Yaqui village. It is a health problem not peculiar to the Yaquis.

The other two facts are, however, more or less peculiar to the Yaquis and deserve special attention because both are important for an understanding of the total contact situation. The governmental agencies might be regarded as medical missionaries. The County Health Department provides a doctor who gives his services free to whomever needs them; hospital facilities in a county hospital for indigent persons; a visiting nurse who gives free advice to mothers and others; and finally a free coffin and mortuary service. The latter is compulsory service; the other three are merely available to any who call for them, although the visiting nurse does not wait to be called, but makes regular visits for educational purposes. None of these services is provided especially, or in any special way, for the Yaquis of the county.

The Yaquis avail themselves of all the county health facilities, but they do so in their own manner and that manner is not understood by the Anglo Americans who administer the services. Thus the county doctor is frequently called to minister to a person in Pascua, or in Barrio Libre. In the majority of cases he is called as a last resort, when an individual has tried the known Yaqui remedies and is finally casting about for any means at all of being kept alive. Consequently, there is a large percentage of unsuccessful treatments by the county doctor, and his reputation as a curer among the Yaquis is rather low. The number of calls which he receives to the Yaqui village of Pascua is directly proportional to the concern of Anglo-American persons for Yaqui health, as for instance in the case of schoolteachers or others who are stationed in the Yaqui settlement all day and consequently know about who is sick. Furthermore, Yaquis invariably reserve the right either not to procure the medicine suggested by the doctor, or to withhold it even if it is procured. It may be refused not only because of its cost, which is not a usual reason for not using it, but on account of its taste or color or some other less obvious quality. In other words, the county doctor remains—whether he knows it or not—merely a consultant who has been called in perhaps by a family already in consultation with a Yaqui medicine woman, and no Yaquis feel an inevitable obligation to follow his prescriptions. The Yaquis do not feel themselves lacking in their own medical resources, though they do sometimes feel that they are not adequate in a particular case; but it cannot be said in general that Anglo-American medical techniques have any higher prestige than Yaqui.

One of the features of Anglo-American medical technique, which meets with most definite opposition among Yaquis, is hospital treatment. A serious case always results in the county doctor's recommending removal to a hospital where the patient may be "kept clean, given good nourishing food, and made properly comfortable." The doctor at the time of making this recommendation is generally looking at a person lying on the dirt floor of an adobe house in a pile of much-used quilts, buzzing flies, and a large group of relatives and compadres sitting and standing about, maintaining a constant murmur of conversation or even singing. Those are the usual conditions maintained by Yaquis for persons who are seriously ill and expected to die.[18] To the doctor they appear insuperable difficulties to getting well. His solution is the hospital, with clean white beds and an absence of solicitous people. To the Yaqui the hospital means death, because the overwhelming majority of Yaquis who have entered hospitals have done so as a last resort and have not come out alive. The hospital also means the elimination of the one thing left that seems worthwhile with death so near, namely, the presence of kin and compadres. A cold, impersonal hospital with unaccustomed sheets and drinking tubes and bedpans, with a strange language being spoken all around, does not, therefore, appear to the Yaqui as the solution, and consequently, he does not follow the doctor's suggestion and go to the hospital except under compulsion or as a desperate last resort.

Yaquis do not kill dogs. They feel that they do not have the right because traditionally dogs belong to San Lázaro, and there is memory in the Yaqui settlements of an old feast which was given annually for all the dogs of a village at which they were given special food in bowls. As part of the community, dogs were as inviolable as human beings, even though they may have been kicked around and, by Anglo-American standards, treated indifferently. Dogs, therefore, go on accumulating in considerable numbers. Then some summer one bites a person or two. If the County Health Department finds rabies, there is a clean-up of the Yaqui dogs. This happens periodically in the Tucson villages and always creates hard feelings on the part of the Yaquis. Even if a temporarily recognized "chief" of the Yaquis cooperates with the dog catcher, the rest of the Yaquis exhibit a determined passive noncooperation, and the clean-up of dogs always remains partial. But the dog round-ups remain a constantly recurring feature of the relations between Yaquis and the County Health Department.

The Yaqui relations with undertakers are an interesting form of contact. As a matter of tradition, Yaquis in the main areas of concentration of population make use of the free county facilities for burial. They always request the plain pine box and the undertaker's services. And the undertaker's helper always appears after the night of a Yaqui funeral with his large black hearse, dressed in coat, collar, and tie as is required by his employer, as a matter of respect for the dead and the family, although the Yaquis are coatless and tieless.

Relations with Religious Groups

The Yaquis in Arizona are recognized by a number of church groups as an urgent and promising field for missionary work. Roman Catholics, Presbyterians, Baptists, Jehovah's Witnesses, and a few lesser-known sects have made and, in most instances, are still making efforts to present their teaching to Yaquis in Pascua and Guadalupe, these being the Yaqui centers that have received general publicity and are therefore known. The work of these various sects has been carried on in extremely different ways and has met with varied receptions. Nowhere has it been without effect;

nowhere has it been completely rejected. The general impression that one gets is that, as always in the past, Yaquis have remained eclectic in their religion. Persons baptized into the Baptist church go on serving in the Yaqui church as important officials. Persons who inveigh bitterly against the Catholic church may make it a point to go to its services more or less regularly. A deep and constant reader of Spanish tracts distributed by Jehovah's Witnesses may be a devout Yaqui Catholic and may at the same time also attend regularly the meetings in the village of a Baptist evangelical group. Only one organized outside agency accepts the Yaqui church as on a par with any of the sects that are busy proselytizing the Yaquis. This is the Chamber of Commerce. It encourages and even promotes in a mild way the most spectacular of Yaqui ceremonies—those at Easter—and by so doing influences Yaqui religious life in an important way. The complex reactions of Yaqui culture to the Anglo missionaries and the Chamber of Commerce constitute the subject matter of the following section.

Protestantism is definitely associated by Yaquis with Anglo Americans, and the Catholic church is associated with Mexicans. This is true despite the fact that the priests with whom Yaquis have had contact in Arizona have not been Mexican and despite the fact that the Protestant sect which has been most influential in the Tucson region has been a Mexican congregation with a Mexican minister. In the present section we shall discuss only the Anglo-American Protestant missionaries and their work. We shall reserve for the next chapter on Mexican-American relations the treatment of both the contact with the Catholic church and the contact with the Mexican Baptist church.

In Pascua the Anglo Baptists have been more active than any other Protestant group. The work of the Baptists has been chiefly carried on through the Mexican Baptist church of Tucson, but there have also at various times been missionaries claiming affiliation with the Baptist church. The work of one of these independent Anglo missionaries will illustrate the character of the contact for which they are responsible. One was moderately active in Pascua in the spring of 1937. He was accustomed to bringing magazines such as *Time* and *Life* and odds and ends of clothing and distributing them to persons in the village. Unable to speak Spanish, he became acquainted with only two persons in the village, one an English-speaking woman who had already been baptized into the Mexican Baptist church and the other a young man, Juan Silvas, who at that time had been inactive in Pascua ceremonial life for a number of years. The missionary was to be seen once or twice a week in the village bringing small gifts and talking English to whomever would listen. On several Sundays he held meetings in the Pascua schoolhouse. One of these meetings was observed. There were twenty-seven in attendance, twenty of whom were Yaquis, the others being Mexicans from Pascua or Barrio Belen. As the people were gathering for the meeting, news of which had been spread during the week through the village by the missionary, the missionary talked rapidly to his English-speaking Yaqui Baptist acquaintance. He told her of his own experiences with prayer and that God had brought him what he wanted because he had faith and prayed, the thing that he wanted always coming to pass. The meeting proceeded:

The missionary talked in English very rapidly, apologizing for the fact that there was no one to speak to them in Spanish. He told them that all he wanted to do was help them and that they had the right to worship as they pleased. He told them that the way to "build mansions in heaven" was not to be good boys and girls, but to have faith. He passed out to all he thought could read the Gospel of John in English, and read and partially explained the fourteenth chapter. He said that he did not see why these people had to pay taxes when the Pimas and Papagos didn't, and he thought that he might, through the proper sources, have their taxes exempted. He mentioned the fact that he knew José María García, the *maestro mayor* of Pascua (with whom he had tried unsuccessfully to have several conversations during the preceding weeks). At the end he passed out song books in English and tried to get the people to sing, but none knew the songs, so after he sang the first verse alone, he read the others. Then he offered a prayer. Then everyone just sat and did not know what to do. Finally the Baptist acquaintance got up and said that was all, and the people left. As the Baptist woman left, the missionary said to her not to give up her religion no matter what people said about her, because she would be happier with it.

The meeting indicates the lack of real contact established between the Anglo-American missionary and the Yaquis. It indicates also the readiness with which Yaquis respond to a call for such a meeting. Twenty people was a respectable turn out. Several more meetings were held of the same kind. Then during the Easter ceremonies of that year the missionary hired a visiting evangelist's sound truck and posted it on the highest spot in the village. While Yaqui ceremonies were going on at the Yaqui church, the truck roared out a message that could be heard over the chants before the altar. It exhorted "to take refuge in the Great Savior, Our Lord Jesus Christ," and thus to "win the Kingdom of Heaven." Several times during the Lenten season the truck appeared in the village and blared forth its message, always in English. This angered the schoolteacher, and these activities were stopped. Sporadically, after 1937, this missionary has held meetings and appeared in private houses in Pascua but has never built up

a personal following or gained any influence among Pascuans. His miscellaneous activities are typical of the casual religiously motivated Anglo
American without an organization behind him who periodically appears
in Pascua under the name of missionary.

More efficiently equipped and more persistent have been the disciples
of Judge Rutherford, generally known as Jehovah's Witnesses. They have
carried on a campaign of proselytization at Pascua since the early 1930s.
They have employed two methods which have resulted in leaving a definite impression on the minds of many Pascuans. Never holding general
meetings, they go from house to house, usually on Sundays, some speaking in English but some also in Spanish to individual Pascuans. They do
not rely entirely on the personal contact, however. They have a large number of publications with vividly colored covers printed in Spanish. These
they distribute for a small sum, perhaps five cents apiece, but they also
express their willingness to sell them for a cake of soap or any other small
useful article. Pascuans have bought probably a hundred or more of these
pamphlets in the past five years and they are circulated widely through the
village. The printed Spanish word is not, however, their only means of
contact. In addition, they carry phonographs and play records in Spanish
which present in effective oratorical manner the ideas of Judge Rutherford.

These ideas have become a part of the thinking of several influential
Pascuans, and it seems worthwhile, therefore, to discuss them briefly. The
pamphlets which have had wide distribution in Pascua have the following
titles: "Universal War Near," "The Crises," "A Just Ruler," "Dividing the
People," and "Escape to the Kingdom." The doctrine is simple and goes
over and over two or three main points. Its kernel is as follows: a cataclys-
mic world crisis is coming, a crisis which had its beginning in 1914. The
rich men, the politicians, and the priests will be destroyed because they
have been part of the invisible "army of Satan," which has been dominant
in the world. Those who love God and consider the Bible—the Jehovah's
Witnesses—will be saved and will go to the kingdom of heaven which will
supplant the "world of doubt and suspicion and insecurity." The authority
for all of this is the Bible and, indirectly, the pamphlets of Judge Rutherford. This simple prophecy of a millennium is set forth with abundant
illustrations from current history and abundant quotations from the Bible,
and with vivid colored pictures showing radiant angels who watch while
fat, rich men, gangsters, kings, and soldiers destroy themselves, as working
men and ordinary people escape to a bright heaven.

This idea of a millennium and the coming of a kingdom of heaven is frequently discussed by the older Yaqui men who have bought copies of the Rutherford pamphlets. These men are also the ones who are the leaders in the Pascua church. They compare the "army of Satan," so vividly described in the pamphlets, to the Yaqui *Chapayekas,* who represent evil spirits during the winter ceremonial season. They interpret world events of recent years, particularly the European war, in Rutherford's language. Thus the doctrine has definitely affected them, but no Yaqui has been found who is intensely devoted to the Rutherford ideas. They use them merely to illuminate present-day events, and they seem to regard the coming millennium merely as a matter for speculation. None has any deep faith in its imminence.

Relations with the Chamber of Commerce

Since the early 1920s, Yaquis have been in contact with the Anglo-American idea of religious freedom. This was presented to them in very concrete fashion at Pascua at the time of the founding of the village. In the words of Lucas Chavez, who was active in the founding of the village in 1922:

Mr. Franklin and Kirk Moore said that they would give this land to the Yaquis and they could pay for it when they were able. Every family would be able to buy a lot for $150 or $100. Then Mr. Franklin said he would give to the Pueblo some more land which they would not have to pay for. This was the big lot where the plaza is. Kirk Moore said that this would be the place where we would build our church, and there would be a fence around it. Then the Yaquis would have their Easter ceremonies here unmolested. They would not be disturbed by bad Yaquis who did not go with Pistola, nor by Mexicans, nor by any other people. They would follow the old customs here unmolested and here they could do just those things which had always been according to legitimate Yaqui custom.

Kirk Moore thus made very clear to the founders of Pascua that Yaqui religious customs were to go on in accordance with the principle of religious liberty enjoyed by all other Americans. Yaqui leaders like Chavez have not forgotten this statement and regard it as legal sanction for the continuation of their church as independent from any other church in the Tucson region.

According to Yaquis in Tucson, it had been Moore's idea that all the Yaquis of the area should come together in Pascua and hold their religious ceremonies in the plaza. He tried to make the Pascua location attractive as a ceremonial place by providing a subsidy for the Easter ceremonies. This subsidy, usually given through the Chamber of Commerce and amounting to as much as seventy-five dollars, began to be dispensed in the early 1920s. In 1923 or 1924 a meeting was called at the Chamber of Commerce at which Moore spoke. Yaquis from both Pascua and south Tucson were invited. The subsidy was mentioned and the south Tucsonans were urged to come to Pascua. They did not come, but held their Easter ceremonies in Barrio Libre as they had done since 1916. They have continued to hold them apart from Pascua ever since that time.

Meanwhile, the annual subsidy at Easter became a Tucson tradition. When it was not given by the Chamber of Commerce, it was contributed by private persons, but gradually it became a recognized institution of the Chamber of Commerce. As the latter slipped into the role of benefactor to Pascua Easter ceremonies, it also began a campaign for publicity for the ceremonies which has been continued and has developed to an ever larger scale.

From the first, the Chamber of Commerce has promoted publicity in the newspapers of Tucson, and this publicity has become one of the major sources for the coinage of popular terminology concerning the Yaquis. In addition, the Chamber of Commerce has issued leaflets and pamphlets each year since at least 1930 describing the ceremonies. In 1933 the Chamber issued a sheet copper leaflet describing the Easter ceremonies as "The 400th Annual Yaqui Indian Oberammergau." In 1941 an illustrated pamphlet of twenty-five pages was printed called "The Passion at Pascua." These publications of the Chamber of Commerce have always been printed and given free to the Yaquis of Pascua who were urged to sell them for small sums to visitors who wished to have some description and interpretation of the ceremonies. The Chamber of Commerce publicity program has had very noticeable results. The attendance of outsiders at the ceremonies has increased steadily and might be conservatively put at the figure of 900 for the year 1941. The parking of cars became a major problem as early as 1936, and consequently the Chamber of Commerce organized a committee known as the Yaqui Indian Passion Play Committee. In 1941 this committee had developed to the point that it was organized in four sections: one devoted to parking arrangements, one to seating arrangements, one to newspaper and radio publicity, and one to the provision of costumes for the performers.

The attitude of the Chamber of Commerce in its activities is that it is assisting the Yaquis economically and that it is developing one of the important resources of Tucson as a tourist attraction. Officially, its secretary in an interview says that he is trying to preserve "one of the outstanding folk festivals of the Southwest and to maintain its authentic folk character."

Relations with Teachers and Others

Some of the most intimate and far-reaching contacts, in their effects on Yaqui culture, have been those between Yaquis and persons connected in one way or another with educational institutions. It has been pointed out that schools have been established at the two most newsworthy Yaqui settlements—Guadalupe and Pascua. The Pascua school has been in existence since 1924, the Guadalupe school since the late 1920s. The company towns, such as Eloy and Marana, also have schools but are not supposed to be designed for any particular one of the groups engaged in work there. At Marana, for example, all the children—Anglo, Mexican-American, and Yaqui—go to the same school in accordance with the general Arizona state educational policy; only Negroes are segregated in elementary school.[19] Yaqui children attend these schools, but in a rather haphazard manner, and attendance is not enforced by a truant officer. The Pascua and Guadalupe schools differ from the company ones in that they have been established for the special purposes of ministering to particular Yaqui communities. The Guadalupe school, taught as far as fifth grade by a Hawaiian woman, has been sponsored by the U.S. Government as a Public Works Administration project. It practices no segregation; Yaquis and Mexicans who are in about equal proportions in Guadalupe go to it together. It may be regarded as a specially subsidized rural school, and it is conducted in that manner.

The school which has been at Pascua since 1924 is not like that existing for the use of Yaquis at any other place. Like so much else in connection with Pascua, it represents a particularly conscious effort on the part of one or a few Anglo Americans to direct specifically the cultural development of Yaquis as set off from any other group in the population. Pascua has always been, since the days of Juan Pistola and Kirk Moore, the center of all such "improvement" efforts. The burst of interest in Yaquis in Tucson in the early twenties when the village of Pascua was being set up resulted also in the establishment of the Pascua school.

In 1923 Miss Thamar Richey, who had been a teacher in Indian schools in various parts of the country, found herself without a post in Tucson and became interested in the Yaquis. Her personal energy was so great that she persuaded the City School Superintendent of Tucson to set up with

Miss Thamar Richey and all her students at the Pascua School, April 1937. *Photograph by David J. Jones, Jr.*

city funds a special school at Pascua, expressly for the Yaquis, although the village was outside the city limits. It was first set up in the Yaqui church at Pascua, but within a year or two an adobe building was constructed just at the edge of the Pascua acres. Miss Richey continued to be its teacher from its founding in 1924 until 1939 when she died. During this period she devoted her life almost entirely to the Yaquis of Pascua. Her job was to teach English to Yaqui children, who were thought of as having a special language handicap, and thus to prepare them for entrance to the city or county schools. Thus the Pascua school remained a pre-elementary school and was not graded.[20] Students, after learning English there, must go on elsewhere for ordinary elementary and grammar-school instruction. With this very limited educational job, Miss Richey took time to interest herself in the lives of all Pascuans.

She became an important power in the village. She had access to various charities, such as the Community Chest and the Big Brothers, and so forth. She came to be known as the benefactor of the Yaquis by various church organizations and other groups in Tucson, and they turned over to her unneeded clothing, food, and other items which she distributed at Pascua. The assistance she gave was real and was much needed, and she asked nothing in return for the help she gave. She knew every Yaqui family in Pascua very intimately and made rounds almost once a day in order to see who was in need of any sort of help. She remained on constant call both at the school and at home for Pascuans who wanted to borrow a dollar, know how to fill out an application, get some relief, and for other endless requests. The set of attitudes which she held must be considered because of her long-continued and very effective contact with the Yaquis of Pascua. A few quotations may indicate something of the nature of these attitudes:

Miss Richey doesn't think the [Easter] ceremonies are being efficiently handled this year, nor were they last year (1936). Last year she went to much trouble to get boards for seats and when she had the boards hauled to the plaza there were no boxes ready to place them on. This, she thinks, is typical of how the Yaquis act. The people of Tucson go to expense and trouble to help them and then they refuse to do anything in return. The Chamber of Commerce sent bleacher seats out once for the ceremonies and the Yaquis simply left them outside the plaza where they couldn't be used. Then, too, the Yaquis never let anyone take pictures. This shows ingratitude.

Implicit in this quotation are certain characteristic features of the school-teacher's contact with Pascua. She was perspicacious enough to know that there was no "chief of the village" of the kind imagined by the Chamber of Commerce and others. She laughed at Tomás Alvarez and disapproved of him because he drank frequently. She herself, therefore, ignored all "chiefs" and did her work directly with individual families. This left her completely out of touch with the larger community enterprises such as the Easter ceremonies which, of course, had their leaders and organizers. She worked always entirely on a basis of face-to-face individual contact. Thus she missed getting much understanding of Yaqui culture. At the same time that she scorned all types of "chiefs," she called limosnas[21] "begging expeditions" and shook her finger at them as they passed through the village. She went on until the end interpreting Yaqui culture and her relations with it in terms of the simple standards of personal relationships in an individualistic society. This was the basis of her approach, and it made her peculiarly acceptable by the Yaquis, because she had no axe to grind.

The other important aspect of Miss Richey's contact with Pascua Yaquis may be thought of perhaps as a buffering influence between interested groups, such as missionaries in Tucson and the villagers. While Miss Richey was alive, Pascua was her field, as it were, and she kept the various missionaries outside. Another quotation may indicate the situation here:

She told me that Gwynn's loudspeaker had made her mad, too, Friday and that she had called up Beal of the local Baptist church to see if Gwynn was connected there and whether they could do something about stopping him. Reverend Beal said that Miss Richey should not try to stop him, that she herself should have done something in all the years she has been in the village to stamp out the religion there. Miss Richey told him that the religion worked pretty well for the Yaquis and that she thought it would be wrong to stamp it out. Miss Richey told me that two years ago Morales of the Mexican Baptist church had come out here and preached, using the schoolhouse. Miss Richey went to one meeting and found "men and women with their arms about each other sitting on the tables." That had made her mad and she had told Morales to get out and stay out.

This quotation illustrates the scope of her religious and moral convictions as they guided her in threading her way among the various lines of contact that reached out periodically from Tucson to the Yaquis at Pascua. She maintained the principle of religious liberty with great intensity and objected to missionaryism. She did not stand as a pathway for cultural influences of any specific kind from Anglo-American culture; she was, rather, an insulation against such influences, as indicated by their influx almost immediately on her death. She regarded her own function in the contact process as the catalyst who was opening up channels through education and English language which would lead Yaquis by a natural route into Anglo culture. Her influence was not profound culturally and would be difficult to trace except in the fields of language and economic contacts through the various charity organizations. Her commitment to the village engendered considerable fondness on the part of Yaquis.

After Miss Richey's death, the Pascua school continued to be regarded by its teacher who worked there as much a mission as a teaching job and the Richey tradition of the teacher taking a part in village problems is a continuing tradition. The school has become a center of a certain type of contact with the Anglo world. Thus, moving pictures are occasionally shown there and, as we have seen, persons who wish to hold religious meetings use the schoolhouse. A W.P.A. needlework class for women has been instituted at the school and Pascua women attend this several times a week. Although the school was designed as a Yaqui school, it has always been attended by many Mexican-American children as well, the usual proportion being about three-fifths Yaqui and two-fifths Mexican American. The same is true of the adult needlework class.

When a child leaves the Pascua school, he is supposed to be able to use the English language, whether written or oral. He then goes into one of the city schools, ordinarily beginning at the Davis school which is located in a Mexican-American district of the city, so that most of the school contacts of Yaquis are with Mexican Americans. By 1941 only a half dozen Tucson Yaquis are known to have gone beyond the sixth grade. One attained the third year of high school. At these higher levels the contacts are increasingly with Anglo Americans. The school contacts will be discussed chiefly in connection with the Mexican-American influences, but it may be of interest here to note one twelve-year-old Anglo American girl's attitude toward Yaqui schoolmates:

The Yaqui kids don't mix much with the Americans and the American kids get along with them all right. The Mexican kids cheat and play little dirty tricks in games, but the Yaqui kids don't do that. The Yaqui kids are sort of slow, though.

This indicates again the consistent tendency of Anglo Americans to feel distinct differences between Mexican Americans and Yaquis with a generally more favorable attitude toward the Yaquis.

There is a certain kind of contact with Anglo Americans which is relatively rare and which might be called, looking at it from the Anglo point of view, a passive contact. Painters, photographers, ethnologists, writers, and even musicians appear from time to time in Yaqui villages actuated by an interest not in bringing something from Anglo-American culture to the Yaquis, but rather in taking something from Yaqui culture for presentation to Anglo Americans. These persons frequently work out contacts with Yaquis such as they would among persons from their own cultural group. Not being in the roles of instructors, administrators, employers, or missionaries, they are dependent for their success on none of the institutions of Anglo-American culture and must accordingly become dependent on Yaqui goodwill, which means learning how to behave in accordance with Yaqui customs. Their influence on Yaqui culture, nevertheless, whether they realize it or not, is considerable, and we shall make an effort here to assess the nature of that influence.

Because Yaquis sometimes gain attention in the newspapers of southern Arizona, some Anglos are conscious of their peculiar citizenship status. Thus it happens that any information about them which is new, not well known, or strange, finds its way easily into the newspapers. Most of such information comes through artists, writers, or scientists who spend a brief period with some Yaquis and report their work to the Anglo world. Ever since 1918 there has been a constant stream of newspaper stories emanating from or based on the work of various students of Yaqui culture.

Without exception, these students have maintained a favorable and even warm attitude toward the Yaquis. They have, therefore, influenced Yaqui culture in two important ways. In the first place, they have heightened the consciousness of Anglo-American newspaper readers toward the Yaquis as a separate group within the population, and in the second place they have tended to foster a favorable attitude toward the Yaquis. Let us consider some of their work and their statements about it.

One of the most influential of such students was Phebe Bogan of Tucson whose study of the Pascua Easter ceremonies in 1925 long served as material for reporters assigned to cover those rites and for compilers of the Chamber of Commerce pamphlets. She wrote of the Yaquis as follows:

They are tall, well muscled, noted as warriors, hunters, sailors, pearl divers, cowboys, farmers, artisans and mechanics. Like the men, the women are high-hearted and of great endurance. As a race they are merry, much given to festivities and often shouting when they walk. . . . In Arizona the Yaqui may work unmolested; he may worship God as he pleases, he may earn a living and help others, for he is not lazy nor idle from choice and he is thrifty. . . . He cheerfully accepts life among a people whose language he cannot understand and whose ways are strange except where they touch his own ideals of independence and liberty (pp. 10–11).

He is married by the priest; his child is carried to the church to be baptized (p. 10).

Their religious devotions are performed with a sincerity that is unquestionable, even to the most casual observer (p. 21).

Like all children of nature these people worship God in the great open spaces (p. 22).

The Yaqui Indian is a Mexican Indian driven from his native land by a long series of wars and persecutions because he has steadily refused to subdue an inherent independence and love of liberty. . . . He is an exceptionally rational and industrious Indian (p. 67).

Singularly tenacious of his ideals, his habits and beliefs, the religion and the mores of the Yaqui will endure so long as there is a Yaqui among them of pure blood, unless civilization with its iconoclastic tendencies gains a firmer hold over them in the future than it has in the past. They are hebraic in their pride of race (p. 68).[22]

Mrs. Bogan based her writing on very intimate personal contacts with Pascua Yaquis. She brought them into contact with Anglo-American culture through her writing which appeared in pamphlet form, in Arizona periodicals, as reprints in the newspapers, and as a small book. Almost all subsequent writers have drawn extensively from her work, and her view has perhaps become a standard one among middle-class Arizonans who have no direct contact with the Yaquis.

While Bogan's contact was intimate and long-continued, the majority of artists, writers, and scientists maintain very fleeting contacts and report their impressions to the press. Thus a well-known portrait painter from Washington spent a few weeks in Tucson one summer, painting various Yaquis of Pascua. He spoke enthusiastically to reporters of the people of the village:

Señora Matus [one of the old women he had painted] is 90 years old. . . . I could not help placing her as cousin in dignity to my typical Boston grandmothers. She lives in poverty, yet she sustains a dignity of bearing of a lady of the old school. You may say she is only a Yaqui, but she is handing down a cultural tradition.[23]

This artist painted some twenty people of Pascua and then exhibited his sketches in a Tucson art gallery and later placed them all on exhibit in the Arizona State Museum in Tucson. His favorable views of Yaquis received considerable space in the newspapers.

An occasional student of anthropology who has studied the Yaquis passes through Tucson and duly gives out an interview to the press. Thus one from California passing through the city from the Yaqui country in 1934 reported:

I feel a genuine friendship for the Yaquis and I wish to correct some current misconceptions about him. . . . I was warned before I went into Yaqui country not to deal with them, but I have since found all such advice misleading as they are trustworthy to the extreme.[24]

The files of newspapers and periodicals since 1910 repeat again and again such views on the part of artists, writers, and scientists. These stories cannot have been without effect on the general reading public of southern Arizona.

The two well-known Yaqui villages, as a result of the considerable mention of them in newspapers and even in nationally circulating Sunday supplements, seem to be singled out by various Anglo Americans whose status in their own culture is, to say the least, aberrant. These persons, some male, some female, pass through the villages during the Easter ceremonies, or occasionally at other times, making casual contacts with whomever they see, Mexican or Yaqui, leaving pamphlets or pictures, telling their unusual ideas to whomever will listen, and they disappear again, perhaps writing one or two letters to some person in Pascua whose address they have obtained in passing. It is not possible to list or even indicate all those aberrants who thus leave their casual marks on the Yaquis, for they are numerous in the course of a decade, and sometimes they make contacts with perhaps only one or two persons whom an investigator does not locate until long after the memory has become vague. It will have to suffice here to suggest their nature by giving the details of one case occurring in 1936, that of the "Prophet Jonas B. Israel," of Flintstone, Maryland:

One afternoon in late August a white-bearded man was reported to be sitting outside the church of Santa Rosa [the Catholic church at the south edge of Pascua]. He wore white clothes of coarse duck, a pair of pants extending to just below the knee and a shirt covered with a cape, which was fastened at the throat with a large horse blanket pin. He was barefoot. His hair was long and white tied up with a string at the back. His beard hung down nearly to his waist. He wore a bright ribbon about his middle in place of a belt. Pinned over his left breast was a nickel star with the words "Jesus Loves You" on it, and there was also another emblem with a red streamer. He carried a long stick to the top of which was affixed an oblong piece of metal like a banner. On this were painted various symbols and the words Zion, Peace, and Truth. Beneath the metal banner was a roll of cloth, which unfurled, turned out to be the American Flag.

He told his life story readily, explaining that he was called Israel. He was 67 years old, a vegetarian, and had been in 11 insane asylums and 26 jails in the United States. He had raised ginseng in West Virginia. He had been an itinerant preacher, had received the knowledge in 1914 that he should part his hair in the middle, and had been wandering over the United States ever since. He carried a sheaf of tracts for free distribution, one called "What is Man? The Hidden Mystery." He further described himself as "an Israelite Messenger and Practitioner of Divine Healing."

This prophet slept in the Pascua church for a night, rolling up first on the altar until he was asked to get down on the floor, distributed some leaflets about the village, wandered here and there but doing little talking, then disappeared. The general opinion in Pascua was that he looked like God and certainly must have been very old, but "if he could cure, why didn't he do some of it?"

Another type of aberrant Anglo American is one we might classify as the Indian sentimentalist. These appear during the Easter ceremonies, make an acquaintance, state that they have some Indian blood in their veins, leave some mementos such as a piece of jewelry and write a sheaf of notes concerning the nobility of Indians and the deep, sweet mystery of the Indian philosophy of life. These, too, seem to fail to leave much mark, except one of strangeness, on the Yaquis.

The aberrant visitors cannot be adequately assessed as a cultural influence. Their contacts are casual and sporadic. Their purposes and attitudes remain unintelligible, but their appearances are usually well remembered. Yaquis do not assent to a classification of them as "loco." Thus Prophet Jonas, mentioned above, was not classified by any Yaqui as simply crazy. He was not thought to act "crazy." He talked "all right" and did not do anything harmful; therefore, he was just another Anglo American, not fully intelligible to be sure, but certainly not classifiable as crazy. One can only speculate that such aberrant persons serve to remind Yaquis constantly of the infinite variety in personality and behavior of the Anglo Americans with whom they come into contact.

Yaqui Views of Anglo Americans

There is perhaps no Yaqui concept of Anglo Americans which could be classified as a stereotype. There is detectable, however, a sort of general attitude toward Anglo Americans, which contrasts with that toward Mexican Americans. Never so inclusive in its application, it is nevertheless a real factor in the relations between the groups and perhaps may be thought of as an incipient stereotype.

The Yaqui use of color epithets is inclined to be exact and literal and the Anglo Americans are not thought of as "white." The term white is regarded as properly applicable to Hispanic Americans, that is, Mexicans, because they are thought to be the color of ashes, but Anglo Americans are regarded by Yaquis as being red, rather than white. Thus Anglo-American foremen on ranch and railroad jobs are spoken of as having "tomato-faces." The first Anglo Americans with whom Yaquis came into contact in Sonora and Arizona are frequently spoken of as having been *muy colorado;* the red-burned faces of the Anglo Americans are one of the most vivid memories of those first contacts, and usually no opportunity is lost to mention the color in the re-telling of the early experiences. The practice of speaking of "tomato-faces" still obtains among the younger Yaqui workmen and children in Arizona.

The usual term applied to Anglo Americans when Yaquis are speaking among themselves, as in sermons in the church and in ordinary conversation, is merely *meikan,* which is to say "Americano." However, there is another term borrowed from the Mexicans which has a good deal of currency. That is "gringo," or, as a Yaqui is more likely to say it, *linko.* Linko seems to have somewhat derogatory connotations and is, therefore, not used in formal discourses such as sermons. The term would seem to be going out of usage in the United States and to have been much more frequently used prior to the 1920s. The general connotations of the terms used for Anglo Americans would seem to be favorable or neutral rather than unfavorable.

The older Yaquis express themselves favorably concerning most of the institutions of the Anglo Americans. The following are typical examples:

English is much more like Yaqui than Spanish is. In fact, you will hear people call Yaqui "little English." That is because many of the words are really the same and are pronounced the same way. It is pretty easy to learn English.

In Mexico there were always spies around looking for Yaquis and we were afraid to act like Yaquis. We found out that in the United States we didn't have to be afraid. We were allowed to have our own religion and so we began to have Holy Week again. The sheriffs said that no one would be allowed to molest us.

Yaqui law is just like the Americans'. It allows any accused man to have someone to defend him. That is just like it was on the Rio Yaqui. The *kobanao* had to go around and get a man's relatives and friends to testify for him before the bow-chief. He was taken care of in the trial. That is like the Yaqui law. It worked the same way.

There are three indications of less favorable attitudes toward Anglo Americans shared by Yaqui communities as a whole. This evidence suggests that the latter are beginning to be recognized as a heterogeneous group, toward different parts of which different attitudes may be directed. Thus, two sub-groups among the Anglo Americans have been singled out for representation by the Chapayekas during Lent. One of these is the Negro. Occasionally, since about 1930, there has been a single Chapayeka during a season who has worn a black mask and an American felt hat. Called *chukui,* or black, he has been spoken of as representing a Negro. Little suggestion of any evil represented by the Negro mask has been forthcoming.

The other Anglo-American group which has been represented by the Chapayekas is the Depression hobo horde which rides through southern Arizona constantly on the Southern Pacific railroad. These have been represented occasionally since the mid-1930s, appearing in groups of two or three during Lent and Holy Week. The stereotype has features of the Anglo American comic-strip tramp. The mask is always pink or red, not white, wears a battered American felt hat, and has the chin and upper lip painted dark brown or black to indicate a growth of beard. These tramps, say Yaquis, are dirty and do not care to work, and sometimes they rob people. They are increasingly popular as subjects for the Chapayekas.

There is still a third group of Anglo Americans of whom Yaquis have in recent years become conscious as distinct from the main body of Anglo Americans. These are the "Okies." Up to 1941 none has been the subject of Chapayeka lampoon, but the term "Okie" is of frequent use among Pascua

Yaquis. It refers, of course, to the refugees from the 1930s Dust Bowl disaster, itinerant cotton and vegetable pickers who live in the same camps or on ranches with Yaquis during the harvesting season. The term "Okie" as used by Yaquis has connotations of poverty, dirt, and unreliability. It is definitely a derogatory epithet.

It can be said that Yaquis in Arizona have been incorporated into the social structure of the Anglo American in connection with perhaps all but one of the major aspects of the latter's culture. That is, among Anglo Americans there are systems of economic relations, political relations, and church-based relations, and from none of these are Yaquis excluded. To be sure, they do not range so far as Anglo Americans in each of these systems of relationship, but they nevertheless have social position in each of them. It is possible to point to only one of the major aspects of the social structure that has not become a means for relating Yaquis to Anglo Americans, that is, the family or kinship system. Arizona Yaquis and Anglo Americans are forbidden by Arizona law to marry.[25] As will be seen below, Yaquis are known to have intermarried with Negroes, Papagos, and Mexican Americans, but no instance is known of an Arizona Anglo-Yaqui marriage.

Each of the areas of contact has its peculiar characteristics, both as regards the nature of the formal relations and as concerns the attitudes in the midst of which the contacts take place. The most unceasing and constant relations are maintained in the sphere of economics. Constant and regular also are the contacts with political institutions of various kinds, but they do not have the character of daily occurrence. Both the economic and the political relations are maintained primarily between Anglo Americans and Yaqui adult males; very few Yaqui women participate except seasonally or indirectly in such relations. The relations with religious organizations or representatives are sporadic and irregular, but when they do take place they are between Anglos and both sexes of Yaquis, and even to some extent with children. The relations with educational institutions are primarily maintained by the very youngest Yaquis, and they end suddenly after the tenth to thirteenth years. The other contacts discussed are extremely sporadic and casual and have the character of affecting selected persons rather than a village as a whole.

The degree of intimacy of the contact in the various aspects of life again differ sharply. The most intimately personal relations between Yaquis and Anglo Americans have been maintained in the economic, political, and scientific areas of contact, but that cannot be held for all aspects of these contacts. Those Anglo Americans who have come to know Yaquis in the most many-sided ways seem to have been the sheriff's men, an occasional lawyer, students of Yaqui ceremonies and culture, a few teachers, and those rancher-employers who have one or two Yaqui families living beside them on their more or less isolated ranches. The tendency, however, in southern Arizona agriculture in which Yaquis engage is toward increasingly impersonal relationships as the Yaquis hire out to the large irrigation companies and are more and more segregated in their own villages on company-owned land. In general, one may say that an intimate personal relationship between a Yaqui and an Anglo American in any aspect of life is rather the exception than the rule, but that whatever attitudes of the latter have general currency are frequently based on the experiences of the occasional Anglo American who has developed an intimate relationship with Yaquis somewhere.

The attitudes among Anglo Americans are somewhat varied, but they all have a general basis of agreement. It is usual to see a clear distinction between Yaquis and Mexican Americans and between Yaquis and other Indians. This distinction is recognized most frequently in an appraisal of their work habits and "trustworthiness." When they are compared, it is usual to rank Yaquis more favorably than any other of the Arizona minority groups. This favorable attitude is reinforced by reference to their history, which is generally interpreted as indicating desirable characteristics such as love of freedom and independence. But there is a definite set of attitudes which is not favorable to Yaquis, indicated most clearly in the thinking of public administrators and Anglo-American neighbors of Yaqui villages. The first of this group is accustomed to viewing Yaquis as a social problem in regard to health and poverty. The second group is concerned mostly with personal habits such as drinking and tends to classify all Yaquis as "dirty drunks."

Whether through firsthand contact or not, the knowledge of all Anglo Americans concerning Yaquis is incomplete and imperfect. This is best exemplified in the belief on the part of most persons that there are only two villages of Yaquis in Arizona. Or perhaps, one might say, that there is only one village, the people of Tucson being aware only of Pascua and those of Phoenix only of Guadalupe. It is generally believed that all the Yaquis in Arizona live in one or the other of these villages, that they are segregated there. Thus Anglo Americans are not generally aware of the fact that Yaquis are scattered through the towns and over the ranches of southern

Arizona and that they are here and there making their way into the general population of the state. The awareness of certain areas of Yaqui concentration results in an inequality of treatment of Yaquis by Anglo Americans. Thus, Pascua Yaquis have become exclusive recipients in Tucson of special charities designed for Yaquis, while the Yaqui residents of Barrio Libre go unnoticed and undifferentiated as Yaquis by the Anglo Americans.

The lack of knowledge of Yaquis extends into other aspects of life, leading to an erroneous view of Yaqui tribal solidarity and customs. This interferes strongly with successful political relations and also results in the creation of a general attitude which tends to place Yaquis in the category of the "American Indian," which is a well-formulated and potent stereotype governing the relations of Anglo Americans with reservation Indians. The tendency is probably more and more to think of the Yaquis in terms of this stereotype, rather than in terms of the stereotype they hold for Mexican Americans.

There seem as yet to be no institutionalized barriers to assimilation of Yaquis into the Anglo-American population. There is no formal legal segregation of any kind, except for a suggestion of it in the immigration service's refusal to grant citizenship status to a single Yaqui on the grounds of his being an Indian. Restaurants, theaters, schools, and other public gathering places have no formal or apparently any informal segregation policies. However, segregation exists, as we have noted, in connection with the agricultural labor camps. Here, if anywhere, are to be found the seeds for formal segregating institutions, but there are a number of factors which are tending to modify this trend.

In general, we may say that the Yaqui view of Anglo Americans is a favorable one. The favorable character seems to go back to a period before there was any intimate contact. At present there is a less clearly defined attitude toward the Anglo Americans as a group, but there are developing certain stereotypes in connection with subgroups. These stereotypes show little difference from the attitudes of Anglo Americans themselves toward such groups.

CHAPTER 3

The Relationship
of Mexican Americans
and Yaquis

A large proportion of the people in southern Arizona are Spanish-speaking, yet they constitute a cultural minority. That is to say that the language of state officials is English, state documents and court proceedings are in English, and public policies are determined by courts, legislature, boards of supervisors, and city councils, the personnel of which are English-speaking in the majority. Moreover, the most powerful financial and commercial institutions are owned and directed by a majority of English-speaking persons. In addition the school system of the state which determines and administers education for Spanish-speaking as well as other children is dominated throughout all its levels by Anglo Americans. There is no question then that Spanish-speaking people constitute a cultural minority and in that sense are in a similar category to that of the Yaquis.[1]

Relations with Mexican Americans

The relations which Yaquis maintain with Mexicans are considerably different from those maintained with Anglo Americans. This is not to say that none of their relations with Mexican Americans are similar to those with Anglo Americans; it is rather to say that there is a whole series of relations with a segment of the Mexican-American population that has no parallels with any relations maintained with Anglo Americans. These relations are close and intimate as compared with relations with Anglo Americans, and they are maintained with the segment of the Mexican population which would probably be called lower-class by Mexicans in general, that is, the lowest income group usually composed of relatively recent immigrants from Mexico to the United States.

The Geography and Terminology of Contact

It is at once apparent that the newspaper-reading portion of the Mexican-American population of southern Arizona refers to and thinks about Yaquis in quite a different manner from the newspaper-reading portion of the Anglo-American population. In contrast with the romance-tinged terms of the Anglo newspapers linking Yaquis with the stereotype of the American Indian as "braves" and "tribal," the Mexican-American newspapers, like *El Tucsonense* of Tucson, report Yaqui affairs in quite different terms, when they report them at all. In the first place they pay considerably less attention to Yaquis, especially those in Arizona, and in the second place they do not glamorize or romanticize such matters as the annual Easter ceremonies as do the Anglo newspapers. The reporting is matter-of-fact; Yaqui ceremonial officials are mentioned by name as individuals rather than as "chiefs" or "headmen"; and the Easter ceremonies themselves are characterized baldly in such terms as "Lenten observances." The reporting of Yaqui political activities in the days of Juan Pistola and since has followed the same pattern of serious and prosaic treatment, showing neither condescension nor the tendency to romanticize. In general, it may be said that the public consciousness of Yaquis as a distinct ethnic group is lower for Mexican Americans than for Anglo Americans. Their interest, as reflected in newspaper treatment, has always been higher in Yaqui political fortunes than in Yaqui ceremonial activities.

This lesser public consciousness of Yaqui distinctiveness is coupled with much closer physical contact between Mexican Americans and Yaquis. Quite consistently, wherever one finds Yaquis in southern Arizona, their neighbors, when they are not Yaquis, are Mexican Americans. More rarely, they are Papagos.

The Mexican-American neighbors of Yaquis may be thought of as two kinds: those who live surrounded by Yaquis and those who live surrounding Yaquis. There are ordinarily two very different types of geographical propinquity. We may discuss first the Mexican Americans who live

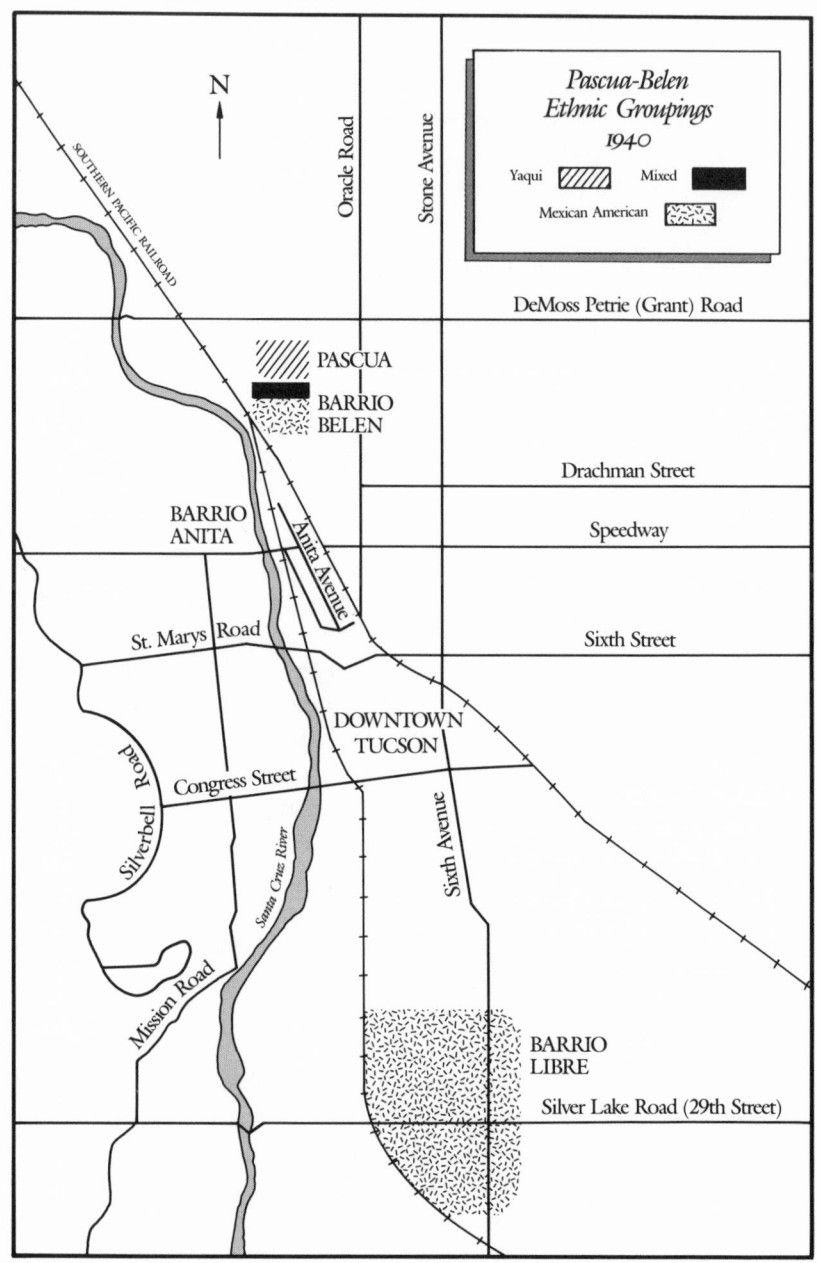

surrounded by Yaquis, using by way of illustration one of the Mexican-American residents of Pascua village. In 1937, for example, there were living within the limits of Pascua proper, that is, not including Barrio Belen, four households of Mexican Americans. Three of these were permanent residents, the other was a transient family which had moved into a vacant house and subsequently moved elsewhere. The latter phenomenon is common: a Mexican-American family moving back from the cotton fields takes over for a time any vacant house that can be found anywhere and lives in it until evicted or until another place is found. Such temporary occupation of Yaqui houses by Mexican Americans is common in Pascua. The other three Mexican-American families in Pascua during the spring of 1937 must be considered in detail, for they illustrate a number of significant elements in Yaqui relations with Mexican Americans.

One household was composed of a woman of sixty and a man of about fifty—Doña Pancha and Joe Bule. Both were of mixed blood: Pancha claiming Mayo Indian and French blood, Joe claiming Anglo and Pima Indian. The claims of Indian blood were never definitely established. No Indian language was spoken by either of them, and they each understood Yaqui only slightly. Pancha kept a small grocery store with a stock of canned goods, cake and bread, soft drinks, tobacco, cheese, and so forth. She turned over perhaps fifty cents a day. She had been in business for fifteen or more years. Joe had come to live with her about four years before. Joe hauled groceries out from Tucson in a Model-T truck and Pancha ran the store. Their relationships with Pascuans may be described as those of friendly outsiders, despite the fact that they were in contact almost daily with a majority of the villagers. The Yaquis themselves regarded them as distinct from themselves on two major counts: in the first place, they did not speak Yaqui and, in the second place, their attendance at ceremonies was sporadic, and when they did go they ordinarily would stay for only a few minutes, although there were instances of Pancha pitching in and helping with the cooking at a funeral or novena for a friend of hers. Joe himself expressed an attitude which emphasized his separation from Yaquis on this count:

The trouble with the Yaquis is they don't make much money and they don't save nothing. They spend it all for *wakabaki* and have fiestas. They would have fiestas every day if they had the money.

Joe should probably be thought of as somewhat similar to the aberrant Anglo Americans who have been described above. He found Pascua congenial perhaps because of its aberrancy from general Arizona culture.

Pancha was quite different from Joe. She maintained fairly intimate relationships with Yaqui families, conversing always in Spanish, and seemed to
have more contacts with her Yaqui neighbors than with Mexican Americans. She lived in the vicinity of Pascua for more than twenty-five years.

Pancha's mother used to play the harp for the Pascolas at Pascua, but
Pancha's only participation in ceremonial life was her occasional cooking
for a ceremony held by one of the Yaqui families with which she is especially intimate. This sort of participation is, however, conventional female
Yaqui participation and serves to identify Pancha more closely than Joe
with the life of the village as a whole. Pancha thus remained apart on the
two scores of language and of religious belief and participation, but she
nevertheless had knit herself into the life of the village very much, even
though she remained essentially a Mexican American rather than a Yaqui.

There is another type of participation in Yaqui life on the part of Mexican Americans represented in the relations to Pascua of the Pablo Olivas
household. The head of the household, Olivas, claimed no Indian blood of
any kind, but represented himself merely as Mexican. The family had lived
in Pascua for more than ten years in the heart of the village. The father,
Pablo, worked as did the Yaquis on ranches or at odd jobs in Tucson. The
children attended the Pascua school, understood and spoke Yaqui fairly
well. The parents understood Yaqui, perhaps more than Doña Pancha,
certainly more than Joe. The children appeared at Yaqui ceremonies with
Yaqui children and stood about for short periods. Pablo occasionally went
to a ceremony for a short while. Relations with Yaqui neighbors were intimate, and there was mutual help and exchange of food in hard times
or during illnesses. Pablo's daughters had been *madrinas* (godmothers) of
Fariseos at Eastertime.

The most notable participation in Yaqui culture was Pablo's part in the
Easter ceremonies. He had been gatekeeper for some seven or eight years,
an office which gave him charge of the limosna bowl in which collections
are taken and of the selling of Chamber of Commerce pamphlets to Anglo-
American visitors. He was often called "chief" by the sheriff's men and
others concerned in the Easter ceremonies and was always assumed by the
visiting Anglos to be a Yaqui. He was one of the principal go-betweens
in Yaqui affairs with sheriff's and other offices in Tucson, often acting as
interpreter (he spoke some English) for the Fariseos and for individuals in
Tucson.

The gatekeeper's office was held for a long period before him by another
Mexican who lived just outside Pascua. In the case of the Olivas family

there is some assimilation into Yaqui culture, the younger generation being more participant in and familiar with Yaqui ways than the older. This same sort of assimilation is apparent in more striking ways in the case of the wife and family of the former gatekeeper who died in 1935. When he died, after a number of years' service as gatekeeper, his death anniversary was commemorated by the Pascua Yaquis in a *cumpleaño* (end of year) service in the Pascua public plaza. Since then his wife and children have taken up residence in Barrio Belen at the south edge of Pascua and the wife's participation in Yaqui ceremonies is constant and regular. She holds no office, but is to be seen in attendance at most ceremonies and frequently, like the Yaqui women, stays throughout the night. This is regarded by Yaquis as one of the essential traits of Yaqui behavior. She understands Yaqui moderately well, but appears always to speak in Spanish.

The behavior of these three families indicates that the assimilation of Yaquis and Mexican Americans is not wholly a one-way process. Not only are Yaquis being assimilated into Mexican-American culture, but very definitely there is an assimilation of Mexican Americans into Yaqui culture. This assimilation involves the learning of the Yaqui language and an integration into the padrino and ceremonial systems of the Yaquis. It is a process that is taking place on a small scale, but is quite evident in all the Yaqui centers of population. It affects Mexican Americans who live within Yaqui villages or near them.

Intermarriage

The assimilation of Mexican Americans to Yaqui culture may be carried a step farther as a result of intermarriage. In the decade of 1930 to 1940 there were five intermarriages involving Yaqui residents of Pascua and Mexican Americans. Four of these resulted in bringing Mexican-American women into the orbit of Yaqui culture and one in bringing a man into it. One of these was short-lived. Juan Silvas, a Yaqui, married a Mexican woman, had one child by her, and then the woman died. The mixed-blood child was turned over to his Yaqui grandmother to keep. The man subsequently married a Yaqui girl. The other three marriages of Yaqui men and Mexican-American women have brought the women into Pascua Village as permanent residents and have, in varying degrees, brought about the assimilation of the women into Yaqui culture. We may consider some of these in detail by way of pointing out the nature of relations established.

Jesús García is a mixed blood Yaqui, his father having been Mexican and his mother Yaqui. His mother lived with her Mexican husband only a short time and then took up residence with a Yaqui, José María Casillas, by whom she had a large family. Jesús was brought up by his mother and his Yaqui stepfather. The latter has been prominent in Pascua life as a harpist and as a founder of the Easter ceremonies in Arizona which were first revived at his household near Tucson. Jesús was notoriously promiscuous among the Yaqui young women in Pascua in his early youth, but finally settled down with a Mexican girl whom he married and by whom he has had six children. He built a house of his own in Pascua after marriage and continued to be prominent in the Fariseo society as a Chapayeka. His wife has never learned to speak Yaqui, but understands it readily. The children speak Yaqui by preference, but hear their mother speak Spanish constantly so that they are bilingual in the true sense. The mother never participates in any way in Yaqui ceremonies, but she and Jesús have promised one of the boys to a ceremonial society. After some eight years of marriage, Jesús and his wife took up residence in Jesús's father's household in Pascua, giving up their own house to the wife's parents and sister who have continued to occupy the house in the center of the village. Like their daughter, they do not participate in the ceremonial life of the village but maintain intimate visiting relations with their Yaqui neighbors, speaking, of course, in Spanish in all of these contacts. In this instance we can see assimilation into Yaqui culture extending through three generations, the youngest being thoroughly Yaqui, the oldest finally swinging into contact as a result of the partial assimilation of the middle generation.

Another example will indicate the more complete assimilation of both a wife and her mixed-blood children. Luis Martínez is a full-blood Yaqui who married a Mexican-American woman in 1923 and has lived with her ever since. They have had five children (surviving). The wife, Francisca, has not learned to speak Yaqui, but understands it thoroughly, and uses isolated Yaqui words. The children speak Yaqui, but seem to have little preference for it over Spanish. The language of homelife is characterized by constant shifts from Yaqui to Spanish and back again, the father speaking most usually in Yaqui, the mother always in Spanish, and the children in whichever language they get started at the moment. Luis has become increasingly prominent in village affairs during the years since his marriage. He belongs to the Fariseo society and is a popular Pascola Dancer. He and Francisca dedicated their oldest son to the Fariseo society as a Pilato and their next oldest son also as a member of the society. The eldest daughter has been dedicated as a Cantora. As a result of his son's being a Pilato,

Luis was elected in 1940 to the captaincy of the Fariseo society and for two years has held the office to the satisfaction of the villagers. This made him the most prominent man in the village during the whole of the winter cere-monial season. As his prominence has increased, his Mexican-American wife has extended her participation in Yaqui ceremonial life until in 1941 she became the director of the public kitchen, supervising the cooking for the Fariseos and other participants during the whole of Holy Week. It is not traditional for the wife of the Captain of the Fariseos to assume this position. She has attained it through her own ability and initiative, which indicates a strong interest in the Easter ceremonies. The family continues to live in Pascua Village surrounded by Yaqui neighbors and seems not to be thought of as different in important ways from other Yaquis.

The one Mexican-American man who has married into the village of Pascua has come into it by a devious route and may not be considered as assimilated. Claiming to have been born of a Yaqui mother in Arizona, he was, nevertheless, brought up among Mexicans in Sonora and speaks only Spanish and a little English. Marrying a Yaqui girl in Sonora, who had long been a resident of Pascua, they returned to the village, and he continues to live in her parent's household in Pascua. He has learned a few words of Yaqui, but he does not participate in or attend Yaqui ceremonies. The nature of his domestic life will be dealt with more at length below.

No instances have been recorded of marriages between Yaquis and Mexican Americans which have resulted in the assimilation of the Yaqui to life in a Mexican-American community. There is very great probabil-ity, however, that this process has been taking place for years in Arizona. However, the cases just mentioned have had certain effects which may be described as partial assimilation of the Yaquis to Mexican-American culture at the same time that the Mexican-American spouses have been as-similated to Yaqui culture. One of the most obvious types of such mutual assimilation is in connection with the godparent system of the Mexican Americans.

Godparents

Yaquis of Pascua are constantly drawing on their Mexican-American neighbors to serve as madrinas and padrinos. The majority of Mexican Americans who come into the network of Pascua society in this manner probably come as godparents of Fariseos at the annual Easter ceremonies, tying colored handkerchiefs on the arms of the godchildren and running with them into the Yaqui church in the final climactic rush as the Judas effigy is burned in the plaza. In addition, Mexican Americans sometimes serve as sponsor of the *hábito* (vestment) in cases of illness. It is, however, extremely rare for Yaquis to ask Mexican Americans to assume the very important position of godfather of baptism for their children. Ordinarily, Yaquis ask Yaquis to fulfill this function. But there are a number of cases of Yaquis serving as godparents of baptism for Mexican-American children. These seem to happen chiefly in the case of those Yaqui families that have intermarried with Mexican Americans. Thus an example may be taken from the case of Luis Martínez, the Yaqui mentioned above as being married to the Mexican-American woman, Francisca:

> Luis Martínez said that he wanted me to take him into the Cathedral of San Augustín about 2 P.M. because he was going to be padrino of confirmation for a Mexican boy named Telles. The Telles family live just south of Pascua Village in Barrio Belen. I (the investigator) took Luis down to the Telles household where we picked up the Telles boy and went into the Cathedral. Standing on the front steps waiting for us were the rest of the party—the father and mother of the boy, Luis's wife, two Mexican girl residents of Barrio Belen, and three other Mexican Americans whom I did not know. Luis was thus the only Yaqui in the group. Luis also stood out from his Mexican-American associates in that he did not pray for a moment just after he assumed his seat. The service involved the confirmation of about forty boys and girls. Luis performed in satisfactory manner, taking the Telles boy up to the rail and bringing him back. The family was in a jolly mood as we went back to the village and a "chocolate-drinking," financed by Luis, was held at the Telles household. Later as the sun set, the party swung into a full-fledged Mexican dance, which lasted late. When I left late in the evening, Luis was still the only Yaqui present and was enjoying himself hugely with chocolate and wine and a good dinner.

This man, Luis Martínez, who so successfully participated with Mexican Americans in a typically Mexican-American sort of ceremony, it must be remembered, became three years later the leading ceremonial official of Pascua and has served satisfactorily for two years in that capacity. The extent of his participation in both cultures is unusual. The fact that he can do it so successfully indicates a certain amount of compatibility between the two.

It is probable that every family in Pascua has links with neighboring Mexican Americans through the ceremonial sponsorship system. A systematic record was made of the sponsor network in which one Yaqui household is enmeshed. Of the seventy-six persons related in this way

Luis Martínez with his *ahijado* (godson) of confirmation on the steps of St. Augustine Cathedral, April 1937. The others are the boy's relatives. *Photograph by Rosamond B. Spicer.*

to the matron of the household, seventeen were Mexican American, and without exception neighbors near whom she had lived at one time or another and who had asked her to serve or whom she had asked to serve. Of the formal systems of social relationship existing among Yaquis, it is the padrino system which is used most frequently and most effectively to link

Yaquis and Mexican Americans. It is in basic structure the same institution in both the cultures and thus intelligible to both groups. Consequently, all that is needed is geographical propinquity to bring it into operation as an assimilating mechanism. The major effect of its operation is to bring Yaquis and Mexicans into intimate contact in each other's homes, where they must eat each other's food, listen to each other's music, and dance each other's dances. It is a notable fact in this connection that the mixed *bolas* seem to be held at the Mexican houses. Dancing is not part of a Yaqui bola; it is definitely part of a Mexican bola. Thus, most Yaquis are some-what Mexicanized in the course of the social fulfillment of the ceremonial obligation.

Trade

There are very few Mexican-American-owned stores at which Yaquis trade. Their trading is chiefly with Chinese merchants. However, it will be recalled that one of the neighbors discussed above has maintained a store within the limits of Pascua Village for some fifteen or eighteen years. Her trade is one that relies on day-to-day needs for little luxuries and on the miscalculation of persons during their weekend shopping which forces them to buy a dab of lard or a cup of flour or something like that in very small quantities. There are two similar stores run by Mexican Americans at the southern margin of Pascua, one designed along the lines of Pancha's store; the other is attempting to expand. Anita Goosby, the proprietress of the latter store, speaks as follows:

They (the Yaquis) won't come and buy anything to amount to anything from me. Oh, they'll spend a nickel or a dime at a time, maybe a hunk of cheese or a box of cookies. But they don't spend nothin' to amount to anything. I had to get rid of my meat stock. They don't want to buy meat from me. They get old stuff in town and dry it out. I don't carry nothin' but wieners anymore. I can't even carry any flour. They won't get it from me. They go in town to the Chinese stores. I got a big lot of beans, dry beans once, and I got 'em pretty cheap, too. But I was a cent or so higher than them Chinamen's stores and those Yaquis wouldn't buy the beans. They all waited till Saturday and went in and got 'em off the Chinamen. You can't turn nothin' over here.

To help her trade, Anita is now beginning to give presents and make friends by performing little services for the families of Pascua. She do-nates food in considerable quantities to funerals, gives a free mail service in competition with the nonfree one of Lucas Chavez, and finds many ways to help people. She is also calling herself half Mayo. It seems probable that she may become an important influence on the life of Pascuans through her interest in trade, but as yet she is not, and we may say the Mexican-American contacts with Yaquis through trade are not an important consideration.

The Mexican Baptist Church

We have discussed briefly above the activities of an Anglo-American missionary claiming affiliations with the Baptist church. This man ultimately joined forces with the Mexican Baptist church in Tucson and has ceased his lone meetings. The Mexican Baptist church has been interested in the Yaquis of Pascua for more than fifteen years and has held numerous meetings in the village, has disposed of much charity, and more recently has developed an organized missionary campaign which has had very definite results.

The Mexican Baptist church is a large congregation of Tucson, composed mainly of bilingual persons with Spanish surnames. Its pastor is a United States–born Mexican American named Morales. There are a number of mixed Mexican-American and Anglo-American persons active in the church's work. One of these, Mrs. Dolores Wright, has been the most effective and most active of the Yaqui missionaries during the past ten years. As a volunteer social worker, she has had much to do with the distribution of county relief supplies in Pascua and Barrio Belen. She established a W.P.A. needlework class for adult women in conjunction with the Pascua school. She, Reverend Morales, and the Anglo missionary, Gwynn, have held almost weekly meetings at the Pascua school in the evening at which there are prayers, sermons, and singing. The activities of the Baptists have resulted in the baptism in their church of four or five Yaquis in a period of ten years. The activities during those years have resulted in the creation in Pascua of strong feelings for and against the Baptists. There is a definite pro-Baptist group, some of whom are baptized in the Baptist church, and also a definite anti-Baptist group composed of all the more prominent leaders of Pascua ceremonial life. A major source of opposition to the Baptists lies in the use by their missionary of the charity supplies and the school in their attempt to gain the favor of Pascuans; they are charged with withholding these benefits from Pascuans who do not care to attend the weekly religious meetings or who go into Tucson to the church services there.

The intimate relations maintained between the Baptist pastor and his Yaqui converts are indicated in the following note:

Lucas and I (the writer) dropped in to see Morales of the Mexican Baptist church. He was composing a sermon in his very dusty office. He greeted Lucas heartily, calling him "Hermano Lucas" and putting his arm half around him. Lucas called him "Señor Morales" and also put his arm half around him. We sat down and Morales asked Lucas why he had come. Lucas explained that we were just visiting. Morales then talked to me for some time in English, saying that he had been interested in Yaquis from the very beginning of his work—he had been in the Mayo country in December 1939, and had preached in several towns. . . . Morales turned to Lucas several times, always addressing him as "Hermano Lucas" and speaking very much as an equal to him.

The relationships are maintained in the Spanish language and the Baptists make no effort to learn Yaqui. The activities of the group receive much support in Tucson generally, particularly through the Tucson Needlework Guild. In their statements in the newspapers on behalf of the Yaqui work, they speak of the Yaqui children as "under-privileged young American citizens."

The Catholic Church

Because the Yaquis invariably think of the Catholic church as a Mexican institution and because its most effective contacts have been carried out by Spanish-speaking priests in Arizona, we shall consider it here in connection with the Mexican-American relationships. Moreover, the Catholic congregations with whom Yaquis come into contact through the church are for the most part Mexican American.

There has been a Yaqui Catholic church in Guadalupe village for fifteen years. It is visited once a month by a priest who conducts mass. There is no orthodox Catholic church within the limits of any other of the villages, but the Santa Rosa Mission Church is situated just a few feet from the southern boundary of Pascua village, and it is surrounded on all sides by Yaqui households, some in Pascua, some in Barrio Belen, so that it may be regarded as geographically in the heart of Pascua. We may consider in detail the origins of this church and by that means arrive at an understanding of the nature of the missionary contact with Yaquis.

During the 1920s and early 1930s, there were two Spanish-speaking priests at the Church of the Holy Family about a mile south of Pascua in Tucson. This Catholic church was frequently used by north Tucson Yaquis for baptisms, marriages, and funerals. The two priests, Fathers Carmelo and Lucas, became well known to Pascua Yaquis. Padre Carmelo said the first mass in Pascua at the Yaqui church of San Ygnacio in 1925. He continued to say mass there about once a month from that time until 1930. He and Father Lucas came often during this period to the village. They became familiar with the Matachin, Deer, and Pascola dances. They even recorded the music of the dances and kept it on file in the church in Tucson. They arranged for periodic distribution of commodities in the village by the Society of St. Anthony and often sent out gifts in the form of old clothing, toys, and dishes.

In 1926 a wealthy Catholic of Tucson contributed money to build a day-altar that Padre Carmelo could use in saying mass at the church of San Ygnacio. Three years later the Council of the Catholic Daughters of America became interested in Pascua. They financed the Church of Santa Rosa, which was dedicated to that saint in August 1930. The church of Santa Rosa was built as what amounted to a replica of the church of San Ygnacio. Only the Pascola ramada was left out. It was assumed that the Pascua Yaquis would transfer their devotions down to this church in the Catholic plaza, since it had all the necessary features. The Yaquis have not done so, however, and there seems to be no indication of any such gradual transfer. The church has been used by Yaqui ceremonial societies only once or twice a year, chiefly on the day of Santa Rosa and of Cristo Rey, when Matachinis dance there. No other organized groups from Pascua perform there, and attendance at the monthly mass is individual.

From 1930 until 1932 there was regular, afternoon catechismal instruction at the church of Santa Rosa, attended by most of the children of Pascua as well as Mexican Americans from Barrio Belen. About this time, however, the two well-known fathers were called to Spain and have not returned as regular priests to Tucson. Catechismal instruction is still held intermittently, and there is an organization called the "Archicofradía del Niño Jesús de Praga" composed of Yaqui and Mexican-American children that tends the altar at Santa Rosa and maintains the daily flower services during the month of May. Otherwise, the church is not in regular use and there is no active prosecution of missionary work, though the dispensations of the Society of St. Anthony continue. There is no recognition, since the building of Santa Rosa, of the church of San Ygnacio by any Catholic organization in Tucson. Priests do not attend it to say mass and it has no formal connection whatever with Tucson Catholicism.

The individuals of Pascua, however, maintain constant relations with one or the other of the Catholic churches in Tucson. Baptisms, marriages, confirmations, and funerals are carried out by priests in Tucson. Also, priests are called out to the village to give confession and to say last rites. The Catholic cemetery provides free ground to almost every Yaqui who is buried, for almost all Yaquis are buried in a Catholic cemetery. A few Yaquis go in to the little fiestas held within the Catholic church grounds from time to time as pure pleasure carnivals. A few Yaquis go in regularly on Sunday mornings for mass. Thus there is an individual acceptance of Catholicism almost in its entirety, but the two organizations remain distinct, one Yaqui and one non-Yaqui.

The following opinions of Catholic officials are not presented as typical but rather as of interest because they concern Pascua Yaquis rather intimately. About 1940 the successor of Padre Carmelo said:

Yes, I have heard about the Yaquis. It is too bad that I know so little Spanish as yet. What would you say is their intelligence? I don't imagine they are very far removed from the primitive tribal level. I should like to do some work out there. I understand there has not been much success. It must indicate a very low level of humanity among them.

Likewise, another Catholic priest witnessing the Yaqui Easter ceremonies at Pascua said:

What primitive actions! This is hardly bearable. It is wholly sacrilegious.

These opinions are different from those of Padres Carmelo and Lucas, one would suppose.

The following note indicates the attitudes of a Mexican-American Catholic layman, a Tucson house builder who had become acquainted with Yaquis in his youth when he sold clothing from door-to-door. He had brought his family out to see the *novena* of a dead Yaqui whom he had been helping with gifts of food in his last days. The writer's wife reports the encounter:

We were sitting on one of the benches watching the matachinis dance at Mariano's novena. There was a Mexican sitting beside me with his wife and children looking with interest at the dancers swinging their plumas to the guitars and violins in the moonlight. We struck up a conversation. After he had told me practically his whole life history, he began talking about Yaqui ceremonies. "They have those big ceremonies at Easter every year. They ought to fence off the place and charge admission to everyone who comes along to see them." "That would change the ceremonies," I said, "because they are purely religious and not commercial." "Maybe," he said, "but they are just pagan anyway and people are very curious to see them." "They are Catholic rather than pagan," I said. "Oh no, there you are wrong. They aren't Catholic at all. They are just pagan. You ought to know that if they were Catholic, then everyone else would be having them, too, not just these poor people. Oh, indeed, they are not Catholic. They are just pagan."

There remains a group of Yaquis in Pascua who maintain rather close relationships with the heads of various Catholic organizations in Tucson and make the effort to have an interchange of church work between the Pascua church and Tucson churches. This group comprises two or three of the major officials of the Yaqui church, namely, the Matachin Kobanao and the head Temasti. On the other hand, there is a strongly anti-Catholic group, which also includes leading officials in the Yaqui church. Others in the church have little clear-cut opinion and merely go on ignoring the Catholic church, their lives being rather full with their activities in the Yaqui church.

Yaqui Views of Mexican Americans

The concept "Mexican American" does not exist in Yaqui thinking. People who speak Spanish, whether they live in Sonora or in Arizona, are "Mexicans" very much as they are for all Anglo Americans who live in the Southwest. The terms which are used by Yaquis in reference to Mexican Americans, are "mexicano," "yori," and occasionally "blanco" (*tosai*). Perhaps when speaking among themselves the term which is most used is "yori." This word is of Yaqui origin and literally means "light in color." It has a long history of usage in reference to Mexicans in the Yaqui country and has for Yaquis in Arizona a number of specific unpleasant associations, the most common of which is a memory of having been frightened by their mothers with this word as children: "Be careful or the Yoris will get you."

The Mexican in Mexico stood as a symbol of bad habits and corrupt ways and is functioning in Arizona Yaqui culture as a sort of devil who may be held up to the young as a bad example. Moreover, he is treated somewhat as a scapegoat, that is, it is his sin rather than Yaqui sin which is responsible for bad Yaqui habits.

The scapegoat "character" of the Mexican is emphasized through one of the major Yaqui cultural institutions, that is, through the Fariseo society. The function of the Chapayekas has already been pointed out; they objectify in dramatic form the evil agencies that are at work among Yaquis, and they are ritually eliminated from the villages in an annual ceremony at Easter. To understand the Yaqui value system, both negative and positive, it is very important to know what is represented as evil through the Chapayekas each year. Study of the Chapayekas over a five-year period has revealed certain recurring representations and also certain passing interests in the definition of evil. One of the most consistently recurring Chapayeka masks is a representation of a human face, ordinarily colored white, usually with a small, black curled mustache, surmounted by a small visored cap. The name of this representation is *"yori sontau,"* which is to say, "Mexican soldier." Again it may be called *"pelón,"* a term which was applied to the troops of the Sonoran government that fought the Yaquis in the last quarter of the nineteenth century. This historical figure, the object of so much hatred during the Yaqui wars, has evidently been crystallized as one of the important evil spirits or agents in Yaqui life. It will be noted that this is not precisely the generalized Mexican of everyday conversation, but he is, nevertheless, quite definitely Mexican.

The historical experiences of Yaquis lies back of their concept-building. These experiences have given rise not only to the stereotype of the Mexican in general but also to a series of stereotypes concerning Mexican institutions and culture:

The Mexican language is totally different from Yaqui and the Mexicans never wish to hear a single Yaqui word. They are incapable of hearing Yaqui.

The Mexican laws in regard to landownership and property are very bad. They require that land always go to the eldest son, which is contrary to Yaqui law and a bad thing because the eldest son may not be any good.

The Mexicans permit the Catholic priests to charge money for everything they do. They keep giving money to the priests instead of devotion to God and Jesus and Mary.

These beliefs are not, of course, held clearly by all Yaquis, but they are sufficiently common to turn up repeatedly in most interviews dealing with Mexicans. They are widespread among Arizona Yaquis. However, a number of Yaquis go beyond the stereotype of the Mexican in their thinking as a result of personal contact and make more or less objective observations in regard to the differences. Three common observations by Pascua Yaquis are the following:

The Mexicans talk so fast you can't understand them sometimes. You can always tell a Yaqui because he talks Spanish slowly and you can understand what he says. But I know some Yaquis who talk as fast as Mexicans.

Mexicans have something like a *luto* [black mourning cord worn at the anniversary of the death of an adult Yaqui], but it isn't the same thing. I've seen them going around with black ribbons on their hats or around their arms. But Yaquis never do that. These Mexicans don't finish up the lutos the way we do either. They don't keep away from work and sit quiet for a day when they put them on. That shows how different they are from us.

You can see what the Mexicans do on All Souls' Day out at the cemetery. They don't really do it right at all. They never have a maestro to say the *responsos*. They just go out there and put some flowers around and maybe have a picnic. I've seen them out there all right just sitting around.

These quotations indicate some of the differences which are most apparent to Yaquis and of which they are most conscious. A definite concept of the "Mexican" has been formulated by Yaquis and applied to Mexican Americans of Arizona. It is an unfavorable picture and a much used stereotype, serving as a definite value symbol in thinking about Yaqui behavior. When it is so used it ordinarily has little relation to real observed differences of the present time.

The contacts between Mexican Americans and Yaquis are on the whole much more intimate than those between Anglo Americans and Yaquis. They partake, moreover, less of missionary character than do the latter, yet when they are of that directed type they result in more extensive and also more intensive contact. There is a great deal of directed culture contact of Anglos with Yaquis, but very little with Mexican Americans. Contact with Mexican Americans is on the level of the kinship relations and the padrino systems. Mexican Americans also seem to lack definite stereotypes in the characterization of Arizona Yaquis.

The basis of this more intimate contact may be summed up as follows: use of a common language in Spanish, similarity in religious belief and ritual, and geographical propinquity. These conditions result in the Mexican-American failure to distinguish Yaquis very sharply from themselves. However, these very conditions result, on the other hand, in the Yaquis' drawing quite sharp distinctions between themselves and Mexican Americans. The similarity is just sufficient to make differences stand out and to make them seem to rest in part on an evaluation of real differences in the ceremonial practices of the two groups.

CHAPTER 4

Yaqui Associations with Chinese, Negroes, and Indians

A few other minor contacts of Yaquis help shed light on the place of Yaquis in the total community. Each of these might be the subject of a special study, but here we shall present only a few of the more obvious contacts and attempt to compare them with those maintained with the larger groups already discussed.

Relations with Chinese

Yaqui-Chinese marriages are reported from Sonora, but none have been recorded for Arizona. A few Papago-Chinese marriages have been recorded in Tucson. On the other hand, Mexican-Chinese marriages are not infrequent. The Chinese are scattered rather widely over the city of Tucson, so that it is rare for Yaquis and Chinese to be neighbors. This is true not only of the urban Yaqui centers, but also of the rural areas, for Chinese are to be found neither on the ranches nor in the railroad gangs as laborers. The Chinese population is almost exclusively commercial in occupation, with an occasional independent farmer. The contacts between Yaquis and Chinese are, therefore, almost exclusively as buyers and sellers. Chinese run the stores in the low-income areas of the cities where Yaquis do their buying, and they are the most energetic hucksters who carry truckloads of goods to the villages and ranches where Yaquis live. Yaquis think of Chinese as primarily grocerymen. Moreover, they prefer almost uniformly to buy their staple goods from Chinese. They say the following things about Chinese:

They give you credit for groceries when you need it. They learn Yaqui so that you can tell them what you want. They always give you a *pilón* (a little something extra with a large order).

The Chinese storekeepers in their turn express uniformly favorable opinions of the Yaquis with whom they deal. The following is typical:

Don Sen Lee had a grocery store in Tucson. He thought that he could sell more if he got a truck and went out to Pascua, where hucksters were not going. He had learned some Yaqui one fall when he had had to pick cotton for a living. He began taking truckloads of goods out to Pascua. At first the old women were too timid, but when they found that he knew some Yaqui they began to warm to him. "Now they buy from me before they will from anybody else, even if they have to wait supper for me. I always make a special effort to get the Yaqui trade. And believe me it pays you all right. Those Yaquis never try to beat you out of anything. They always remember their bills. I let a lot of them go from one cotton season to the next and they always take up their bills right where they left off the year before. I think they are very honest people. If you treat them right, they never forget you and they always treat you right.

This sort of opinion applies to those Chinese who deal regularly with Yaquis as customers. To other Chinese who do not have much dealing with them, they are strange creatures:

I had to buy some chickens once from some Yaquis. I wanted to buy them quick and get back, but they sure didn't act in a hurry. They all got together in a family conference and it took hours, I tell you. They gabbled like a bunch of chickens themselves. They're sure funny people and their language just sounds like a lot of cackles.

Relations with Negroes

The intermarriage of Yaquis with Negroes began in Nogales in the early 1900s where they were living in an adjoining part of the town. The writer has record of at least six intermarriages. Every marriage recorded has resulted in separation after a few years, but the result has been the production of a number of mixed-blood Yaqui-Negroes. Aside from Nogales, Yaquis and Negroes live as neighbors only in the Marana company town, where again their areas adjoin each other. Unfortunately, the writer has no data indicating the attitudes of Negroes toward Yaquis.

Contacts with Papagos and Pimas

Guadalupe is only thirty miles from the Pima Reservation with its agency at Sacaton in the Gila River Valley. Many of the present residents of Guadalupe have lived for a time on the Pima Reservation, some of them having held land there for several years under a regulation passed in 1910 that anyone clearing an acreage on the reservation could have the produce of it for three years thereafter. There were some intermarriages among those Yaquis who took advantage of this regulation, and as a result there are some Yaqui-Pima mixed bloods on the reservation and a few in the villages around Phoenix.

The Yaquis of Tucson have had more intimate contact with the Papagos, there being the reservation of San Xavier twenty miles south of Tucson and several hundred Papagos living in the city away from the reservations. Many of the Tucson Yaquis made their way into the United States north-ward from the Altar Valley and spent short periods in residence on the Sells Reservation at various villages, most notably at Sells and at Coyote Village. The first place of settlement in Tucson by Yaquis was at Mezquital, or Huupa, between the San Xavier reservation and Tucson proper, an area also occupied by off-reservation Papagos. Papagos lived in Barrio Libre as well. Yaquis often live as neighbors to Papagos during the cotton-picking season in the vicinity of Marana, Eloy, Casa Grande, and Coolidge, where Papagos come from the reservation to work for wages during the season.

There have been marriages between Papagos and Yaquis, as well as in-formal domestic alliances. The writer knows of at least a dozen such unions and believes that there have been many more. These have involved, as in the case of the Mexican marriages, chiefly, but not exclusively, Yaqui males and Papago females. In two instances the Yaqui men have learned Papago and now speak both languages, but with the exception of only two cases on record, the women have not learned Yaqui. The children speak both languages. None of these mixed couples have taken up residence in Yaqui centers of population and, consequently, there seems to have been no as-similation of Papago women to Yaqui culture. It appears rather that the tendency has been for Yaquis to live in and become assimilated to Papago culture.

In general, Papagos and Yaquis would seem to have held each other at a distance insofar as their ceremonial life, the core of their cultures, is concerned. The notorious split between north and south Tucson Yaquis over the Easter ceremonies was furthered by an incident in connection with Papagos. The south Tucson Yaquis came to Pascua to join the north Tucson Yaquis for Easter in the early 1920s. They brought with them a number of Papagos who wished to attend and help with the ceremonies. The north Tucson Yaquis objected, saying that their ceremonies were not understood by the Papagos. The south Tucson Yaquis stood up for their guests. The dispute ended in a general fight, and the south Tucson Yaquis went back to Mezquital with the Papagos and never came back. Again, when Francisco Matus was attempting to continue the Pistola tradition as a warden of ceremonies, he brought Papagos from south Tucson to help him police a ceremony at Pascua. The Pascuans objected, chased the Papagos away, and remained bitter toward Matus ever after that. There is no record, however, of Papagos being anything more than spectators at Yaqui ceremonies in south Tucson. Although Yaquis have maintained their own ceremonies apart from Papagos in Tucson, it happens that they have participated frequently in Papago ceremonies on both the San Xavier and Sells reservations. It was usual for a number of years during the 1930s for Papagos from Sells to send a truck into Pascua to get a group of Pascola and Deer Dancers to perform at a New Year celebration in the vicinity of Santa Rosa, although Papagos do have Pascola Dancers who, the Yaquis say, learned the dance from them. More traditional and intimate in the character of the contact is the annual attendance of Yaquis at the mission of San Xavier on the day of that saint. Yaquis from every village and rural center come in their cars to San Xavier and camp among the visiting Papagos surrounding the mission. Here they attend the services and march in the processions (in 1940 a Pascua maestro chanted in the procession in a prominent position immediately behind the image of San Xavier) and dozens of them carry out ceremonies of donning the San Francisco hábito. In addition, Matachin Dancers and sometimes Pascolas from both Guadalupe and Pascua dance before the church in traditional Yaqui fashion in full costume. After the ceremonies Yaquis and Papagos, if they know each other, dance together in a general social dance.

It has been difficult to find any definite expressions of opinion by Papagos about Yaquis. One Papago girl who had attended the University of Arizona in Tucson expressed herself as follows:

We don't think of Yaquis as Indians. They aren't like us and they aren't like the Apaches either. I think it would be all right for a Papago to marry a Yaqui, but I never heard of any Papago doing it.

Again:

Down there in south Tucson where I live there are lots of Yaquis around. They drink an awful lot and go around at night singing.

Yaqui Views of Papagos and Other Indians

A stereotype current concerning Papagos persists in spite of close contact with Papagos in Tucson and on the ranches which should serve to dispel it. An example of such attitude comes from a Pascua youth of seventeen who has lived apart from Papagos:

Those Papagos put paint on themselves and dance around that way. They are like savages that my schoolteacher has told us about. They used to go to war with paint on, too. The Yaquis are not like that. They aren't savages like the Papagos.

Insofar as there is a stereotype of the Papagos for Yaquis this statement defines it. They show a close relation to the Anglo-American concept of the Indian in general, that is, the American Indian. Undoubtedly, the young man's opinion has been colored in school by an Anglo-American teacher who had such a concept of the "Indian."

The Yaquis, however, are less inclined to lump together all Indians under a single rubric. They make a distinction, for instance, between Papagos and Apaches. The Apaches (and together with them the Comanches) are characterized not only as wild savages who dance with warpaint but also as dark-redskinned people who wear feathers and use bows and arrows. Thus, for example, in the 1941 Easter ceremonies there was a Chapayeka who was classified as either an Apache or a Comanche, but more often as an Apache. He fit in many ways the Anglo-American concept of "the American Indian." His mask was colored a deep Indian red and had a large, high-bridged nose. He wore a feathered war bonnet and his long and short Chapayeka sticks were used as a bow and arrow in pantomime, the long stick having been selected with a curve for that purpose. It might be added that a swastika (an old Indian symbol) was painted on each ear. This characterization was not only consonant with the Anglo-American concept of Indian, but also, at least in its meaning, if not also its form, with the longstanding Yaqui concept of the Apache as a fierce and savage raider—a concept based on experience during the era of the Apache wars through the nineteenth century. The Chapayeka was not linked in any manner, however, with Papagos, thus confirming one's feeling that

Yaquis draw a sharp distinction between Papagos and "American Indians," even though there are features of their stereotype of the former that do not depart far from that of the latter.

Yaqui Views of Themselves

This section would not be complete without some consideration of how Yaquis view themselves. No Yaqui calls himself a Yaqui except when he is talking with an Anglo American or Mexican American and knows that he has to use the term in order to make himself understood. Typically, a Yaqui would say, "I do not understand that word 'Yaqui'. There is no such thing. I am a Yoeme, no less." Yaquis are well aware that other persons do not know the term "yoeme." The only indication of a tendency to adopt the outsiders' terminology is in the occasional use, when speaking Spanish, of the word "Yaquicitos" to apply to Yaquis in general. This term has a friendly, perhaps brotherly connotation quite different from "Yaqui" itself. Ordinarily, in speaking Spanish "Yoemem" is translated literally and becomes, therefore, *la gente*, which is to say "the people." Similarly, the word for the language, "yoem," becomes *el idioma*, or "the language" or "dialect." Another Yaqui term for themselves in general is *wawaim*, or "relative," that is, "kin." This, too, is translated directly when speaking Spanish, so that it is not uncommon in a Spanish conversation to hear the term *parientes* applied by one Yaqui to Yaquis in general. In accordance with Mexican usage, the term "Indio" is used very rarely, and the Mexican term *indigenas*, or *indigenes*, has not been adopted. Yaquis who speak English, however, consistently use "Yaqui" as their group name. It is our purpose in the present section to set forth the Yaqui connotations of the word which they apply to themselves. The original basis of distinction between themselves and Europeans seems to have been color. It has been pointed out above that the term applied to Mexicans or Spanish was and still is *yori* or "light-colored." The standard creation myths describe the making of Mexicans from ashes, that is, a gray substance, and the making of Yaquis from earth or clay, that is, a brown substance. Thus, one of the primary connotations of these two terms, which are set against each other as opposites, is a color distinction. One of the terms which had great currency during the nineteenth century wars was *toroyori*. This was applied to any Yaqui who turned against his own people and helped the Mexicans. It became synonymous with "traitor" and in 1941 was widely used in Arizona still with that connotation. Literally, its meaning in Yaqui is "dark-colored person," more freely, a yori who looks like a Yaqui.

A good deal of attention is paid to the color of a person's skin and hair. There are a number of Yaquis in Arizona who have light brown or yellowish complexions, light brown hair, and occasionally blue or hazel eyes. It is not always assumed that these characteristics are due to mixture with Anglo or Mexican Americans, although facetious references are sometimes made to such possibilities. On the contrary, there is a widely held belief that Mayo Indians may be blonds, or *hueros,* and that it is more likely that a family which produces a huero has Mayo blood in its line. Thus, these light-colored persons are not necessarily regarded as mixed bloods, for Mayos are regarded as practically identical peoples with Yaquis. No stigma of Mexican admixture, therefore, attaches to the hueros unless it is positively known to be present. Even in such cases there is no indication of a conventional attitude of either approval or disapproval. The skin color or eye color usually becomes the source of a nickname and often the term "Mayo" is applied, but the attitudes toward such persons are as varied as are the attitudes toward individual Mayos. The belief that any Mayo may be white-skinned and blue-eyed is one widely held not only by Yaquis, but also by Mexican Americans and some Anglo Americans of Arizona.

It may be said in view of these facts that although racial characteristics are rather carefully noted and are kept prominently before people through such devices as nicknames, there is no correlation of social status with skin or hair color in Yaqui thinking. Even though Anglo Americans, who are economically dominant over Yaquis in Arizona, and the Virgin Mary and Jesus are all represented as light-colored, there seems to be no accepted view that light-skinned babies are more beautiful than dark ones, or that it is desirable to lighten one's complexion. The attitudes in regard to color and racial characteristics are definitely neutral and the color term "yori" has unfavorable rather than favorable connotations, these stemming not from the color itself, but from other characteristics.

In 1939 there was in Tucson, in common with other parts of the United States, a sudden development of patriotic sentiments. One citizen of Tucson expressed his sentiments by buying at the ten-cent store a number of little placards which he gave free to Mexican Americans in the city. The placard contained the following words: "God Bless America. I am proud to be an American." One of the placards was given to a twenty-year-old youth in the village of Pascua. He accepted it gratefully and hung it on the wall of his house, but only after he altered it to read: "God Bless America. I am proud to be an American Yaqui." This was done in all seriousness and was subsequently shown to an Anglo American friend of his. It indicates the tenacity with which Yaquis maintain their sense of nationalism in the United States even among second-generation youths who have been to Anglo-American schools and speak English easily. There is no tendency or desire to lose their sense of national separateness. This is indicated further in connection with applications for citizenship made occasionally by Sonora-born men. Fifty-year-old Francisco Valencia in his application, wherever it called for a statement of nationality, put "Mexican (Yaqui)." Forty-year-old Marcelino Humo always wrote "Yaqui Mexican Indian," and thirty-year-old Felipe Gastelo omitted "Mexican" entirely and wrote "Real Yaqui Indian." It is obviously not satisfactory to a Yaqui to classify himself either as American or Mexican. He must assert that he is Yaqui, and this happens even in the case of citizenship applications where he prejudices his case against himself by refusing to be classified simply as a Mexican.

This sense of national pride in Arizona Yaquis is maintained in conjunction with feelings of both superiority and inferiority in connection with other groups. There is no question of the existence of a feeling of superiority over the stereotype of the Mexican.

But Yaquis have also their feelings of inferiority. This is most notable among the older Yaquis. Among them one of the most common ways of referring to themselves is as *nosotros pobres,* "we poor people." Lino Saurez, the Pascola Mayor of Pascua, recalls his past in Mexico:

I was working hard there. We all worked hard. We started early in the morning and we came back after dark from the fields. That is the way it was with all of us poor people. We had no shoes and never any money and only a little food sometimes. The rich people owned the haciendas and we worked for them. We worked hard all the time, almost every day. We had no time for anything but work. We never went to school. That is why I don't know how to read and write. My sons have learned here in this place in the United States, but we never learned. We were just poor people, you understand. We understood nothing; we had nothing.

Again, we may consider the statement of an old Yaqui woman from Guaymas in connection with filling out an alien registration blank:

Nosotros pobres, we don't know how to read or write. We are just *tontos.* We Yaquis don't know any of that sort of thing. We don't know when we were born, the day, the year, or anything. We just don't know. We are ignorant people, poor innocents, we old Yaquis, because we don't know anything at all.

These views of themselves indicate a feeling of inferiority based on lack of wealth and also on lack of the techniques of literacy. These feelings are widespread among all the older Yaquis and crop up again and again in conversations with Anglo-American students. There is a constant effort to explain their weaknesses in these respects in terms of the hardships and slavery of the years in Sonora before coming to the United States. On these two scores they recognize the superiority of other peoples around them, although the superiority is not definitely allocated to any one group. Just as it was recognized that there were Mexicans who were superior in the matter of wealth and literacy in the early days, so it is recognized that there are some Mexicans, Papagos, and Anglo Americans who are superior in these respects today. The younger people are beginning to feel inferiority in another respect. For example:

When I was working for Americans in Tucson or when I was going with some friends, they used to come home with me sometimes. They were always surprised to find that I lived in a house like ours is, just a Yaqui house, you know, kind of dirty and poor and everything.

Different Yaqui villages maintain distinctive views concerning other Yaqui villages. There seem to be definite feelings of village consciousness in at least four of the villages—Pascua, Libre, Scottsdale, and Guadalupe. The others are perhaps too new to have attained such consciousness and still regard themselves as satellites, at least ceremonially, to the older centers. There is a definite intervillage competition in ceremonial matters, such as obtaining the best Deer Dancer for Holy Week and securing the greatest number of Chapayekas for an Easter season. There is also developing a little intervillage competition in baseball, this being noticeable most between Libre, Pascua, and Marana where baseball teams have been organized within the past five years. There are certain special attitudes connected with special conditions in each of the villages. Thus it is common at Scottsdale to hear remarks of the following kind:

No, we never go over to Guadalupe anymore. There are a lot of Mexicans over there. Here we don't have any Mexicans. This village is just Yaquis. That's why it's better to live here. You don't have any Mexicans around.

In Pascua there is a similar feeling about Libre:

They're all mixed up down there. They don't even have room for a Way of the Cross at Lent. They're all mixed up with Papagos and Mexicans.

These feelings are accompanied with expressions of distaste and disapproval. In Pascua and Scottsdale it is clearly regarded as a virtue for Yaquis to live in more or less distinct groups, separate from Mexicans and Papagos. In Barrio Libre, however, there is no such view current, and Pascua is generally regarded as very far from an ideal Yaqui village. One of the chief sources of criticism of the Pascuans springs from the Chamber of Commerce aid to the Easter ceremonies. It happens occasionally that Libre Chapayekas come to a *fiesta de promesa* at Pascua to perform. When they do they vigorously oppose the taking of pictures, which is permitted under certain conditions at Pascua. This antagonism to picture-taking has a profound effect on Pascuans. They say that since they get so much help from Anglo Americans for their ceremonies that they cannot very well prohibit all picture-taking because that would be ungrateful. They stipulate, however, that pictures must be taken from a hidden position, because, they say, "If the Libre or other Yaquis think that we are letting pictures be taken they will talk about us, saying we give the ceremonies for money." The Libre people classify the Pascuans as "crazy" in connection with the Easter ceremonies because of their welcoming of publicity. The Pascuans, in turn, regard the Libre Yaquis as ultra-conservative and say that they are foolish because they "won't talk about their ceremonies to Americans."

Summary of the Yaqui Point of View

Yaquis, like other peoples, find it easy to make generalizations both about themselves and about everybody else. They have, in other words, stereotypes which simplify their thinking about group relationships. These stereotypes are in some measure based on real experience, but like all generalizations they depart sharply at many points from reality. Nevertheless, no matter how far from the truth they may be, these group labels continue to be of significance in governing their relations with others.

Yaquis distinguish Mexican Americans from Anglo Americans rather sharply, generally maintaining a favorable or neutral point of view toward the latter and an unfavorable attitude toward the former. The stereotype that they have in regard to the Mexicans is precisely formulated and plays an important part in Yaqui evaluations of their own and other people's behavior. The Yaquis further distinguish between themselves and the Papagos and other Indians, showing some tendency to adopt the Anglo-American stereotype of the American Indian, but keeping themselves separate from this stereotype.

There are definite feelings of superiority to the Mexican and Indian groups, and no clear-cut feeling of inferiority to the Anglo-American group. The respects with which there is inferiority feeling are literacy and wealth and cleanliness, all of which, of course, are marks of class status in Anglo-American and Mexican-American society. The older Yaquis do not seem to be conscious of the cleanliness mark of inferiority, but the younger Yaquis are.

In all their group relations, the Yaquis maintain a strong sense of national consciousness which seems as strong in younger as in older persons, and there is a tendency to regard segregation from other Indians and from Mexicans as a desirable state.

In general summary of Yaqui contacts with Anglo Americans, Mexican Americans, and Chinese, Negroes, and other Indian groups it can be said that it is obvious that the relations of these three groups with Yaquis have been quite different in each case, and seem to be dependent in all cases on both the degree and type of contact.

PART II

The Selection of Behaviors by Yaquis

CHAPTER 5

Older Yaqui Men

In the next four chapters case studies of individuals from the Arizona Yaqui settlement of Pascua will be presented. The purpose will be to show in as concrete a manner as possible how Yaqui individuals have adjusted to the complex cultural situation in which they find themselves. The case studies give a view not only of the nature of individual adjustments in the present, but also of antecedent adjustments.

The case studies of the men presented in this chapter carry us back to the Yaqui River pueblos in the 1870s and 1880s and the Sonora cities before 1900. Through their eyes we see the nature of their initiation into some of the distinctive Yaqui customs which they still practice. We see in what manner they became acquainted with the customs and ways of thought of other peoples with whom they came into contact at different times. In following their experiences up to 1941, individual by individual, we shall be looking for clues as to what possibilities were open to them at different times in their lives, what patterns of behavior and belief they were aware of, and what led them to choose one or the other of the patterns that were available. It becomes clear from the consideration of this group of older men, who might be supposed to have been most irrevocably disciplined as Yaquis in their childhood, that there has been much opportunity for choice. It is the basis of choice for this group of men over fifty that we are chiefly interested in determining. Why have they remained Yaqui to the extent that they have?

Case Study of Lucas Chavez

In 1940 the third Maestro in the Pascua church organization was a man of sixty-nine named Lucas Chavez. He was fairly regular in his attendance at Yaqui ceremonies and was a consistent participant as assistant to the other two Maestros in all the most important ceremonies, such as All Souls' Day, the fiesta of Saint Ignatius of Loyola, and Holy Week. He was outspokenly antagonistic toward the Catholic Church organization of Tucson and especially to some of its affiliated organizations which were carrying on instruction and other activities in Pascua. At the same time, however, he was undergoing conversion—as the term was used by the Mexican Baptist church—to that church.

Lucas Chavez, October 1936.
Photograph by Rosamond B. Spicer.

Lucas Chavez, third Maestro, *left*, and Maestro Lo'i (José María García), *center*, at the Palm Sunday service in the Pascua church, March 1937. *Photograph by David J. Jones, Jr.*

Chavez had held office in the Pistola political organization of the 1920s and was as a consequence rather well known to a half dozen or more Anglo Americans of Tucson. These acquaintances had led him to a number of other specialized relationships with Anglo-American students who were seeking information about Yaqui culture, relations which had heightened his own consciousness of that culture. Chavez was also widely known among Yaquis in Arizona, having compadres or godchildren or formerly intimate associates in every Yaqui settlement.

Of slight build, weighing about 115 pounds, and below medium stature for a Yaqui man, he was unobtrusive in his appearances in public ceremony. Despite his advanced years, his hair was black and abundant. His skin was of medium to dark brown as compared with other Yaquis, and his face was moderately seamed and wrinkled. A widower without children, he was living alone in his own house on land not his own in the village of Pascua.

Life History

The life of Lucas Chavez may be considered as comprising five periods as follows:

Age 1 to 15, living in Torim, Sonora, on the Yaqui River.

Age 15 to 21, working in various parts of Sonora.

Age 21 to 40, living in Nogales, Arizona, and vicinity.

Age 41 to 60, living in Pascua Village with his wife.

Age 60 to 69, living in Pascua alone as a widower.

Chavez was born in Torim in 1871 and lived there continuously until 1886. This was the period of most intensive warfare on the Yaqui River, and his departure from the river country coincides with the final defeat of the Yaqui leader Cajeme. Chavez's parents were Indian, his father, Loreto, being a Yaqui of Torim and his mother, Antonia, a Mayo from Echojoa. His father combined several different kinds of activity in all of which the boy Lucas participated from perhaps the age of six or seven. The father was a Maestro who visited the smaller settlements of Yaquis around Torim, there being "enough Maestros in Torim itself." He was also a *cargador,* taking loads of native tobacco, cheese, salt, corn, and parrots for sale to Guaymas and bringing back needles and other metal goods and various cloth products. The range of his trading activities extended throughout the Yaqui country from Guaymas to the Mayo River. As a small boy, Lucas went with his father and helped drive the burros. They used no wagon, for "there was only one wagon in the whole of Torim in those days and it had solid wheels cut from cottonwood trees." Between expeditions and when there were no ceremonies requiring his services, Loreto tended stock (horses and cattle) for his more well-to-do relatives in Torim. He and Antonia also had a small herd of pigs which Antonia and Lucas tended. Their home was on the outskirts of Torim rather than in the village proper.

Chavez remembers the whole of this period in Torim as one of continual disturbance. He dates events in relation to battles, particularly to the battles of Echojoa and Santa Cruz on the Mayo River in which his three older brothers were killed, the battle of Añil near Torim in which some uncles were killed, and the battle of Buatachive north of Torim in the Bacatete Mountains in which he saw his father and mother killed. One of the most vivid and easily recalled of his memories is that of General Cajeme and his troops riding in scattered units through Torim, singing the

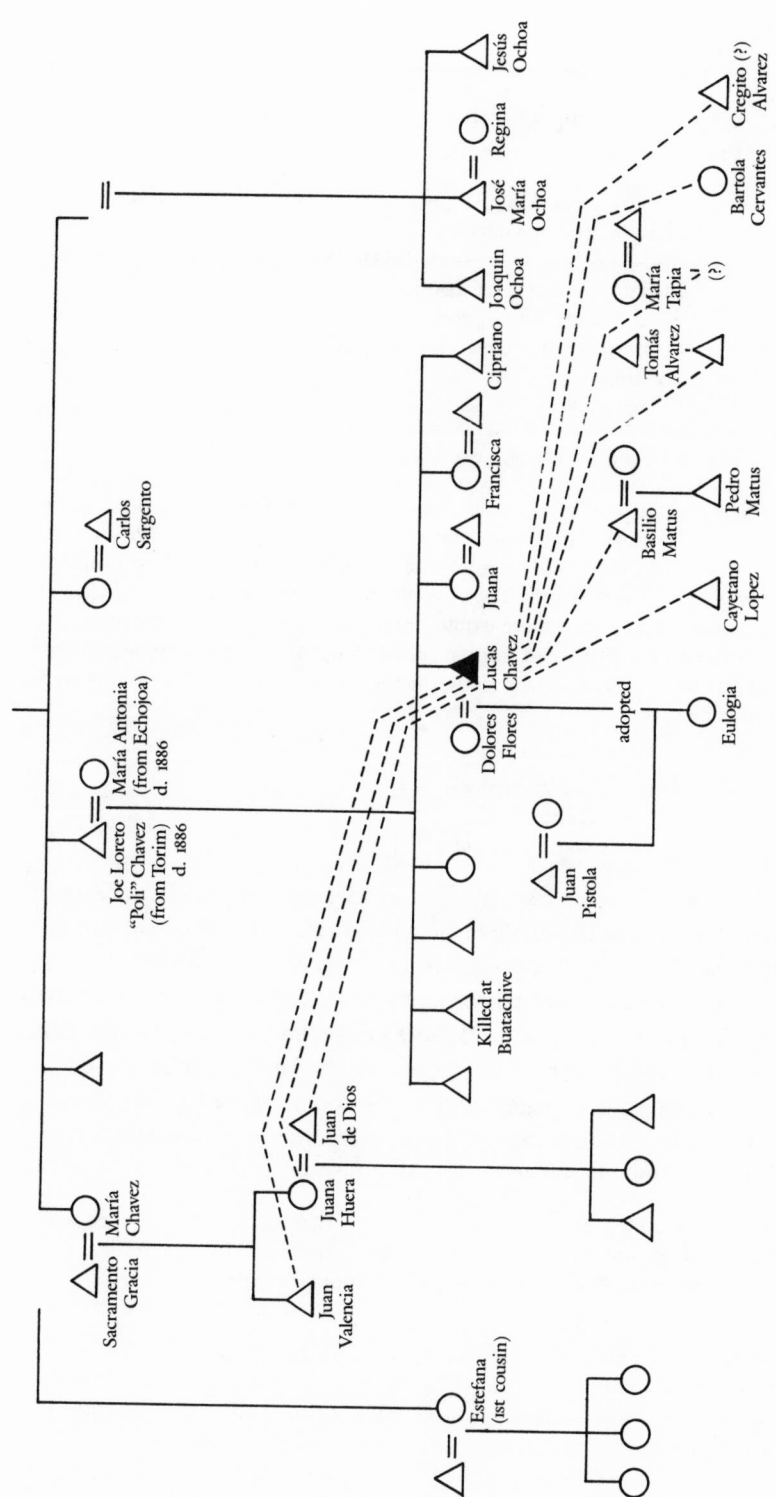

Partial Genealogy and Padrino Relationships of Lucas Chavez

current songs of the campaign, such as the Yaqui corrido, which may be translated as follows:

> Yes, my friend Don Augustín (a Mexican general)
> I have a little business with you
> And there will be no money in the transaction
> I want to change this wooden bow
> For a shining Remington.
> I want to change these carrizo arrows
> For some cartridges.
> We have a little business, you and I.

He remembers Cajeme himself very vividly:

The soldiers would pass by the house when they were fortifying Añil. Cajeme would sing in Spanish. They would go by in file past our house. Ten men on horses with Cajeme. He would be riding with his leg hooked around the pommel, singing very slowly, very gently. There would be one man on each side of Cajeme on horses. Then a mile back there would be ten more men and then ten more. He would usually go by with about thirty men that way, then maybe there would be a hundred infantry in the rear back along the trail. Cajeme was always singing. Oh, what a man he was:

> Says the general Cajeme
> I do not fear the federals
> Nor yet the nationals.
> *Ai manabe, ai manabe.*

The memories of his last days in the Yaqui country are of events of violence, particularly the battle of Buatachive where Cajeme made his last effective stand against the Mexican troops. Cajeme made the stand in the Bacatete Mountains where he fortified a peak and took within his own lines the wives and children of those Yaquis who were supporting him. Lucas and his father and mother and younger brother and other close relatives were among the besieged. During the course of the fighting, Lucas's father was killed, and during the mopping up afterwards his mother was killed. Lucas escaped with an uncle and some others. He says:

How well I remember the defeat of Cajeme. I remember the cry of lamentation that the people raised when they were in the mountains. We were hiding there where the Yoris would not see us. The people would cry out:

Kaita Dios ha:ni. (There is no God here.)
Kate nacion itom nokriamachi. (There is no nation can defeat us.)
Elapo Elapo. (No matter, no matter.)
Kaibu te ta'apo enemigota mampo ito su tohine. (Never will we let ourselves fall into the hands of the enemy.)

After the battle we had no food, no water, no clothes. We had only water we were carrying about in the stomachs of animals and the water stank. We had only a little meat and that without salt. The old people were afraid, but to us children would say over and over: "Better for our lands to fall into the hands of any other people than the Mexican." That is what they said.

After three weeks in the mountains, Lucas and his uncle managed to get back to Torim, where they were rounded up with other Yaquis and put on a boat for shipment to Guaymas, about twenty miles up the coast. The voyage is one of Lucas's most terrible memories. They ran out of water. The small boat was extremely crowded. They were required to stand off Guaymas for a full day, while everyone suffered greatly from thirst. The sea became rough and when they were finally landed at the port, everyone was in a state of exhaustion.

In his fifteenth year, his parents dead, in the company of two of his father's sisters, Lucas began the second period of his life. He was sent in the company of a large number of Yaquis to work on a hacienda near La Misa, fifty miles northeast of Guaymas. With other Yaqui boys he was sent to do odd jobs such as scaring the crows away from the harvested wheat and corn. He speaks of his patrón as a good man who developed a liking for him and finally made him a houseboy. His duties consisted in waiting on the table, fanning the mistress of the hacienda, and to some extent overseeing the activities of the other boys. He quickly learned a little Spanish and even got some help from his patrón in learning his letters. But he did not become attached to the life of the hacienda and, hearing that his younger brother was at the Hacienda Torres farther north, he ran away and joined him. Here he worked for a few months and then with his brother ran away.

Again he went north until he located his godfather of baptism on a hacienda north of Hermosillo. Here he got a job on the Southern Pacific Railroad and began to work his way north to Nogales. Finally, in 1891, at the age of twenty, he moved across the line into Nogales, Arizona.

He remembers vividly the corridos that were sung by the Yaquis and Mexicans as they worked together on the railroad. There was one which made fun of Cajeme and which the Mexicans sang when they were drunk to make the Yaquis angry:

> Good morning, Don José María (Cajeme)
> I am going to put you to the yoke
> With twenty-five *pelones*
> And a single *don nacional*.

> This is the Indian Cajeme
> Who appeared at a ranch
> And an old laundrywoman
> Was the one who betrayed him.
>
> Coming from the little war,
> They commenced to chat,
> Guaranteeing his life,
> Thanks to a single *don nacional*.

The corrido recalled the capture of Cajeme at San José de Guaymas after the defeat of Buatachive. Chavez says of the song:

The drunken Mexicans would sing this and I used to feel very sad. I didn't like it at all, but I heard it so much that I learned the music and words.

This period in Lucas's life was one characterized by constant association with Mexicans, albeit in the company of his brother and a few other relatives and godparents. He was learning Spanish, but was still using Yaqui. It was a period of freedom and new experiences and seems to be remembered as pleasant and exciting, not as difficult and sad.

The next fifteen or twenty years constituted a period of acceptance of and adjustment to the life of a railroad worker in the United States. Lucas crossed the line at Nogales because "there were better wages, a dollar a day in Arizona as against a peso in Sonora, for the same kind of work." He never went back across the line. For the first few years he lived in Nogalitos, a Yaqui settlement at the edge of Nogales, Arizona. Here he was closely associated with Teofila Lopez and other Yaquis. He worked with Teofila at learning to read and write in Spanish, and also with her he studied church ritual, until his younger brother, Cipriano, was killed "by Mexicans" while working as a trackwalker north of Nogales. Then Lucas wandered some more, working as far as Yuma, Sasco, and Patagonia, but finally came back and settled down with a woman, Dolores, from the Yaqui country. The memories of this period are predominantly of warm, friendly relations with Yaqui neighbors and of Anglo-American foremen and bosses. The general tone of the period is, however, one of insecurity and fear of being sent back to Mexico.

When he was nearly forty, about the year 1910, Lucas and Dolores, whom he had now married through a church ceremony, moved to north Tucson, where they settled as squatters in old Barrio Anita. They had had no children. Lucas continued to work for the railroad, but also took jobs on the surrounding ranches. Within a few years he became associated with

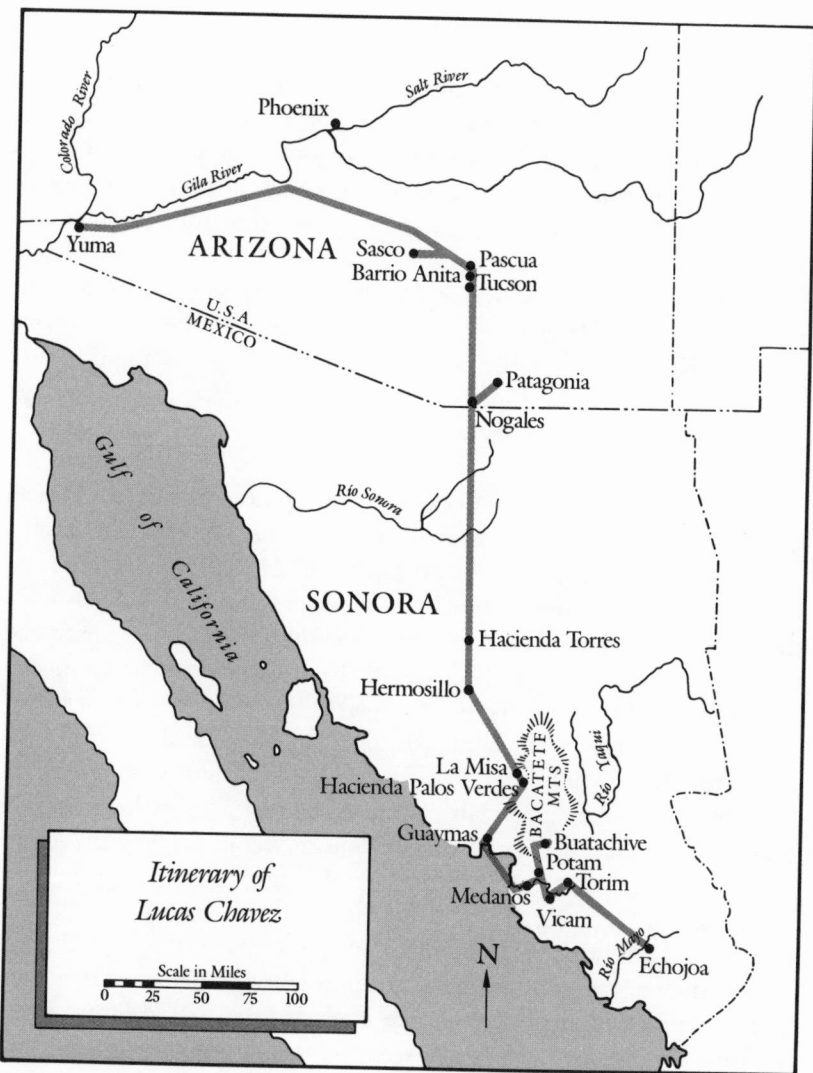

Itinerary of
Lucas Chavez

Juan Pistola as secretary of *la colonia de las tribus Yaquis*. As the only literate member of the Pistola junta, he became well-known not only among
Pistola's followers, but also with Tucson Anglo Americans. He accompanied Pistola to meetings with the lawyer, Kirk Moore, in the city, and he
received Tucsonans who came to Barrio Anita to talk about "the nation
within a nation" and took notes on the meetings. Through Pistola he

began to get better jobs and for several years was a gang foreman, first on the railroad and later on the highway. He became more prosperous, built a substantial adobe house with pigeon roosts on the roof, and secured a horse and wagon. After Pistola's death he continued to be prominent in north Tucson Yaqui affairs. He kept possession of the papers and documents of the Pistola government and was generally known by the title of "secretary of Pascua." He began to take part in church ceremonies as a Sacristan and, having the only mailbox, assumed the position of mailman for the village. In 1931, his wife died. Having no other relatives, he continued to live in his large house alone. This period of Lucas's life was one of achievement of high status as a Yaqui both in relation to Yaqui culture and in relation to the surrounding cultures. It was characterized by feelings of great security, both socially and economically, and by a tone of satisfaction and pleasure.

In the ten years since then, Lucas's Anglo-American friends as well as all his influential Yaqui associates have died. His status as secretary has lost its meaning for both Yaquis and Anglo Americans. He has devoted more and more time to service in the church, yet while he has occasionally assumed the duties of Maestro, he has not developed into either an able Sacristan or Maestro. He is increasingly disregarded as an important church officer. Economically, he has become steadily worse off and for the past four years has been permanently on charity aid, being rated as physically unable to work steadily. His horse has died, and he has been unable to replace it. His house is deteriorating. His clothes are almost all gifts from various charitable agencies. His major activity consists still in fulfilling the job of postman for the village, but people are objecting to his charge for this service and are securing mailboxes of their own. He is, in general, either ignored in the village as an unimportant person, smiled at as a slightly crazy old man, or definitely distrusted as a schemer who extorts money in connection with mail delivery. He interprets this period of his life as one of sad decline in which he has seen "his people going the wrong way, forgetting the good things, and wishing to become like Mexicans." He has taken to drinking occasionally and has been in jail twice in Tucson for disorderly conduct.

Orientation in Yaqui Society and Culture

During the fourteen years that Lucas Chavez spent on the Yaqui River he seems to have passed through an ordinary Yaqui boyhood, with ordi-

nary family, godparent, and ceremonial relations in process of establishment. He spoke no language except Yaqui until after he left Torim, in his
fifteenth year. He was the fifth of six children, having three older brothers,
and one younger brother, and one older sister. He lived with his immediate family in a house apart from any other family group, but was intimately
associated with both his mother's and father's relatives who lived in or
near Torim. He was acutely conscious of the relative poverty of his parents.
He repeatedly described his father as a "poor man" and one who had no
property of his own. His mother's family, who had moved from the Mayo
River to Torim, are also described as poor and referred to apologetically
as "pig-keepers."

Lucas does not speak readily of his mother. He remembered her name,
Antonia, with great difficulty. The mention of her death at Buatachive
consistently brings tears and a great show of emotion, but the interviewer
could never be sure to what extent the memory of her was distinct in
such instances from that of the general terrible scene. Once, however, in
response to a direct request to tell about her appearance and mannerisms,
he broke down completely in tears and was unable to find words for several
minutes. When he recovered himself, he said, "My mother often told me
not to go with the bad boys who were around there in Torim." He never
elaborated directly on this theme, but as we shall see one of his ruling
concepts is of a humanity divided into evil men who are constantly trying
to give him and others "bad advice" and good men who give out "good
advice." His mother remains a shadowy figure who did not accompany
her husband on his trading trips or his occasional stays in Hermosillo, but
remained at home "to look after my brothers" and tend the pigs.

His father, Loreto, who was more often called "Poli," is remembered
as a physically vigorous, very active man who was always extremely busy.
"He was not a runt, like me. I have seen him lift up the hundred-pound
sacks of corn to load them on the burros without any effort at all." The
memory of his father is tinged with worship:

I remember how my father used to help when my mother was going to have a baby.
I remember how he stood near with water and how he gave *pinole* to my mother so
that the baby would come out all right. . . . There were many persons who talked
against my father constantly. They had bad advice, just like a lot of people here in
Pascua. My father used to tell me not to go out and see those people. They were
very bad. But my father was like God: He liked everybody. That is the way you
think of God. He doesn't dislike anyone and my father was like that. Yes, my father
was very poor, but he was like a judge in the pueblo and there were people who
respected his word. Only he never really was a judge because he liked to wander
around and he was always getting burros together for a trip to Guaymas.

Loreto took Lucas along on his trading ventures, and Lucas enjoyed the strange foods of Guaymas and the life on the trail, but his father was not easy on him. As Lucas remembers it, he worked harder than the other boys of Torim:

I used to go out with my father. He would be planting, always in someone else's fields. He used to take care of Sacramento Gracia's fields (a brother-in-law). Then I would guard the field from the little animals. It was not far away from the pueblo, and sometimes I would be on a horse, guarding the crippled horses. I used to work with the irrigation, too, with the *norias*. There was what we called *molko vaso*, getting up water with a rope. Sometimes I wasn't very happy doing this because as you would know there would be other boys around and they would come along calling to each other and then they would take off their clothes and go in swimming, while I had to work. . . . I would be guarding the watermelons and they would come along calling to each other to play ball. . . . Or they would go by with their bows and arrows for some shooting and I couldn't go with them. I always had to work, and this made me a little mad with my father. He wouldn't let me go with the boys. I was always where the animals were, working, but it was a good thing for my father to be hard that way.

There was strict discipline in Lucas's family in the matter of prayer and religious observance. One Yaqui custom was strictly adhered to:

When I was living in Torim with my father and mother all of us children in the family had to go out to the cross in the houseyard once a day and kneel there and put our hands together in front of our breasts and pray. We had to say over three times the Ave María Purísima then slowly in Yaqui: "Greetings and God aid you, our mothers, our fathers, our relatives, all the elders. Keep us in good health throughout the night and until morning comes." Each afternoon my father would come and tell us to do that until we learned it all perfectly.

Lucas's father and mother saw to it that he took part in the children's processions during the month of October, and sometime before he left the Yaqui country they promised him to service as a Sacristan, although he never had opportunity to serve as such.

Lucas does not remember much about his brothers and sister, with the exception of his younger brother, Cipriano, who accompanied him on his Sonora wanderings and for whom he developed a deep affection. He does not remember the names of any but Cipriano:

How should I remember that? I never called them anything but *insai* [Yaqui kinship term, my older brother]. I don't have any idea what their names were. They didn't use names very much then. You know, they used to all stand around when a baby was born and each person would call it something. One would say *tutuli* [pretty]; another would say *tosali* [white]; another might say *ilichi* [little one]. You know the way people do when they stand around and look at a new baby. Well, the one of those that people remembered would be the name that the baby would have. Of course, they had almanacs and there is a day for each saint, the patron for the day, but they didn't use that very much. My brothers called me *yunki,* which means blacksmith's anvil.

Lucas apparently had little to do with his older siblings. The brothers were a great deal older and went off to fight with Cajeme while Lucas was still very young. They and the older sister had been killed by the time Lucas was ten years old.

Lucas prefers to talk about his aunt María Chavez and her husband, Sacramento Gracia, to talking about his own parents. María, he thinks, was his father's sister, but he is not sure. She and Sacramento took care of Lucas and Cipriano during the battle of Buatachive, and María for a short time after that, when they had been sent to La Misa. Lucas never fails when he mentions Sacramento Gracia to point out that he was "very well known in Torim." He dwells on the importance of Sacramento at every opportunity.

Sacramento was one of the *Susuakame* [village elders] and as such wore his hair long. It reached down as far as his buttocks. Only the Susuakame wore their hair this way. My father had short hair like the other men; the maestros didn't wear long hair. I remember the big hats that Sacramento used to wear. The hat was big because he had to put all his hair inside it.
Sacramento was a very well-known man. He was one of the *communes,* one of the older men of the pueblo, and people came to him to settle disputes and to get advice as to what they should do. There were four other men with him at Torim who made up the Susuakame. I remember the names of those other four very well. . . . They used to meet together and walk and decide things and sometimes there were other Susuakame who came from other pueblos and discussed. They were very important men.
My uncle, Sacramento Gracia, had the only wagon in Torim. He made the wheels himself, because he was very skillful in making things out of wood.

The concern that Lucas shows in interviews to point out his own relationships to an important and well-known man like Sacramento Gracia is typical of him. His tendency is to attach himself to an able and prominent person and by that means attain status in his society. Evidently, one of his major problems in his orientation in the life of Torim was the low status of his father. He respected and honored his father, but he knew that he had little standing in the community because of his restlessness and lack of office. Lucas sought compensation for this condition in identifying himself with Gracia.

The kinship orientation of Lucas in Torim remained imperfect. We may note his uncertainty as to the relationship of Sacramento Gracia's wife to him. He used the usual kinship terms in his relations with his elementary family, but he did not learn the terms for more distant relatives. At present he is unable to give a complete list of Yaqui kinship terms and, like other Arizona Yaquis, falls back on the use of Spanish ones. This characteristic imperfect knowledge of the kinship system and its obligations cannot, in the case of Lucas, be attributed to a lack of relatives in the Torim situation. He was associated with many of his mother's relatives, as well as his father's. It more likely indicates the characteristic Yaqui emphasis on ceremonial sponsorship relations. Lucas was identified, through the godparent system, with the family of Sacramento Gracia. He remembers more vividly his relations with his godparents of baptism than those with his mother and seems to have been more intimate with the former than with either his father or mother.

He says of his madrina:

I remember my godmother *de pila* [baptism] so well. Her name was Juana Huera. She was very well known, the daughter of Sacramento Gracia. She had a brother who was called Juan Valencia. . . . He was very Mexican in appearance, very white, and very well known. When a person's skin is very white, they always call him *huero* [Spanish for blond]. No, I don't know how Juana got her light color. They used to say that sometimes when the Yaquis went off to the haciendas outside the Yaqui River to work for money that they came back with children who had Spanish blood, because both the men and the women would get together with the men and the women on the haciendas. They used to go out and work that way because there was no money on the Yaqui River. . . . Juana spoke only Yaqui, like all the others in those days. No one was speaking Spanish. . . . I remember how my godmother used to say to me, "Now this is your little sister," pointing to her daughter. "Call her sister, don't say '*ahijada*.'" Juana used to say that I was her son. I was very dark, but I had white brothers and they were very nice. They were white like my madrina and I liked her because she was always giving me food to eat and then she sometimes gave me shirts. I liked her as much as my mother. Her husband, my godfather, was light and very tall. They called him Juan de Dios sometimes and he was very famous in Torim.

My madrina used to say to me sometimes, "You are not a little white one." I used to be a little mad at that, but not much. That was worth more. The whites are worth more.

To reach Juan de Dios later became a goal for Lucas after he left the hacienda at La Misa. He finally joined him with Cipriano north of Hermosillo and through Juan became established as a railroad worker at Carbo.

Lucas's orientation in Yaqui ceremonial life has been disjointed and imperfect, and yet it is this aspect of Yaqui culture which has come finally to give him the most secure status in a Yaqui community, in fact, the only status which he now possesses. It has been mentioned that his parents made a manda that he become a Sacristan sometime before his fifteenth year. The reason for the manda was the usual one, illness as a baby.

No, I didn't go to school. There were no schools in the Yaqui country. My father never had time to teach me anything. He learned what he knew at a Maestro's school. The Maestros used to get together and dance and chant and pray and the young ones learned from the old ones. They had dances like the *Pastores*. My father didn't teach me to be a Maestro. I remember some people wanted him to and they told my mother about it, but she said that I had been promised to be a Temasti and no more. Thus it wasn't necessary to teach me all that a Maestro should know. The pueblo thought it would be better for me to be a Maestro, but my father said he didn't have any time to teach me because of the fighting and troubles.

I remember the jokes they used to make with me about being a Sacristan. People used to come to our house and ask, "This fellow is going to be a Sacristan?" They would point to me and say, "Well, that little boy is surely going to be frightened. Because everybody knows that a Sacristan has to serve for the dead. He will have to do the *alba* rites at four o'clock in the morning, when he is all alone in the dark. Oh, that poor little boy is certainly going to be afraid." I used to listen to this talk and I didn't like it.

Others would say, "In those hours there are not people around, only the sound of the dawn. There are only the dead who may come and meet him. The Sacristan has to fulfill all this. Yaqui law requires it!" Others then would say things to frighten me more, "Yes, it's the truth. The dead come and just touch the Sacristan ever so lightly." I was terribly frightened, being a boy, because it made me think of what my mother would say when the baby cried, "Careful, now the dead will come and maybe the Yoris will come, too."

Thus Lucas had it impressed on him that he was to be a Sacristan and, as he remembers it, people outside the family regarded him as good material for the more exacting office of Maestro. But his activities in the ceremonial life remained, during the whole time he was in Torim, those of the ordinary, untrained small boy. He saw the Matachinis dance, the Fariseos come and go in season, and sometimes he participated in the October processions:

I used to be with the other children in the processions in the month of October. There was the procession of the *Koba yuyeste*—the skull and bones—every afternoon. This was the procession when we carried the skull of an old padre on a little table. These were bones from an early time, of a Catholic father who was good for the Yaquis. He had worked well for the eight villages and then he died. So they kept his skull and bones and marched with them in procession each year to honor the head. We children all carried candles. The skull was in the center of the table. We went from the church to four different crosses outside in the churchyard. There was a new maestro each day for this procession. The crosses were like the ones in the plaza at Pascua which we use on Holy Week—Saint Luke, Saint John, Saint Mark, and Saint Matthew. . . . We sang "*Salgan, Salgan, Salgan*" in the procession. There was always a *piskanyaut* who came and directed us children in this ceremony.

There were the Matachinis who came to all the houses. They would come with the blessing of María Santísima, who is their patroness. I think they came singing sometimes. I used to hear the alabanzas that belonged to each part of the Matachin ceremonies. There was the one for the genuflection:

> Sea bendito alabado el Santísimo José
> Por fe del eterno Padre en el mundo imagen fue.

That one always at that time. I heard it often with pleasure.

Kuasepe is a hill near Torim that is very high and is all rock without anything growing on it. It is this hill that they used to burn fires on during the vespers of Santa Cruz. I remember seeing the luminarias there. On the other side of Torim near the bend in the river is Abasokawi (which means "hill of the alamo"). Here is where they had a procession at the cumpleaño of Santa Cruz, perhaps on May 2 which is the day of Santa Cruz. This was when we burned the old crosses in fires. I remember the big cross that they always put on the hill of Abasokawi. It was very beautiful at the vespers of Santa Cruz.

There were aspects of the ceremonial life that Lucas does not remember with pleasure, for instance, the Fariseos:

I remember how much I used to be afraid of the Fariseos in their season. I didn't like them at all. I cried a great deal in the time of the Fariseos until I was twelve years old. I never went to the *capilla* [chapel] because of this fear. But my mother used to tell me what to do. She would say, "Now whenever you want to get rid of bad things, turn away evil, just say Ave María Purísima. Don't fear them. The Fariseos cannot work harm if you say this." Then the Fariseos used to come to the house on a limosna and my mother would give them a plate full of fruit and tobacco. My mother would say to me, "Now don't be afraid or they will punish you. If the Fariseos make a bad sign or movement, just say Ave María Purísima. As soon as you say that the Fariseos will fall down and die." You know yourself how the Fariseos fall down and shake all over when they hear those words, as though they were about to die. You know, too, how they shake their rear ends instead of saying thank you when they leave a house on limosna. That is the way they used to behave in Torim.

Lucas's reaction to the Fariseos has much of what may be noted among Arizona Yaqui children today, but the note of fear is much stronger and his emphasis on his fear indicates an unusual degree of timidity in regard to them.

Lucas's further orientation in Yaqui ceremonial life was sharply interrupted by the battle of Buatachive. He had begun to be interested in "the old stories." He was working hard from the time he was eight or nine years old and says that "there was no time to sit and listen to the Susuakame." But occasionally he did listen to Sacramento Gracia and learned a few of the important Yaqui myths such as "Yomumule," the "Emperador and Omteme," "Santiago and the Milky Way," and a few others. But just as his interest was roused, he was wrenched away from the Yaqui community life and for more than twenty years had no connection with an original Yaqui village.

While he was in Nogalitos, however, he met Teofila Lopez, a Yaqui woman who had been trained as a Cantora on the Yaqui River. Lucas had meanwhile taught himself to read and write, and he began a notebook of alabanzas and responses, apparently remembering his manda to become a Sacristan. He worked evenings and Sundays with this woman whom he describes as "very wise" and from "a very good family," but he never practiced as a Sacristan during this stay at Nogalitos. It was not until later in Pascua, and after his political activities with Pistola had declined, that he began actually to appear in the church and participate in the ceremonies. He has become during the last fifteen years of his life a moderately competent Sacristan and at times attempts to serve as a Maestro, when the regular Maestros are absent. He is not regarded, however, as having ability as a Maestro. The son of Teofila Lopez, himself an exceptionally able Maestro, says:

That Lucas don't know his business. He can get along as a Sacristan, but he don't know much. He had been studying twenty-seven years to be a Maestro and he don't know how to do it yet.

The general opinion of the villagers bears out this view. Lucas is rarely sought for a ceremony in the capacity of Maestro, although his participation in church ceremonies as a Sacristan is frequent. He speaks of himself, however, as a Maestro rather than a Sacristan and spends the greater part of his leisure time studying the ritual which Maestros must know. He has never held any other ceremonial offices nor been a member of any other ceremonial societies.

Lucas's integration into the formal aspects of Yaqui society, after the period of Mexican association in Sonora, came first in the field of political organization. He became one of the leaders in the effort to organize Arizona Yaquis under the "chieftainship" of Juan Pistola. The process by which he became attached to Pistola's organization has not been discovered fully. There is no indication of any contact with or participation

in the government of Torim during his youth there. We may recall his
devotion to Sacramento Gracia, the Susuakame, and his early desire to sit
at Gracia's feet and learn about Yaqui culture from him. Throughout his
interviews there is constant mention of *"la ley Yaqui"* which he regards as
as definite an entity of social regulations as Blackstone, and his mind is
full of formulations of "the Law." But so far as can be determined, these
formulations of the law were worked out by him and Pistola and their
associates in conversation during the period of their cooperation; most of
the men were equally inexperienced in Yaqui political behavior and thus
their organization was based on boyhood memories. Lucas always thought
of himself as subordinate in the Pistola government. Pistola appeared to
him and still appears as the ideal type of Yaqui man:

Juan Pistola was not able to read; he didn't know a single letter, for he had to work
all his life. He went to work in the placer mines in Sonora and always had to escape
after a while so that the Mexicans wouldn't capture him. He was a Mayo, but he
was like the best of the Yaquis because he suffered terribly at the hands of the
Mexicans, like the rest of us. Oh, as I shall tell you, he suffered. He went without
food and without drink. He hid in the hills for weeks to escape the soldiers. He
knew what it was to suffer. And that is the reason that he was a good man. He
came to know truth (*luturia*) in this manner.

Don Juan Pistola was a good man for his people. He knew how to act. He
understood that he had to keep everyone in knowledge of what was going to
happen. He would call a meeting when something was to be decided. He had the
strength of voice and heart to talk in the meeting; he was not backward when there
was talking to be done. But he talked quietly and firmly. He had the voice Yaqui.

Pistola never forgot his people. Everyday he walked from house to house to
find out if anything was needed. He was like the Pueblo Kobanao on the Yaqui
River, always working for his people. He could help in these things, because he
knew the important people in Tucson. He used to drink a great deal before he
became Kobanao and as a result he frequently got into the courts and learned the
ways of judges and all about court procedure. It was this that made him successful
in freeing the *prisioneros* in 1918. Don Juan had a very good head for those things
and he knew how to get help for his people.

Lucas had known Pistola in Nogalitos and describes him as wholly undis-
tinguished among Arizona Yaquis until the prisionero incident in 1918.
From that time forth Lucas revolved as Pistola's satellite and remained
rigidly loyal to him long after Pistola's death.

The political concepts of which Lucas became a devotee through his
association with Pistola must be regarded as a combination of those which
actuated the autonomous Yaqui River folk communities, and some newer
ones developed in response to the special needs of Arizona Yaquis. The

major concept was of Yaquis as a political entity distinct from other peoples in Arizona and maintaining their own organized government. This government was to be administered by elected officials (an ideal which was never realized). It was to take care of Yaqui interests in the economic, political, and social fields; the organization called for the creation of work groups among all the Yaquis with Pistola as go-between for employers, the establishment of trial courts for settling all disputes among Yaquis and a police force of Yaquis which was to cooperate with Arizona authorities, and the establishment of regular channels through which benefits such as charity relief and medical aid would flow from the surrounding community to Yaquis. In return for the freedom granted Yaquis to establish such a government, Pistola and Chavez believed that they were obligated to keep track of all Yaquis entering the United States and to report their whereabouts to immigration officials and also to discourage the running of guns and ammunition across the international boundary, a practice which had its center in south Tucson among the members of the Society of the Little Jesus.

This political orientation preserved at least two features of traditional Yaqui life, namely, the preservation of integrated social and economic life among Yaquis and also a large measure of autonomy in political action. It departed from the older tradition in eliminating the close linkage of Yaqui political and ceremonial life and in admitting the partial economic dependence of Yaquis on the surrounding peoples. These ideals of political life have remained with Lucas Chavez up to the present. He is still a vigorous spokesman for them, both in the village and outside. He takes special pains to promulgate them to all non-Yaquis who will listen.

Lucas Chavez's political ideals have become a source of separation between himself and the developing mode of life and organization in Pascua. He measures all leaders or would-be leaders in terms of the Pistola ideal. Speaking of the present Matachin leader, who also tries to serve as "Pueblo Kobanao," he says:

Tomás is not able to talk to men in the way that Pistola was and moreover he doesn't know the true meanings of Yaqui words. He has never made a sermon when he should at the close of the dancing because he doesn't know how to talk. He is without the spirit to speak vigorously to the Americans and moreover he doesn't know anyone of importance.

That Tomás has never called a meeting, so that we never know what he has in his mind to do.

Tomás came from Hermosillo and knows nothing about the Yaqui River. He doesn't understand the ritual of the Matachinis, and yet he acts as Matachin Kobanao. He doesn't understand what a Kobanao had to do and doesn't know the meaning of the word *Wikoi Ya'ut* [bow chief].

Lucas speaks in similar vein of the head of the Fariseo society and the older Maestros who manage the church ceremonies. In his opinion the people of Pascua have undergone a steady degeneration since the days of Juan Pistola. They are *"muy izquierda,"* that is, they are weak and ineffectual like the left hand is, compared to the right. They don't want a leader, but are like the anti-Pistoleros who preferred to follow evil ways instead of uniting themselves behind a good leader. They have become bad and are teaching their children to behave badly: "They wish to be like the Mexicans."

Lucas's separation from the other villagers is apparent in not only his behavior and attitudes, but also in the other's opinion of him. To them he is "a little bit crazy, perhaps," an evaluation which may be elaborated as follows:

That Lucas wants to have a chief here. He says he has a lot of papers that show that Juan Pistola is chief, but everybody knows that Pistola died a long time ago. He don't know what he is talking about.

Orientation in Other Cultures

Lucas was ejected suddenly and painfully from Yaqui life at the age of fifteen and found himself faced with the problem of adjusting to a new language and a new culture. His sudden and terrifying removal to La Misa left him without any of the Yaqui kinsmen under whose influence he had grown up; his father, mother, younger brother, and even Sacramento Gracia and his beloved godparents of baptism were no longer with him. Only Sacramento's wife remained. His adjustment, however, was rapid, and insofar as can be told from his accounts, not only successful but accompanied with feelings of achievement.

It is interesting to encounter such ready adaptation, especially in view of his early encounters with Mexicans.

Yes, I went to Guaymas many times with my father. It took us eight days with mules, burros, and horses. I would ride a horse and go along clucking and saying *"hyu"* to the burros. We would go into Guaymas and all we boys would be very much afraid of the Mexicans there. The Mexicans always went around talking as though they were mad and saying evil things. They would say *"Chinga, chinga"* all the time. It scared us because they would keep saying, *"Yaki, Yaki, Yaki,* Indio" at us and then a lot of bad words. I didn't like to go into Guaymas on account of the way they talked. I used to stay out at the edge of the town while my father would go into the market and sell his things. I would guard the animals.

He insists that he wanted very much to fight the Mexicans and suffered because he was too young to be accepted as a soldier.

Why should I not have wanted to fight. The idea came from the games that the boys sometimes played. There was a game in which we set up two posts, each called *wasa'i*, about fifty feet apart. Then each of us would shoot to win with our bows and arrows. The one who hit the post would win. Playing this game made me want to fight the Mexicans, and why should I not have wanted to fight. I was a boy. They killed my father, but before that they killed my brothers on the Mayo River. They killed my relatives everywhere. Yes, I wanted to fight. . . . I say that it was not without cause. . . . You ask who does something wrong to you and then you want to punish them. I was thinking of the unjust things which the Mexicans were doing which made me want to fight. There were my relatives who were killed near Tanques between the Yaqui and the Mayo rivers. They burned the house of Cajeme. These were evil Mexicans who did those things. Was it not what I should have done to have wished to fight with them?

And then there was the lamentation of the defeated old people after the battle of Buatachive: "Better that our lands should fall into the hands of any other people than the Mexicans." This was one of his most vivid memories of his last days in the Yaqui country. Nevertheless, in spite of these experiences Lucas's adjustment to life on the Mexican hacienda at La Misa was rapid and for a time satisfying.

He thinks of the adjustment largely in terms of learning a new language and very probably his ability to learn had a great deal to do with his feelings of satisfaction during this period. His father had had to learn some Spanish in order to carry on his trade, but he knew very little. Occasionally, his father had read Spanish prayers to Lucas, sounding out the vowels and the consonants, but Lucas had never learned the meanings of the words nor even to associate the letters with any particular sounds. Now in La Misa he encountered a patrón who was helpful. This man, Tapia, whom the Yaquis called "Money Bags," seems to have taken a special interest in Lucas. He took him in as houseboy and thus forced him to learn Spanish so that he could wait on tables properly. Lucas learned quickly and as Tapia saw his quickness, he even made sporadic efforts to teach him to read. For the first time, Lucas began with a great feeling of wonder to realize what the meaningless sounds his father had intoned to him really signified. "Ah," "eh," "ih," "oh," "uh" became the symbols for letters and he began to experience the excitement of getting meaning from a printed page. This is one of his most stirring memories.

But there was an interruption, and he began his wanderings, and did not take up his efforts to read again for five years. Meanwhile, as he worked on the railroad he absorbed spoken Spanish. Spanish corridos were drilled into his head, whether he wanted them to be or not, as he worked with the singing gangs along the railroad. He was speaking Spanish fairly easily by the time he crossed the line into the United States and here he again took up his reading with Teofila Lopez. Within three or four years he was reading and writing Spanish easily. He was keeping his own notebooks of Spanish hymns and prayers and was reading newspapers and the little collections of Christian sermons and Catholic ritual which circulated among the Mexican population. He had passed from the nonliterate world of Sacramento Gracia to the literate Mexican world by the time he was twenty-five. Up to the present he has continued to live to a large extent in the world of Spanish Christian tradition, reading deeply in collections of Bible stories, but chiefly in a handbook of the essentials of Catholic ritual called the *Ancora de Salvación*. Nearly all of his leisure time has been spent during the past nine or ten years going over and over the prayers, the hymns, and the *oraciones* (sermons) of the *Ancora*. So important are these in his life organization, as well as in those of older Yaquis, that space must be taken to quote some verses from his notebook, portions of which will indicate the point of view which they embrace:

Sea bendito y alabado	Blessed be and praised
El santísimo José	The holy Joseph
Por fe del eterno padre	Through faith of the eternal father
En el mundo y magenfue	In the world and magnified
Sea bendito y alabado	Blessed be and praised
Porque con sumo placer	Because with highest pleasure
Pues venerando por padre	Then honoring the father
Al verbo eterno también	For eternal word also
Sea bendito y alabado	Blessed be and praised
Porque sustito es	Because sustained by
Del espíritu divino	The divine spirit
Guardandole entera fe	Guarding the whole faith
Sea bendito y alabado	Blessed be and praised
A cesar de lucifer	To check the devil
Por los siglos de los siglos y	For centuries of centuries
Los siglos santos amen Jesus	The holy centuries. Amen, Jesus.

It must be emphasized that it was Lucas's literacy above all that gave him the highest status he ever attained in Yaqui culture and that the title of secretary which he assumed rested wholly on his ability with letters. In this sense he was a go-between, between the nonliterate Yaquis and the literate Mexican culture.

We know nothing about Lucas's sexual needs and interests prior to his fifteenth year. This aspect of his personality was not probed very determinedly for the boyhood period and no data came out voluntarily. But we find that at fifteen he began to be vigorously interested [in the opposite sex], and that the first object of fixation was a Mexican married woman. Don Pancho Tapia's wife was in the habit of taking off most of her clothes in the hot weather and lying down in the house. At these times Lucas was called to fan her. Lucas himself was pleased and proud at the show of confidence which this indicated in him on the part of Don Pancho Tapia, but more than that he found himself becoming sexually excited. The emotional stress during the recollection of these scenes is extreme. There are no details, but it seems fairly evident that Doña Tapia was Lucas's first sexual fixation and that very probably he left La Misa on account of her. His interest thereafter continued to be taken by light-colored girls. His own descriptions of such interests indicate that he never went farther than looking at such girls, but he did eye them and remembers such ogling in detail. Thus after he had crossed the line at Nogales, he was working under a majordomo who had married a Yaqui woman. Their daughters were light-colored and Lucas says that they were "good-looking" and that he could not keep his eyes from them. Lucas admits to no affairs during his youth. He finally settled down with a Yaqui woman whom he and others describe as "very light-colored." It seems fairly clear that light-colored women have attracted him from an early age and that undoubtedly his godmother Juana Huera at Torim was greatly influential in establishing this focus of interest in him. He loved Juana Huera dearly and she became a female ideal for him. However, it should also be noted that his preference for light skins in women is not consciously associated with any concepts of social status. There is no indication in the mass of data about Lucas that he regards color as in any way a mark of status. If there is a consistent attitude in regard to color, it is a somewhat unfavorable one concerning hueros in general, which he may bring to bear in an evaluation of someone whom he wishes to decry because of interbreeding with other races.

Lucas's first contact with Mexicans after the shock of Buatachive resulted in the shattering of the stereotype that his family had developed for him. Mexicans were not vicious beasts, blood-thirsty and mean. On the contrary, his good fortune in his first two places of employment made him feel that Mexicans could be kindly and fair and helpful. His praise of Don Tapia and also of his patrón at Torres is unlimited; they were "very fine men," and they were "good patrones." The attitude which he adopted in relation to them was made up of the following elements. He admitted his subordination; he set out to adapt himself and to seek their goodwill; he was genuinely pleased and happy when he found that he could win their confidence and trust. But he did not accept their dominance over him as in the inevitable scheme of the world. On the contrary,

> They sent us to La Misa and then out to the hacienda of Palos Verdes. It was pleasant there. The patrón was a good man. General Martínez and the hacendados were good to the Yaquis in those early days after Cajeme. They took good care of us and we were grateful. We were the defeated ones. There was nothing we could do. It was good to live peacefully for awhile after the fighting. They made us work hard, but that was all right. Had we not been defeated? Was there anything that we could do?

He goes on to describe his own rise to houseboy at La Misa with great satisfaction. Then why did he leave so suddenly? He will not tell us about this, and one is forced to guess that Doña Tapia had something to do with his departure. One feels also that there was no sense of loyalty or obligation. As a member of a defeated tribe, he regarded himself as footloose and obligated to no one. We may note then that his first orientation in Mexican society was as a forcibly subordinated individual whose loyalties remained outside that society. He was also oriented as an economically dependent person who admitted from the first that his welfare depended on currying the favor of his employers by any means whatever. His attitude appears further in the following:

> Then I left Torres with my brother Cipriano. Like other young boys I told a lie to my patrón. I told him that my aunt was sick in La Misa where we had been and that I had to go down there and see her. He believed me and then I asked him for five pesos and he gave it to me. So I left Torres and got my brother Cipriano and we went north to Hermosillo on foot and never came back. My patrón in Torres was a very good man.

His attitude toward the Mexicans now in superordinate positions was one which he shared apparently with the other Yaquis of La Misa:

> At Rancho Palo Verde there were 130 Yaquis as laborers. There were no fiestas because the patrones had much work to do. We worked six days a week only, but they did not want us to have fiestas. There were no Matachinis at the funerals. The people prayed and burned candles, that's all, only the family of the dead one being there. It was not as now in the United States where they have their religion. It was

the punishment of the Mexicans. We were Indians. There was peace there then, though under the law of the Mexicans. What could we have done? That is what the people asked. The patrones required work. Sentence had been passed.

Thus the suppression of Yaqui ceremonial life was keenly felt, but it was accepted with resignation. The employer-employee relationship here was not voluntary with recognized obligations on both sides. Lucas's reaction to the situation seems to have been to remove himself as quickly as possible from it. He did not stop moving once he had started until he began to have Anglo Americans as bosses in the vicinity of Nogales. One does not know in detail, but one may infer that this was more acceptable to him than to be subordinate to Mexican employers.

During his fifty years in the United States Lucas has been definitely wishing to disassociate himself from Mexicans and to become identified with Yaquis. He has consistently sought residence in areas occupied by Yaquis, and today he lives in the heart of one of the principle Yaqui villages. He was quite evidently dominated during his first twenty years in the United States by a fear of being sent back to Mexico, where he was fully aware that conditions were growing steadily worse for Yaquis since his youth at La Misa and Torres.

We went on without Pascolas for many years in the United States. We did not know who might be around. There were Mexican spies everywhere. We were afraid to act like Yaquis. It was not until 1909 that fear began to leave us and there was a celebration of Semana Santa.

The revival of ceremonies was for Lucas a signal for general Yaqui unification and assertion of themselves as a distinct people. Emphasized perhaps more than anything else in his account of the founding of Pascua is the protection that would be afforded from interference by "Mexicans" in Yaqui ceremonies. He is inclined to include the Catholic priests and also the Catholic Daughters of America as Mexicans and to oppose them doggedly. His great contention is that "the Catholic priests have never done anything for the Yaquis in the United States" and that "their counsel is evil." He considers them to have developed a conspiracy along with the C.D.A. to break up Pascua through the establishment of the church of Santa Rosa. He opposes all contact with the Catholic Church for this reason and refuses to attend any ceremonies at Santa Rosa. He speaks bitterly against the priests at every opportunity and maintains that Yaquis suffer through contact with the Mexican-American congregations of the Catholic churches. He has, therefore, never identified himself with any Catholic church in Arizona.

Lucas's aloofness from the ceremonial aspect of Mexican culture in the United States has, however, broken down in the last few years. He has not weakened in his opposition to the Catholic organization or its followers, but he is one of the few Yaquis who has become a member of a Protestant sect. In his seventieth year he was baptized into the Mexican Baptist Church of Tucson, thus becoming one of four Pascua Yaquis having this formal affiliation. Describing his experience at the church in Tucson on the night of his baptism, he says:

Sunday night it was very pleasant in the Baptists' church. They came up to me and shook my hand and called me brother. They are on my side and I am for them. They are good people and they are all on the side of God. I am there, too. They are not like the Catholic priests who have never been on my side. The people at the Baptist church called me brother. They said, "There is only God, only God." They prayed for me. They called me brother, as they patted me on the back. It was pleasant. That is not the way it was on the Yaqui River when I was there. Then there was trouble and people were evil.

This conversion, however, does not conflict with his activity in the Pascua church. When asked if he expected to continue serving in it, he said:

Why should I not? I am living in Pascua, am I not? I expect to go on being a Maestro. As long as I live in the village I am expected to be a Maestro. The people want me to come and help them out that way.

He does not think in terms of strict sectarianism and sees no contradiction in his position as a practicing official in the Catholic-oriented Yaqui church, as a baptized member of the Mexican Baptist church, and as a determined opponent of all Catholic priests wherever they may be. He says:

We expatriates, we poor Yaquis, yes, we are Catholics. But we do not care for the priests. I have told you again and again that they have never done anything for us here. We don't have any reason to like them. Have they helped us in our troubles either here or in Mexico? They never have. They are not for us. But we are for God, and I am for everyone who is for God. I am with those people, the Baptists with Señor Morales. They are good people.

Lucas's baptism has followed a three-year period of intimate acquaintance with a Mexican American Baptist missionary who has distributed food regularly to him and to others who attended her meetings in the schoolhouse in the village.

Lucas's friendly relations with Mexican employers in Mexico and with the Baptist congregation in Tucson have not stood in the way of his construction of a stereotype of the Mexican. Two quotes are examples of his attitude:

The Yaquis dance for the purpose of devotion, for no other reason. Some think it is for pleasure, but it is not. It is not like the Mexicans who dance with pretty women for the fun of it. That kind of thing is not permitted in the religion of the Yaquis.

Right from the start the Mexicans have gone around giving bad advice to the Yaquis. That is the only reason that Yaquis drink so much. The Mexicans used to come around and tell the Yaquis to drink. "Come on, no use being sad," they would say. "Get happy." The Yaquis began to drink and that is why we are lost now.

Mexicans remain for him morally inferior beings and constitute the scapegoat of all his moral reflections. His manner of use of this stereotype in his thinking will be taken up below.

The orientation of Lucas Chavez in Anglo-American culture has remained incomplete. His contacts with it have never been as intimate as they have with Mexican culture. His first conception of it came when he was working on the railroad north of Hermosillo and he along with his fellow-workers began to realize, as they said in their song, that Anglo Americans had certain technological abilities that placed them in a different class from either Yaquis or Mexicans. This gave rise in Lucas to a high respect for Anglo-American ways, which he has never given up. His first personal contacts with Anglo Americans, moreover, were pleasant ones. In Nogales, Sonora, he began to have section bosses who were Anglos. These men he consistently describes as remarkable. They were remarkable in the first place for their capacity for work. Most of them were prodigious workers and several of them were prodigious drinkers. Both of these characteristics gave rise to some awe in Lucas. Then he became acquainted with the wives of some of them, and these he uniformly describes as "very good people," a phrase much used by him to indicate persons who behave politely and speak quietly. Later he had Anglo-American bosses, one at Sasco, who invited him to eat in their houses. He discovered that they said grace at table and this appealed to him as a respectable Yaqui-like custom, which he thought set them off from Mexicans. He noted that they said grace before instead of after like the Yaquis, but this difference he regarded as insignificant.

His high opinion of Anglo Americans continued to develop during his years of contact with Pistola's sponsor, Kirk Moore. He speaks as though he felt no subordination to Anglo Americans as he had to Mexicans in

Sonora, but rather an obligation to do what they might wish because they uniformly treated him as an equal and because they furthered his and Pistola's aims for a "Yaqui nation." The sense of obligation has increased steadily through the years. An example of his use of it to rationalize behavior that he does not actually approve is the following:

After all are we not foreigners here? If the Chamber of Commerce says that it needs Yaquis to dance at the rodeo then we must go. Didn't we go last year? Didn't Tomás and Molonko and I go and didn't we carry bows and arrows in the rodeo parade? Of course, we went because they needed us. That is the way it should be. Doesn't the Chamber of Commerce help us out each year with the Gloria? Why shouldn't we dance for them if we are needed? Angel [a Matachin Monarca] may object, but he has never been grateful to the Americans for anything. He is always against the Americans when they need something. He has always been rebellious.

Perhaps because of his conciliatory attitude, Lucas has had wider contacts among Anglo Americans than anyone else in Pascua. These contacts began in the Pistola period when Lucas came to know all of the businessmen and lawyers who became interested in Yaqui affairs. Each of the students, from Bogan on, who have studied Yaqui culture has become more or less intimate with Lucas. He has even spoken to classes in anthropology at the University of Arizona. He regards himself as a somewhat official interpreter of Yaqui culture to the Anglo-American world.

Throughout these contacts he has never learned English, except for a few words of greeting. He is not literate in English and therefore reads neither newspapers nor magazines which would put him in touch with Anglo-American culture. Spanish remains the medium through which he deals with all Anglos as well as Mexican Americans.

Modes of Thought and Value System

The historical description of Lucas Chavez's life experience just completed indicates some of his characteristic beliefs and behavior, but it does not give an adequate picture of the man as he thinks and acts at present at what must be nearly the close of his life. We shall in this section make the attempt to show what he has become as a result of the experiences just passed in review.

Still physically active, he keeps in close touch with events in the village as a result of his post as mailman which requires that he visit every house in Pascua and many in Barrio Belen almost every day. He is a man of extreme deference and courtesy who observes probably more meticulously than any other Pascuan the niceties of Yaqui greeting and departure ritual. He is similarly careful of polite observances in all his dealings with Anglos and Mexican Americans. He is unusually wordy in all conversational preliminaries concerning health and wealth and is likely to enter into long flowery speeches of praise concerning the persons before him or their relatives. He is talkative in any gathering, having a ready flow of words in either Yaqui or Spanish, but Yaquis are inclined to disregard what he says and to consider him somewhat boring. He is, however, welcome in every household in Pascua and also in many in the other villages, where he makes himself at home quickly without strain or backwardness. His great social ease and verbal readiness makes it possible for him to dominate ordinary conversations, and he evidently enjoys doing this.

On the other hand, it is very noticeable that he does not attend gatherings of the older men that take place during the fiestas. He is evidently not formally excluded from such social gatherings, but he maintains the air of being alone and self-secluded, remaining silently in the altar side of the ramada or sitting alone on a bench. He attends the fiestas and ceremonies only spasmodically, even though he has no other business to keep him occupied. Characteristically, he appears an hour or two after a ceremony has started and leaves for home long before it is over, attending strictly to his work as a Sacristan or subordinate Maestro while he is there. He gives the air, more than any other older man, of coming purely to fulfill his duties and not for any social purpose. He almost never engages in even the casual chatting that takes place among the Maestros and Cantoras between prayers and alabanzas. He stands out, in other words, at all public gatherings as a somewhat withdrawn figure, even though he participates in the formal ritual.

His approach to both Yaquis and Anglo Americans in ordinary social intercourse is that of a man who will not under any circumstances overstep the rules of polite discourse, but who nevertheless is dominated by a desire to keep the conversation in his own hands and to use it as a vehicle for expressing his own ideas. When he fails to do this among Yaquis, he is likely to lapse into complete silence for extended periods. He appears to enjoy particularly conversations with women who are not talkative and with persons who, through kinship or godparent obligations, are required by custom to defer to him. In such situations he assumes authority immediately, and verbally expands tremendously. These, it should be borne in mind, are the only occasions on which he may become authoritative, for he no longer holds any village office which carries much authority as a perquisite.

He has a number of dominant foci of interest which he verbalizes frequently with great intensity of speech, accompanying gestures and dramatic actions, and often considerable show of emotion. These are in a sense all interrelated, but they may be distinguished as follows: Yaqui nationalism; contempt for Mexicans; disapproval of modern Yaqui ways; and belief in Christian doctrine. In any discussion of these interests he reveals on the one hand the manner in which he manipulates ideas and on the other the values in terms of which he rates persons and customs. The vigor with which he pursues his ideas and the clarity with which he develops them make it necessary to consider him as an exceptionally intellectual person in Pascua, in whose mental life we may see most of the contradictions and most of the adjustments that constitute Arizona Yaqui culture.

Let us consider first his "Yaqui nationalism," for in analyzing that, we may see his conception of what Yaqui culture should be and its relation to other cultures. He holds, still with considerable passion, to the set of ideas developed under the influence of Juan Pistola, and Pistola remains for him a sort of personification of the ideal. He says:

I shall tell you how it was. In those times in the eight pueblos (here he has fallen, perhaps consciously, into one of the traditional phraseologies which every Maestro uses in his sermons) on the Yaqui River there was justice and order. There Don José María Leyva Cajeme was just one man among many. Here Pistola was the only one and there has been no one since. You have to remember how it was. There were men who were strong for their people and knew what to do.

Harking back to the pre-Cajeme days on the Yaqui River, Lucas thinks constantly in terms of an irrecoverable "Golden Age." His own experience of that age was slight and incomplete, but it nevertheless has become for him a standard and a goal:

In each of the Eight Towns there was the Pueblo Kobanao. He knew the wants of everyone. He went from house to house and spoke to everyone. He found out what was wrong, what was lacking, and then he got help. He told others and everything was made all right. The Kobanao was like a father to the people of the pueblo. It was he who found help for an accused man. He had to find the relatives and the friends of the man and they pled the case before the bow-chief. The bow-chief was severe; he administered the punishment, lashes to the evildoer, or sometimes they put him in stocks. All the evildoers were punished as they should have been. There was no divorce, because they put the man or woman who had been wrong out to the wolves. Everything was very much in order, just as it should be.

Thus Lucas envisions a benevolent but a strictly disciplined society as the Yaqui ideal.

This is the kind of society, fitting his views of nineteenth-century Yaqui society, that he hoped to see develop in the United States. He says:

We had our land. There is still a paper somewhere from the King of Spain marking off the boundaries of the Yaqui country. We owned everything from Guaymas to the Mayo River. We were happy until the Mexicans came in, until the land was stolen and the federal government had to send their soldiers to hold the land and send the Yaquis away. We did not wish to bother the Mexicans. We only wanted to stay where we were, but the Mexicans were always fighting. They are still stealing land and they cannot be trusted. They have promised, oh, they have promised many things at different times, but they have never kept a peace. We cannot believe anything they may promise. If Governor Yocupicio promises land to Arizona Yaquis now if they go back there is no guarantee. We might be killed the day of our arrival. The Yaquis will not be safe until they have the strength to fight back, their own soldiers and their own government. They have always known that and they only want to have their own government on their own land.

Here is the idea of a Yaqui nation distinct from the Mexican nation, one held not only by Lucas but widely among older Yaquis in Arizona and probably also in Sonora. It was this, of course, which lay back of the "nation within a nation" concept developed by Pistola and Kirk Moore. Lucas has remained its vigorous devotee in the United States and desires mergence with Anglo Americans no more than with Mexican Americans, although he believes that it would "be better for Arizona Yaquis to learn English and move out of the villages than it would be for them to go back to Mexico."

Lucas's passionate devotion to the idea of Yaqui independence is closely coupled, of course, with a profound and deeply felt hatred for Mexicans. We need not elaborate further about this hatred, for Lucas's attitude and beliefs here are all of a piece with the usual Yaqui. Thus one of his basic distinctions:

Sometimes Mexicans used to come to me and say: "You are a Mexican. Yes? The same as I. You come from Mexico." But they were wrong. I am not a Mexican. A Yaqui is not a Mexican. I do not come from Mexico. I come from Sonora and the people of Sonora are Yaquis. Once in the time of Juan Pistola they asked me to make a list of all of my people because they had work for them up near Casa Grande. So I made a list and when I was doing that the Mexicans would come and say: "I'm a Yaqui." Yes, they wanted work and so they said that they were Yaquis. They were people from Sonora, but when I asked them to speak in the language they couldn't do it. . . . We would all laugh at them because they couldn't say the words right. . . . I was born in Sonora and that country does not belong to the Mexicans.

Again a basic distinction:

The Mexicans have many different beliefs, all kinds of beliefs and religions. They have so many different kinds that sometimes they call them *cualqueristas* [whatever-you-pleases]. But the Yaquis always have and have had only one belief. There are old stories about the only belief that they have had. The old men knew all these things. They couldn't read and some people say that they didn't know anything at all, but they actually knew everything that was going to happen. They knew about the Conquest and they were waiting for it. There was the old woman Yomumule who told them. They wanted the Conquest to come because they would be baptized. So Yomumule took a river and rolled it up under her arm and all those Yaquis from whom we came went with her and the others went into the sea. And those Yaquis who believed her were baptized and waited for the Conquest. Then the Mexicans came and the trouble began.

Yes, they are cualqueristas. When I was working for Mr. Nolan near Nogales on the Southern Pacific we used to find Mexicans who didn't know anything at all. They didn't even know how to cross themselves and sometimes Mr. Nolan would get down on his knees to show them how. They knew less than any Yaquis; they had cattle and fields out in the hills. I have never seen any people who were more ignorant.

Lucas lets this last picture stand as his type of the Mexican and never draws distinctions between kinds of Mexicans. He does not recognize a better and a worse type among them as he does among Yaquis quite consistently. All Mexicans are for him, whenever he speaks in general terms, "persons of bad counsel" who have always and still are engaged in misadvising Yaquis. He sees them as a host of evil spirits waiting everywhere to turn Yaquis on the wrong paths.

Closely allied with his intense disapproval of Mexicans is Lucas's disapproval of modern Yaquis, for he believes that the younger Yaquis born in the United States "want to become cualqueristas and evildoers like the Mexicans." He says:

There was a Yaqui named Jesús Valdenegro who used to live in south Tucson. He ran a bakery and made a great deal of money. Then he bought some houses. He was very rich. Yes, he spoke Yaqui well and he was very much a Yaqui, but his children aren't. The sons and daughters are married and one of them lives in Tucson somewhere. They don't speak Yaqui and never did. They want to be Mexicans. They are just the same as Mexicans, even if they do use their father's name. They are a lot like the Papagos who live in Tucson and are just like Mexicans.

The desire "to be like Mexicans" is one of Lucas's favorite themes. All the young people of Pascua, he says, have forgotten how to behave properly. They are careless in their greetings especially. They greet you casually with a *"Chania"* instead of a dignified *"Dios em chania"* (a contrast like that between "Hi!" and "How do you do"). Moreover, they leave off the kinship terms of address like "achai" and "mala" and all the others. They do not use any respect terms at all. All this is precisely like the Mexicans who also use a single casual disrespectful word in greeting. But there are many worse things taking place. For instance, they do not get married properly, never go to the priest, and then are very likely to separate right away. On the Yaqui River everyone was properly married, and no one dared to get "divorced" because of what the pueblo officials would do. The young people are "just the same as the Mexicans" in their light regard for marriage. Besides this the young men are sometimes drinking and singing during ceremonies, "off in the bushes out somewhere with the Mexicans, learning evil ways." They also go to dances and dance with women, which again is a Mexican custom and was never permitted "under the Yaqui Law." Even the village leaders, like the Matachin Kobanao Tomás Alvarez, are in league with Mexicans, seeking to break down what is left of the village solidarity.

Lucas makes a distinction between Yaquis as he does not between Mexicans. He constantly classifies Yaquis of Pascua as of "good family" or "not of good family." The precise content of his categories is not altogether clear, but one finds him applying the former classification to persons who observe the traditional Yaqui greeting forms and the latter to those who do not. His evaluations of this kind seem to have no reference to wealth, to ceremonial participation, or to prominence in village life. He seems to regard all the older persons of Pascua as of "good family" and bemoans the fact that their children are not being brought up as if they were "of good family."

The final major interest of Lucas which we shall discuss is Christian doctrine. He spends a great deal of his time reading in this field and enjoys discussing it and relating it to Yaqui ritual practices. He has a clearer conception of God as distinct from Jesus than other Yaquis in Pascua and expounds his ideas in this matter readily:

All the churches are for Jesus Christ and that makes them all the same in the eyes of God. It doesn't matter a great deal which one you go to; that is the way I think about it and that is what I was telling Miss Kanen [the schoolteacher at Pascua]. I told her that all which is evil comes from Satan and all which is good comes from the angels. The angels are all around us, just as they are now in this month of

October and they never had bad teaching for anyone. There are bad angels, too, who give bad advice. They are from Satan. (Lucas rose from his chair and swung his arms about to indicate angels flying about us. He was sucking in his breath, as he talked, for emphasis in his usual manner.) Everything good which God permits comes from the angels and that is all that you need to know. But the bad angels come to you at any time. They are like the little boys who use to come to me. My mother would say, "Go, get the wood." And then the boys would come and say, "We are going to play ball; why don't you come along?" Talking evil that way, always like little boys keeping their friends from good work.

This is a ruling concept with Lucas, the idea of a world peopled with good angels and evil spirits, all of which are competing for his ear to give him either good advice or bad advice. One listens to one or the other group and acts accordingly. He often identifies Mexicans with the evil spirits and accounts for disapproved Yaqui behavior as the effect of listening to them. This is the basis of his moral system. It is a passive sort of system, but also one which permits of a certain amount of self-determination.

His concept of God is not very divergent from a general Christian one:

It is like the example I will give you. Once down on Meyer Street there was a window in a drugstore. It was owned by Señor _____. He had many snakes and turtles and other small animals in the window. I used to go down there often and look at those animals. They crawled around. They moved over each other. The snakes would spit out their tongues at each other and at the other animals. They crawled around that way and I watched them by the hour. I couldn't keep away from there. Well, the druggist would come and feed them. He took care of them like that, giving them food and they went on living together, even when they got in each other's way. The druggist was like God to them. He held them all in his hand like God. We are all the same way. We are all here and God is looking down on us and watching out for us. We are like the animals in the drugstore window.

He has arrived at his concepts of God and the basis of moral behavior as a result of much thinking over a long period of years. His recent conversion to the Baptist Church has been a more casual event, related more to his disintegrating social relations among Yaquis than to any changes in his general religious concepts. His social relations with the Baptists have been the outstanding feature of this conversion in his mind.

The Yaquis like myself on the Río Yaqui never learned anything about our own people, about *la raza*, because of two things. Always there were the evil ones, *los leperos*, the bad people, who talked against us all the time. They gave bad counsel and my parents always told me to keep away from them. Then there was the revolution. There was always trouble. My father never had the time to tell me anything.

I never could sit and listen to the Susuakame, because there wasn't time. I had to work, work, all the time. But Sunday night it was pleasant in the Baptists' church. They called me brother. They said, "There is only God, only God." They prayed for me. They called me brother. That is not the way it was on the Yaqui River when I was there.

Evidently, in retreat from a world that has been full of confusion and unpleasant social relations, he has welcomed this simple solace and accepts it not as a new revelation so much as a friendly, pleasant experience.

However much Lucas may have entered into Christian ways of thought and formal relations with Christian persons, he nevertheless retains a head full of Yaqui religious concepts.[1] He is definitely in process of renouncing that tradition for the Christian mythological tradition. The role of the latter is that of a force which is constantly before him on the printed page and which therefore assumes authority over the more dynamic oral traditions which derive from his Yaqui orientation and which are not reinforced by constant repetition now. The following may indicate one of his approaches in such matters:

I asked then if it was true that the Pascolas had come up from the devil. Lucas answered, "It's not certain. No one knows for sure whether they did. All we have are a lot of people who tell these stories about the Pascolas. But how should they know for sure where the Pascolas came from? They have not been to school and they have not read books; they only repeat what they have heard and they don't know. There are people who talk like this and they may be right: On the Yaqui River there are beautiful mountains with many peaks. They are high. In these mountains there is water, water which flows very fast and is very clear. It flows with much force. The people say that this is where (he enumerated with his fingers) the Maestro, the Cantora, the violinist, the *Tampaleo*, the Temasti, and the Pascola come from. This was where the Pascola and his violinist learn the things that they know." I pointed out that the Maestro learns what he knows from a book. Lucas agreed heartily, saying that everything the Maestro does has come from a book. "This is where he is different from the Pascola who does not learn what he knows out of a book. This makes me think that the stories about the Maestro are wrong, and if they are wrong about the Maestro, then perhaps they are wrong about the Pascolas, too. But who knows?"

This same careful intellectual approach is pursued vigorously by Lucas in discovering explanations in Christian terms for aspects of Yaqui ritual. His method is to find in his books of Christian doctrine some statement which he may apply to a puzzling trait, so that he explains the beard of the Pascola mask as a representation of the beard of one of Christ's disciples. It is not necessary to approach these matters either historically or logically;

it is necessary only to find authority of any kind in the Bible. His ultimate justification for the Yaqui rituals is as follows:

Many people say that it is bad to have Chapayekas, that they do evil things and are bad examples, but they do what they do to show the poor Yaquis who can't read and don't know anything about the Pharisees who were evil. There is no other way for them to know these things.

An Interpretation of Lucas Chavez's Relations to Yaqui Culture

We have been considering not a typical Yaqui, but a particular type of personality in Yaqui culture. What we wish to know as a result of this analysis is in what ways Yaqui culture has met or failed to meet the needs of this kind of personality. If we can point that out, we may understand more clearly why Yaqui culture has the characteristics which it has in Arizona. The present section will include a discussion of the relations between the culture and the personality of Lucas Chavez. No claim is made that the data is sufficiently complete to delineate the whole nature of the personality, but enough have been presented to indicate some major characteristics.

Lucas's concern with social status and his interest in securing status were evident in his boyhood days in Torim. He was sharply sensitive to the low status of his family and himself attempted to identify with Sacramento Gracia whom he and others rated as of higher status. The effort here was to raise his own status not by acquiring wealth, which he recognized as one of the marks of status, but by associating himself with the higher status individual and by acquiring knowledge which gave that individual status. The means which he adopted here was consonant with Yaqui culture in general, which placed types of knowledge and official position higher than wealth as status attributes. Lucas's efforts in this direction were constantly frustrated by Mexican interference while he was in Torim, or at least that is his view of the causes back of his father's behavior in preventing him from acquiring the status attributes which he sought.

Again we find him at La Misa seeking higher status immediately and achieving success in becoming houseboy. Here his efforts again were directed to the acquisition of knowledge which was associated with the high status, namely, the Spanish language. Similarly, he found satisfaction in achieving mere proximity to the representatives of higher status, Don Pancho Tapia and his wife. It would be worthwhile to know what interfered with continued progress in status acquisition at La Misa. Was it his fixation on Doña Tapia or was it, as it seemed to be later, growing fear of the general Mexican aggression against Yaquis?

Once Lucas had removed himself from the Mexican world to Nogales, we find him turning immediately to ways and means of acquiring status in the transplanted society. Though Yaqui society was insufficiently organized at this time in Arizona for the acquisition of Temasti-Maestro knowledge to confer much status, it was in that direction that Lucas's activity turned. One reason might be the promise (manda) which his parents had made that he would become a Sacristan, though there is no mention that he suffered any illness at this time which might have freshened his fears of supernatural sanctions and resulted in his effort to fulfill the promise.

Whatever the immediate causes back of his choice for Yaqui status at this time, it is certain that he was constantly blocked in his efforts. Although he acquired the Temasti knowledge, he was unable to practice because of his ever-present fear of Mexican "spies." He remained frustrated in his efforts to secure status in Yaqui society; his only satisfactions during the period appear to have been his fairly intimate associations with Anglo-American bosses. These experiences indicate again his characteristic sense of achievement in securing proximity to persons of recognized higher status, but they also raise a complication, for they suggest an absence of any formal barriers between himself and status in Anglo-American society. He might have "worked his way up" to section foreman but apparently chose not to pursue what would have been normal procedure for an Anglo American. Instead, he followed Yaqui modes of status acquisition, despite the impossibility of public recognition for his work.

It was not until his association with Juan Pistola that his status needs began to be fulfilled. Here, in a short time, he found himself in a position in which his special knowledge, literacy in Spanish, gave him a title and therefore status in Yaqui society in Arizona. Moreover, in the very process of acquiring status in Yaqui society he found himself also with status in Anglo-American society, for the Pistola government was essentially a go-between institution. So long as Lucas was "secretary" to the Pistola Yaquis, he was also "secretary" to all the Yaqui nation in Arizona in the eyes of the Anglo Americans. This marks the climax of satisfaction of Lucas's status needs, and as a result this period in Yaqui history stands for him as the period of ideal relations between Yaqui and surrounding cultures.

With the decline of the Pistola government, Lucas turned to his Temasti knowledge increasingly as a source of status. His abilities, however, were not up to the society's requirements, and we find him steadily losing status in Yaqui society. His estimate of himself as a Maestro does not jibe with the Yaquis' estimate of him. Refusing to acknowledge their judgment, he nevertheless obviously feels himself considered unimportant. This time the source of frustration is clearly Yaqui society itself, rather than the Mexicans. His reaction is one of verbal aggression against Yaquis. Until this period in his life, he has been able to assign all his frustrations in status-seeking to Mexican interference. Now he is forced to construct a new devil, which he identifies, however, with the old devil in a new guise. "The Yaquis are becoming like Mexicans."

What, we may ask, other satisfactions and frustrations has Lucas derived from Yaqui culture? We have discussed the relation of the culture to what appears to be his dominant psychogenic need, that of status and role in society. But his status interests do not, of course, comprise the whole of his personality. We should describe him as a man who inclines to lean heavily on others, who avoids doing anything of which he is doubtful, who requires sociable, friendly associations, who defends his own actions, and who justifies himself and his beliefs with elaborate verbal expression. He is, in short, something of a timid soul with a strongly developed superego, dependent and social. These characteristics are ones which are consonant with Yaqui culture in its unbroken form, for Yaqui culture puts a premium on the mild, egalitarian, highly socialized individual who does not put himself forward. It rewards the man who recognizes the degrees of status and abides by them, and this above all is the trend of Lucas's personality. He is a personality well adapted to Yaqui culture in its old form. His frustration in the culture must be attributed not to these basic traits, but rather to other traits which he possesses, namely, a tendency to evaluate himself rather than to let others evaluate him and accept their evaluation, and some tendency to put himself forward. There is a fundamental and inevitable conflict in the personality of Lucas rather than in the cultural determinants. However, it seems probable that the special conditions of the Pistola period, which gave Lucas prominence not through a skill recognized by Yaqui culture but through the skill of literacy which constitutes a value in the outside culture, contributed to individualizing him to such an extent that he could not readjust to Yaqui culture once the Pistola period had come to a close.

Lucas's life during the period of status decline for him has been one of intellectual effort. This intellectual activity, however, has not turned inward on himself. It has turned to the various elements of Yaqui culture.

His major activity is the rationalization of these in terms of the Spanish Christian tradition. He has elaborated a system, in the first place, of Yaqui society which corresponds most nearly with that which he and Pistola tried to develop. He lives largely in this world of a vanished utopia of autonomous Yaqui society. In the second place, he has been at work thinking the Pascolas and other aspects of Yaqui culture into harmony with Christian doctrine. This is not a conscious intellectual process; that is, it does not have a conscious goal, but represents his need for order and intellectual harmony. He must harmonize what he sees about him with the thoughts to which his reading has given rise. The thought processes are definitely those of scientific scepticism and classification by qualities or traits. The technique is scientific so far as it goes, but the objective is not.

Comparisons

No brief is held for Lucas Chavez as a "typical" older Yaqui man. He is a type of personality, and he illustrates a type of utilization of Yaqui culture for the meeting of individual needs. He departs sharply in the nature of his personal organization, as well as in his integration into Yaqui society, from many other men of his age group in Pascua. Before we can understand the relation of Yaqui culture to his general age group, we must consider the details of the experiences of a number of other older men. None of these will be presented at as great length as was Lucas Chavez. We shall have to resort to the presentation of briefs and resumés of these other life histories, and there will naturally be a selection from the data with reference primarily to the questions of social mobility and Yaqui cultural stability.

Tomás Alvarez, Matachin Kobanao

It appears fairly clear that Lucas Chavez's limited success in Yaqui culture is closely related to his failure to receive training in a recognized Yaqui skill until relatively late in life. There is no record of his practicing the Temasti skills regularly until he was about forty. Similarly, Tomás Alvarez lacked early training in Yaqui ways, and yet, his adjustment in a position requiring technical skill and knowledge has been fairly successful. The difference in the two adjustments has been largely a matter of personality differences.

Tomás was born about 1894 somewhere near Hermosillo, Sonora, of Yaqui parents who had been born in Yaqui River towns. Both parents died before Tomás was five years old, and Tomás seems to have had little to do with them before their deaths. He remembers himself as a homeless waif for the first twelve years of his life with a feeling of extreme insecurity, hard-pressed constantly to get enough to eat and never clothed in anything but rags. He remembers no brothers or sisters, but thinks that he may have had some. He became completely disassociated from Yaquis when he was eight or nine, perhaps earlier, and after wandering, at the age of ten, found a job as table boy at a hacienda near Magdalena.

I don't remember my father and mother. I guess I didn't have any. I just remember carrying wood. All the time. I was not eating very much because I had to get all my food by hauling wood. That was a bad time. I had no food or clothes. I was wearing a manta which came just below my waist. That was all the clothes I had. I had to carry wood in small loads, because my arms were small and I had only my arms to carry it with.

He remembers vividly the extreme kindliness of his Mexican patrón and the great plates of food which it was his duty to handle. He worked there a year and then was picked up by some relatives of his mother who were making their way across the line.

He entered the United States in 1906 and went immediately to Benson, Arizona, where he got a job for himself the morning of his arrival in the commissary of the railroad.

In Benson, when we arrived that first night, I was sleeping under a wagon because of the snow. In the morning I got up and left Chepa and went over to a big house where there was an American named Monchado. I had on just a ragged shirt and pants. He asked what I wanted. I said I wanted to work. He said that was very good, that he knew a lot of boys just my age who only wanted to play. He said he had some work in the commissary. He asked me where the rest of my clothes were and I told him I didn't have any. He said, "Poor little fellow," and there were some other men there and they said the same thing. Then Monchado said he would give me some clothes and maybe some food and he said he would give me some cigarettes. I told him that I didn't smoke. He said he was glad to hear that, that there were many boys around my age who smoked all the time. I told him that I had not yet received permission from anyone to smoke. He said that was very good and maybe I would like some candy instead. I told him that I would like that.

He continued to be associated more or less with the Araiza family with whom he had come across the line, but economically he remained self-sufficient just as he had been when he was alone in Sonora.

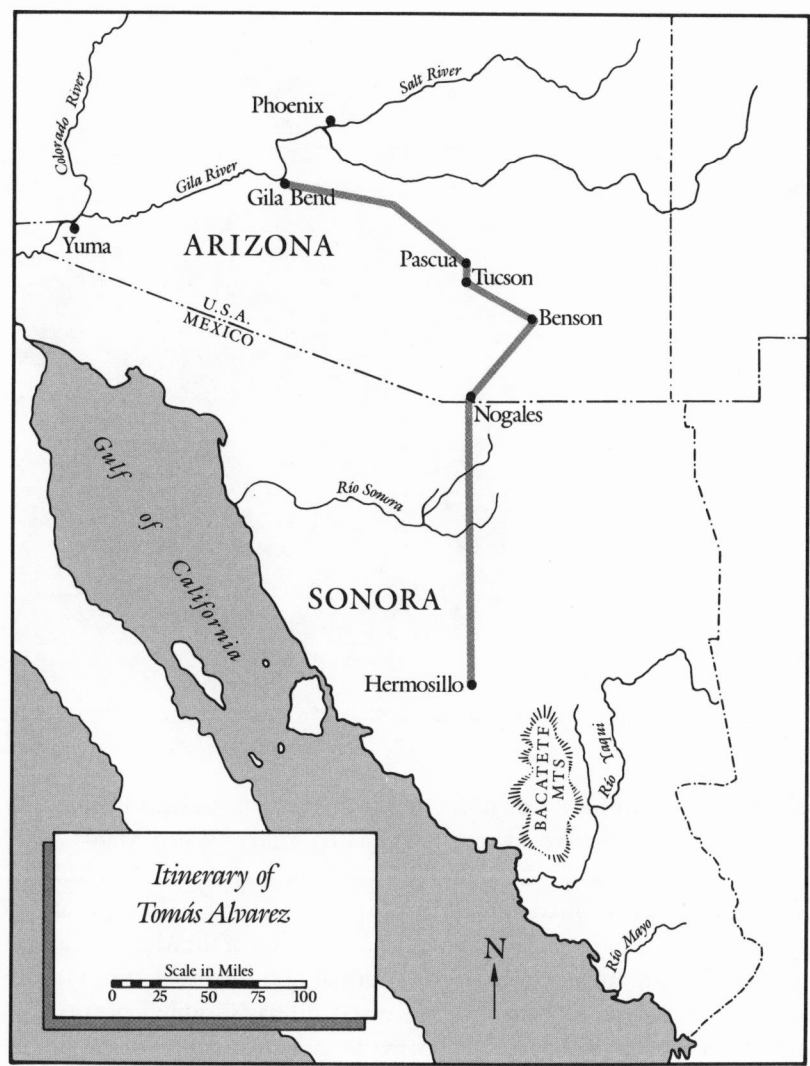

Itinerary of
Tomás Alvarez

Tomás worked in various capacities for the railroad for the next ten years and became an assistant section foreman and held down other jobs of trust. He lived at various places between Gila Bend and Benson and finally settled down in Barrio Anita in north Tucson. Here he became associated with Juan Pistola. Married in 1916, his wife died a few years afterward, and there were no children. Tomás stopped working for the railroad and

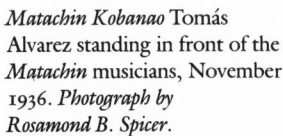

Matachin Kobanao Tomás
Alvarez standing in front of the
Matachin musicians, November
1936. *Photograph by
Rosamond B. Spicer*.

began to devote much time to serving as an assistant to Juan Pistola and
to Pistola's less effective successor, Francisco Matus. When Matus died,
Tomás was regarded by the Catholic Church in Tucson as "chief" of the
Yaquis, and he permitted himself to be spoken of as such. In 1931, at the
age of about thirty-seven, he assumed the leadership of the Matachin dance
society without any election or other formal means of selection. He has
served as Matachin Kobanao for ten years and has steadily increased his
activity as "Pueblo Kobanao," that is, as official representative of the village
who calls the doctor, seeks charity aid, and so forth. He rarely works, but
increasingly asks for assistance from the villagers in return for his activity
as Kobanao.

Tomás is short, being only an inch taller than Lucas Chavez, five feet five
inches, but he weighs 145 pounds. His manner is moderately aggressive.
Although he talks with difficulty and is ill at ease in a public gathering
where he has to talk, he nevertheless tends to dominate a group and is
never ignored as Lucas is in either casual or purposeful gatherings. He has

an air of authority at church ceremonies, where he carries on his duties as Matachin Kobanao. He is jovial and friendly in ordinary social gatherings.

Tomás had no orientation in Yaqui society until perhaps the last fifteen years of his life. As a child he had no close relations with family or relatives and during his early years did not live in close proximity to any sort of Yaqui community. He learned to speak Yaqui first, but then abandoned it for a number of years and spoke a very limited sort of almost pidgin Spanish. He came back to Yaqui when he entered the United States, but neither his Yaqui nor his Spanish is recognized as being up to any accepted standard. He is a "poor talker." His later contacts with relatives were of a very tenuous kind, and he took pride in his own independence, so that he remained rather outside the pale of Yaqui society until about 1916. Then, his attempt to enter the society met with disapproval from Yaquis, for he was regarded as not having taken proper care of his Yaqui wife and, by some, as being responsible for her death. Her illness, however, resulted in his making a manda to serve the Matachinis, a manda which he regards himself as fulfilling now in the capacity of Matachin Kobanao. His first orientation in Yaqui society came almost wholly through his political activities. Tomás was accepted by Juan Pistola as an able executive and was regarded by him and Francisco Matus as material for a leader of the Yaquis. He is spoken of by all who participated in the Pistola government as an "assistant chief," though his name appears in none of the documents.

With the decline of the Pistola government and the failure of Yaquis to offer him any other office, Tomás took matters into his own hands. In fulfillment of his manda he began entering into the activities of the Matachin society. He knew nothing whatever about the dances or the management of the society. His ignorance was regarded as greater than that of almost any other Pascuan on such matters. However, there was no one else willing to assume the duties of Kobanao, the man who had just been elected to the office feeling that it demanded too much of his time. Unattached and willing to spend whatever time was required, Tomás took over the leadership, learning constantly through the years. At present some people grudgingly admit here and there that Tomás fulfills his office moderately well, but in general opinion has not changed. He is still thought of as largely ignorant. His integration into Yaqui society at present rests entirely on his official office and a few godparent relationships.

The orientation of Tomás in non-Yaqui society began earlier than did his orientation in Yaqui society. His early unimportance and even namelessness may have encouraged an aggressive manner, for it is clear that he early learned how to approach employers and secure jobs. He was intent, apparently from his twelfth to his twenty-fifth year, on making his way in Anglo-American society. He worked into positions of responsibility that few Yaquis have held, such as assistant foreman on the railroad. But his attempted adjustment to Yaqui society through his marriage interfered. His marriage resulted in his beginning to drink, according to his account and that of others, and he sank to the level of track laborer again. From perhaps his thirtieth year on, he ceased entirely to be sensitive to the pulls of Anglo-American socio-economic life and turned steadily toward securing status in Yaqui society.

The dominant element in Tomás's personality is the desire for authority and importance. It is not a simple desire for status in the sense that Lucas desires status. Tomás sees himself as an important and central figure in Yaqui life: "First there was Juan Pistola; he was a great chief. Then there was Francisco Matus. Now there is I, Tomás Alvarez. That is the way it has come down. I am in the line." There is no leaning on others for help up the ladder of status as in the case of Lucas. Tomás is independent and self-sufficient. Tomás is even able to ignore the whole village, in a sense, in his quest for power and assumes the Matachin leadership in spite of all the people. Yet it is notable that he seeks power through an established and functioning Yaqui institution. Despite his lack of technical knowledge of the Matachinis, he was sufficiently a Yaqui in his orientation to understand that only the ceremonial societies have remained as vital and functional means to position.

That Tomás has been capable of disciplining himself to obtain what he wants has been apparent throughout his life history. He did not smoke or drink until after he was twenty-three. This was obviously not a result of primary group controls, for there were none such operating on him. It was a discipline which he regards as important for fitting himself to get a satisfactory job and work his way upward. These controls over himself broke down only after his marriage. Again, there has been discipline in the taking over of the Matachin society, a discipline which must not always be easy for him to conform to. But he says repeatedly, "No, I cannot decide that. If I say that such and such a thing should be done, then no one will do it. It is necessary to talk with the Monarcas, get them all together, and then we can decide. We must all talk it over." He is here in later life submitting for the first time to definite social controls and quite clearly for the purpose of maintaining his personal power. Lucas Chavez says of him:

Tomás is doing better now. He is going around from house to house as Pistola did. But he is full of evil advice. He has been in the pay of the Catholic Daughters of America. He has gotten money from them and then he takes the young men and drinks with them. He drinks with the Matachinis on that money. He wants to be like a Mexican.

Tomás has many of the beliefs which Lucas has concerning Mexicans. He is also capable of disparaging someone by saying that "he wants to be a Mexican." But the Mexican stereotype with Tomás is a minor thing, not the passionately held attitude which it is for Lucas, and he uses it only casually for the purpose of making a joke or pointing a story. His actual relations with Mexicans are fairly intimate, having a Mexican mistress and many friends in Barrio Belen. His ideal of life ("if he had a million dollars") is to build "a little store" at the highest place in the village and sell cheap goods to "the gente." He feels that when he gets old he can "beg limosna from the gente" and so he need not worry about a job now or in the future.

Tomás has no interest in, or consciousness of, Christian doctrine as in any way distinct from Yaqui doctrine or ritual. He believes the stories of the origin of the Pascolas and the common interpretations of the Matachin paraphernalia which link it with the story of Peter and the Betrayal. He is not concerned to rationalize or intellectualize. He believes whole-heartedly that there is a body of true Yaqui doctrine which he unfortunately does not know, but that if he had the energy he could inquire into and acquire for himself. But his interest does not lie in that direction. His interest is in the mastery of the technical details of Matachin dancing. This occupies his mind and time.

Guadalupe Balthazar, Head Sacristan

One of the younger Yaqui men said once during a discussion of village leadership: "If some Yaqui tells you he is the chief, you can be sure then that he isn't. A real chief never says he is. The people just make him serve." This represents the usual attitude toward public office, as it is expressed publicly and collectively. Tomás defers to it in public and so does Lucas, but their private attitudes do not quite conform. This is especially true of Tomás, less so of Lucas. In Guadalupe Balthazar we have a man who behaves and appears to think in conformity with the Yaqui ideal. He has never sought any office and does not wish one at present, yet he is considered to be the head Sacristan of Pascua.

Guadalupe Balthazar in front of
his house, September 1937.
Photograph by Rosamond B.
Spicer.

Balthazar was born in San José de Guaymas in 1873. His parents were
Yaquis, his father from Rajum and his mother from Belem. They had
moved out of the Yaqui country, taking up residence voluntarily on a Mexican hacienda at San José, because of the fighting and violence in the Yaqui
country. They retained, however, fields in the vicinity of Rajum and returned periodically to plant and cultivate them. Thus Balthazar remained
in close contact with life on the Yaqui River during his boyhood. He saw
much of the fighting in the western Yaqui country and like Lucas was one
who escaped into the hills after the battle of Buatachive. After this for a few
years, he continued to live with his parents at San José de Guaymas. Then
they attempted to return to the vicinity of Belem. At the age of sixteen,
Balthazar was confirmed as a Temasti in Belem, but had only a few months
practice. Meanwhile, his father had been charged with murder by a Yaqui
court and the judgment involved loss of his land. The family returned to
San José de Guaymas where Balthazar stayed until 1911.

Guadalupe was married about 1905 and had four children. At the be-

Temasti Guadalupe Balthazar and *Maestro* José María García at a service on Día de la Santa Cruz, joined by a small worshipper, May 1937. *Photograph by Rosamond B. Spicer.*

ginning of the Madero revolution there was fighting near San José and Balthazar moved his family to Guaymas. Later, he moved to Hermosillo and obtained work as a gardener. He saw a great deal of the fighting in Sonora during the Revolution. In 1916, weary of disorder, he took his family and came to the United States, settling immediately in Barrio Anita. He obtained a job as gardener for a wealthy Anglo-American family and continued in that post until he was retired with a pension in 1935. At present he lives alone in Pascua on a lot for which he has paid. He has served as a sacristan in Pascua for twenty years and has been recognized as head Temasti since 1938.

Balthazar's orientation was primarily as a pro-Cajeme Yaqui, his father having participated in most of the fighting with Cajeme. But before the final defeat of Cajeme there was a cooling toward the latter as a result of what the family regarded as an unjust judgment in the murder case. The Balthazars, however, remained Yaquis culturally and attended ceremonies in Belem, Rajum, and Vicam regularly until about 1900. There is no evidence of anything significant in Guadalupe's family relations. The family was religiously strict, Guadalupe experiencing the same daily prayers be-

Itinerary of
Guadalupe Balthazar

Scale in Miles
0   25   50   75   100

fore the houseyard cross which Lucas remembers. He was also required to memorize the catechism in Yaqui. Family life was smooth, pleasant, undisturbed by anything except the wars. There was no want or privation except for a brief few weeks after the battle of Buatachive. Contact with Yaqui communities was brief and sporadic, so that the family remained a separate nucleus of Yaqui custom at San José:

The church at San José was kept locked. Neither we nor the Mexicans had any fiestas at the church. Nobody used it. We used to have a little celebration of Noche Buena in the houses, that was all. Then we always put food out for the dead on All Souls' Day. We never celebrated Holy Week. On the day of San Juan there used to be a little chicken pull. . . . Now that I think of it there were never anything but funerals in the private houses at San José. But we used to go to Belem for many of the fiestas.

Once when the family went to Belem he was impressed into ceremonial service:

Some men took me to the church and told me that I was going to be Temasti now. I said that I didn't want to be one, that I lived far away in San José de Guaymas.

After his confirmation he went occasionally to Belem and practiced as a Temasti a little. He became acquainted with all the Maestros in Belem, Rajum, and Potam. After 1900, however, most of the Yaquis were dispersed from the towns and he ceased to have contact with any Yaqui communities. It was only after he came to Tucson in 1916 that he began to serve again:

After I had been here awhile, they began saying, "Guadalupe Balthazar was a Temasti on the Yaqui River. He should help us here." So they began asking me to come to the church. There was nothing I could do about it. I have been helping ever since.

The opinion of him held by Pascuans is extremely high. He is regarded as having a great deal of knowledge of church ritual and is thought to be the only man capable of making the proper arrangements for Holy Thursday and other events of Holy Week.

Balthazar's orientation in non-Yaqui society cannot be thought of as a distinct process. He does not remember learning to speak Spanish, but believes he learned it right along with Yaqui. He is similarly unable to remember the process of learning to read and write, but is at present thoroughly literate in Spanish. He makes no sharp distinctions between Yaquis and Mexicans, but regards himself as a Yaqui because he is more at ease in speaking that language. He never makes use of the Yaqui stereotype of Mexicans and is without any expressed hatred of Mexicans, although he says:

The Yaquis here all pay a great deal of attention to All Souls' Day. They observe it properly because they regard it as a penitence to perform, but the Mexicans say that it is too much work to do that. They do not pay enough attention to their religion.

He believes that the Yaquis ought to make more use of the church of Santa Rosa "because it is cleaner and more comfortable than San Ignacio." But he continues to serve in the latter church regularly. He is, however, a conscientious helper in the few ceremonies which take place at Santa Rosa. He also attends the Catholic churches in Tucson regularly and frequently, where, unlike most Yaquis, he observes Roman Catholic rituals precisely, such as making the proper genuflections before sitting down.

His major interests lie in the details of ritual performance and in a dispassionate concern with Yaqui history. He has read considerably in the latter field, less in the field of ritual. He is a stickler for detail and correctness in both historical fact and ritual procedure. He thinks in an objective methodical fashion, seeming always to seek the highest degree of order. He is also deeply concerned with plants and trees and maintains an interest in their care and their characteristics. He is unable to talk for long about himself, invariably departing into detailed descriptions of wholly impersonal events or things. He is totally lacking in the animal lore and Yaqui beliefs which are so important in Lucas's mental baggage.

Balthazar's physical appearance is commanding. He is tall, five feet eleven inches, and imposing. His manner is aloof and dignified, not retiring and withdrawn as is Lucas's. He is never talkative except in small gatherings of older people who question him about life in Sonora. On this subject he expands for hours.

His drive seems to have been always toward quiet, ordered living. Unconcerned with status and uninclined toward assuming authority, he has always been impressed into public service. He has never voluntarily sought an office and does not desire one. He is the most universally admired man in Pascua. No one criticizes him or finds fault with any aspect of his behavior. It appears that he has been perfectly suited to Yaqui culture in temperament, but it nevertheless also appears that he lacks intensity of expression in his commitment to Yaqui culture.

Rosario Escalante

Like the three men just discussed, almost all of the Pascua men over forty have some sort of village office, some skill of a Yaqui kind which they are able to practice and which gives them satisfaction and some status in the community. Some have been promised to the service of one of the ceremonial organizations during infancy, as Lucas was or as Tomás Alvarez was promised later in life. Some have developed skills late in life, as Tomás has, under the influence of obtaining some sort of status in Yaqui society. Some have through various accidents of their careers learned Yaqui skills, like Guadalupe Balthazar, and have subsequently been drafted for service in Arizona. The writer has known only two men over fifty in the village of Pascua who have never assumed any community office and who are not regarded by anyone in the village as capable of assuming such office. If such men moved outside of Yaqui society, their peculiar lack of status would excite no interest, but the fact that they are as definitely Yaqui as any of the men so far discussed raises the question: what are they gaining by remaining Yaqui? If they have none of the specially Yaqui community statuses, then why do they remain in Yaqui communities? These questions bring us to an aspect of the meaning of Yaqui culture to individuals which has not so far been disclosed at length. In order to develop an approach to them we may consider the life history of one of the men in Pascua who has no village office, and moreover, has a record of minimal community participation.

Rosario Escalante was born in 1888 in Hermosillo. His parents were both Mayo, he believes. He grew up in the vicinity of Hermosillo and remembers the life as a difficult one. Beginning at the age of seven or eight, he spent his days in the fields, cultivating and tending crops. He remembers no Yaqui or Mayo neighbors, but thinks he must have lived among Mexicans. Just before he was twenty, in 1907, the climax was reached in shipments of Yaquis to central Mexico and Yucatán. His family was all caught in the net—two brothers, three sisters, himself, and his parents. They were separated, but all, except perhaps a sister, were sent to Veracruz and kept at work there on a large hacienda, growing beans, wheat, and garbanzos. Rosario worked there for over a year. The peons were not given sufficient food. They were beaten unmercifully with clubs if they did not finish assigned stints of work. Rosario's brother died. Rosario himself felt unable to endure the life and escaped. He walked northwest, passed through Mexico City, and worked a few days there, worked a few more days in Jalisco. Eventually he reached Hermosillo again.

With the outbreak of the Madero revolution, Rosario's parents also returned to Hermosillo and attempted to settle down. However, within five years they had been rounded up again and were sent about 1917, "by Calles" to work on a hacienda at Toluca, D.F. Panic-stricken at the thought of being sent to another place like the hacienda in Veracruz, Rosario walked north to the United States and entered Arizona in 1918. He heard, meanwhile, that his parents had died in Toluca. He thinks it proba-

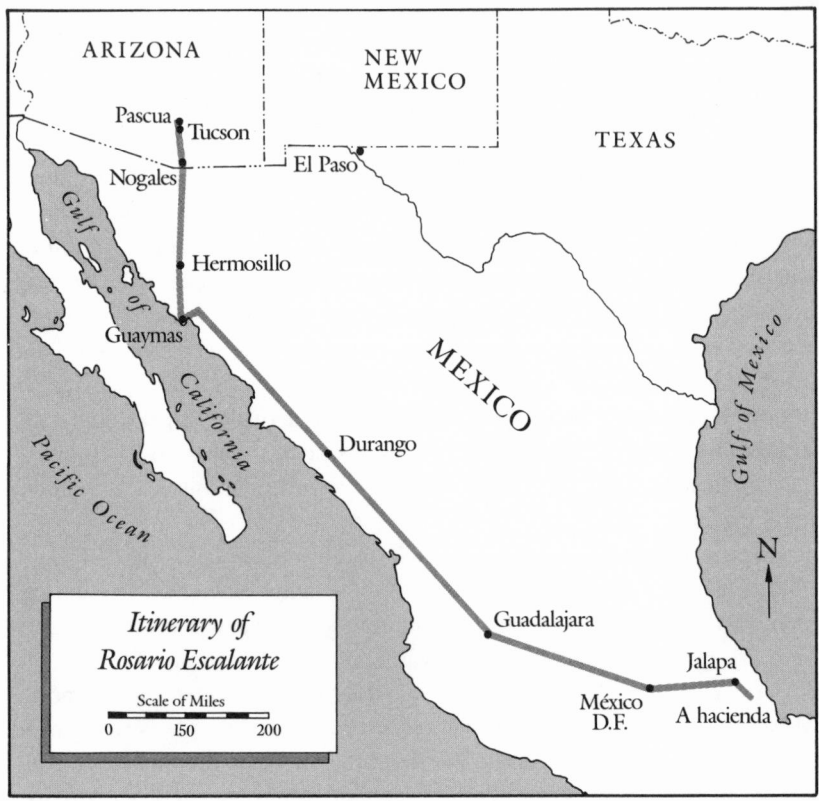

ble that a sister is still alive in the vicinity of Toluca; except for her, he believes he has no relatives anywhere.

Rosario settled in Barrio Anita and was one of the first to move out to Pascua in 1922 with the other Pistoleros. At Barrio Anita he began to live with Josefa Araiza, a prominent Yaqui woman who has been head *Kiosti* (altar tender) at Pascua for many years. He has lived with her ever since in her large household of daughters. He has worked steadily since 1922 and is one of the four in Pascua, along with Guadalupe Balthazar, who has paid for his lot. Rosario has supported the large family at a rather higher level than most in Pascua, receiving help from the unmarried women of the household. Rosario has never had a village office of any kind and is not interested at present in developing any skill which will enable him to. He is conspicuously absent from all the ceremonies which his consort, Josefa, attends as head Kiosti. His appearances at any village ceremonies are extremely rare and always brief and casual, unless they are at his own household. Here he does whatever is conventionally required. He leads, for example, the procession of relatives at a funeral involving some relative by marriage. He provided money for the cumpleaño commemorating the death of Josefa's father and served as fiestero at the cumpleaño fiesta. In other words, in the case of all private ceremonies which involve his own household or its closer connections, he behaves as any proper Yaqui, but his ceremonial activities do not extend beyond those limits.

As a result probably of his careful attention to his family ceremonials, he is not a target for gossip as are other persons in the village who are regarded as lax in their ceremonial obligations. It is recognized that he has no manda to perform any ceremonial service, and it is thought that he is serving sufficiently in taking care of his family interests and in permitting practically all the members of his household to fulfill their mandas in the ceremonial organization. He rarely drinks and is not obtrusive when he does. This also helps his general village reputation. He is respected in the village as a hard-working man, just as he is respected as such in his own family. He lacks, however, any prominence whatsoever in the village, unless someone happens to think of his exploit of escape from the dire conditions of the haciendas in Veracruz and the courageous walk home to Sonora. This gives him a certain minor importance and notoriety in the village.

Rosario's orientation in Yaqui or Mayo society apparently did not begin

The house of Rosario Escalante, March 1937. *Photograph by David J. Jones, Jr.*

until after he was thirty and had moved to Tucson. He describes no contact with Yaqui culture in Hermosillo. The period from 1907 until 1918, when he was between nineteen and thirty years of age, was one devoted entirely to work and escape from Mexican masters. He has not been influenced by any desire for status in Yaqui society, but rather apparently by desire for security. His interests and activity are constantly directed toward securing steady jobs, and he has perhaps one of the best reputations of any Pascua Yaqui with the Anglo-American employers for whom he has worked.

His orientation in non-Yaqui society is characterized by the familiar hatred for Mexicans. His experiences, of course, explain the vigorous persistence of that feeling in him. He believes that all Mexicans dislike all Yaquis. He recognizes that they do not hate Mayos, but they "do not distinguish between Yaquis and Mayos when they are living together." He suffered as a Yaqui, even though he was a Mayo, and he has reacted like a Yaqui toward Mexicans. Mexicans, he believes, are "very bad people" because of what he regards as wholly irrational hatred for Yaquis which operates even without reference to whether or not its object is actually a Yaqui. His attitude has an interesting element in that he says repeatedly, "It is not possible to live in Hermosillo because the Mexicans say that the Yaquis are bad; they say that they kill people." In other words, the Mexicans make unreasonable charges against Yaquis constantly. Since they are unreasonable, there is nothing that can be done except to avoid Mexicans. Here would seem to be the core of the doctrine so well known to Yaquis that the Mexicans are constantly "angry." This angriness is unreasonableness, irrationality about the Yaquis. Rosario came to this country, he says, in order to avoid being stopped and molested constantly and because of his fear of the physical violence on the Mexican haciendas. Within the past few years he has learned to read in Spanish and is learning a little in English. His spare time seems to go into this activity rather than into the development of any Yaqui skills.

Rosario is not completely lacking in knowledge of Yaqui culture. He has picked up a general acquaintance with its ceremonial aspects since coming to Arizona. He knows the Pascolas well and has watched them and listened to their talk sufficiently to be able to give a good account of them. He moreover thinks they are very funny and is especially impressed with the humor of their addressing little animals as saints. He knows little about the church ritual, however, and has no interest in it. He appears to have lost interest steadily in Yaqui culture since his first acquaintance with it in Barrio Anita.

Rosario is a Yaqui only through the historical accidents of his life which have given him a common background with other older Yaquis in Arizona. He is also a Yaqui through his present affinal and some godparent ties, but the distinctively Yaqui elements of culture have no appeal for him, and he does not relate himself to them in any significant way. He is definitely a member of Yaqui society, tied to it by many different strands of obligation, but he is not a full participant in Yaqui culture and gives no indication of becoming so.

The four lives which we have considered do not represent the only four existing types among the older men of Pascua. There are other kinds as would be evident if we were to consider Juan Flores ("Shorty") the seventy-year-old hard drinker who entered Arizona in the early eighties and has been drinking and making adobes ever since. It might be interesting to try to analyze his curious casual participation in Yaqui ceremony. There is no other way to describe him except by saying that he participates as a *Moro Ya'ut* (manager of the Pascolas) only when he feels like it. He feels like it frequently, however, and the Pascuans are conscious of him in two manifestations, one as a serious and conscientious Moro directing the activities of the Pascolas, the other as a drunken bachelor who sings self-made ditties to himself in the shade or in the moonlight under his mesquite tree.

We might find a different type if we should stop to consider José María Casillas, the harpist. Small in stature, busy making harps or Pascola masks, thought of as the repository of Yaqui lore, but almost inarticulate about it, he was the man responsible for the first Tucson revival of the Easter ceremonies, a man now with no official post in the village life, but impossible to classify except as one of the "most Yaqui" of all who are living in Pascua. There are other types of persons and other types of adjustment to Yaqui culture. The four we have selected are significant for the purposes of this study. They indicate four significant manifestations of Yaqui culture.

The four men may be thought of in a continuum or series. Thus Lucas Chavez represents the most thoroughly Yaqui of all. He possesses and makes use of Yaqui concepts; he knows the content of Yaqui culture and understands its meanings. He proceeds in Yaqui fashion to obtain status in Yaqui society because he is moved by Yaqui motives. He shows conflicts between his personality and the cultural set, but these are resolved largely in good Yaqui fashion. Tomás Alvarez is more a member of Yaqui society rather than someone who could be called truly a Yaqui. He has status and he participates actively and at various levels in the social structure of Pascua, but Yaqui culture is not apparent to him as an entity, and its meanings are ones which he has constructed for himself as of the moment to suit his needs. He is in process of adjusting Yaqui culture to his own personality, but this process, of course, cannot help but be reciprocal. Guadalupe Balthazar is less fully a participant in Yaqui society than is Tomás Alvarez, but he is perhaps more of a participant in the culture. Yet his connection with society or culture is tenuous, and there is no doubt that the elements of Yaqui culture that he knows are the least distinctive and the most like corresponding ones in Mexican-American Catholic culture. Guadalupe might slip out of Yaqui society very readily despite his cultural acquisitions from it. He could be equally content in the Mexican-American culture of Tucson, if his command of the Spanish language were equal to his command of Yaqui. He could have moved easily into that culture, if any incentives had arisen, but none did. Rosario Escalante is purely a member of Yaqui society. The culture as a community expression might disappear tomorrow, but Rosario's life and certainly his system of values would be practically unchanged. He is the farthest from the core Yaqui culture, though still a member of the society.

CHAPTER 6

Younger Yaqui Men

The younger men of Pascua whom we shall consider here are men who have been born in the United States or were brought as infants to this country by their parents. They have had more continuous and uniform contact with Yaqui parents than the older Yaqui men. Their experiences in general have been of a different type from that of the older men, lacking chiefly the unpleasant and fear-inspiring experiences with Mexicans characteristic of their elders. In following their lives backward to about the threshold of 1900, we are taken back to the period of the reorganization of Yaqui culture in Arizona, to the early days of Yaqui settlement and introduction to the complexities of life in the United States among the different ethnic groups. In tracing out these different backgrounds we are again interested in looking for the clues to choices of cultural behavior on their part. Why have they moved out of the influence of Yaqui culture at different times, as all of them have? Why have they moved back at different times to participate in that culture?

Case Study of Cayetano Lopez

In 1940 Cayetano Lopez was a man of considerable fame among Arizona Yaquis. Although widely known and recognized as an able Maestro, he was not participating as a Maestro and had not done so for several years. He was living alone, having never married, in a tiny house built for him by a very dear friend, a Pascola Dancer of high reputation in Pascua. Identifying himself thoroughly as a Yaqui, Lopez was, nevertheless, probably characterized by less participation in the distinctive Yaqui behaviors than any other Yaqui of his age. He is of special interest for detailed study because his life has interlocked intimately with that of Lucas Chavez.

Cayetano Lopez is of medium height as compared with other Yaqui men, being about five feet six inches tall. He is heavily built, weighing about 155 pounds. He dresses in accordance with the mode of Arizona laborers generally. His appearance is usually careless and even sloppy, a manner accentuated by his awkward and ungraceful body movements. He is exuberantly healthy, reporting no serious illnesses at any time in his life.

Life History

We may divide Cayetano's life into six significant periods as follows:

1894–1903   Lives in Tucson and Nogales with mother.

1903–1909   Lives with godparents and others after death of mother; school and other Anglo contacts.

1909–1917   Learns to be Maestro and serves in Guadalupe.

1917–1927   Serves as Maestro in Barrio Libre.

1927–1931   "Chief of Arizona Yaquis."

1931–1941   Lives in Pascua and Libre, no village office.

Cayetano Lopez was born in Tucson in 1894 in a Mexican-American area, there being no developed Yaqui centers of population in the city at that time. His father, José Lopez, was a Mayo Indian who was one of the first to arrive in Arizona, having entered in the late 1880s just after the defeat of Cajeme. His mother, Teofila Lopez, was a Yaqui from Torim where she had served as a Cantora. José was making his living as an adobe maker, and Teofila was helping out by taking in washing "from Mexican families." This first period of Cayetano's life was characterized by considerable moving about—from Tucson to San Xavier where José farmed for a time, then to Nogales, then to a railroad section house near Yuma, and finally back to Nogales. There were also visits to Magdalena in Sonora. For Cayetano it was a confused and not a very pleasant period, ending with the shock of his mother's death in Nogales in 1903.

Cayetano Lopez, September 1936. *Photograph by David J. Jones, Jr.*

The following period was definitely an unhappy one. His father had left the family before Teofila's death, and Cayetano now found himself homeless. He was taken in, however, by his godfather Lucas Chavez. Chavez treated him harshly and he ran away, and was befriended for a time by an Anglo-American family—the Nolans—in Nogales. He went to school in Nogales, then lived with a Mexican family. Later he lived with an aunt, and then with another godfather in the vicinity of Tucson, and for a while lived at Sasco where he went to school again. All together he completed five years of school during this period, and this has constituted his total schooling.

At Sasco he began to study as a Maestro, although he was only fifteen years old. He continued his training during the next eight years, and after many different jobs in mining towns and travels as far as El Paso, he began to practice, as a young man of twenty-one, in the Yaqui village of Guadalupe. For two years he continued at Guadalupe and began to feel that he had an established place, for he was recognized as a very able Maestro.

Sometime after 1917 he returned to Tucson and has lived more or less regularly in that vicinity ever since. From 1917 to 1927 he was constantly

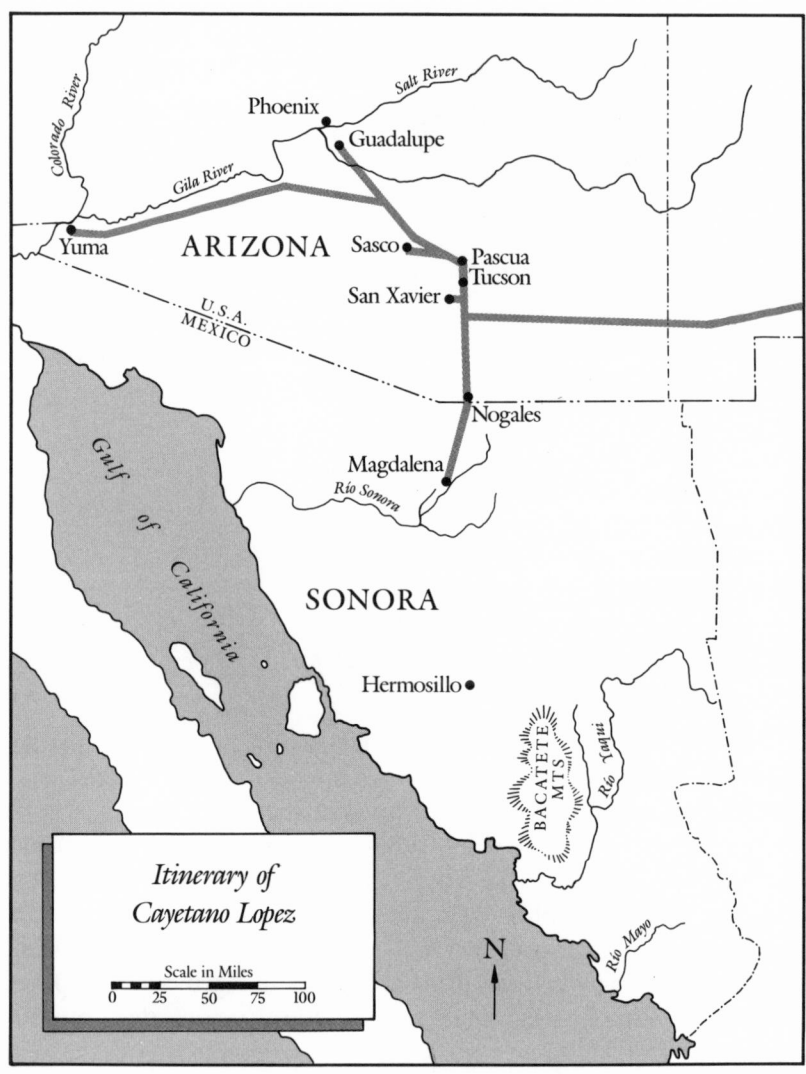

Itinerary of
Cayetano Lopez

Scale in Miles
0   25   50   75   100

N

practicing as a Maestro in Barrio Libre and became prominent in Yaqui affairs also as a go-between with Anglo Americans. Like other Yaquis in Barrio Libre, he kept aloof from the Pistola organization in Pascua, although he was not a leader of the Nestor Muñoz group which actively opposed the Pistola faction.

In 1927 Muñoz, as a result of participation in a court case, was forced to leave Tucson, and Cayetano became the most prominent political figure among Yaquis in south Tucson. He was extremely active as a go-between in many legal cases, particularly the bootlegging cases of the period.[1] He was thrust forward in 1929 on behalf of the Arizona Yaquis who were opposed to the Guadalupe Flores plan for the return of Yaquis to Sonora. As a result of these activities, which included writing letters to the governor of the state and even to the President of the United States, he was declared to be "chief of the Yaquis of Pima County" in 1931. Never satisfied, however, with the Yaquis' response to his leadership, he resigned from the "chieftainship" in 1932 after one year's service and turned the office over to a Yaqui of Barrio Libre. The period was one of great prominence for him in Yaqui affairs, but also of constant frustration resulting from his failure as a leader.

Since 1931 he has relinquished his political leadership and has also ceased to practice as a Maestro, no longer taking part in any regular way in Yaqui community life either in Libre or Pascua where he has finally taken up residence. He drinks with increasing frequency and does less and less in the way of acting as go-between for Yaquis with official Tucson. The period for him is one of resignation to failure and constant preoccupation with his numerous frustrations. It is notable, however, that he continues to live and maintain a house in a Yaqui village, showing no tendency to move out into any of the Mexican-American areas of the city.

Orientation in Yaqui Society and Culture

Cayetano's very earliest years were not spent among Yaquis, with of course the exception of his immediate family. As he says:

My father go away before my mother die and we had always live around with Mexicans, where Mexicans were. My mother live around that way, not so much where Yaquis was.

None of the Arizona Yaqui communities had yet crystallized, so that there was little opportunity for the family to identify with Yaquis until Cayetano was seven years old. At that time they moved to Nogalitos where some twenty Yaqui families had settled.

Cayetano has several vivid memories of events in his family life before he was eight years old:

My mother and my father were fighting a lot. I remember that when we were in Nogales. My father was playing around with that Papago woman. I didn't hardly know my father. One time when we was living in Nogales, Arizona, there was a Papago woman playing around with him. And he was coming along by my godmother's house and he was carrying a gallon of wine on his back and this Papago woman come along and she started playing with my father. My godmother she came in and she saw this Papago woman and the Papago woman said, "I don't care how many wives he's got, I'm going to have a good time with him." And she kept on playing with him and my godmother told my mother about what she said. Then my father come on home with this gallon of wine over his shoulders and my mother ran over and she fought hard with the Papago woman and chased her away and then she took a stone and hit my father with it. It hit him where the gallon of wine was and it broke all over him. I remember when all that happen. I was just beginning to get my eyes to look around and I remember that one of the first.

This seems to have been typical of the relations between his father and mother. The father was irregular not only in his marital relations but also as a worker. Cayetano remembers his mother as spending all her time washing clothes "for Mexican families" in order to keep her family going. The father apparently shifted about a great deal, and the family would follow him to a new location only to have him shift again in a few months somewhere else. He deserted them for good in Nogalitos shortly after the incident related above. Cayetano's statement that he "hardly knew him" is illustrated further by the following incident:

Later on my father was working at Jaynes Station and I was living in Tucson with another godfather which I had. We were on the street in Tucson and my father come along. I guess I was maybe eleven years old. This was maybe about 1908. I didn't know my father who he was and he didn't know who I was, but my godfather said, "José, do you know who this is?" And my father said, "Who is it?" And my godfather say, "It's your son." And my father say, "My son!" And then he look at me and say, "Which son is it?" Then I didn't see him for a long time after that and he never send me no money or anything and never send any clothes to my godfather for me to wear. He didn't never pay no attention to me.

Cayetano's accounts of him are, however, quite free from any moral censure, and he has remained loyal to him to the last. He says:

My father died last winter (1940) in Casa Grande when he was 103 years old. He was with my sister there when he die and the newspapers in Casa Grande tell all about him because he was so old. I went there for the funeral and then I stay in Casa Grande for about three months after that.

This devotion to family and refusal to make any judgments of a moral kind on any relative is thoroughly typical of Cayetano, as it is of other Yaquis.

Cayetano's relations with his mother were much happier. He was deeply devoted to her. She began teaching Cayetano to read Spanish when he was barely seven years old. Having been a Cantora in Torim where Cayetano says she "sang with the priests," she was well acquainted with Yaqui church ritual and before her death had taught Cayetano some of her lore. Teofila, as related earlier, had considerable fame among Yaquis in Nogalitos as a learned woman, and it was with her that Lucas Chavez studied after he came to Nogalitos. Not long after Cayetano's birth, he became ill with colic. Lucas Chavez happened to be in Tucson at this time and as part of the effort to cure Cayetano, Teofila called Lucas in to act as godfather of the rosary. Lucas placed the rosary about Cayetano's neck and the illness was allayed. This established a relationship between the two families which had important consequences. Cayetano speaks of his mother as follows:

My mother always treat me all right. She told me how to say prayers every night and I used to say them. And she always tell me what she beat me for when she beat me and then she didn't beat me very hard.

She died when Cayetano was nine years old, and he immediately came to realize how much more secure and pleasant was even his broken home than life with his godparents and others. Cayetano still is overcome with emotion and breaks down into tears at his mother's grave in Nogales.

His father, José Lopez, came to live with Cayetano's mother when he was already about fifty years old and after he had had at least three children by another Yaqui woman. By Teofila he had four children: Francisco, who was ten years older than Cayetano; Juanita, who was four or five years older; Cayetano; and a daughter, Agustina, who was younger. Juanita died the same year as her mother in Nogales. Agustina seems to have been taken and cared for by José. Cayetano remembers only his very much older brother, Francisco. When Cayetano was about five years old and Francisco fifteen, an event took place which Cayetano records as follows in his fragmentary autobiography:

My brother Francisco Lopez start to drink and he cut the throat of my godfather and he went in to Magdalena, Sonora, Mexico . . . and my aunt was living (there). Her name was Juliana Yuku . . . And then after my brother went in to Mexico, we went after him because in that time, the Mexican government was sending the Yaqui Indians in to Yucatán.

The family brought Francisco back with them to the United States and he, young as he was, immediately assumed the responsibility for them which the father was not showing. He obtained a job on the Southern Pacific and took the family with him to a section house near Yuma. Teofila's illness, however, brought them back to Nogales, and after her death Francisco failed to assume the care of Cayetano. Working here and there on the railroad, he returned frequently to Nogales, and for a few years appeared to Cayetano as his only protector in the unpleasant household of his godfather, Lucas Chavez:

> When my brother Francisco was around, Lucas and Lola always nice to me and didn't beat me, but that was just because my brother was there and Lucas was maybe afraid of my brother.

Francisco's protectorship, however, was soon ended, for when Cayetano was fourteen Francisco was killed "by a Mexican" while he was working on the railroad tracks near Sonoita, Arizona.

Cayetano has visited his younger sister and his half-brothers and sisters occasionally during his life, but has never maintained any close relations with any of them.

Before Teofila died, she had arranged that Cayetano be taken by her sister, Juliana Yuku, whom they had visited in Magdalena. But there was no way to get Cayetano across the line, and so he was taken by godparents. It was not until after five trying years in Nogales and Tucson that Juliana brought her family across to Arizona and Cayetano began living with them. The relationship, however, never worked out. Cayetano says that Juliana's son of his own age was "always fighting" with him and that he "could not stand to be with him." So he left the Yuku household. Still, Cayetano has had many more intimate relations with his relatives than has Lucas Chavez, for example, and this shows in his more accurate knowledge of such things as the kinship terminology. But since the death of his mother and older brother, his ties with Yaqui society have been through godparents and ceremonial relationships rather than through kinship. He has had miscellaneous relatives near him throughout his life in Arizona, but none have played an important role in his development.

When Cayetano's mother died, it was his godfather of the rosary, Lucas Chavez, who assumed care of him. At the time, Lucas and his wife Lola were taking care of several other orphan Yaquis. Cayetano was treated very harshly, according to his accounts. The autobiography says:

> Lucas Chavez's wife used to make me wash clothes for the Mexican people and make me sell *tortillas de maiz*. Lucas was working for the railroad at Nogales, Arizona. We were in the section houses, and then one Mexican woman that she was my godmother told Lucas Chavez that she has a little land and told him to build up the house and so we live there and then an American lady the name of Mrs. John Nolan was looking for a boy to work for her, and Lucas told her about me and so I started to work for her.

Immediately, trouble developed. Cayetano says that Lucas had told him he was "too dumb" to go to school and had therefore put him to work with Mrs. Nolan, who was the wife of Lucas's foreman on the track. Lucas says that Cayetano had refused to go to school and had gotten into trouble over the theft of some money and that therefore he had decided to put him in Mrs. Nolan's care. He found Cayetano "*muy duro*," that is, unwilling to be told anything and constantly disobedient. "He would never come home at night. He stayed away all the time." Cayetano's autobiography says:

Mrs. Nolan put me in the public school and then she started to teach me until sometimes of the nights and Lucas got disappointed with me because I didn't come home quick and so he start to whip me like a beast without a shirt on me. So I couldn't sleep at night. And one morning I told Mrs. John Nolan that I wasn't going to school anymore and she got surprised about what I have told her. So she told her husband Mr. John Nolan to ask me about it and I told Mr. Nolan about what happen to me the night before. So Mrs. Nolan told me to show my back to them and so I did, and then she called for Dr. Birdy. So that day I didn't went to school. Mrs. Nolan started to fix up a room for me so I could live there with them and then a week later Lucas met me at the gate of the fence and ask me why I didn't come home for a week and I told him to ask Mrs. Nolan about it and so he went in but I never knew what Mrs. Nolan told him. And so I got afraid of Lucas and went to a Mexican's house to work for them.

The memory of the beating which Lucas gave him is a repeatedly retold event in all its bloody details in Cayetano's interviews. He evidently suffered an intense fear of Lucas throughout the rest of his boyhood and avoided any meeting with him until he was a grown man. For the past twenty years, however, he has had frequent contact with Lucas, and in their meetings there is no evidence of overt hostility. Both recognize and behave in accordance with their godparent-godson relationship. Cayetano addresses notes to Lucas which always begin: "My esteemed godfather." He has assisted Lucas frequently as a godson should in little matters such as buying medicine for him and even food when Lucas has been without money. Lucas introduces Cayetano to strangers as "my son" and in writing to him always calls him either "son" or "my fine godchild." To others on many occasions, however, both speak harshly of each other. Cayetano does not hesitate to describe Lucas as "mean," "hard," and even "dishonest." Lucas speaks of Cayetano as "a very bad man, who drinks too much." His favorite characterization of Cayetano is as follows:

That man, my godson Cayetano, he has a very good head and his mother taught him all the good things, but he is very wrongheaded, and he has never done what he should.

In response to a suggestion once that Lucas does not like him, Cayetano said:

What makes you think he don't like me? He is my godfather. He has always been trying to take good care of me.

Thus the godparent relationship continues, overlying the well-developed feeling of hostility that each has for the other as a result of the unpleasant incident in Nogalitos.

Cayetano never went back to live with Lucas and Lola. He lived with Mexicans in Nogales and with the Nolans for two or three years and then with other godparents briefly in Tucson until his aunt arrived from Mexico. He continued to seek out godparents to live with until he was past eighteen, but never stayed with any of them for any length of time. A few months at the most was the limit. His godparent relationships were thus never happy or helpful to him except very briefly in moments of emergency. One of his most permanent and satisfactory relationships, however, was worked out later in life, after the age of about thirty, with a compadre named Francisco Valencia. Valencia was a large, strong Yaqui who seems to have been regarded by Cayetano as a sort of protector. Cayetano was associated with him in the political affairs of Barrio Libre and later, when Valencia moved to Pascua, Cayetano followed him, and Valencia built a small house for him on his lot. Cayetano lived there for seven or eight years until after the death of Valencia and remained doggedly devoted to him. Cayetano says of him:

Francisco was the best Yaqui I ever knew. He was good to me. He help me out every time. He made that place for me to live and he tell his wife to keep me there after he die. He was always trying to help me out. He always take good care of me. He was a good guy.

It was a compadre relationship then, which developed into the most lasting and deeply felt of all of Cayetano's personal relationships.

Cayetano's orientation in the ceremonial life of Arizona Yaquis was begun by his mother. Teofila, we have seen, taught him prayers and some of the church ritual. She did not promise him to the service of any ceremonial organization, perhaps because he was never seriously ill. But when Cayetano was fifteen he came into contact with a Maestro who influenced him profoundly. Living at a small mining camp, Sasco, west of Tucson, where there was a large group of Yaquis building railroad, Cayetano was supporting himself by hauling and selling water. He became acquainted with a Yaqui named Ignacio Valenzuela. Valenzuela and Cayetano had nothing to do in the evenings, and so Valenzuela began teaching Cayetano how to conduct services. He taught him the rudiments of chanting. Cayetano learned quickly because it was all familiar to him as a result of his mother's chanting at the house in Nogalitos. Coming to Tucson, Cayetano continued his studies with Valenzuela's mother-in-law and another woman who had been a Cantora on the Yaqui River. Off and on for the next four years, between jobs on the railroad, he returned to Barrio Libre and continued his apprenticeship under Valenzuela's mother-in-law. He was regarded as a capable Maestro in Barrio Libre by the time he was nineteen. His unusual ability at an early age is one of the recurrent stories among all Arizona Yaquis. The myth has it at present that he was leading services better than old Maestros when he was only fourteen. It was not until he was twenty-one and had taken up residence at Guadalupe Village that he settled down to a regular practice. This lasted two years; then there was more wandering, and finally in 1922, at the age of twenty-seven, he returned to Barrio Libre and lived there more or less continuously as a leading Maestro for eight years. He had never taken a manda, but he had undergone a long apprenticeship and his status in the Yaqui church was assured. Yaquis in general expected him to become the best Maestro in Arizona.

Orientation in Other Cultures

Cayetano learned Spanish as soon as Yaqui. He does not remember a time when he was not able to speak Spanish, and his mother taught him to read Spanish while he was still a very small boy. He entered school in Nogales at the age of nine and continued in school there through the third grade. He completed two more years of public school before he was fifteen and by that time was able to read in English as well as to speak it fluently. His command of English is sufficiently good to have permitted him to hold the job of court interpreter for several years in Federal Court in Tucson. He reads and writes English readily, with many errors, but can make himself understood adequately. He is thus definitely tri-lingual. His preferred conversational language is, however, still Yaqui.

As already touched on, Cayetano's contacts with Mexican culture in Arizona have been extensive but miscellaneous. After running away from his godfather in Nogales, he had lived for a few weeks with a Mexican family and worked for them in their store, during which time he spoke Spanish exclusively. His mother had secured a Mexican godmother for him in Nogales and his relations with her were friendly and intimate; it was

she who gave Chavez a piece of land on which to build a house so that
Cayetano could "be raised properly." When he was sixteen, Cayetano had
become associated with a Mexican family. They had borrowed thirty dollars from him in small sums, and they repaid him by giving him a job in the
mining town of Ray when they started a restaurant there. He worked in
the restaurant for six or seven months, again speaking Spanish exclusively.
A good part his life has been spent in Barrio Libre and Guadalupe where
there are many Mexicans and where he has always had Mexican neighbors.
He says:

I have been with Mexicans all my life, but I never forget how to talk *la lengua*
(Yaqui). I never live in a real Yaqui village much and I never dance Matachin or
anything. My mother always live out with the Mexicans. She live here in Tucson
before there was any Yaquis much here. That was why she live with Mexicans.
But we went to Nogales and there wasn't much Yaquis there then. She was always
out washing for the Mexicans and doing all kinds of work for them. I have a
lot Mexican good friends. There was some boys who got killed in the last war,
(World War I) and I haven't seen them since that time. They was Mexican boys
and they was my good friends. They were all right. These Yaquis who say they
hate Mexicans, they haven't never live with them. I have live with them all the time
and they are all right. No, they don't never make fun of me for being a Yaqui,
except sometimes they make fun of la lengua and talk about the Yaqui language
being a funny language. I am working with some Mexican fellows now on the
Forest Service and they are all right. They are my friends. They ask me for words
in Yaqui and I write them out for them and they learn them. There are Mexicans
around who know how to talk Yaqui. They make a little fun of it but the Yaquis
make fun of them, too, because they try to speak la lengua and they don't talk it
like we do. No, the Yaquis don't make fun of the Mexicans' language. Don't they
talk it themselves the way the Mexicans do?

Cayetano's attitude toward Mexicans contrasts strongly with that of the
older Yaqui group. His tolerance toward all ethnic groups is a notable
feature of his make-up.

    Cayetano's sexual life has an interesting passive character. In fact, he
expresses himself as follows concerning Yaqui women:

I am too old now [1940] to think about marrying anybody. I guess maybe I'm
forty-eight [actually forty-six]. Anyway I never think about these Yaqui girls. I
never have one for a wife, because they don't know anything, those Yaqui girls.

The first sexual experiences which he had are briefly recounted in the autobiography:

And they was making a Yaqui Indian celebration for Saint Joseph on the 18th day
of March, 1909, and in the celebration my aunt took me with them over to El

Sasco, Arizona, and I just being with them in Sasco four months, and I run away from them because my aunt whip me because a woman was playin' with me. That woman name is Antonia, wife of one man the name of Guadalupe; they comes to Pascua Village. But they are now living over at Marana.

He was fifteen when this Yaqui woman began "playing with him." It was four years later before he began having regular sexual experiences. He says of his sexual life:

I never was married. I always lived with old women. [Embarrassed grin on Cayetano's part.] First time I live with an old Yaqui woman. Then she leave me and I live for awhile with a Papago woman, an old Papago woman, then she die. Next I live with another Papago woman. I stayed with her a pretty long time.

The relations with Papago women developed during his long residence in Barrio Libre. Although he is familiar with Mexican prostitutes in Tucson, he is disinclined to discuss any experiences with them or any other women in terms of sexual exploits. His attitude in such discussion is rather a passive one. He speaks of a woman as having "got to him" or "playing with him." As he tells it, he is always the passive agent, never the active one. He claims he is not attractive physically to Yaqui women.

As in the case of his associations with Mexicans, he has had many contacts with Papagos during his residence in Barrio Libre other than those with the women with whom he has lived. His father left his mother to live with a Papago woman, and for a brief few weeks Cayetano lived with them when he was about fifteen. He has one half-brother, therefore half-Papago, through this union, whom he visits occasionally at present. He says:

The Papagos in Libre used to have a lot of fiestas, but they have stop all that now. The old people is dying and the young ones don't do that. They drink and they dance with women. They fight a lot. The young ones are worse than the Yaquis. They drink more and they fight more.

But, in general, he thinks the Papagos are good people:

These Yaquis don't know nothing about the Papagos. I live around them for a long time and never have anything to say about them. They are all right. They never bother anybody.

Most significant of Cayetano's intercultural contacts has probably been the experience with the Nolan family in Nogales. It will be recalled that this took place shortly after his mother's death and that the Nolans replaced his Yaqui godfather, Lucas Chavez, as his guardians for a time. For the beginning of this period of close contact with Anglo Americans, we turn to an interview account which represents some of the material already recounted in the autobiography:

Well, Lucas tell me that I was no good in school. I guess he think I was too dumb. And I went to work for Mrs. Nolan. She was a white woman who didn't speak very much Spanish, but her husband Mr. Nolan he speak Spanish very good. Then Mrs. Nolan told Lucas that she was putting me to school and Lucas didn't like that very much and tell me that I would be no good in school. Then he didn't like it when I come home late one night and he beat me. He took all my clothes off and he beat me until my back was all black as that suitcase there. I ran away to Mrs. Nolan's then and I want to tell her what Lucas had done, but I guess she couldn't understand, so she call Mr. Nolan and he come and speak to me in Spanish. This was when I was about eleven years old, I guess. He ask me what I want and I tell him that Lucas had beat me until I was black, and they look at my back and see how it was. Then Mrs. Nolan said that I was going to stay at her house and she started right then to fix a room for me. She put a rug in this room and got a table and then they got a bed and they fix it all up for me. I stay there that night but I told her I was not go to school again, because Lucas didn't want me to go. But then I went to school again and then sometime Lucas come for me. I was afraid for go to him. I was terrible afraid from him for a long time and I not go to live with him again. Lola come for me but I didn't go with her. I lived with Mrs. Nolan for a long time.

For about a year, after a brief residence with a Mexican family to whom he fled once when Lucas came for him at the Nolan's, Cayetano continued to live in his clean little room in the Nolan household. Mr. Nolan had been born in Ireland and had come to the United States while still a boy. He was a bluff, hearty, hard-drinking, kindhearted man, engaged in working his way up to road supervisor on the railroad. Mrs. Nolan was childless, a kindly, warmhearted woman as Cayetano and Lucas remember her. Cayetano lived with the Nolans, learning English, going to school, and coming into contact with middle-class Anglo-American customs. The influence on him at a time when his Yaqui world had disintegrated from around him must have been profound. Why he left has never been revealed in any of the interview material. That it was not painful is indicated in the fact that he has returned frequently to visit up to the time of Mrs. Nolan's death in 1940. Cayetano believes that Mrs. Nolan wanted to leave him some money just before her death. She asked to see him, and he neglected to go until after she died. When he did go, she was buried and Cayetano spent a tearful afternoon in the Nogales graveyard, going first to the well-kept, fenced plot of Mrs. Nolan and then to the weedy heap of orange gravel without even a cross which marked his mother's grave. At each he broke down completely, and before Mrs. Nolan's grave he murmured over and over, "She was a good, good woman."

It is impossible to classify Cayetano's participation in Yaqui political life as either an orientation in Yaqui or in Anglo-American culture. It brought him into intensive contact with both. At the age of twenty-seven, as a man who could read, write, and speak English fluently, Cayetano began to be called on by Libre Yaquis to interpret for them when they were called into court. His behavior at this time and the manner in which he impressed lawyers with whom he had dealings are indicated in an interview already quoted.[2] The lawyer further says of him:

Cayetano used to come with a myriad of small, personal problems—I can't remember what they were all about—but his interests ranged from Litchfield Park (near Phoenix) to Marana. . . . Cayetano would have no respect for office hours. He called me at home a number of times, and one night called me after three A.M. The second time I told him that I had my .38 right there and the next time he called I was going gunning for him. I saw him the next day at the office, but he made no reference to the incident. He was calling up about some ceremony, something he wanted me to do. I never could understand him when he made those night calls; he seemed drunk. He seemed to chant, in English, as he talked.

I was surprised that the Mexican element had not touched Cayetano. If he were acting like a regular Mexican, he would have approached me with a proposition to split the fee, but he never asked me for compensation—even when he worked directly for me in interpreting in jail.

Another funny thing about these Yaquis. I would spend hours with them sometimes in the offices and then would meet them on the street fifteen minutes later, and there would never be a sign of recognition. They would walk right past me, looking straight ahead. Cayetano was not like that, however. He had a firm, brisk handshake. So many foreigners have a soft handshake. He would spot me on the street and as we approached each other he would quicken his pace and come up to me. He would extend his hand and give mine a good shake. He apparently allotted a certain length of time for these casual visits. He would talk with great enthusiasm for a short time and then, "Good-bye, Mr. Allen," and he was off with a click.

Cayetano did not impress all the Anglo Americans so favorably. Some regarded him as a shady character, but in general he impressed the court officials sufficiently to obtain a job as court interpreter and served in this capacity for several years. He was engaged in the prohibition cases by Yaquis caught bootlegging, in insurance-collection cases, in disputes over house lots. He was also recognized as early as 1923 as sufficiently important to be called in as a Yaqui leader in a Chamber of Commerce meeting at which the effort was made to bring Libre and Pascua together, at Pascua, for the Easter ceremonies. Cayetano was then a representative of Barrio

Libre, and he personally refused the fifty dollars which was offered to effect the union of villages.

It was not until 1927 that Cayetano became widely prominent in southern Arizona. In that year Guadalupe Flores entered the country and began promoting his scheme for buying up land in Sonora and shipping the Yaquis back to it. Cayetano heard about the proposal and decided that he himself did not want to leave the United States because "there wasn't anything to do in Sonora. This is the only country we know." He found another Yaqui in Libre who thought as he did, Henry Savala, and the two began talking against Guadalupe Flores among Arizona Yaquis. Cayetano was widely acquainted in Guadalupe, Scottsdale, and the Yaqui villages and made trips to them to talk to Yaquis. Eventually, he was persuaded to write a letter to the governor of the state, saying that there was no general desire on the part of the Yaquis to go back to Sonora. The letter was sent to President Hoover and there was a good deal of publicity in the newspapers:

Then Governor Hunt gave Cayetano a letter in which he said that all the villages would have to elect a chief each. Cayetano came back to Pima County and found that some of the Yaquis of Pascua were for him and some were against him. They went to see a lawyer named Edward Aboud about the matter. He explained that they could make up a resolution and publish it. This they set about doing. They appointed Cayetano chief over his own protest. They made Francisco Valencia assistant chief and gave José Alipas a similar title. Henry Savala was made secretary. Then they embodied what they had done in a resolution and this was sent to Governor Hunt in 1931 and copies were sent to Washington. It was also published in the newspapers. Then Cayetano was officially recognized as chief by the state district attorney, by Mr. Hall of the Immigration Service, by Bailey, the Pima County sheriff, and by the governor.

Thus Cayetano became "chief of the Yaquis." He secured a typewriter, bought a number of law books, and hired a young lawyer to "explain" them to him at fifty cents an hour. But Arizona Yaquis were not interested in chieftainship. Some came to the meetings which were called in each of the villages, but nothing was accomplished. Cayetano began to feel strongly that he was accomplishing nothing and resigned the office to Henry Savala in 1932. Cayetano says of his withdrawal:

I didn't want to be chief when they made me chief in 1931. I told them that I didn't want to do it. I liked to go different places and didn't want to have to stay around and be chief. I told them to get a man who could read and write and talk good English and who had a family. I didn't want it. But they made me chief because I had written a letter to Governor Hunt about Guadalupe Flores. So they elected me chief. I was chief for just one year, but I didn't like it. They didn't trust me [embarrassed grin]. I knew Mr. Scott and the immigration men and I talked with them when Yaquis was deported and some men I got off, but some of them I couldn't and the Yaquis would blame me. They said that I was really shipping men to Mexico just like Guadalupe Flores. Well, there wasn't nothing I could do in lots of these cases. The Yaquis always blamed me. They are saying that I got men deported. That is why I don't like to be chief, because they don't trust me and they are always talking against me.

With Cayetano's resignation the chieftainship became even less important, and finally entirely disappeared with no claimers. We shall have more to say about Cayetano's activities in the office in a later section.

Since abandoning participation in Yaqui political life, Cayetano has also completely abandoned his activities as a Maestro. He claims that he does "not believe in the Yaqui religion anymore." He says:

When I was being a Maestro at first, I used to think that everybody believed that way. I didn't know there was anything else. Well, I began getting around places and I found out different. There was these priests. A man died in Barrio Libre. Mrs. Parker gave the family a good coffin and furnished six cars for the funeral. They drove up to Santa Cruz Cathedral and I went in to see the priest. The priest said it would be $7.50 to have the body brought into the church. I have only one dollar and that family was poor. Then the priest say, "Well, you have nice-looking coffin and a lot of cars there." I said it wasn't none of his business what we had. Then the priest say that it would be $7.50 and if we didn't pay we couldn't have no grave in Holy Hope cemetery. I guess I got mad and I say, "Well, he is only going to sprinkle some water around anyway and I tell that fellows with the coffin to take it back to the hearse. Then the priest say they can have it for a dollar. I never like priests after that. I was only nineteen then, I guess, but I fight with them ever since that time. But I had my First Communion at the Church of the Sacred Heart in Nogales when I was about fourteen.

As he has "been getting around," Cayetano has gone to other churches:

I thought I would try out all these churches around, so I have been going to many of them. I went to different Methodist ones, and some Presbyterians, and this man Morales' Baptists. I go to all of them. The Methodists is about the same as the Presbyterians, but the Baptists acts different from them. They are more friendly and the preacher he talk better. But me and Francisco like to go in to the Pentecostal better, because they don't take up no collection in there.

Although Cayetano no longer attends the Yaqui church where he lives in Pascua, and although he does occasionally visit the Protestant churches, his most frequent attendance at present is at mass on Sunday in the Tucson Catholic churches.

Modes of Thought and Value System

Lacking the intellectual equipment of a Lucas Chavez and the facility of the latter for self-revelation through words, Cayetano Lopez is at once less sure of what he believes and also less clear in his analysis of the world about him. From Lucas one obtains the impression of a rather self-sufficient and positively oriented mind; from Cayetano one obtains the impression of an unorganized mind. His interests, which he appears to discuss no more readily with Yaquis than with Anglo Americans, and his attitudes have a more negative quality than do Chavez's in connection with Yaqui culture. The positive element in Cayetano's thinking is derived from Anglo-American culture.

The starting point in Cayetano's evaluations is an acceptance of Anglo-American values, an acceptance rather than a devotion to them. This passive quality is dominant in him in most respects. His acceptance of Anglo-American values has not, however, resulted in a tendency to identify himself with any group other than the Yaquis. He states repeatedly, as will be recalled, that he has never "forgotten la lengua." This mark of Yaquiness is one which he has never wished to reject. He identifies himself with Yaquis in another way:

Those Yaquis in Pascua always talk against me and say I did bad things to them. But I always try to do good things for them. Don't I have the same blood? Why should I try to do bad things for them?

He recognizes that he has lived out among Mexicans more than most Yaquis, but he also points out that he has never claimed to be a Mexican out of economic or other motives:

That ——— ——— has got to telling them in Tucson that he is a Mexican when they ask him. I never tell anybody I'm a Mexican because I never be anything but a Yaqui.

Throughout his period of disaffection with Yaquis, during the past ten years (1931–1941), he has continued to live in Pascua and thereby to identify himself with Yaquis more effectively in the eyes of Anglo Americans than at any previous period in his life, for Pascua is preeminently the Yaqui center in the view of Anglo Americans.

This identification with Yaquis, as in the case of Lucas Chavez, however, does not mean at all an acceptance of Yaqui culture. His rejection of many of the most significant of Yaqui cultural values is revealed in his discussions of his chieftainship:

Well, when I got to be chief they came to me and they said we want to have the old customs. We want to take the man we catch in bad things on Good Friday and tie them to a cross like we used to. Well, I told them that they was not to do that. I said that I had been to Governor Hunt and that I talked with him and to American judges and asked them about it and they had told me what Americans can do. Then I said that these things were not what the Americans do and they don't want us to do them. We are in America and we have to do what they want us to do. I told them that they couldn't tie men to crosses and do those things. So they didn't like me. I just told them what American judges had told me. I just say that this was a shame thing to whip men on Good Friday like they want to do according to the old customs. That was all I tell them, but they get mad with me and it got worse and worse. So then in 1932 I quit being chief. I never want to be that anyway. Because they always fight with themselves.

Here perhaps he indicates a rejection of Yaqui customs for reasons of practical expediency in relations with whites. But his disapproval of the older customs goes deeper than that:

The trouble is they have things like the Pascolas. And these Pascolas go to fiestas and they are always talking dirty. They are telling these things about getting to women. This is a bad thing. The Yaquis say it is an old custom and that it is what they used to do and they go on doing it. But it is making them all bad. My best friend was Francisco Valencia and he was a Pascola but he never talk that I hear at home about these thing and he not go and tell Felix [his young son] all these bad things. He was a good man. He tell Antonio and Carmen [his wife] when he die in the hospital to take good care of me just like he always done for me. He take the best care of me all the time and I was always have bad luck in everything. I never have no family to live with. Well, these Pascolas always say bad things and that is why everybody is living bad. I tell them when I was chief that I want to stop these Pascolas because they was bad and that is why they don't like me.

He feels also that the Maestros are a bad influence, somewhat in the category of the Catholic priests whom he regards as money-grubbers:

I learn them [the Maestro skills] from a man who die in 1916. He was a good Maestro, not like these men who try to do it now. He knew everything and I learn some from my mother before she die. They were good and know how to do it. My mother was a big Cantora in Torim and used to sing with the priests. These Maestros don't know how. Puri [present Maestro Mayor of Pascua] has a big book and so does Anastasio [a prominent itinerant Maestro living in Pascua], but these books are in Latin and they read them and they don't understand them. José María García [former Maestro Mayor of Pascua] was the same way.

One of the Yaqui customs, that of ceremonial participants taking the excess food from a fiesta table, has embarrassed him:

That's what make me ashame. I ashame for that. They not suppose to do that. Once there was a lot of Matachinis dancing at San Xavier [on the Papago Reservation] and the chiefs of the Papagos say that they want to give them to eat. So they set a table with a lot of food and the Matachinis go over and sit down but there was not enough room for them at the table. So they begin to pass out cups of coffee and food to the Matachinis who was standing there. This made the Papagos mad. Then the Matachinis was putting the bread from the table in their shirts. They reached over and pulled it to them and made their shirts full of it and kept on passing out any food to other Yaquis. The Papagos didn't like this and they don't feed the Yaquis like that anymore.

Much like Lucas Chavez, Cayetano maintains the attitude that present-day Yaquis are not behaving properly. Much more than Lucas, Cayetano censures their sexual mores when talking with Anglo Americans:

The young boys and girls is always going and getting together. They do that when they have fiestas. That is the first thing they do around midnight. The trouble is their mothers and fathers don't tell them nothing. They ought to explain to them what to do, but they don't do that.

There is boys like this Dolores Escalante. He go to high school and everything, but he is still think like those old people. He hear what they have to say all the time. When those Matachinis is dancing he can't keep from it. He have to dance and he is dancing all the time, but he go to high school just the same. He ought to understand what he read in the books, but he is like those other Yaquis. He read and just go over it. He ought to think what it say in those books.

The trouble is they don't read nothing and nobody explain it to them. Morales [the Baptist preacher] he pass out Bibles and other books, but those Yaquis don't read nothing. They take the books home and throw them away, that's what they do. Morales ought to explain things to them but he don't do nothing. He just give them a few prayers and that is what they already got.

Unlike Lucas, Cayetano does not refer back to a standard of reference in an earlier period of Yaqui culture which can be regarded as more nearly perfect. The Pistola period means nothing to Cayetano, although he regards Pistola as a very "good man, because he put many flowers on my mother's grave." Nor is there any tendency whatever on the part of Cayetano to consider the Yaquis of Sonora as at any time better than Arizona Yaquis. His major political activity, it will be remembered, was based on the conviction that Arizona Yaquis had nothing to gain by a return to Sonora. He has inquired about life in Sonora from recent immigrants and says that they all tell him, "The Yaquis down there is all just the same as here." Cayetano also has, like many other Arizona Yaquis, a knowledge of various recent events on the Yaqui River, particularly concerning crimes and court trials. He recounts at length a murder case involving a Yaqui woman who had lived in Arizona until 1922. She murdered an unfaithful husband and made use of her son as an accomplice. Both she and the son were convicted of the murder and executed. Cayetano, in common with others in Arizona, feels strongly that the son should not have been executed. In summing up the case, he says:

Those Yaqui peoples down there did wrong. They have old rules that they do things by in the old way. We know that it was wrong what they did.

Lacking much background in Yaqui history, he is unsympathetic with the hatreds of the older people. He says that he knew nothing "about the Yaqui business" (meaning the gun-running which took place in the early part of the twentieth century from Arizona and the motives behind this activity) until he was about twenty. He says also that he is "tired of hearing these old Yaqui peoples talk about what happened in Sonora. They do better to forget all about it."

There is a constant note of frustration in all of his accounts of ceremonial and political participation in Yaqui affairs. He says repeatedly that "those Yaquis won't never do the right thing. You can't tell them what is the right thing to do. That is why I quit being chief." Again and again he ends up the telling of an incident during his chieftainship with the remark, "Now they are against me." He described his efforts to tell "them what they have to do in the United States because they is here in this country, but they don't want to hear me. So they get so they don't trust me, just because I try to tell them what is right." He believes in the final analysis that "there is nothing to do" about it. He says of his discontinuance of his Maestro's duties: "They don't never ask me anymore. How I do that, when they never come and ask me to."

Notes on Personality

Cayetano is seen by other Yaquis as *muy coyote*, that is, as a man who cannot be trusted in any deal involving money. He is thought by a majority of the younger men to have cheated in favor of himself in most of the insurance and court cases in which he has been involved with Yaquis. There are many stories in Pascua and Barrio Libre concerned with shady deals in which Cayetano has participated. We have seen that Anglo Americans who have come in contact with him have had a similar impression, but the only Anglo American who has had extensive legal dealings with him did not have such an impression. It seems certain that whether or not he actually has been dishonest (and the writer is inclined to believe that he has merely been careless) he is not trusted by Yaquis generally. He has, moreover, never gotten along with Yaquis with whom he has lived for any length of time. His life is a series of movings from one household to another, a few months or a year with relatives or godparents or compadres, then a shift and a few more months in another household. His longest residence in one household seems to have been in Pascua from 1931 to 1940, and in this case his friend Francisco Valencia built him a separate one-room house of his own. This repeated inability to adjust himself to any intimate domestic group for any length of time must be taken into account in any analysis of Cayetano.

At present Cayetano's manner is one of submissive diffidence. He defers and submits to Lucas Chavez, for example, obeying Chavez's command that he accompany him on an expedition to Nogales even though Cayetano had made a definite resolve not to go because he had no clean clothes to wear in which to visit Mrs. Nolan. His submissive attitude is apparent not only with a godparent who had a legitimate claim to deference, but also with all Anglo Americans, and in company with other Yaquis he is disinclined to assert himself. He submits to the wishes of Anglo Americans to the point of making himself an object of ridicule, as the following example will indicate:

The schoolteacher at Pascua had told some Presbyterian friends who wanted to have "an Indian dance" at a church social that they should get hold of Cayetano as interpreter and he would help them find someone who would perform the dance. The two men came out and found Cayetano and told him what they wanted. Cayetano said that he knew no one who would want to dance and then attempted to leave them. The men were insistent and began telling Cayetano that he himself would do. Cayetano grinned embarrassedly and said nothing. He tried to tell them that his friend Francisco Valencia was a professional Pascola Dancer and would dance for them. Francisco appeared, immediately dominating the group, and told the men, through Cayetano, that he did not wish to dance. His answer was definite and the men felt it for they said no more to him. But they had become aware of Cayetano's softness and spent a half hour making foolish gyrations and persuading Cayetano. Finally, Cayetano gave in, went in to the party in an old blanket and gave a little meaningless dance. The men said afterward that "Cayetano was a natural clown and they had laughed themselves sick over him."

Cayetano thus gives indications in most of his relationships of never being certain about what he wants to do and ready to be persuaded to do anything at all.

He has been drinking with increasing frequency for the past ten years. He customarily goes on a two- or three-day spree at the end of each two-week pay period, spending most of his pay during the course of it. He becomes fawning and affectionate when drunk, never loud or aggressive. He often turns up at a fiesta after midnight or in the early morning and stands unobtrusively, swaying by one of the mesquite-root fires. He tries to buttonhole a person and talks endlessly to him.

When he is sober, Cayetano keeps very much to himself in the village. He never visits around, although young men often seek him out in his little house to talk with him. With the young men he is not silent, but he speaks most frequently in reply to questions and generally keeps in the background. He never attends a public ceremony except when drunk and then ordinarily remains for only a few minutes or an hour. Since Valencia's death he lacks any close associates. When working, he is lethargic and complains of being sleepy most of the time. His typical attitude is one of complete relaxation, sprawled on a bench in the shade of his little house. He has a passion for sending notes to people to ask a favor instead of appearing in person himself.

Interpretation of Cayetano's Relation to Yaqui Culture

Cayetano's personality is of a kind eminently adapted to successful attainment of status in Yaqui society. He possessed the capabilities which enabled him to attain skill in the Maestro profession; he was, in fact, outstanding in this ability and was recognized by Yaquis generally as exceptional. He had the ability to speak at length in public meetings. He had a passive tendency, which made him shrink from public office, and he even found it painful to be singled out for leadership. He had no tendency to individualize himself and act alone in any capacity; he worked effectively only in the company of others. All of these characteristics indicate his temperamental suitability to Yaqui culture, and they did, in fact, result in his attaining a high status in that culture. This being the case, how does it happen that in his later life he has ceased to participate in the society at the level of his abilities and feels himself that he no longer participates even mentally in the culture?

One answer to this question is to be found in the unique set of circumstances which brought him into exceptionally close contact with Anglo-American culture. His experience with the Nolans was of profound influence in his development. Coming as it did at a time when his Yaqui associations had become actively unpleasant and his mother no longer constituted a link with Yaqui culture, he absorbed the Anglo-American values of the Nolan household and has never since relinquished them. Unlike Lucas Chavez, his separation from Yaqui culture began long before he was rejected in actual fact by Yaquis; Lucas's strictures on modern Yaqui culture seem to proceed largely from his frustration in status attainment within the limits of that culture. Cayetano brought Anglo-American values to his "chieftainship," which resulted merely in acquainting Yaquis publicly with the gulf between himself and them. His opposition to the Pascolas and his objection to inhumane punishments proceeded from his basic Anglo-American point of view. Public insistence on these non-Yaqui values marked him in the eyes of other Yaquis as a person apart from them.

Moreover, Cayetano's interest in social status has never been highly developed. He differs sharply in this from Lucas Chavez. Cayetano has been motivated by a desire for acceptance by others; his drive has been toward conformity. He has honestly avoided prominence, and when it came to him he was unable to bear it. It may be thought that his insistence on the abolition of old Yaqui customs when he was chief indicates an independence and resolution at odds with any drive toward conformity. His actions in that case are, it appears, rather to be explained on the basis of his clear awareness of Anglo-American viewpoints and his strong desire as representative of Yaquis to conform and to have his associates conform to Anglo-American desires. His motivation here was consistent with his usual tendencies. It was the cultures which remained inconsistent and which Cayetano was unable to harmonize. The fact that he was unable to harmonize them indicates rather definitely a deeper absorption of the Anglo-American than of the Yaqui point of view. If he had been more culturally Yaqui, he might have understood how to proceed in accordance with Yaqui techniques of persuasion and discussion. His approach, however, was clearly an Anglo-American one. Nevertheless, Yaqui society remains his society, particularly since his withdrawal from the go-between position, and the source of his unhappiness and frustration at present is that he is not accepted by Yaquis. He does not care particularly about status, but he would like to be liked and appreciated. The obvious fact that Yaquis do not understand his intentions and efforts on their behalf is his most often reiterated sorrow.

Why, then, does he not proceed to some extent as Tomás Alvarez and even Lucas have proceeded? That is, why does he not take up his trade as a Maestro in which he had once won the approval of Yaquis and win back that approval? Tomás has worked his way through active disapproving attitudes on the parts of Yaquis to a rather secure status in the society.

Cayetano himself recounts the example of Anastasio Velasquez, the itinerant Maestro, who forced himself into prominence despite the objections of the Fariseo society in Libre. The answer is that Cayetano is too good a Yaqui. He does not want the status; he wants merely the acceptance. He feels unable to force his way back into ceremonial participation unless "the Yaquis ask him to." He is powerless to act without the feeling that there is social approval of his actions. He remains, therefore, utterly frustrated in his dearest wish and utterly prostrate, as a good Yaqui should be, before the wishes of the society.

Is there no form of aggression in response to these frustrations? There is the simple one of verbal assault on Yaquis in the presence of Anglo Americans, an assault which it will be noted takes the form of an attack on Yaqui sexual mores. This again indicates his extreme sensitivity to Anglo-American values. He chooses a weapon which he knows will take with Anglo Americans. Other than this, there is only drinking. But drinking in his case is hardly an aggression; it is purely an escape which permits him to find temporarily the acceptance and sense of liking people that he has always sought. The assault that he constantly wages on Yaqui sexual mores is also an assault on himself, for his own sex life has been lived in constant accordance with Yaqui forms. This again indicates the passive, self-punishing attitude which is dominant throughout his life.

There remains the all-important question of his continuance as a Yaqui. Least of any Yaqui who has so far been considered does Cayetano have reason to remain a Yaqui. He knows the mores of surrounding peoples. He has the linguistic abilities for participation in the surrounding cultures. He has no status to lose by shifting his loyalty. He possesses a sense of inferiority about Yaqui cultural values. He lacks the historical biases of the older Yaquis and feels tolerant and friendly toward surrounding people. Why, then, does he continue as a member of Yaqui society and insist on his identification with Yaquis? The answer probably lies in a historical consideration of his development. It is only in Yaqui society that he has attained acceptance, except for the brief period with the Nolans. If we knew more of the final days there and the circumstances of departure, we might understand better his relations with Anglo-American society. It seems probable that those final days were haunted by a fear of Lucas Chavez that eventually rendered the life too insecure for him. In leaving the Nolans, he was probably eliminating the physical fear of Lucas. His contacts then became Yaqui, and his general acceptance as a Maestro came quickly afterwards. Sixteen years of acceptance as a Yaqui conditioned him irrevocably. It is entirely possible that his sense of persecution and nonacceptance by Yaquis will drive him out of Yaqui society eventually, but it would be necessary that he have a feeling of acceptance in a group somewhere else. There is no group with whom he has been sufficiently identified. He remains powerless to move, meanwhile, for only such group acceptance can move him to action.

Comparisons

Cayetano Lopez is a younger man who has had the unique experience of living in the domestic household of an Anglo-American family. This has colored his life deeply, and hence a study of him gives us valuable information about the relations of cultures in southern Arizona. However, we cannot permit Cayetano to stand as our only example of the younger Yaqui men. In this section we will consider four other Yaquis under the age of forty, some born in the United States, some born in Sonora. We will present their lives briefly, including only a selection of material which seems most relevant to the study in hand.

Refugio Savala

In Refugio Savala we have a man of high intellectual ability whose participation in the more formal institutions of Yaqui society has been minimal, but whose acquaintance with and understanding of Yaqui cultural traits is unusually extensive. We have in him an example of a person saturated in Yaqui culture who paradoxically has moved outside of Yaqui society more than most younger Yaquis. The facts of his life may shed some light on this paradox.

Refugio is thirty-seven years old, having been born in 1904 in Magdalena, Sonora. His mother was a Yaqui, born in one of the Yaqui River towns, who escaped, after the fighting of the 1880s, to Hermosillo and then to Magdalena. His father, Martín, spent all his boyhood and young manhood on the Yaqui River, in the vicinity of Torim and later at Cocorit. During the battles which Cajeme led, Martín in the company of other young men did not fight, but remained in the Bacatete Mountains living off the country. At the age of thirty-five, he was a "member of the council" at Cocorit, a title the meaning of which is not clear. He left the Yaqui country in the early nineties at the age of forty in order to escape capture and shipment to Yucatán. After a short period in the vicinity of Magdalena, he left for Arizona, taking his wife with him, and got a job on the railroad between Nogales and Benson. Refugio had been born in Magdalena when his mother returned to her maternal relatives' household so as to have Refugio under their care. A few weeks after Refugio was born, there was a round-up of Yaquis in the Magdalena region and his mother was caught in the net. The family legend has it that she pled recent motherhood and so softened the jailer's heart that he let her, alone of all the Yaquis in the round-up, go free to take care of Refugio. It was a year, during which she existed by selling tortillas on the streets of Magdalena, before Martín was able to find them and take them back to the United States in a burro cart.

Refugio grew up in section houses at Patagonia, Benson, and finally Tucson. In 1921 he and his mother took up residence in Pascua Village as one of the first families to move in under the aegis of Juan Pistola. Martín lived with them for awhile, but then moved to Barrio Libre where he lived until he died in 1932. Refugio went to the Catholic parochial school and later to public schools in Tucson and also night school, completing about the equivalent of the second year of high school. In his late teens he went to work for the Southern Pacific and has continued as a railroad laborer ever since, with only occasional excursions into cotton picking.

There was no break-up of Refugio's family until he had reached adulthood. His relations with his parents were warm and affectionate. He remembers his mother especially with great affection. She had a great deal of charm, so much that Yaqui and also Mexican women came daily to Refugio's house to chat with her wherever they were living. She told stories of life on the Yaqui River, which Refugio listened to and remembered later and wrote down in English. She knew some Spanish, but preferred to speak in Yaqui and so Yaqui was the language of Refugio's homelife. When she died, Refugio felt "a great loss" and described his feelings in an English poem of despair. Refugio's father was a man of great mental energy, who taught himself to read and write Spanish at the age of fifty in order to be able to keep accounts for himself and other Yaquis who had had unsatisfactory dealings with a Mexican-American storekeeper at Patagonia. He also talked a great deal to Refugio about his life on the Yaqui River, about which Refugio said:

My brothers never used to listen to my father talk like I did. I would even ask him to tell me the stories sometimes because I liked to hear them. But my brothers didn't never listen like that. They were just like the Mexican kids. They thought

that they knew more than my father did and they would run away just as soon as he began to talk.

But Refugio's most intensive contact with old Yaqui culture came through a visit of his mother's uncle to Arizona when Refugio was about thirteen. He explains:

That was Loreto Hiami. I guess he must have been my grandfather, no, he was my uncle, because he was my mother's uncle. He used to tell me so much things I couldn't get it all. I used to ask him questions. By God, I would make a lot of questions, because it was hard for me to understand. I was just a kid. There was so much for me to get in one year. He came up from the Yaqui River when I was about thirteen. He walked all the way up to Tucson. There was a bunch of men that came together and he was very old, but he wanted to come up and walked all that way. He came up here when we was living in Barrio Anita there by the place where the flume comes out. He came over to our house and my mother was there.

He says, "Don't you know who I am, *nana* (which is like *hija* in Spanish) and she says, "No, *hapchi*, I don't know you." Then he told her to look at him harder and he told her his name. Then my mother was sitting down, but by God she got up quick and she went over and put her arms around him. She knew who he was right away. He said that he guessed he would stay a couple of months but he stay with us for a year. He was a great warrior down there and he used to tell us everything. ... So I listen to old Loreto all the time and then I used to go out and tell the kids those stories. I would be playing ball or something in the evening and I would say, "Come on, boys, I bet I can tell you a story you won't understand." Then they would listen to me and I would tell that one about Jesus, Mary, and Joseph and the hierarchy of angels. They used to like it and sometimes they would ask me to tell it the next night and I wouldn't mind, because I liked to get it in my head. That was what I was trying to do. So I was telling those stories of Loreto's a lot then.

Loreto awakened Refugio to a tradition which his parents had not given him. Refugio says that his mother "didn't know a thing about the Bible stories. She would get me to tell her about Joseph and she would listen." She and Martín had had little contact with organized ceremonial life and the Christian tradition that went with it on the Yaqui River. They seem to have been "country people" rather than town dwellers until late in Martín's life. They had told Refugio the Yaqui myths of the great bird monster and the boy monster slayer, the story of the talking stick and Sea Hamut the translator of it, the story of the old woman of the sea called Yomumule, and the other myths little touched by Christianity. Loreto, however, was full of the Yaqui-ized versions of the marriage of Joseph and Mary and the birth of Jesus through Mary's contact with a flower. He described to Refugio the old Yaqui version of the meeting in the heavens between God and the morning and evening stars before the decision to send Jesus to earth. These awakened a deep interest in Refugio which has continued; he is still at work in odd moments at putting the stories into both English verse and prose.

When Refugio was about seven, after the family had come to Tucson, he was ill and his mother promised him to serve in the Matachin society. She did not think that he was very ill, and so she promised him for only three years. When he recovered he served in the society and danced Matachin for the three years. Since that time he has never participated in any of the ceremonial societies and has had no formal contact with Yaqui ceremonial organization. His father, however, was instrumental in bringing him into touch with Yaqui culture in another way. His father had been a harpist in Cocorit, and at Pascua and Libre he played his harp for the Pascolas whenever he was called on. He took Refugio around with him to the fiestas and Refugio sat in the Pascola ramadas and watched the dancers. He

became familiar with the music and the songs and the dances of the Pascolas. He has been interested for the past three years in recording in English
the sermons given by the Pascolas, and he has written out in English prose
the little dramas that the Pascolas formerly gave as well as typical stories of
exaggeration and humor that the Pascolas tell. His continued participation
in Yaqui culture is not the result of any formal obligations established by
his parents or other relatives or by himself, but rather a result of a personal interest, which quite evidently springs from his early contacts with
his parents and Loreto Hiami.

During the depression in 1929 and 1930, Refugio's family was on relief,
and Refugio could find no work. He began writing poetry and prose in
Spanish, Yaqui, and English, and during a five-year period produced some
hundred and fifty pages of original composition. During this period, he
fell in love with a Yaqui girl in Pascua. He used to wait for her in the evenings underneath a cottonwood tree north of the village. He wrote poems
in Spanish about this tree, not about the girl. After two years of happy
meetings with her she became pregnant. Refugio built himself a small
house in Pascua, and the girl came to live with him. The baby was born
and died almost immediately. The girl refused to stay with him. Refugio
was grief-stricken for several years after she left him. He told friends in
Pascua that he "wished to die." He wrote a poem which began:

> There was a night of deadly melancholy
> And I could see only that one called Death.
> She was there and looked like an angel
> And I was going to follow along with her.

He turned with more determination to writing the story of Jesus, Mary,
and Joseph in verse. He finished a large portion of it. One stanza ended:

> Jesus with infinite patience
> Waited for blessed death.

Then his mother died in 1932 and he felt that he "could no longer stay in
Pascua." He became an itinerant, working his way throughout the Southwest, riding freights up the West Coast, being impressed to fight forest
fires, working with extra gangs, and cooking for himself on the railroad.
A Mexican girl hobo liked him and traveled with him for a while. Always
the poet, he writes now of women:

To love a woman is the same as to love God. When you love a woman you go
to her and tell her everything. You admit all your mistakes to her. This is just the

same as you do when you confess to God. But loving a woman is different from loving a man. A woman has a hold on you that is different and once you have been with her, she will always have this hold on you because you will get to thinking of her and will go to her. She doesn't have to do anything at all to make you come back to her.

His experiences have made him subscribe to an old Yaqui custom:

I used to be with Juan Pistola's wife a lot down there in Barrio Anita. She was just fifteen and Juan Pistola was about seventy. She was just a kid. She used to have dolls in the house there when she was married. She was a good woman in every way. I used to go up and light the candles at their house and we used to read together. Juan Pistola didn't care. She was just a kid. She was sure young, but you know how it is with those Yaquis in those things. The first come the first served maybe you would say. There was a lot of those marriages all the time and, by God, those are always the best ones. Always, by God. When a man come into a village and he can make the marriage right away, there is always a girl which is given to him. And by God, those are good marriages. But whenever a boy marry his girlfriend they always go wrong. Maybe they wouldn't ever know each other before, but they always got to be happy marriages. Dolores [Pistola's wife] was just a Yaqui woman, she wasn't trying to fix anything. She just made a pigtail out of her hair, she wasn't fixing it up.

Refugio's contacts with other cultures have been extensive and even intimate. He has studied grammar and dictionaries and read textbooks of English literature, though, as he points out, at present he is reading only the "comic magazines" because that is all you find around the section houses. He was encouraged in his writing by the Pascua schoolteacher, about whom he says, "I ought to have written a poem about her because she was doing so much for my family in the depression, but I guess I forgot to do that." Refugio finally developed a very good ability in speaking English as a result of working with a railroad gang of Negroes with whom he "got along fine. They was talking easy and taught me all the time." His living in intimate contact with the gang of Negro laborers he remembers as one of his most pleasant experiences.

He has lived a great deal in the company of Mexicans in the course of his railroad work and has no feeling of hatred for them, such as the older Yaquis have. He believes that the poor Mexicans suffered as much as the Yaquis in Sonora at the hands of the "rich ones." He writes poems recalling the suffering of his mother at Magdalena and the injustice which the Yaquis in general felt at the hands of the Mexicans, but he is more inclined to see this period of upheaval in Sonora as a struggle between the rich and poor rather than between Yaquis and Mexicans. Yet he uses the Yaqui stereotype of the Mexican almost as freely as any older man. He says, for example, concerning modern Yaqui boys:

Those Yaqui kids are getting to be just like Mexicans. They don't stay around when their fathers get to talking. They don't listen to them. They just run off and think their fathers don't know anything—just like Mexicans.

Wherever Refugio goes in his travels, he stops to seek out Yaquis and stay with them for a while: His visits are looked forward to with pleasure by his Yaqui relatives in Yuma, where he stops occasionally and stays long enough to write out a few alabanzas for his uncle to use in his duties as a burial official for Yuma Yaquis. When Refugio comes back to Tucson, he stays with his half-brother in Pascua or Libre and drinks with Yaqui friends rather than with Mexican. He thinks of himself very definitely as a Yaqui and shows no tendency to lose his identity in the Mexican-American population.

Refugio possesses none of the negative attitudes toward Yaqui values or Yaqui society that are shown by Cayetano Lopez. His only antipathy is toward the institution of "chieftainship." He says:

In Arizona the Indians don't want chiefs because this has been the cause of their separation in Tucson into the north and south sides. It has been similar in the Salt River Valley. There shouldn't be chiefs and it probably happen that when a Yaqui tell you he is chief, he isn't one.

Refugio's criticisms of Yaquis are never couched in the general terms characteristic of Cayetano, but they always refer to specific individuals. He does not object to Yaqui sexual mores; in fact, he shows no consciousness of their being different from any other peoples'. He is very far from feeling ashamed of the Pascolas. Instead he has a vivid interest in them:

I always listen whenever I can to that morning Pascola sermon, because I want to hear just exactly how he say it. That has many beautiful things in it. He speak of the people staying through the night and hope that they have been enjoying themselves all the time. He apologize for everything he say that might have hurt anybody and he ask pardon and say that all what he say be in pure fun.

He has studied the Pascola ritual intensively and probably knows as much about it as any Yaqui in Pascua, including the Pascolas themselves. He knows less about other aspects of the ceremonial, but returns to Pascua for the Easter ceremonies and finds the old Yaqui explanation of the Cha-payekas as "soldiers made ugly because they work harm to Jesus" very satisfying and even "beautiful." Refugio observes his kinship obligations scrupulously, even to the point of impoverishing himself temporarily to contribute to a second cousin's funeral. He says that whenever he comes to a new town, he always goes first to the Catholic Church, because he says:

My father was a very customary man and he would always do that. I cannot deny that I am a Catholic because my family was always that way. But I guess you would say maybe I don't have no religion. There are certain things which if you are a Catholic you have to do. But if you don't do them, life is just the same and nothing happens.

He says that he went through a period, just after his "failure as a lover," when he was mixed up and didn't understand "the correct things." He says:

I was writing in those days and I didn't know enough to understand about God. My head wasn't big enough to take Him in. What I wrote that time I do not like to think about now. I wish to ignore it. It was that time when I want to die. I saw Death like an Angel in my dream. She was like a pretty lady and I kept after her. Then I went on to talk about God. I say that I do not know Him. I know only about some who have know Him. I mean those prophets. I say that I do not know Him myself. I write those things because I could not yet understand. It was like imagination and I saw it that way and just wrote it down when it came. But in the end I say something about asking the pardon of God for what I wrote.

In those days of creative activity he had the feeling of tapping a spiritual world outside himself. Even his agnosticism seemed to come from that world to him. He still has that sense of being in touch with a world outside himself, from which his poems and many thoughts come. He describes it in old Yaqui terms:

It is like prayer because the songs are inspired. They [the Deer songs] come from the wilds—just like when you dream. When you dream you go to a place of nature. Nature is the source of inspiration—and prayer. The songs are about nature and were inspired by natural objects. Therefore, the songs are like prayers.

Refugio would seem to be as much a Yaqui culturally as anyone we have described. His conflicts are not cultural ones, but those of a sensitive man frustrated by the ordinary events of living, such as death, disappointment in love, and the difficulties of making a living. He has never been interested in social status but remains entirely outside the world of status either in his own or any other society. His devotion to Yaqui culture is to be explained only in terms of the devotion of any man to what he has been brought up with and knows something about. Why is he not subject to the disaffection of men like Cayetano and Lucas? Perhaps merely because of his insensitivity to status. He is the creative man who loves whatever is before him, and for its own sake.

Jesús García

Jesús García is a mixed blood who shows his ancestry in his physical characteristics. His skin is a yellowish-gray, very light in color. He is spoken of universally in the village as *huero* (blond), and he is sometimes spoken of as not a Yaqui, but "half-Mexican."

The father of Jesús was "a Mexican," but he left the household and died before Jesús was three years old, and consequently, Jesús has no memory of him. The mother was a Yaqui woman living in Santa Ana, Sonora. As soon as the Mexican deserted her, she began to live with a Yaqui from Cocorit, José María Casillas, but continued to assign the Mexican's surname to her son by him. When Jesús was six years old, the family, driven by fear of the raids in the Santa Ana region against Yaquis, put their belongings in a wagon and headed north. They crossed the line somewhere on the Papago Reservation, ran across a mine which had just been opened, secured work in connection with it, and settled down for two years there on the reservation. This was in the year 1904.

In 1906 the family moved to Tucson and got work on a ranch just north of the city, Tierra Floja, as it was called. Other Yaquis joined them there and the ranch became a center for Yaquis in north Tucson. In 1909 it was Jesús' stepfather who opened a new era in Yaqui culture by getting a permit from the Tucson sheriff to hold the Easter ceremonies. The ceremonies were held for the first time in the Tucson region at his house, and the young son Jesús, eleven years old, served as a Fariseo. José María continued to promote the Easter ceremonies, uniting south and north Tucson Yaquis at his house annually for several years, yet he himself never held an office in connection with the ceremonies.

Jesús went on for ten more years living with his parents, his two younger brothers, and two younger sisters, full-blood Yaquis. He never worked on the railroad, but always as a ranch hand, and he says that it would be impossible for him to change: "I always got to work on the ranches, because that is the only kind of work I know." He was notably promiscuous as a young man. Eventually, however, at the age of twenty-nine, he married a Mexican girl and settled down with her in Pascua, building himself a new board house. He has had five children by her, and they have continued to live together. They have, however, turned their house over to her Mexican parents, and they live with Jesús' stepfather, who is now a widower, in his large house in Pascua. Their time is divided between a cotton ranch sixty miles north of Tucson and Pascua. The summer and autumn months they spend on the cotton ranch, the winter and spring in Pascua during the Fariseo season and after.

Jesús' stepfather is described by other Yaquis as "muy Yaqui," a phrase frequently applied to a person who is at home in no language except Yaqui and is therefore reticent in his contact with Anglo Americans and even Mexican Americans. José María was born in Cocorit of Yaqui parents who owned an exceptionally large tract of land near Rajum. They were wealthier than most river Yaquis until the early 1880s when, as Jesús says, "the Mexicans came in and stole the land." José María's father then fought in Cajeme's army until he was killed just before the battle of Buatachive. José María, at the age of seventeen, came to Magdalena and lived on an hacienda there among Yaquis. He is typical of the ranch-raised Yaqui as contrasted with the Yaquis who have worked on the railroads. He speaks Spanish very poorly and with difficulty and is devoted to old Yaqui customs. He spends his time now as an old man carving Pascola masks, making harps, and occasionally (although he is too old for much of it) serving as a harpist at Pascola Dances. The only village office which he has ever held in Sonora or Arizona is that of Pascola harpist. We have no information about the Yaqui woman who was Jesús' mother, except that she was also "muy Yaqui."

Jesús lived as the oldest son in this strongly Yaqui family. His mixed parentage has always been widely known, but there is no evidence of either discrimination against him or favoritism in the family. His father promised Jesús first to the Matachin society and then to the Fariseo society. In each, Jesús rose to prominence. He danced for many years in north Tucson as a Malinche and developed sufficient skill in the dance to become a Monarca, leading the dances. In accordance with Yaqui custom, he has gradually discontinued Matachin dancing since his marriage, feeling that he has fulfilled his manda. He says, however, that the chief reason why he no longer dances is that he simply doesn't feel like it after working all day. He has served in the Fariseo society since he was eleven years old, being one of the youngest Fariseos at the time of the revival of the Easter ceremonies. He is recognized as one of the two ablest and most experienced men in the society and serves each year in the capacity of Chapayeka Ya'ut, that is, as leader and coordinator of all the Chapayekas. His leadership here, however, is a result of skill in clowning and pantomime, and he is not thought

of as timber for administrative head of the whole society. He attempted
once to learn Pascola dancing, but his teacher went away and he lost interest. His brothers have also been promised to and served in the Fariseo
society. The atmosphere of his father's household has been one of active
interest in Yaqui ceremonial life, and each member has been a participant
throughout his or her life, but none has distinguished himself beyond the
sort of leadership which Jesús has achieved.

Jesús was popular with and much favored by the Yaqui girls of Pascua,
but his marriage with a Mexican-American girl has been and remains a
thoroughly stable one. The family has lived either in Pascua or on the ranch
where there are four households of Yaquis ever since the marriage. Both
Spanish and Yaqui are spoken in Jesús' home, he preferring Yaqui, the
wife preferring Spanish, although she understands everything that is said
in Yaqui. The children have been sent to Tucson and other schools, and
they speak English, Spanish, and Yaqui readily. As the boys have grown
up they have been promised to the Fariseo and Matachin societies and are
now serving in those societies. Jesús remains devoted to his father and has
been supporting him for a number of years.

It is noticeable that Jesús has more Mexican-American associates in his
leisure hours in Pascua than other Yaquis of his age. He has entered into
numerous compadre relationships with Mexican Americans, and he fre-
quents the houses of his wife's friends in Barrio Libre. Yet his identification
with Yaquis is unmistakable. He maintains Yaqui as the language of his
homelife, has always lived in Yaqui villages or among Yaqui families on
ranches, and participates regularly in Yaqui ceremonies. He speaks often
with feeling of the injustice done by Mexicans to his stepfather's family.
There is no indication of a derogatory attitude toward Yaquis in any of his
statements or behavior. He makes no use of the Yaqui stereotype of Mexicans. He seems, in other words, to be a well-adjusted Yaqui man who also
maintains considerable Mexican-American relations in which he is also adjusted. His mixed blood is well-recognized, but it carries no implications
of status with it. He is culturally, and to a large extent socially, a Yaqui.

Juan Silvas

More than most Yaquis of thirty-five, Juan Silvas has mastered the techniques of getting along in the Anglo-American economic world, though
he is not better off financially than his neighbors. His knowledge of Anglo-
American ways and attitudes is extensive. Yet he has identified himself with

Juan Silvas, January 1937.
*Photograph by Rosamond B.
Spicer.*

Yaqui culture in one of the most usual and normal Yaqui ways. The contradictions of his life are perhaps more typical of his age group than in the
cases of the young men that we have discussed so far.

Juan Silvas was born in Oro Blanco, Arizona, near Nogales. His father
was a Yaqui from Potam, a retiring man who has served in Pascua for
many years as a Moro for the Deer Dancers. Juan's mother was also a
Yaqui. Juan, however, was with his parents very little during his boyhood.
His mother died while he was still an infant. He ran away from his father
when he was eight or nine years old, lived for a time with his father's
brother-in-law, a Mayo, and then struck out on his own when he was not
more than twelve years old. He worked as a waterboy on the railroad near
Phoenix and gradually took his place as a track laborer. He worked as a
section hand in southern Arizona and California, in the company mostly
of Mexican Americans.

When he was about twenty, he was seriously injured while at work on
the railroad and was sent to the hospital in Sacramento with a crushed

hip. It was eighteen months before he was able to leave the hospital. Here he learned to speak English very well and had intimate dealings with an Anglo-American lawyer who insisted on pushing a suit against the railroad. The suit was successful and when Juan left the hospital he had $1,500 in his pocket. He also had a manda to serve in the Fariseo society at Pascua. He had thought that he was going to die when he first entered the hospital and immediately promised himself for nine years' service as a Captain of the Fariseos. As he puts it, "I promised that I would help those Yaquis in their religion."

He came back from Sacramento to Tucson and in a few weeks spent all his money, using most of it to buy "clothes for his relatives." Then he began a two-year period of wandering. He says he "was just a hobo," working wherever he could, moving about in New Mexico, Arizona, and California. Tired of wandering he came back to Pascua, married a Mexican girl, and got a job as a truck driver in the city. He says that he "didn't wait around any. I just went to the head of the street department and told him I wanted a job and he gave me one. When they asked me what I was, I always had to tell them I was a Yaqui because I am sort of light-colored and they thought I was maybe a Mexican." Shortly after the birth of a boy, Juan's Mexican wife died, and he sent the boy to be brought up by an aunt in Pascua. Juan wandered about some, but always returned to serve at the Easter ceremonies, where he was made a *Cabo* so as to get training for the fulfillment of his manda as a Captain of Fariseos. He served for the next nine years, thus completing his manda, but was never elected to the captaincy. He refused to serve further at the end of the nine years.

Two years after his Mexican wife died, Juan began to live with a Yaqui woman and has remained with her ever since, having four children by her. He is harsh with her but provides for her well because of his ability at getting himself good jobs that pay a little more than the average job that a Yaqui gets. His aggressiveness in getting work has resulted in his having rather better furnishings than most Yaquis in their houses, including an icebox. But the exterior of his house has the same appearance as the most ill-kept of Pascua wattle-and-daub houses. His treatment of his wife and his periodic drinking have resulted in his incurring the disapproval of the whole village. He is given to aggressive behavior when drinking and often turns up drunk at fiestas in the middle of the night, often causing disturbances. His wife has become a devotee of the Baptist meetings at the schoolhouse, but Juan says he has no interest in what the Baptists say and does not believe that they are telling the truth, "because what they say isn't what Catholics think."

Juan insists on his being a Yaqui, but he has no Yaqui prejudices against Mexicans and makes no use of the Mexican stereotypes. He drinks frequently in the company of young Mexican Americans. He says that he does not like Yaqui ceremonies, particularly weddings, and always speaks, to Anglo Americans at least, rather objectively of "the religion of those Yaquis." However, he has at present a definite interest in the Fariseo society. He feels that he has sufficient knowledge to be made Captain of the society and resents the fact that he has never been given that office, since he was promised by himself to it. He tells Anglo Americans that he would like to be "chief" of the Easter ceremonies and that if he were, he would run them better than the present leaders. He says that the first thing he would do would be to build "a better church." On the occasion when he attends the Easter ceremonies, he observes very carefully the ritual and the procedures, quite evidently with an eye to himself assuming the office of Captain. He is, however, no longer considered even a member of the society because his manda has been fulfilled and he has refused to serve for four or five years. The general opinion of him in the village is that "he drinks too much and never has given a single fiesta." None of his children has been promised to ceremonial service. Still, he has not turned his back on Yaqui ways, and he identifies himself as an active participant in Yaqui life.

The four younger men whom we have considered differ from the older men in certain important respects. They have had more intimate contact with Anglo Americans, they have been to Anglo-American schools, and they speak English. In some instances, they have had less contact with Yaquis during their youth, but in general they do not differ so much from the older men in this respect. Two of them at least have grown up with as much early Yaqui contact with Yaqui communities during their boyhood and young manhood as did the older men, and this is reflected in the fact that all have had longer periods and earlier periods of intensive participation in Yaqui ceremonial life than any of the older men.

The younger men differ from the older in having shown a greater amount of mobility. They have had the ceremonial participation mentioned, but they have also moved out into other communities and have traveled more widely in the United States than the older men. It is an important fact that, despite this mobility, they have all moved back into Yaqui society finally and seem rooted there at present. Lacking in general the older generation's prejudices against Mexicans, they have nevertheless not tended to identify with the Mexican Americans, despite even intermarriage and much closer association with them than the older men.

Not all of them have achieved status in Yaqui society, but it is noticeable that neither have they sought status in any other society. They show in two instances a sensitivity to Anglo-American cultural values, but little interest in status in Anglo-American society.

CHAPTER 7

Women of Pascua

The women of Pascua in many ways repeat in their lives the experiences of the men who have been discussed. The general pattern of the experiences of the older women shows a great similarity to that of the older men. Moreover, some of the younger women show the same mobility that characterizes the younger men, moving in and out of Yaqui society at various times under various circumstances. There are, however, some experiences which are characteristic for the women and do not appear in the sketches of the lives of the men. In this chapter we shall consider the lives of four women from different age groups in an effort to make clear the distinctive female experiences and the relation of these experiences to their present participation in Yaqui culture. The first whom we shall present is the only one of the four whose life carries us back to the Yaqui River pueblos in Sonora.

Case Study of Juana de Amarillas

One of the most consistently active women in the ceremonial life of Pascua is a Cantora whom the people call "Juana Matayaki." She lives in a characteristically fluctuating household, but she, together with a man who is her third consort, remains in the household constituting its focus for

Juana de Amarillas seated
outside her house, 1941.
*Photograph by Rosamond B.
Spicer.*

some four or five others who come and go, including a son-in-law and a
daughter-in-law and the latter's children.

Physical Characteristics

Juana de Amarillas is in 1941 eighty years old. She is about five feet five
inches tall, which is exceptionally tall for a Yaqui woman. Her tallness has
been the source of the nickname that Yaquis have applied to her for many
years—*Bue'u Cantora*—which is to say "Big Singer." She has always been
slender. Her skin is dark in comparison with other Yaquis and now her
face is extremely wrinkled, but her black hair is untinged with gray. She is
and has always been very active physically and possessed of great physical
endurance.

Life History

Juana de Amarillas was born in Bacum, one of the eastern towns on the
Yaqui River, in the year 1861. Her parents were both Yaquis, her father
from Bakum, her mother from Torim. She was promised by her parents to

be a Cantora while she was still a baby, and she served before her marriage as an *Alpes* (church flag-bearer). When not more than fifteen or sixteen her parents arranged for her to marry a young Yaqui named Luis Buitimea in Cocorit. She went to Cocorit to live and immediately began intensive studies as a Cantora, working with the Maestros of Cocorit. She says:

What a hard religion we have! We used to work hard there. I worked with old Lo'i [the man who later became Maestro Mayor of Pascua]. He was a Maestro. There were a lot of Maestros, not just the one. I was a Cantora. There were other Cantoras. We learned to sing because the Maestros taught us. That was all they did. There were Matachinis to teach the young Matachinis, and there were Pastores teaching how to do that. We would go and the Maestros would tell us how to use the voice, just so, like this, you understand. That was hard work, but we went on and I learned how.

Juana had three sons by her first husband, before the fighting began in earnest on the Yaqui River. Then her husband was killed and she was separated from her sons. She lived in Guaymas for a time and then came back to Cocorit where she married another Yaqui. Sometime before 1900 they left the Yaqui River and went to Hermosillo.

Then we came to Hermosillo and that was when I lost my husband. The soldiers took him away. We didn't know anything about what happened to him. He was fighting the pelones somewhere. I don't know where he got killed or whether they sent him to Yucatán or what happened. My son was killed in La Paz. He was taken there by the soldiers. He died and they sent me a paper saying he was dead. That was all I ever knew about it. That was a sad time. That's the way it is in Sonora.

She came across into the United States with another son about 1910 and lived for a while in Nogales, then came to Tucson. She had had six children by her second husband. All but three of these were killed during the fighting before 1910, or were sent out of Sonora and died elsewhere in Mexico.

In Tucson she began to live with another man, Mariano Matus, and has occupied a house with him in Pascua since about 1920. They have had no children, but her son and her daughter lived with her at various times with their families. Her son died a few years ago, and her last surviving daughter, after returning to Potam, died in 1940. Juana has outlived all blood relatives that she knows about.

In Pascua Juana has been an important and active participant in the ceremonial life. She has been a leading Cantora for the past twenty years and still serves in practically every ceremony whether at the church in Pascua or at private households. Every Yaqui speaks of her as Doña Juana, and she is regarded as having one of the most distinguished records of

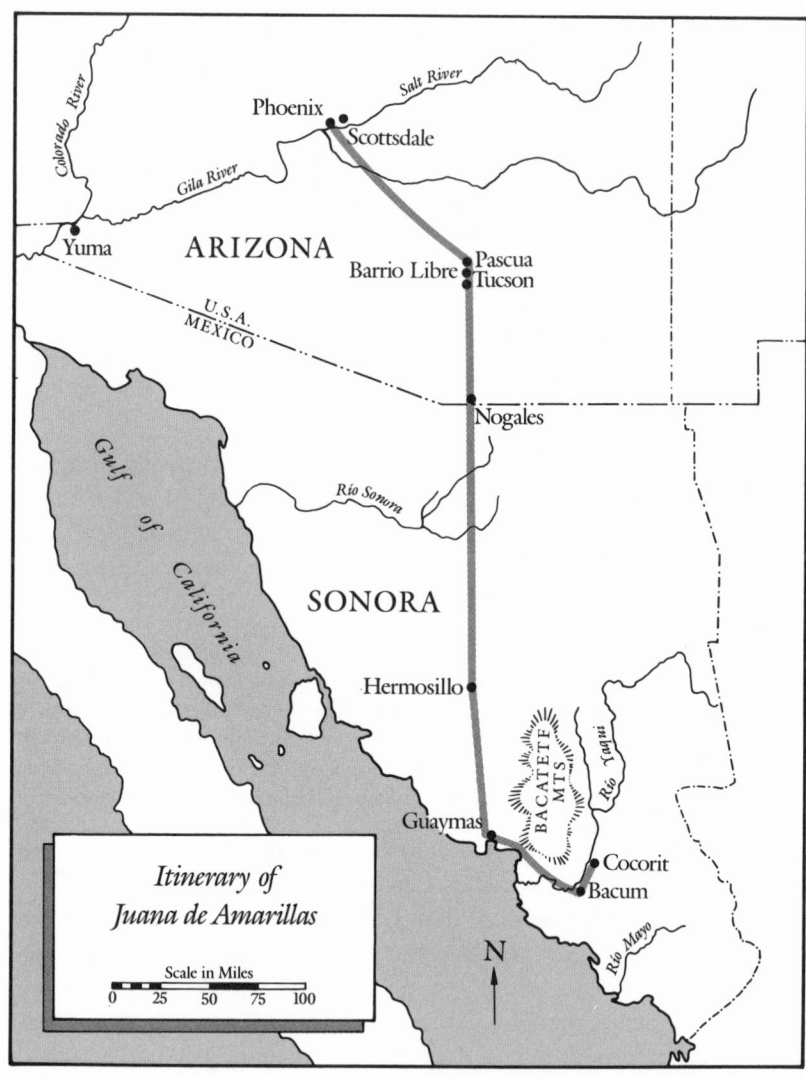

Itinerary of
Juana de Amarillas

Scale in Miles
0   25   50   75   100

N

ceremonial service of any Arizona Yaqui. Her third man, Mariano Matus, died in 1941, leaving her alone in her house in Pascua.

Orientation in Yaqui Society

Juana de Amarillas had a thoroughly Yaqui upbringing in Yaqui communities which had not yet been disorganized through war and social disturbance. She went through the conventional cycle of baptism, dedication

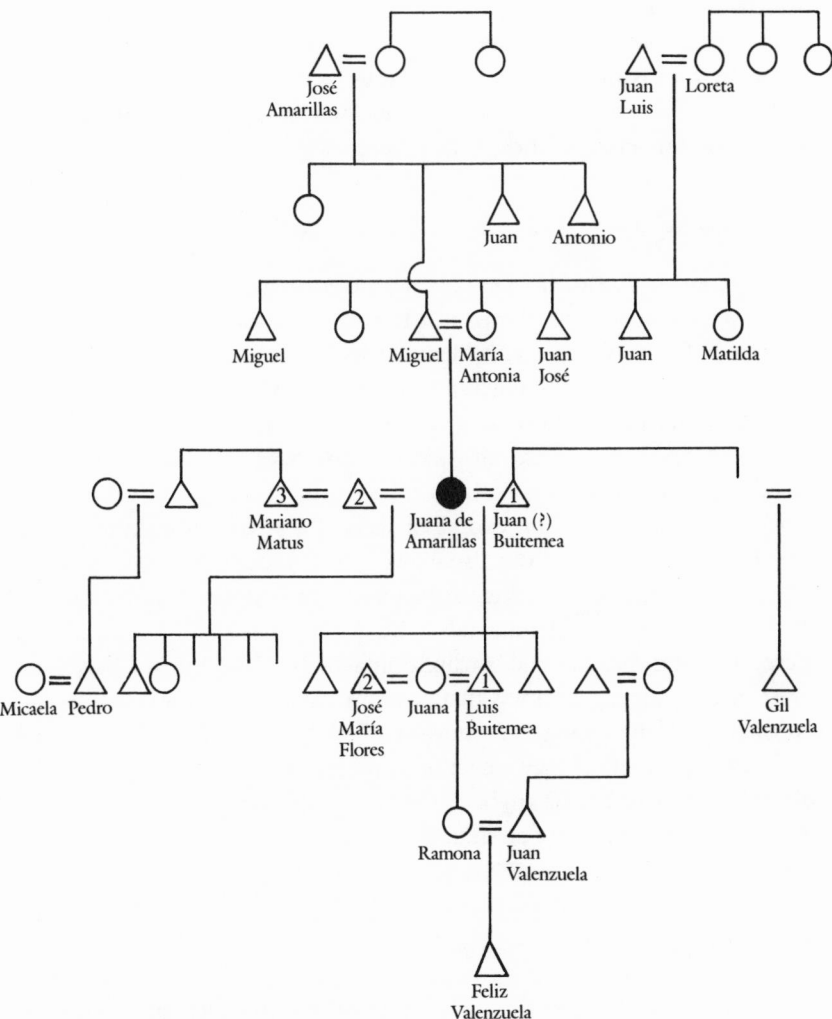

Partial Genealogy of Juana de Amarillas

to a ceremonial society, acceptance of a marriage arranged by her parents, service as an apprentice Alpes, and finally arduous training for full partici- pation in the Cantora society. She was a mature woman who had been married and was bringing up a family and had assumed a definite place in Yaqui ceremonial life before her own family was broken up and she was thrown out among Mexicans in Hermosillo and Guaymas.

Once removed from the disordered situation in Sonora, she reoriented herself in Yaqui society in Arizona. She took up life with another man from Potam and, in accordance with Yaqui custom, did not sanctify this union by means of any ceremony. She went on assuming obligations as a madrina. She continued her service in the Cantora society, acquiring a higher and higher reputation in this capacity.

Orientation in Other Cultures

Her contacts with Mexican-American culture have been minimal. She has never learned to speak Spanish fluently, and although she can carry on a sort of conversation with Mexican Americans, she uses Yaqui almost exclusively. She is wholly illiterate and has learned her Cantora ritual entirely by oral means. There has been no intermarriage in her family with Mexicans. She has no Mexican-American associates in Pascua, except the storekeepers from whom she buys tobacco for cigarettes. She has never worked outside her house except occasionally in cotton-picking season when she has gone out from Pascua with large groups of Yaquis to work on nearby cotton ranches. She has had far fewer outside contacts than any of the men discussed. Her attitude toward Mexicans is based on the usual stereotype of the Yaquis and is wholly unfavorable. Like Lucas Chavez and most of the others, she holds that customs such as wearing short dresses on the part of the younger Yaqui women, so "people can see the flesh on their legs, see whether they are fat or slim," and marriages not arranged by parents—"now in Pascua anybody marries anybody, no matter whether of good family or not"—are an indication of the Mexicanization of Arizona Yaquis.

Modes of Thought and Value System

Juana appears to have three major interests, two of which occupy her conscious thought and the third of which takes up all her physical energy left over from caring for her small household. These are the fortunes and history of her children, the comparison of kinship customs in Arizona and in Sonora as she knew it, and the business of being a Cantora. As an old woman whose household has disintegrated around her, she is left with only old Mariano to cook and care for. Consequently, she finds herself free to attend almost every ceremony in Pascua and leaves the village at every opportunity to sing at Libre or even on rare occasions at Scottsdale. She complains constantly of the rigorous ceremonial demands made on her: "This religion of ours is very, very hard. There are so many things to be done when anyone dies. It is very, very hard work to stay up all night, night after night. There is so much to do." But there is no one of whom we have kept track who is so regular in performance of duties. Her participation record for 1936–37 contains more entries for the year than that of anyone else in Pascua. She served as a Cantora at all but a half dozen of the year's ceremonies, which means that she was so occupied for almost half the days of the year. Her record of service has increased rather than decreased as she has grown older. She keeps one of the important crucifixes used in the church services in her own house on her household shrine and has this taken to the church for every service. She also keeps one of the images of the Virgin and carries this over herself for each ceremony in which it is needed. Her own household shrine is well-kept, and she constantly performs private devotions before it. Her attitude toward the work that she does as Cantora is that it is an exacting but inexorable duty. There is no question of avoiding it in any way: "I have been a Cantora for many years. That is what I have to do."

Another important focus of interest in Juana's present life organization centers about a feeling of cultural change. She is very conscious of the difference between herself as a Yaqui woman wearing long Mother Hubbard skirts and embroidered shirtwaist covered by voluminous undecorated blouse and her young *ahijadas* (goddaughters) and others whose skirts come to just below their knees and whose shirtwaists are tight-fitting and bright-colored. This difference between Yaqui women in Arizona is apparent to her every time she goes anywhere in the village, and she regards it as an indicator of degeneration—a typical older generation view, of course, in almost any culture. The specific content of her view is somewhat as follows: Arizona Yaquis are morally inferior to the old Sonora Yaquis because they dress differently, showing more of their bodies, and because *novios* and *novias* (sweethearts) get married instead of waiting for their parents to pick their mates. Furthermore, they do not remain together after marriage. These types of immoral behavior have been learned from the Mexicans, and it is obvious that the young people "wish to be like the Mexicans." The sense of moral degeneration is backed up by a feeling of laxity in ritual observances. Although Juana complains constantly about the tremendous number of things that "have to be done" in any Yaqui ritual in Arizona, she also feels strongly that much of the ritual is left out. She compares ceremonies here to the ones she knew on the Yaqui River and speaks again and again of omissions. Thus she calls attention often to the failure to en-act the "Running of the Old Man" during Holy Week and the failure to tie misbehaving individuals to the cross on Good Friday for punishment of their sins. She is also much concerned about omissions in the wedding ritual, such as the failure, in many instances, of the bride's family and the groom's family to make the ritual exchange of food during the course of the ceremony. Her devotion to a more nearly orthodox Catholic behavior than is customary among Arizona Yaquis is also significant:

The old people here are ready to die, but the young people are not. A Yaqui on the Yaqui River could not marry until he was confirmed. Here people don't even get confirmed. They don't confess once a year, which is what every Yaqui ought to do. Some confess, but the majority are afraid of the padres. They don't understand confession.

Her feeling about Mexicans and their contrast with Yaquis seems to have some element of class feeling in it:

Here in Pascua anybody marries anybody, no matter whether they are of "good family" or not, just like the Mexicans. And then they run away from each other, like Mexicans.

This sense of "good family" and bad family is rather strong in Juana and her ratings agree with those of Lucas Chavez. She herself is thought of by Chavez as of "good family," in fact, of exceptionally good family, and it should be emphasized again that every Yaqui in Pascua refers to her as Doña Juana.

The third focus of Juana's interest is in her own kin. She speaks often and at length of what has happened to her daughters and sons. Her interest in kinship is reflected in the fact that she knows more accurately than anyone else in Pascua the old kinship terminology and that she is one of the few who remembers the details of the old Yaqui joking relationship between brothers- and sisters-in-law.

Notes on Personality

Juana is direct and outspoken and has the forwardness in her personal relations that deference to the aged fosters. She speaks in short bursts, rather than in monologue, but asserts herself often in conversations. When she enters the church for a period of active work as a Cantora, she ordinarily has a word and a joke for everybody and for nobody in particular. She laughs often. She is affectionate in greeting compadres and comadres and invariably uses the old-style Yaqui greeting, both as to terms and as to the pat on the breast and the half-embrace. She is as forward with Mexican Americans and Anglo Americans whom she has come to know as with Yaquis and inspires the Mexican-American storekeepers in the village with as great a deference (and it should be added with as great devotion, for they both contribute heavily to her support when she is in need, which is most of the time) as she does the Yaquis. She is liked, respected, listened to, and enjoyed by all Pascuans.

Interpretation

Juana represents the well-adjusted Yaqui, fully oriented in Yaqui society and without contacts with any culture except old Yaqui culture. As a Cantora of ability and as a mother of a large family, she has realized fully the meaning and the security assurance of Yaqui culture. Her world has been disrupted and disoriented only through overt acts of Mexicans in Sonora, and so she views Mexicans as symbols of external malevolence. These are a part of Yaqui culture, however, and do not introduce to her any non-Yaqui cultural values. She remains insulated to any but Yaqui values, and thus her life remains ordered and clear.

It is a significant fact that it has been easy thus far to consider individuals as individuals apart from their families because many of the older men and women of Pascua were removed from families at fairly early ages and few have developed large households into which they are integrated in Arizona. Yaqui culture has been carried and preserved by these individuals as individuals and, as time went on, by them as parts of larger communities. The culture has not been maintained and passed on within large family units as must have been the case during the periods before the Mexican wars. The re-integration of Yaqui culture in Arizona has resulted in creating a primary social structure which more nearly resembles that of Anglo Americans than it does the older Yaqui social structure; that is, the individual and the territorial community or village have become the primary units of the society, not the household and the village. It would be a mistake, however, to ignore the role of the family household unit in Arizona Yaqui culture. As has been pointed out above there are large stable household groups, at least a half dozen, in Pascua which comprise from three to four generations and imply, therefore, a more continuous and stable cultural tradition than is apparent in a consideration of the more or less uprooted majority of individuals. These larger households with their several generations of individuals seem to be developing rather than to be breaking down in Arizona, a condition which is largely the result of biological factors, although economic ones play a part. That some of these households are matriarchal in character has just been indicated. We shall consider here one such "matriarchal" household unit, breaking it down as much as possible for purposes of analysis into its individual components. The one selected is the Araiza household, of which one male member has already been considered, Rosario Escalante. The other members of the household are as follows: Luis Alvarez, a man of more than eighty and its oldest member; Josefa Araiza de Escalante, Joaquina Araiza de Martínez, Susana de Matus, Andrea Escalante, Josefina Escalante, Dolores Martínez, Cleofa Martínez, Gloria Martínez, and Manuel Araiza. The relations of this group to one another may be made clearer in the following diagram.

Case Study of Josefa Araiza

Physical Characteristics

Josefa is the oldest woman of the household and the physically largest woman in Pascua. She is both tall and heavy for a Yaqui woman, having a stature of about five feet seven inches and weighing at least 230 pounds. She is large and solidly built without being fat. Her skin is moderately light as compared with other women of Pascua. Her features are not in contrast with other Yaqui women. She is and reports always having been physically active and capable of doing a man's work, as for instance in digging a well. Her voice is low and soft.

Life History

In 1941, Josefa turned sixty-five years old, having been born in 1876. Her father, Luis Alvarez, was a Mayo, and left the Mayo country as a young man and came to Hermosillo where he married a Yaqui woman. Josefa was born in Hermosillo. When Josefa was still a baby in arms, the family (including five older brothers) were impressed for service in a mine between Hermosillo and Altar. They lived at this mine, Placera, for the first nine or ten years of Josefa's life. Working conditions were very bad and life was hard and unhappy. Food was high-priced and sometimes unobtainable and often the family was forced to beg for clothing. The Mexican employer

Josefa Araiza drawing water from the well, March 1937. *Photograph by David J. Jones, Jr.*

forced men to work when they were sick, and he beat them. Josefa's family eventually was able to get away from Placera and for the next ten years shifted about from mine to mine in the vicinity of Altar and Magdalena. In most places they encountered bad living conditions, and as soon as they became unbearable they moved to another place. Almost everywhere they found the Mexican employers acting as though "they were angry with Yaquis." They searched for but never found one who was not.

When Josefa was fifteen, her father and mother arranged for her to marry José Araiza, a Yaqui. Araiza had been born in Hermosillo also and had been brought up by a Mexican. He "looked like a Mexican and spoke Spanish like a Mexican." They had one daughter, Joaquina. Araiza did not provide for Josefa and often tried to beat her, a practice which she did not like and which she was able to prevent because of her size and strength. She left Araiza after five or six years to live again with her parents. Disturbances in Sonora increased and the periodic Yaqui pogroms became more frequent. In 1903 the family, now consisting of Luis and his wife, Josefa, and her daughter Joaquina (the five brothers having died of fever in the mines) decided to cross into the United States. They entered at Nogales and went to work on the railroad at Benson.

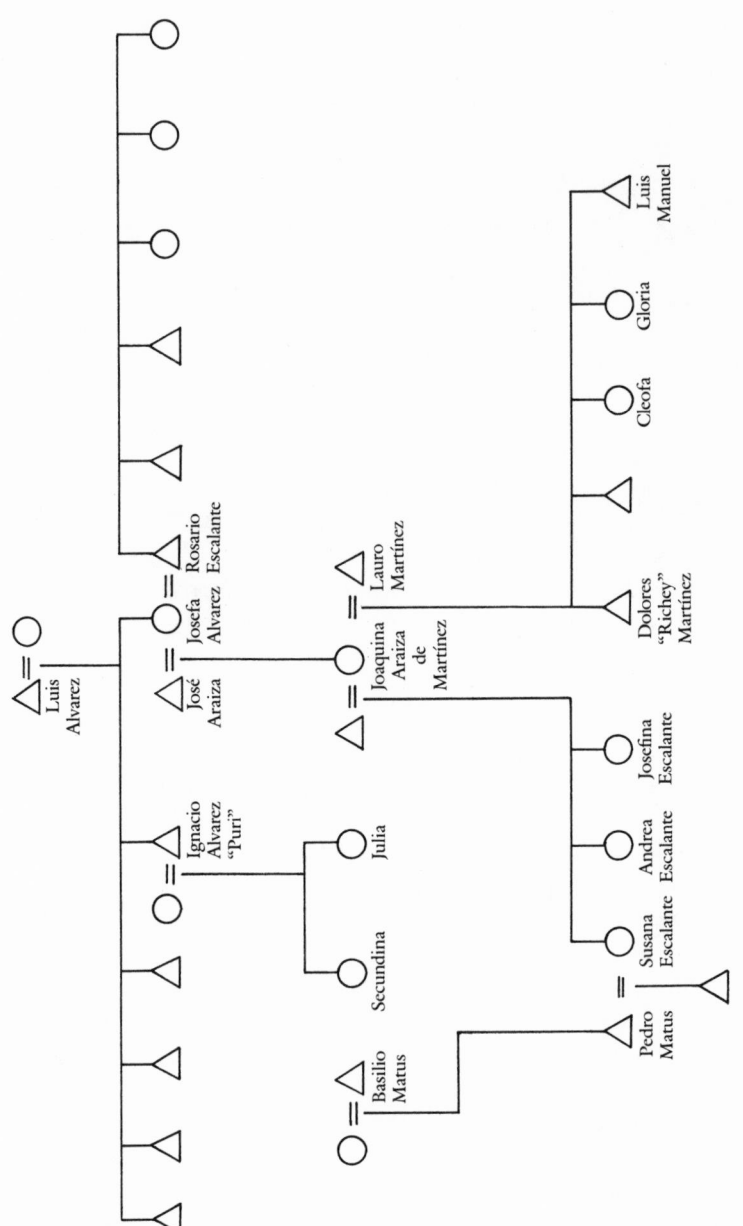

Partial Genealogy of the Araiza Family

About 1912 they came to Tucson and have lived in Barrio Anita and Pascua ever since. Josefa's father, Luis, became the head Temasti in Pascua, serving as such until his death in 1938. Josefa herself became the head Kiosti and still holds that office. About 1915 she began to live with Rosario Escalante and has lived with him since that time. They are one of the four or five families that own their own lot in Pascua. They remain in the village the year round, or at least a portion of the household remains in the village, even though some go away during cotton season to pick elsewhere.

Orientation in Yaqui Society

Josefa says that she is "Yaqui-Mayo" and believes that "Yaquis and Mayos are all the same thing." She has lived with Yaquis, even though "mixed in with Mexicans," throughout her life and says that she prefers Yaquis now and would not live in Barrio Libre because there "Papagos and Yaquis and Mexicans are all mixed up." She uses Yaqui as her preferred language and always has. Her Mayo blood does not give her a feeling of distinctness from the Yaquis of Pascua. In this she is like her Mayo consort, Rosario Escalante.

Although they lived among Mexicans in the mining towns of northern Sonora, there were always many Yaquis present in the villages. The Yaquis who were there had the background of warfare and escape that Josefa's father had. Unlike Yaquis settled in other regions, they did not seem to be afraid of revealing their identity as Yaquis, perhaps because in this period before 1895 there was yet no intensive campaign of Yaqui extermination. As a result, the Yaquis of the mining camps came together for community ceremonial life. Luis Alvarez served whenever he could as a Temasti at Placera and other camps. Josefa grew up in an atmosphere not only of economic hardship but also of Yaqui solidarity in the face of that hardship. She remembers her father as a Temasti and recalls that there was a regular round of Matachin dances, Pascolas, and all the traditional Yaqui ceremonial life. She herself was promised as a Kiosti, but seems not to have served until the family came into the United States when she was about twenty-seven years old. From this time on she has worked regularly as a Kiosti. Her presence in the Yaqui church at Pascua is essential in all the more elaborate ceremonies and her knowledge is regarded as great. She is charged with the special obligation of building the bier for the body of Christ annually on Good Friday. Her house is the repository for two of the important images of the Virgin. Her participation in ceremony is to be equated with that of Juana de Amarillas and the respect which she has from the villagers is of about the same degree.

Of greater interest for the purposes of this study is Josefa's orientation of her household in Yaqui society. For twenty years before his death her Temasti father was too feeble physically and too retiring to exert any influence on the behavior of the members of the household. Josefa assumed that authority herself and became regarded by every member of the household as the final arbiter in everything. Her daughter Joaquina who is forty-five years old says that her own seven children "belong to Josefa. They will belong to her until Josefa dies. Then they will be mine, unless they get married. Then they will belong to their husbands." Rosario, Josefa's consort, is recognized as a "good man who works steadily." But he has no children in the household and is looked to for nothing more than occasional advice. The discipline and orientation of the children in society is in the hands of Josefa, and in minor degree in those of Joaquina. For a time Joaquina's consort was influential, an assertive Yaqui who was prominent in village affairs, but who was killed in 1936.

Josefa has assumed that bringing up children in Yaqui society means giving them ceremonial duties. Her own daughter, Joaquina, however, has never been promised to any ceremonial service; we shall consider her case below. Thus skipping the generation immediately below her, Josefa has taken in hand the children of Joaquina and has placed each in turn in the system of ceremonial participation in Pascua. Joaquina's oldest daughter, Susana (Trinidad), was promised as an *Angelita* (little angel in the Easter ceremonies) first, then as an Alpes, and finally as a Kiosti. She completed her service as an Angelita, worked as an Alpes until marriage, and is now serving as a Kiosti. Joaquina's second daughter, Andrea, was promised as an Angelita and served for ten years, but has taken up no other duties because of an unconquerable shyness, which will be considered below. The third daughter was promised as a Cantora, the oldest son as a Matachin, and the next daughter as an Angelita. Thus each of Joaquina's children, through the influence of Josefa, has been knit into the ceremonial framework of Pascua. Each of these has been a formal promise, never an apprenticeship. When it is remembered that every manda results in the establishment of ceremonial sponsorship relations with at least two people, the importance of Josefa's activity becomes apparent.

A glance over the list of ceremonial sponsors who have been called in by Josefa to sponsor these children indicates clearly the nature of her influence. She has served in a few instances, but for the most part she has called in Yaquis with whom she was associated in Sonora and who crossed into the United States about the time she did. They are thus of her own generation, but more important, they are also of her own outlook and are almost as noted in Pascua as she is as participants in the church ceremonies. They include Pascolas, Kiostis, and prominent Fariseos. These persons, it should be emphasized, have been held up to her daughter's children as due a special respect in their capacity as sponsors. They have been trained in such regard from the age of five or six onward. It should be mentioned in this connection also that Josefa herself has served as madrina of baptism for three of her daughter's children and that she selected again the Matus family with whom she was intimately associated in Sonora as sponsors of baptism for the others. Thus her own authority and respect has been reinforced within the family through the sponsor system.

Orientation in Other Cultures

Josefa speaks Spanish, but neither fluently nor well. She is wholly illiterate, like all the women of her age group. She has lived among Mexicans in Sonora, but has tried to live apart from them in Arizona. She believes that Mexicans are untrustworthy and holds to the usual Yaqui stereotype. Her husband, José Araiza, who beat her and whom she remembers as a bad man, is classified as Mexican-like. Her contacts have always been and still remain very remote from Mexican-American and Anglo-American culture.

Modes of Thought and Value System

What Josefa believes to be important, and the manner in which she justifies the values that she accepts, must be inferred from her behavior; certainly, they are not to be discovered in conversation with her. She remains inarticulate about her beliefs and regards talk as an instrument for accomplishing definite ends, not as a means for expressing her feelings or what thoughts she may have. One of her most definite objectives is to have a household that has sufficient food, is moderately clean, and takes adequate care of its various members, so far as their physical wants go. She believes that there should be a hardworking man, at least one in each household, who provides the money and food to maintain it. She judges a man as to whether or not he brings his money home or spends it on himself for drink and as to whether or not he works regularly. Her present consort, Rosario Escalante, meets these requirements, and she respects him for that. She thinks also that he is a good man because he works quietly and cooperatively with her around the house. She illustrates his excellence by describing how he and she worked together digging the well on their lot, he down in the well putting the dirt in buckets and she above hauling the dirt away. She despises men and women who are not industrious. Her granddaughters she keeps busy at cleaning and cooking and washing clothes, and she speaks disapprovingly of neighbor girls who "do not know how to work."

Another value which rules her life is the system of ceremonial life that governs the community of Pascua. This is an absolute value with her which has evidently ruled most of her existence, judging from her own devotion to it and the efforts she has made to knit the life of her household into it. She does not permit herself even to speak of it as laborious and exacting, as Juana de Amarillas does. It seems to her to be beyond criticism or objective view. It is a part of her and she a part of it. On being questioned she asserts that she goes to every ceremony that is held in Pascua. She asserts that this is something about which it surprises her to have been asked. There is no question that she appears at every ceremony. To ask whether she attends them or not is like asking someone whether or not he gets up each morning. Her own personal ceremonial obligations are equally as much a part of the scheme of the universe and are not to be admitted as even possibly avoidable. She waited a year beyond the normal time for holding the cumpleaño for her father because they did not have sufficient funds, but it was the younger people in the household who were sensitive to the talk of the villagers about the tardiness. She did not mention the talk because to her it was an absolute fact that the ceremony would be held even though it would be late. Other opinions did not disturb her.

For her there is similarly no possible attitude of disapproval for separate elements of Yaqui ritual or doctrine. The Pascolas are Pascolas. There is no possibility of disapproving them. They say what they say. That is all. You have the Deer Dancer at a fiesta if you have the money. All these things are beyond reason and beyond question. They are a part of the scheme of life.

Similarly, it is the custom for Yaqui parents to arrange the marriages of their children. That is what is done. It is true that the marriage that her parents arranged was a complete failure. But that was the fault of the "Mexican-like" man, not of the system. Thus she went ahead and arranged her own daughter's marriage. The man died; then it was up to her daughter to work out her own unions for herself. Josefa again arranged the marriage of her daughter's oldest daughter. The two were not sweethearts; they were obviously not a good match. The marriage broke up and the man ran away to Sonora with the child. But that was because he was "a bad man" and, as Rosario said, "like a Mexican in his head."

The world of Josefa, then, centers about two things—a well-ordered household and a functioning ceremonial system. She sees herself, if she sees herself at all, as a part of these systems. They are not to be viewed objectively. Moreover, you do not know about what you are not a part of, and therefore, how can she know anything about what the Mexicans and the Anglo Americans do? The house and the ceremonies with Jesus and the Virgin linked to them must go on working. That is all life is. Outside of that, who knows what there is?

Case Study of Joaquina Araiza de Martínez

Josefa's household is not so Yaqui as she thinks it is. Joaquina and Joaquina's children have not been insulated from other cultures to the extent that Josefa has. Joaquina was born in Hermosillo and came with the family to the United States before she was seven. She remembers nothing of the hard and anxious life in the mining camps. She remembers first a friendship with Tomás Alvarez, the independent little boy cousin of hers whom they picked up in ragged clothes in Magdalena and brought across the line with them to Benson. Then she remembers hard work, washing and ironing clothes, while the family lived in Barrio Anita. She was married when she was fifteen, like her mother, to a Yaqui boy of twenty-six, "so that I wouldn't have to work so hard, my mother said." But the man died the year of their marriage, and she was a widow at sixteen. There was no child. Joaquina continued to live at home and another man, perhaps a Mexican American, came to live with her. There were three daughters, but the man was too drunken, and Joaquina sent him away. She worked harder than ever, taking in washing for Mexican Americans and Anglos in Tucson. Her grandfather was getting older and Joaquina became increasingly the chief means of support for the growing household. But then Rosario Escalante came to live with Josefa, and not long after, a Yaqui from Hermosillo, Lauro Martínez, came to live with Joaquina. Joaquina had three more children, two girls and a boy, by Lauro. Lauro drank, too, enormously, but he always gave her money before he went off on the sprees. He was an aggressive man. He taught himself some English. After a few years he began to be prominent in Pascua affairs, as a go-between with the Anglo Americans. He got permits from the sheriff's office for fiestas. He acted as collector for one of the real-estate companies. Large as the family had become, it was well-to-do by Pascua standards because it had two good providers. Then Lauro was run over by a train. Joaquina has gone back to washing clothes for people in Tucson harder than ever. She provides as much of the income as Rosario does.

Joaquina looks like a "Mexican." Her skin is light tan and pockmarked. Her lips are thin and her facial expressions change rapidly and often. She has Mexican friends who say she looks like a Mexican, not like a Yaqui. She speaks rapidly in Spanish and is proud of her ability to speak it. Anglo-American observers have never felt that she was a Yaqui. Her mannerisms, her speech, her way of wearing clothes never seemed Yaqui to them, yet she lives in a household containing two generations of persons, one above and one below her, that always seemed Yaqui to the observers.

Joaquina claims to have the blood of her mother and the Yaqui José Araiza. Village gossip says that she is the daughter of Josefa and a Frenchman who lived with Josefa for a short time in Sonora. The opinion is based not only on her physical appearance and her linguistic virtuosity, but also on her behavior. Joaquina does not participate at all in village ceremonies unless they be at her own household. These non-Yaqui qualities of Joaquina's need explanation, or at least further description.

Joaquina says that she remembers nothing of the life in Sonora and, therefore, that she knows "nothing about the trouble with Mexicans." She says she has only heard this talked about. She herself does not voluntarily discuss such things; she is not interested. She has never had a manda to serve in any way in the ceremonial societies. In view of her mother's care in promising all of Joaquina's daughters and her son to service in the church, this seems strange. Why did she never promise Joaquina? Joaquina says, not by way of excuse, but in simple explanation: "I always had too much work to do." This seems inadequate, and yet it is all we have as an explanation. If Joaquina showed any evidence of being regarded as outside the family now, or if she showed evidence of being resentful of her treatment in the family, we could suspect some other explanation. But there is no such evidence. And the fact is that the family was hard-pressed to support itself when it first came to Arizona. Joaquina did have to work. Whatever may lie back of the failure to promise her, it is clear now that her lack of participation in the ceremonial life has definitely affected her. She says of the ceremonies: "I never go to them. I get tired standing around. They sing and sing and pray. I get a headache. If I go at all, I just stay a few minutes." She points out that one of her daughters, Andrea, also feels this way

Joaquina Martínez, January 1937. *Photograph by David J. Jones, Jr.*

about the ceremonies, as though in extenuation of herself. Not only does Joaquina fail to go to ceremonies herself, but she permits Josefa to perform all the necessary preparation for her son when he goes in accordance with his manda. As a Malinche, he has to be dressed at the church just prior to the dancing. Josefa always takes his dress and puts it on for him, an action which is properly carried out by mothers or sisters. Joaquina never assumes this responsibility. Similarly, she points out herself that "Josefa is the one who makes Dolores go to the dances. She says he has to go because he has a manda." She seems unconcerned about his fulfillment of the promise. Furthermore, she is critical of the Matachin dancing. She believes that staying up late at night as a Malinche and dancing may have made Dolores nearsighted. She believes it is too great a strain for a young child. Yet she has never put herself in the way of Josefa's desires in these matters, and there is no evidence of conflict between the women over this matter. Joaquina accepts wholly the authority of Josefa and gives no indication of rebellion.

Joaquina is as devoted to a proper orientation of her children in Anglo-American society as Josefa is to their proper orientation in Yaqui society. Joaquina wants her unmarried older daughters to work as housemaids in Anglo-American houses. She wants them to learn English, to learn to answer the telephone, to learn how to cook in American ways, and to learn how to keep Anglo-American houses clean. She goes out of her way to find jobs of this sort and has been successful occasionally in placing them for short periods. She believes that this would be the best life for them, short of good marriages. She was opposed to the marriage of her oldest daughter with a Yaqui in Marana and was able to say "I told you so" when it failed and the man ran off to Sonora. Equally as significant is her ambition for her oldest boy. She has kept Dolores in school up to the third year in high school and has the definite intention of keeping him there through high school. This is the boy who has also danced Matachin for the past twelve years of his life. He is the first Yaqui to go so far in school in Arizona. Many people in the village disapprove, saying that he should be at work supporting his mother and the rest of the household. Joaquina is thoroughly conscious of this gossip and mentions it frequently. She says that she does not care about it. She wants Dolores to go through school and then to get a good job, perhaps as a brakeman on the railroad. Her devotion to this ideal is proven by her continued hard work taking in washing. She is proud of Dolores' ability to read and speak English and subscribes to an English-language newspaper so that he will be able to read it each day. It is apparent, therefore, that Joaquina is definitely sensitive to certain values of Anglo-American culture and is orienting her children in that direction, despite the pull in another direction by her mother.

Joaquina's attitudes toward Yaqui culture are largely negative. We have discussed her feelings about the tiresomeness of ceremonies and her disinclination to attend them. She also dislikes the language and pretends to Anglo Americans that she does not know how to speak it. If she is able, she will convince non-Yaquis that she does not know any Yaqui and will proceed to speak Spanish in rapid Mexican fashion to prove it. Yet the language of her household is Yaqui, and she herself admits that her oldest daughters have no adequate knowledge of any language except Yaqui. She boasts that she is teaching her youngest son to learn Spanish as fast as she can. She says disparagingly of Yaqui: "Oh, he will pick that up around. But he is going to learn Spanish." She has no apologies for Yaqui culture, because she does not seem really to consider herself a part of it. She likes the Pascola talk. "Yes, they talk bad sometimes, but I like them. They crack

good jokes." In spite of herself, she becomes enthusiastic about the Pascolas and even the Deer Dancer when she has been forced to watch them at a
fiesta given at her household. She notes new actions that she has not seen
before and describes them with great interest.

Despite her pretensions of not being Yaqui in her interests or speech,
she is full of the usual prejudices against Mexicans. Once she has been
discovered to be able to speak Yaqui as well as any other Yaqui, she insists
violently on her Yaquiness. She claims not to get angry when people take
her for a Mexican, but actually she does get angry and resentful. Given a
free hand in conversation with Yaquis, she voices all the usual stereotypes:
"Mexicans are liars. They are robbers. You can never trust one of them.
They are all bad." It is to be noted, however, that she does not make
use of the Mexican stereotype in criticizing the behavior of her children
or the younger generation. She maintains high standards for her son and
daughters, which include not permitting them to stay out late at night or
"run around" or drink, but she does not liken them to Mexicans when they
falter a little in those directions.

Interpretation

The Araiza household, dominated by two strong women, Josefa and
Joaquina, is one in which two traditions are being furthered at the same
time. The dominant woman is Josefa, and she is at present establishing
the Yaqui tradition as dominant. There has been full participation in Yaqui
society in the household for three generations: Josefa's father's, Josefa's
own, and that of her grandchildren. Somehow, in a manner which is by
no means clear, the generation immediately below Josefa has failed to become oriented in Yaqui society beyond the sphere of kinship. But it has
been effective even in that generation, and consequently, Joaquina defers
to Josefa as her mother and head of the household and Josefa's influence
extends to the generation next below Joaquina. This influence results in
a thorough-going participation in the Yaqui kinship, ceremonial sponsorship, and ceremonial systems for the youngest generation.

The interesting thing is that at the same time Joaquina has been at
least partially successful in establishing skills that will give status in the
Anglo-American world. Language, literacy, and domestic habits have been
implanted from that world in her older children as a result of Joaquina's
individual efforts. This seems to have been accomplished with no apparent conflict between the two dominant women. They are at work in two

different compartments. Unquestionably, Joaquina has recognized conflict and given in to Josefa on occasion, as in the case of Susana's marriage, for example, and perhaps now and then in connection with Dolores' dancing. But in the main, there has been no conflict because there is a minimum of incompatibility in the behavior which the two women demand of their children. Joaquina has been able to give them what she has wanted in addition to what Josefa has been able to give them. The household remains at least in external behavior dominantly Yaqui in obedience to Josefa's wishes, but Joaquina makes no pretense of being Yaqui so far as ceremonial behavior is concerned, and the children, as we shall see, carry on both patterns demanded of them.

If there is important conflict, it may perhaps be seen in an examination of the attitudes and behavior of the children. We shall reserve such examination until a later chapter dealing with the youngest generation in general.

Joaquina's position in relation to Yaqui culture remains unexplained. No amount of probing has resulted in uncovering the influences which have been at work on her. We cannot regard those influences as purely negative. That is, she cannot be regarded as responsive to Anglo-American values and unresponsive to Yaqui ones purely as a result of the fact that she was not brought into Yaqui ceremonial life by her mother and therefore not trained in the most distinctive Yaqui behavior. There must have been some positive conditioning there. Was it merely the hardness of her economic life and consequently the development of a better sense of what is necessary in Anglo-American culture for easier living? One is inclined to see something more there, such as the influences that are responsible for her unusual knowledge of Spanish. These, however, have not been revealed, and it is necessary to take Joaquina merely as she is, for what she reveals of the interweaving of the cultures.

Case Study of Salamina Valenzuela

The interweaving of the various cultural traditions of southern Arizona cannot be illustrated better than by a consideration of the Juan Valenzuela household. Neither wholly matriarchal nor wholly patriarchal in character, this household perhaps tends towards the latter because of predominance of strong male personalities. But it possesses a woman who, while not a dominant personality in the household group, has been an important cul-

Salamina Valenzuela holding her sister's child, March 1937. *Photograph by David J. Jones, Jr.*

tural influence. Salamina has, perhaps more than any other woman in Pascua, been in intimate contact with Anglo-American rather than Mexican-American culture. She may stand as an example of the younger Yaqui women of the village, not by any means a typical example, but one that illustrates in her progress thus far through life most of the possible contacts that a Yaqui woman may make with Anglo-American culture. At the same time, she is evidence of the influences that Yaqui culture continues to exert on Yaqui women who have been born and who have grown up in the United States. The story of her life is of a person who has swung as far out of the orbit of Yaqui culture as possible, and then has gradually moved back in, while continuing to seek to move out again. The path of the new outward movement has become a little different from the first, but it is nevertheless outward again.

Physical Characteristics

Salamina is twenty-four years old. She is of medium height for a Yaqui woman, being five feet four inches tall, and slender. Her skin is medium brown, neither dark nor light for a Yaqui, but perhaps tending toward light. Her hair is medium brown rather than black, and she has a permanent wave. She is considered physically attractive by Yaquis as well as by Anglos and Mexican Americans in general. She is physically vigorous, rarely ill, although not particularly strong.

Life History

Salamina was born in Barrio Anita, Tucson, in 1917. Her father, Teodoro, is probably half Yaqui and half Mayo. He was born in Hermosillo and was brought up in a Mexican household for the first few years of his life, speaking no Yaqui but only Spanish until he was perhaps nine or ten years old. Salamina's mother, Manuela, was a Yaqui whom Teodoro married when she was seventeen. Teodoro was a railroad worker, and five years after Salamina's birth he took the family on a job into California. Able to read and write Spanish, he began to pick up English and to work his way up to assistant foreman. The family moved up into Oregon. Salamina was perhaps eight years old. She remembers the big trees and the many flowers with pleasure. She played with Anglo-American children and found life very pleasant.

Still working for the railroad, Teodoro moved to Oakland. Salamina saw the ocean and liked it. Again she had Anglo-American playmates and a few Mexican-American ones. The family continued to move about in California and even lived for a while in New Mexico. But Manuela's health was bad. She had borne three more children after Salamina and began to show signs of tuberculosis. They had come all the way back to Pascua for the birth of each new baby. They decided to return to Pascua and live there

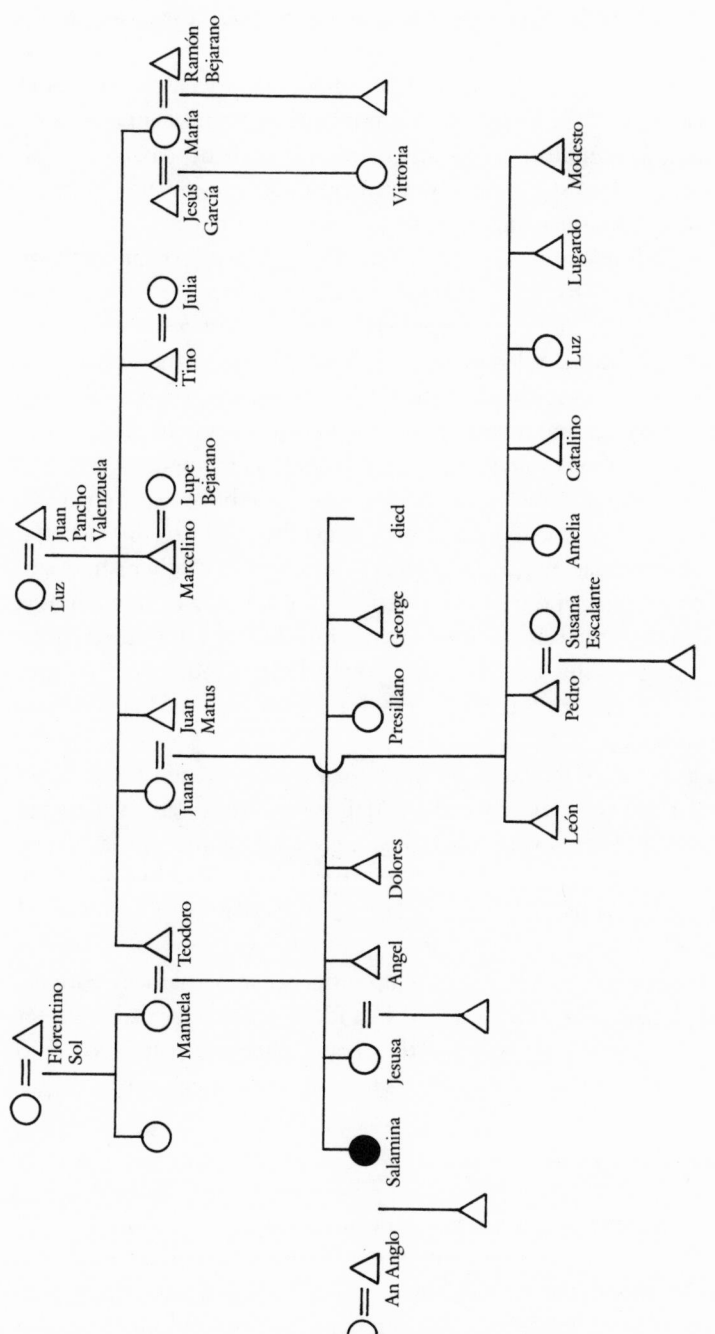

Partial Genealogy of Salamina Valenzuela

permanently, where Manuela could have an easier time close to Teodoro's parents' household.

Salamina was eleven when the family came back to Pascua and built themselves a small adobe house. For the first time Salamina went to school. She already knew English. She learned quickly, and the Pascua schoolteacher took an interest in her. She went on to school in Tucson where teachers showed a similar interest in her. She completed four grades before the family decided that she would have to work to help support them. Teodoro had begun to drink heavily, Manuela was sick, and there were three other children, all younger than Salamina, to support.

At the age of fifteen, Salamina got a job in an Anglo-American household through one of her schoolteachers. She worked for two or three years taking care of babies and acting as housemaid for Anglo-American families. Then she got a job in a restaurant as a waitress. Her employer, a young Anglo American, was attracted to her, and a baby was born. Salamina went to stay with a relative to avoid her father's anger, but the baby died when it was a little over a year old, and Salamina returned to her father's house in Pascua. Her mother, who had had a fifth child, was dying of tuberculosis. Salamina assumed the care of the household until her mother died. After that, her younger sister eloped with a young Pascua Yaqui, the younger boys began to work, and Teodoro left, leaving the care of his youngest child to Salamina.

Taking a trip to Magdalena, Salamina met a young man of half-Yaqui origin, and the two were married in Magdalena. They returned to the United States, and her new husband, Jesús, got a job on the railroad. They tried to live in a section house between Tucson and Phoenix, but they heard that Teodoro had returned to Pascua, and Salamina felt obligated to go back and take care of him. He was drinking constantly as never before. She and Jesús returned and took up residence in her father's parents' household. A baby was born and died in a few months. Her sister left her husband and returned to Pascua with a baby. Then the sister died, and Salamina had the care of this baby as well as of her mother's youngest.

Orientation in Yaqui Society

It can be said that Salamina had no orientation in Yaqui society until she was about eleven years old. The first five years of her life were spent in Barrio Anita and Pascua in association with Yaquis, and she learned Yaqui from her mother as her first language, but beyond recalling that

it was a pleasant period in her life, she remembers little about those early years. The next six years were spent at section houses with Mexican-American and Anglo-American neighbors in regions far removed from Yaquis. Neither her father nor her mother had ever had mandas to participate in Yaqui ceremonial life. Her father had no interest in that life. His earliest years had been spent among Mexicans, and his outlook was not Yaqui. He even tried to use Spanish as much as possible instead of Yaqui in the home. He made no mandas for his children.

When Manuela became ill, however, and the family returned to Pascua, Salamina was thrown immediately into a Yaqui household. Teodoro built his house beside that of his father and mother, Juan and Luz Valenzuela. Juan may be part Mayo (at least Salamina claims that), but both he and Luz are "muy Yaqui" in the Pascua sense of speaking little but the Yaqui language and are extremely reticent in all non-Yaqui contacts, although both were born in Hermosillo and not in the Yaqui country. The grandfather, Juan, is a Coyote Ya'ut (head of the Coyote dance society), and the grandmother is a famous curer, that is, one who cures spells cast by bad witches. They use Yaqui kinship terms within their household exclusively. They had promised the son next oldest to Teodoro, who unlike Teodoro had grown up with them and not Mexicans, to the Coyote society and the son next below him to the Matachinis. In this household, besides the persons already mentioned, were Teodoro's three younger sisters, one of whom was married and had promised her two oldest sons to the Matachín society in which they were participating regularly.

Into this household Salamina came as practically a non-Yaqui, with the language as her only link. She heard herself called *hakala* (granddaughter) by the grandmother and herself adopted the Yaqui terminology in speaking of her younger siblings, but she never learned the terminology for her father's siblings, because the old people had themselves forgotten these terms. She saw her father begin to play his violin for the Matachín dances, although he had no manda as a Matachini. Her younger brother, influenced by the new ceremonial interests around him, began to try to learn to dance Matachín, although he, too, was without a manda. None of her immediate family had ceremonial obligations, but all were making spasmodic efforts to participate. Salamina, however, never did until she was twenty years old and had been home for nine years. Then, when her mother died, she participated briefly in Pascua ceremony for a few months, acting as a *Tenanchi* (virgin-bearer) frequently. This, however, required no manda and established no obligations. She stopped as soon as her sense of loss for her mother abated.

Meanwhile, as a member of a Yaqui community, she was asked to serve as madrina of the rosary, of the hábito, and for Fariseos many times. She accepted the obligations and was knit into the ceremonial sponsor network. She also found herself assuming the social personality of an *ako*, or older sister, increasingly as her mother became less and less able to take care of the family. The responsibility for the household of her father became more and more hers, as the oldest of the siblings.

Salamina's grandmother, Luz, was an important influence in the household. As a curer, she was well known among Yaquis all over Arizona. Her views of witchcraft and Yaqui medicine were strongly implanted in Salamina, as well as in the rest of the family. Salamina says of her:

Luz has intelligence; she knows about these things because she died once. She was very sick when she was a little girl. When she was about fourteen she died. After that she got well, but when she was dead she had a dream. She saw a little table and the table had a lot of little cups and dishes on it. There was a different kind of medicine in each of the cups and dishes. In the dream Luz learned what each of these medicines was for and after that she remembered this and she could cure people when she wanted to. But she didn't cure much until she got to be an old woman. She kept all this intelligence in her mind all the time. When she was a little girl at the time she died, a horse stepped on her head. You wouldn't believe it, but all the bones in her head are still broken when you feel them.

Salamina witnessed cures that her grandmother made on her daughter and a son and others. She came to believe in her powers and in witchcraft as Luz explained it.

The household was a relatively disorganized one in comparison with other Pascua households. The men were without exception hard drinkers. The yard was not kept up. The houses were poorly furnished. It was a contrast not only with the fairly clean section houses in which Salamina had been living, but also with the majority of Pascua households such as, for instance, the clean and well-kept Araiza household. Salamina was extremely conscious of this contrast as she grew up.

Orientation in Other Cultures

Coming back from the varied experiences in California and Oregon, Salamina with her knowledge of English continued her contacts with Anglo-American culture with enthusiasm. She went to the Pascua school and made a friend of the schoolteacher, who regarded her as "the brightest of all the Yaqui girls" and pushed her rapidly to more advanced grades in the Tucson schools. Salamina worked hard and learned to read and write quickly. She took school very seriously and became a sort of interpreter to the Anglo-American teachers for both the Mexican-American and Yaqui children. When she finally had to stop school, she bought a dictionary and used it constantly, looking up English words whenever she needed them.

It was her teachers who found work for her when she was forced to stop school. At fifteen she became familiar with the internal organization of middle-class Anglo-American households. She learned standards of cleanliness and modes of dress. She wore American dresses and used rouge and lipstick when she went to work. She learned how to make up food formulas for babies in accordance with Anglo-American custom. She speaks proudly now of the fact that she was the "first Yaqui girl from Pascua ever to work out. There is only one other who was doing it besides me."

Her first sexual experience seems to have been with her Anglo-American employer after she had begun to work as a waitress when she was about eighteen. She says that she was "in love" with this man. She wanted to marry the man and felt that he was in love with her. When the baby came, she was pleased, but understood that they could not be married because he was already married: "We couldn't because we couldn't." Their relations continued friendly, and he was with her a great deal for nearly two years after the baby was born. He contributed some to its support and helped her to get doctor's care when the baby became sick. She continued to be loyal to him even to the extent of testifying in court on his behalf in a suit which was brought against him. Through him she became more aware of the skills of Anglo-American doctors and began to believe in their efficacy to some extent.

From time to time, Salamina has had miscellaneous brief contacts with Anglo-American students and writers who have become interested in Yaquis and have gone to her for information. She has liked and cultivated these contacts.

At the same time that Salamina's orientation in Yaqui and Anglo-American cultures has proceeded, she has also developed her contacts with Mexican-American culture. Her father taught her Spanish almost as soon as she learned Yaqui. She could read in Spanish before she could in English, although her literacy in English soon developed far beyond her Spanish. Her father, with an early orientation in Mexican ways, has brought Mexican customs into the household in Pascua. For example, when Salamina's baby was baptized, the ceremony took place in Teodoro's household. It was in no sense a Yaqui ceremony. There was a padrino and a madrina to be sure, but there was no Yaqui Maestro to perform a ceremony after the child was brought out from the Catholic church in Tucson. And there were no Pascolas. Instead, in keeping with the custom of the Mexican Americans, there was dancing, men and women in couples, to the music of a small orchestra of violin, guitar, and clarinet. Also when the baby died after baptism, there was no ceremony with Pascolas in Pascua. Instead, the baby was taken quietly from the village and buried "with the Mexicans" in south Tucson. Later, when Salamina's mother was critically ill and it became apparent that she was going to die soon, Salamina began going with her to the Church of the Holy Family in Tucson. They went regularly, as long as the mother was able, attending mass on Sundays. Then Salamina continued to go for a time after her death, while she was also serving as Tenanchi in Yaqui ceremonies in the village.

These tendencies to behave in accordance with Mexican-American custom have probably contributed to her choice of a husband. The man she married in Magdalena two years after the death of her half Anglo-American baby is a man whose father was Yaqui, but who was brought up in Sonora by his wholly Mexican mother. He went to school and acquired an imperfect reading knowledge of Spanish in Sonora. He was brought up entirely out of contact with Yaquis, and he knows nothing of the language, but speaks Spanish exclusively in his household now with Salamina. His whole life up until the time of his marriage with Salamina was lived in Mexico among Mexicans.

Salamina had none of the feelings against Mexicans that older Yaquis show. The stereotype of Mexicans used by Yaquis never appears in her thinking in any form.

Modes of Thought and Value System

It seems safe to say that Salamina places no value on anything Yaqui *qua* Yaqui. She says:

There are very many people in Tucson who are interested in me because I am an Indian. I guess they are interested in Indians because they don't know much about them. If you get to know all about them, there isn't anything interesting to it.

She is surprised to find that students continue to be interested in Yaqui customs over a period of years. To her such interest is "funny." She herself is avidly interested in learning whatever she can about the language and customs of Anglo Americans and goes on studying English with her husband and asking questions about the medicine and food of the Anglo Americans with whom she comes in contact.

She does not dwell on the fact that she is a Yaqui, but oddly enough expresses pride at having Mayo blood, which she claims comes through her grandfather. This may be connected with her definitely expressed preference for light-skinned persons. She says to her interviewer that the "Indians" she has "admired and liked best" have been "nearly white." She has herself applied concoctions to her hair which have lightened it temporarily. She carried on this practice most extensively when she was involved with her white employer.

Salamina believes that there is no value in maintaining the Yaqui language. She says, "It's so much like Spanish anyhow, and Spanish is more useful. Everyone can talk Spanish." Like Joaquina Martínez, she insists that she will not "teach Yaqui" to the babies of the household. She knows that they will "pick it up," and since it is much more important for their welfare in the world, she sets out consciously to "make them talk Spanish and English from the start." She has applied this principle to her mother's youngest boy, to her own child, and to her sister's boy. She claims that both she and her father would "not let the children talk Yaqui at first." She claims little knowledge of Yaqui for herself and under questioning about kinship terminology or names of ceremonial paraphernalia always dismisses the questioner with: "Oh, I don't know. We don't know any of those things." She never uses the full old Yaqui greetings, and she makes use of "*gracias*" always instead of "*lios em chiokwe utesia*" when speaking Yaqui. An evening in her house makes it clear that, as she herself says, the languages "are all mixed up together." Spanish, Yaqui, and English phrases occur in an amalgam which is perhaps predominantly Spanish.

As has been indicated, Salamina has never really participated in Yaqui ceremony. Her failure to participate is not based wholly on the failure of her relatives to establish obligations for her, nor is it based on social backwardness. She definitely does not like the ceremonies, and furthermore she lacks belief in the ideas which actuate them. She occasionally appears for a few minutes at ceremonies, but she says, "It makes me tired to stand around and listen to them pray. I don't like them." She says of the belief in the presence of the spirits of the dead in the village at certain times, as for instance in the month of October, that it makes her laugh:

Everytime I hear someone say something like that I always have to laugh. I don't know why, but I do. There are old people around in the village who believe that. But I think it's funny. We don't put any table out for them to eat from like a lot of Yaquis do.

When her mother died, the funeral and novena were put in the hands of her mother's family since Teodoro was drinking. There was a conventional series of ceremonies with a large number of Matachinis, and in these Salamina participated in orthodox fashion as an eldest daughter, but her private opinion was that "those things that they do aren't very important." She keeps no Book of the Dead with her mother's name in it, but she prays for her mother at the Catholic Church in Tucson.

She can see no purpose that the Pascolas serve whatever. She mentions

that her father and mother had no Pascolas when they were married and
"didn't want any." She announced definitely before her marriage to Jesús
that she would never have any Pascolas when she got married and, of
course, she did not. It has been noted that her baby was not given either a
Pascola baptism or a Pascola funeral. She never watches the Pascolas when
she attends a Yaqui ceremony. She does, however, enjoy the antics of the
Chapayekas and occasionally goes out to watch them come in from the
fields during Lent. This is just "because they are funny to watch."

Like other members of her household Salamina has had a deep belief in
witchcraft and in Yaqui medical techniques. As she grew up, her belief in
her grandmother's medical abilities was absolute, although she is inclined
to tell Anglo Americans at present that she does not now believe in them.
Her attitude in regard to witchcraft is indicated in her reply when she was
told, during the course of a witchcraft case in Pascua, that Anglo-American
judges did not believe in witches: "How do they know there aren't any
witches? How can they prove that?" Evidently, she starts from the opposite pole from an Anglo American in her thinking, chooses the opposite
assumption, and asks for same sort of proof from the Anglo American that
the latter would ask from her to prove her position. She is familiar with
the Anglo-American position, but regards her own as just as valid, and she
has many items of experience to back up her beliefs, as for example, the
following:

Luz knows all about these things. Julia [an aunt living in the Valenzuela house-
hold] was sick once in her left breast. A lot of pus came out of the sore above
the breast. Then Luz saw a dream that a witch had made Julia sick and she began
to cure her. She got a lot of thorns and put them on Julia's side and pretty soon
a water-bug came out of her breast. The bug was about as big as the end of my
thumb. After that Julia wasn't sick anymore, but there was a big hole above her
breast and now there is a scar there still. Her breast never gets big now and it just
hangs there.

Salamina knows the lore of witches:

A witch works at midnight. She has a little olla and she puts thorns in this and
mixes them with food. This is what she uses to make people sick. My grandmother
has seen these things done.

The reason that Chica [a woman accused of witchcraft in Pascua in 1937] has
the sores on her legs is that Angel [Salamina's uncle] had a sore on his hand for a
long time. Then it was cured by my grandmother. When the witch makes somebody sick, then if they get cured, the witch begins to get sick with the same kind
of sickness that the other person had.

She holds these beliefs with a good deal of conviction and at the same time has much faith in Anglo-American medicine. She recognizes the efficacy of both Yaqui and Anglo techniques and is perfectly willing to use whatever ones will bring about the desired effects.

One of Salamina's ruling principles is that of "getting ahead in the world." And she uses those words to express it. She respects her present husband because "he is ambitious" and will work hard with her at learning English, "so that he can get a better job maybe." She tries hard to get her younger brothers to work steadily and worries when they lie around at home and refuse to go to C.C.C. camp or do anything else. She believes that "all the Yaqui children should be put in school somewhere so that they would learn English well, instead of going off all the time to pick cotton." She believes that all Yaquis "would be better off if they would try to be like Americans instead of always getting together with other Yaquis wherever they go." She urges her younger brother to get some kind of work so that he "will get somewhere." Clearly, she has picked up not only the Anglo-American values but also the phrases in which those values are expressed in English.

Coupled with this attitude toward the ultimate goal of living is an acute consciousness of the situation in which she finds herself. She repeats again and again that "my friends always get surprised when they find what kind of a place I live in." They always say they never thought my house was like that until they see it. They get surprised to find that my family is really related to me."

Notes on Personality

Salamina has an easy, quiet manner in which all Anglo Americans who have been associated with her find a great deal of charm. She is soft-spoken, but enthusiastic and animated on occasion. At home she is moderately talkative, easy-going, and not inclined to give orders, although as an older sister she is entitled to do so. She defers to her father on all occasions as she is expected to do, but evidently despises his drinking behavior and suffers intensely, particularly in the presence of Anglo Americans, when outsiders are given an opportunity to see him in his customary form of behavior. She is motherly and affectionate with her brothers and children and nephews. She gives no evidence of maladjustment in her family, except for occasional glints of hatred or anger at her father's behavior. She seems neither aggressive nor frustrated in her overt behavior.

Interpretation

Salamina emerges from analysis more clearly than any individual who has been discussed as one engaged in the net of Yaqui society without being a participant in Yaqui culture. Yaqui culture does not mean enough to her to give rise to feelings of disapproval for its elements. Her values are the values of Anglo-American culture.

Such a condition has come about through contacts. Salamina has had an abundance of Anglo-American contacts, and, moreover, intensive contacts that have made her privy, through reading and intimate experience in Anglo households, to a large part of the range of Anglo customs. It can be easily demonstrated that by 1941 no woman in Pascua and no man has had the type or intensity of contacts that Salamina has had. And she was a relatively clean slate for the Anglo-American values to impress themselves on. She is resolving them more or less successfully by taking the next best thing to actual Anglo-American status. She is taking a Mexican-American husband new to the country in whom she can implant Anglo-American values. She is moving successfully again in the direction in which she started before her ties to Yaqui society were clear to her.

Brief Summary of Data on Women

A consideration of a few women in Pascua has revealed to us a rather different world from that of the men. Among the women we have found two opposite poles of Yaquiness that exist in Pascua. At one end there is Juana de Amarillas, completely insulated from any outside contacts, a participant Yaqui with no values or standards that have been derived anywhere except from old Yaqui culture. At the other end is Salamina Valenzuela, wholly insulated from Yaqui culture, with very few values, outside of the kinship sphere, that derive from Yaqui culture. Both these women are well knit into the society of Pascua. Salamina, to be sure, has a much simpler social personality in Yaqui society than does Juana de Amarillas; that is to say, she is without ceremonial society facets of that personality, for example. But both are, nevertheless, functioning in Yaqui society.

The insulation of the older women is easy to explain and to understand. Lacking the contacts with employers, moving within the limits largely of the domestic household, they rarely developed the primary means for communication with an outside world, that is to say, languages other than

Yaqui. Even when they did develop these, the opportunities to use them were limited. They remained in the Yaqui world of status and security exclusively, because the outer world did not impinge upon them. They lacked contact in the fullest sense of that word. And those women who were so insulated have become a major force for social stability and cultural stability of Yaqui culture in Arizona.

The case of the younger women is perhaps equally as clear. If we ask the question: why should we find among the women at least one person who is farther removed from Yaqui culture than any of the men? The answer might be: because the men who have been similarly removed from Yaqui culture have also been able to move out of the society, and consequently we do not find them available for study in the village of Pascua. We should have to search for them somewhere outside the village in the Spanish-American areas of southern Arizona cities. And this indicates the peculiar position of the women as compared with the men in Yaqui society. Their mobility is not so great; it is fraught with greater difficulties. Given early kinship ties in Yaqui society, it is much more likely that they cannot match any growing cultural mobility with an increased social mobility. The man is freer to move in accordance with his own needs. The woman is more subject to the press of her family obligations in Yaqui society. Moreover, if she remains in Yaqui society and has a family, then her whole life appears to be within the Yaqui sphere, for she has no economic relations that pull her out as a man does. She looks more Yaqui in her daily behavior because she is bound by the Yaqui community, even though she is culturally far removed.

The women whom we have considered probably represent more accurately, and in more of the significant details, a general cross-section of Pascua women than the men represent a cross-section of Pascua men. There is less variation in detail among the women's lives and adaptations. Paradoxically enough, however, there is also this greater extreme of contrast. Women are more generally wholly Yaqui or wholly non-Yaqui in their behavior and outlook than are the men. The men show more kinds and degrees of Yaquiness. The general significance of this situation will be considered in a later chapter.

CHAPTER 8
Youths of Pascua

From the year 1890 until perhaps 1920, covering the span of a generation, it would have been impossible to predict even within rough limits what experiences a Yaqui would live through. That perhaps is overstating the case. It would be more accurate to say that predictions could have been made along, say, fifteen or twenty different lines. There were thus many universes into which any given Yaqui might find a way, and once established in a universe, the course could have been predicted within reasonable limits. In other words, the prediction of Yaqui behavior would have been a very complex activity, calling for knowledge of a very large number of social environments. Between 1920 and 1940, or thereabouts, the number of universes within which Yaquis might move was reduced. In considering southern Arizona Yaquis alone, the number is reduced still further. Yaquis here have limited their world again to few paths, but these paths are new. They are obviously not the same ones which existed on the Yaqui River before 1890. They involve dual and even triple orientations for all the children.

In this chapter we will consider, though briefly, some of the young people who have grown up in Pascua. It will be our concern to indicate the nature of their family backgrounds, their behavior at present and up to the present, and their attitudes and beliefs. The picture of the people of Pascua that we are attempting to sketch would not be rounded out if it lacked some indication of what the youngest generation is feeling and doing.

Dolores Martínez

In 1941 Dolores is sixteen, having been born in Pascua in 1925. His mother is Joaquina Araiza, whose life story was told in the last chapter, and his father was an Hermosillo-born Yaqui, Lauro Martínez. Dolores has been sent to school regularly and is now in the third year of high school, a degree of schooling which no other Yaqui in Arizona has so far experienced. He speaks clear English, reads an English language newspaper daily, and at the same time speaks Spanish readily, and uses Yaqui constantly in his home. He addresses Anglo Americans as "Mr." and "Mrs."

Three *Matachinis* and their *Kobanao* on a trip to Picacho Peak, 1940. *Konanao* Tomás Alvarez, *lower left*, and Dolores Martinez, *lower right*. *Photograph by Rosamond B. Spicer.*

and always adds "sir" and "ma'am" to his replies in speaking with Anglo Americans, although he often confuses genders and reverses the Anglo usage of these terms. He finds his teachers "nice" and is inclined to accept their statements, such as "all that is in the newspapers is not true" and "the Indians were primitive people," with finality. He dresses more in the mode of middle-class Mexican-American boys of his age than do the majority of other Yaqui boys in Pascua. He wears dress pants and bi-colored shoes often, particularly at Yaqui fiestas.

Dolores is regarded as well behaved and a good boy by his family. He does not stay out late at night and has never been drunk. He defers readily and equally to his mother and grandmother and is quiet and unobtrusive in the household. He obtains jobs in the summertime and contributes what he makes to the general household funds. He wants to complete high school and believes that he must finish in order to get "a good job." His ambition is to get a job as a brakeman on the railroad because he has heard that "brakemen make as much as eighty dollars a week." He wants to get a "good house." At present he is determined never to get married: "I am going to be a lone bachelor. I will get old that way." He expresses no interest in Yaqui or other girls and does not go with them at fiestas. His associates outside of school are Yaqui boys his own age.

Dolores is one of the best dancers in the Matachin society. He has recently been promoted to Monarca, that is, dance leader. He began dancing at the age of four in accordance with a manda made by his grandmother. His mother says:

Dolores was only four years old when he danced first. The Kobanao would hold him by the hand and lead him around to make him do the dance right. He didn't like to do it and would get sleepy, because he had to dance all through the night. He was very pretty in his Malinche dress, but I think that is the way he got so nearsighted. But he likes to dance now whenever they dance and he always goes.

He is one of the most regular of participants, but it is notable that he, as well as his mother, places his schoolwork above Matachin dancing as a value. Whenever the Matachinis dance during the week at a ceremony that cannot be postponed until the weekend, Dolores appears and dances, but he explains that he cannot dance all night because, "I have to go to school in the morning." He never stays later than midnight on such occasions. Both he and his mother, as well as the rest of the family, are proud of the fact that Dolores has become sufficiently skillful to dance as Monarca. His mother made a special trip to San Xavier Mission to see him dance in that

Dolores Martínez dancing as
Malinche, left, Palm Sunday,
March 1937. *Photograph by
David J. Jones, Jr.*

capacity in 1940, an unusual action for her since she ordinarily pays no
attention to Yaqui ceremonies outside her own household.

Significant attitudes of Dolores are indicated in the following:

You know, those Papagos are very primitive. They do things in the old ways.
They follow the old customs. The Yaqui were never primitive like that. They never
did those things. They were always like they are now. But the Papagos used to
paint themselves when they danced and they still do that. Then they used to paint
themselves before they went to war. The Yaquis never did that. The Yaquis weren't
primitive like the American Indian. We have been studying about all those things
in school and my teacher has been telling us how primitive the Indians are.

He is aware of differences among Yaquis and has opinions about their
significance:

Those people down at the other place (Barrio Libre) they call us the crazy village.
They don't like what we do. They think we are crazy because people take pictures
at the Gloria and because we have let them take phonograph records. Maybe they

are jealous. I have heard a lot of people talking that way. They don't like it because we send Pascolas out to dance at the Papago Reservation. They don't like it because we had Matachinis dancing at a house in Tucson where there wasn't any santo. They say we are a crazy village and they don't know why we do that. Maybe they are just old-fashioned.

Still under the protective care of his family, Dolores's personality is not subject yet to the conflicts that his dual orientation provides material for. He is living simultaneously, unquestionably, in the two cultural worlds that his mother and grandmother represent. If there is to be conflict, there is no sign that it has yet developed. In a sense his situation is like that of a woman such as Salamina Valenzuela. He is in Yaqui society, but many of his values and hence much of his cultural participation lie in Anglo-American society. His opportunities for social mobility have not yet arrived.

Josefina Escalante

Dolores has a half-sister named Josefina. She is eighteen. Her mother is Joaquina Araiza. She has gone through eighth grade in Tucson schools and speaks and reads English moderately well, but she is not so much at home in the language as Dolores. Having stopped going to school, Josefina now picks cotton with the family in the autumn and winter months, usually staying in Pascua and going to nearby farms. She dislikes picking cotton intensely and wants to get work "taking care of babies and cleaning" in Anglo-American households. She is positive about not wanting to work for Mexican Americans. She also has the ambition of wanting to be a teacher "like the white teachers I had in school." But she has no notion of how to become one.

Josefina tells Anglo-American interviewers, "I don't talk good Yaqui. I don't know how to talk it very well. My grandmother has to tell us how to say words." She is proud of her ability to speak English. She and the young girls with whom she went to school speak English among themselves in the village. At school she developed some very definite feelings about other ethnic groups. She did not like "the Mexican kids"; they play "mean" and "fight all the time." She insists that she liked "white kids" better and had a "lot of white girl friends." When she was at Flowing Wells school the teacher was very strict about not permitting any of the children to speak Spanish or Yaqui during school hours. She used to make them bend over

Josefina Escalante, March 1937.
Photograph by Rosamond B.
Spicer.

and whip them if they used any language but English. Josefina is proud of the fact that she never got whipped for this offense. She did not like Davis School where "all the kids talked in Spanish all the time even though they weren't allowed to." She says of a Yaqui family living in Pascua:

You know those people over there? They can't talk Mexican or English, they just talk Yaqui all the time. If I talk to them in Mexican they just hang their mouths open and don't know what I'm talking about.

Once she volunteered the following in the midst of a talk with an Anglo-American interviewer:

I don't feel like a Yaqui. I don't know anything about what they do. (The interviewer suggested that she had seen her singing as a Cantora at the Yaqui church.) Yes, but I don't know anything about it. I just don't feel like a Yaqui or anything. I just feel like people.

During another interview that took place while she was watching a Yaqui fiesta at which she should have been singing, but had refused to, she said,

"I wish I was a white woman, and then I would like to be a teacher all my life."

Josefina was promised by her grandmother to be first an Angelita during the Easter ceremonies and then a Cantora. The grandmother insists that she has a manda, but Josefina tells Anglo Americans that she does not have one. Nevertheless, she participates frequently as a Cantora in the Pascua ceremonies and has developed some knowledge and skill in the work. She maintains, however, that she does not like to sing and gets out of it when she can.

She is very conscious of what "those Yaquis" (the other villagers) say about her family. Thus in discussing the cumpleaño, which the family was to have in memory of her great-grandfather's death two years before, she told an interviewer that "it wouldn't matter if they (her family) didn't have that fiesta." The interviewer then asked why they were going to go through with it. Josefina said, "Those Yaquis wouldn't like it if they didn't have it. They say things about our not having it, about not having it last year. They said that he (the dead man) must have been her (the grandmother's) stepfather." Similarly, she is very conscious of the village disapproval of her mother for letting Dolores stay in school so long, but she has no particular feeling about the value of his staying in school. Her feeling that nothing bad would happen if the death anniversary ceremony was not held is parallel with her feeling about the Matachin Kobanao's belief that it is bad to permit the Matachinis to dance at private Anglo-American houses where "there is no santo." This she thinks is just a "funny" idea, and she laughs at hearing it.

Josefina is a blithe girl and says she feels as if she is "about twelve years old instead of eighteen." She spends her time at home cleaning and washing clothes and goes out in the evening with Yaqui girls her own age and younger, wandering through the village giggling and stopping in at ceremonies (if she has not been commanded to serve at them as a Cantora). Since leaving school, her life is wholly in the village and her friends are all Yaquis. But her point of view, like her brother's, is such that she places little value on anything that is distinctively Yaqui. The ceremonial life is incomprehensible to her and her ceremonial participation, unlike her brother in this instance, is drudgery. Yet the moral sanctions of the villagers are strongly operative on her and tend to make her behavior conform to the Yaqui standard. She is externally a Yaqui girl, if she is not so internally.

Presillano Valenzuela

Presillano comes from a household that is as far below the Pascua standard of cleanliness and order as the Araiza household is above it. We have already indicated the nature of the drinking and disorder apparent in this household in our discussion of Salamina. Presillano, at age twelve, has never been promised to serve any ceremonial organization. Unlike his older brother, Dolores, who was also never promised, he has not been moved even to associate with the Matachinis and to learn the dance steps for the fun of doing it and for the sense of comradeship with the other young boys. Presillano stays at home most of the time and looks at comic books. He went through two or three grades in school and is able to speak English, but rarely tries it. He was not quick in school, although for a time he worked hard under the inspiration of his sister, Salamina. When asked what his ambition is, he says simply, "I won't be anything." He has gone

Presillano Valenzuela playing with his little brother, George, April 1937. *Photograph by David J. Jones, Jr.*

out to a C.C.C. camp, but won't stay and comes back to Pascua. He draws pictures—of soldiers in uniform, of long streamlined automobiles, and of airplanes. He likes to color these pictures with crayons. He has learned to play the guitar and sings with his uncles and brother and father sometimes in the evening—songs in Spanish, the current popular songs that they have on their phonograph records. He never appears at a Yaqui ceremony. His interests are crystallized in no direction beyond playing the guitar. He has recently begun to drink a little.

Dolores Romero

In 1941, at the age of twenty-one, Dolores was drafted into the army, but at seventeen he was a Matachin Monarca. He danced at every ceremony. He had dropped out of school after the fifth grade, when he was thirteen, because he didn't "like to sit inside." He says, "I would get sleepy. So I just didn't go anymore." But he learned to read and write and continued to take pleasure in writing, even composing some poems (about a beautiful horse) of his own. He speaks good English and uses it whenever opportunity presents itself.

Dolores's mother died when he was very young, and he was brought up in Pascua by his grandmother, who had been born on the Yaqui River. His grandmother was "muy Yaqui" and promised Dolores to the Matachinis. The household was maintained by her married son, and so Dolores was not forced to work after he stopped school. Before being drafted he devoted most of his time to making Matachin paraphernalia, dancing Matachin, and just visiting with his friends. He never drank. He was very friendly with Tomás Alvarez, the Matachin Kobanao, and went with him on limosnas to other villages. He spent a great deal of time just talking with him.

Dolores felt that the Maestros were a mysterious and awesome group. He did not understand what they were doing when they went to sing for a dying person. He wondered whether they were trying to make the person die. He was interested in the stories he had heard about a water serpent from whom the Pascolas got their knowledge. He wondered if it would be possible to go down to Sonora and find out if the story were true. He doubted it. He did not have any explanations for the Easter ceremonies in which he took part each year as a Caballero. He participated faithfully, marching with the Fariseos and carrying his aluminum painted lance on

A group of *Matachinis;* Tomás Alvarez, *Kobanao, top center,* Dolores Romero, *lower right,* February 1937. *Photograph by David J. Jones, Jr.*

which he had spent a good deal of time. He obeyed orders and carried out his duties carefully, but he had never understood what they meant. He saw the ceremonies in terms merely of the specific actions which he and others carried out. Occasionally, he felt some understanding of ritual meanings, as when he volunteered, for instance, that the whipping on Wednesday night of Holy Week was "to make people clean." But ordinarily, a discussion of such an event would lead him to say: "The father whips his children and compadres whip each other." That was all, the simple fact of what was done. Moving in the round of yearly ceremony, he was a part of it all, but its meanings went no farther than the social relations in which they involved him.

Before leaving for the army, Dolores had no ambitions that he could express. He had no preference for railroad work as against cotton picking and ranch work. He took what he could get when he found it became necessary for him to get a job. He went on from day to day with no plan and no apparent desires other than to take part for the pleasure of it in the Matachin dances. He was happy, easy going, friendly, and inclined to take life easily. He was energetic only when dancing Matachin.

Untouched by Anglo-American values and unreflective about Yaqui values, Dolores represents a common type of youth in Pascua. A participant to the full in Yaqui society, allowing himself to be molded easily in its ways, enjoying the rhythm of its dancing and taking delight in the color of its ceremonies, the culture on which it is based remained outside the range of his grasp. He was not conscious of it in any way because he had never paused to set it in contrast with anything else. In his life there is no conflict and hence no decision to make. Now that he has been taken into the army, will there be a change?

Dolores Romero, *center,* dancing *Matachin,* November 1936. *Photograph by Rosamond B. Spicer.*

Summary of Data on the Youngest Generation

The young people whose behavior and attitudes we have considered in this chapter introduce few new elements into our discussion of Yaqui individuals. It is not new to find the dual orientation such as characterizes Dolores Martínez. The whole-hearted evaluation of Anglo-American ways above Yaqui ways, such as we find in Josefina, is not new either; that again we may duplicate among the younger men and women. The sharper distinctions in the matter of skin color and cleanliness which the younger people make are perhaps new, but they are new only in the matter of degree. They are also prominent in the views of older Yaquis.

We might have expected to find more evidence of conflicts here, but it is a significant fact that we do not. These young people are not obsessed with conflict. Their personalities are smooth running and their tones are happy, much more so than in the case of either the younger or the older adult group. We can see material for conflict; we can detect potential conflicts arising, but as yet, conflicts have not sharpened. The young people seem to be poised to take their places in a conflicting world. They are equipped to move either into or out of Yaqui society and culture. They have not yet suffered frustrations, though we can predict that a boy such as Dolores Martínez is almost certain to have them. We must return to the adults if we wish to study the kinds of conflicts to which Yaqui culture contacts give rise.

It is impossible to say that in this youngest generation we have evidence of uniform dual orientation in Yaqui and Anglo-American cultures. The data on Dolores Romero belie such a statement. It is still possible in this third Arizona generation to find individuals whose orientation in spite of a little English is wholly within Yaqui society. Before being drafted, Dolores Romero was such an individual. And yet careful note must be made of the fact that although he has been thoroughly oriented in Yaqui society and although he was almost free of contact with Anglo-American culture, he remains a nonparticipant in Yaqui culture; he does not know much about it. We have no evidence that he has been injected with its values. It remains a mystery to him, unexplained, and outside his thoughts and his life. It does not indeed have value for him any more than Anglo-American culture has value for him.

PART III

Cultural Processes

CHAPTER 9

The Revival of Yaqui Culture

The Yaquis did not enter Arizona as a society, that is, as an organized group of persons. They came as individuals or as small groups of miscellaneous kin and ritual kin. The odyssey of Lucas Chavez was not unusual, a lone young man searching for relatives, compadres, and godparents. His search extended over a period of fifteen years or more, and he did not settle down among any considerable number of Yaquis until he was more than thirty years old. The Araiza household, holding together as an extended family of three generations, was unusual, representing, in fact, an extreme in the cohesion of any Yaqui group during the dispersal. Few Yaquis had as many Yaqui associates so continuously over the period from 1890 to 1905 as did Josefa Araiza. But even the Araiza household was isolated for years from other households. Yaqui society, even those units that had formed in the Sonora cities and haciendas after flight and deportation from the homeland, was thoroughly broken up.

Consequently, the Yaquis who came to Arizona and settled there just before and after 1900 did not constitute a transplanted segment of Yaqui society. They were individuals with varying degrees of enculturation in the Yaqui way of life, who for the most part had not known one another until their arrival in Arizona. They sought one another out, however, and began to form little groups within the Arizona population. These groups had no generally common background in the sense of childhood residence

253

in communities of the same type and indoctrination in a common set of understandings for meeting the whole range of individual needs. It is true that those, like Chavez, who were brought up in Yaqui River villages, even though the villages may have been at different ends of the Yaqui country, had closely similar backgrounds. But the Arizona immigrants were by no means all from Yaqui River villages. As many had been brought up in Hermosillo or some other Mexican community as had received early training in Yaqui communities.

There were, however, common features in their experience. The most important of these, and the one which tied together the common experiences, was maltreatment by Mexicans. It was this that gave meaning to their flight, to their goal of reaching refuge in the United States, and to their determination to settle permanently outside of Mexico. Other than this there was not even the common experience of having learned Yaqui as the language of earliest childhood. Although all who called themselves Yaquis in Arizona spoke the Yaqui language or the related Mayo by the time of their arrival, it is not certain that orphans like Tomás Alvarez and some others learned Yaqui as their first language. Yaqui was a common language for those who formed the Arizona settlements, but Spanish was also a common language, and it seems likely that there were as many who were as deficient in Yaqui as there were others who were deficient in Spanish. It was the same for other Yaqui customs. Individuals who joined the new Yaqui congregations had to be instructed and trained in the Yaqui ways by those who knew them.

It was, then, a consciousness of being classified as Yaqui by Mexicans that constituted the common background of the immigrants to Arizona. This brought together individuals of Mayo parentage, individuals who had lost all contact with Yaqui groups during formative years, as well as individuals who had been more or less fully disciplined and indoctrinated in the Yaqui customs of the River villages. It was on the basis of the common experience of having suffered as Yaquis that they came together and began to organize themselves apart from others in Arizona.

The Motives for Revival

The revival of Yaqui culture in Arizona was not immediate and wholesale. It has depended on the emergence of a Yaqui society, which grew slowly at first, became accelerated after 1910, and has continued steadily since then. The growth of Yaqui society has, in turn, depended on eco-nomic adjustments to the new situation in Arizona. As the economic life has stabilized and certain occupations have become traditional for Yaquis, the Yaqui settlements have taken form, and in these settlements Yaqui cul-tural traditions have found expression. The Yaqui cultural revival may not be regarded then as a sudden, sweeping response to any special condition or set of conditions in Arizona. It is to be understood, in its inception, as a number of individual responses to particular individual situations. Some of these responses have been revealed in the life stories that we have re-viewed.

Families who came across the line after 1900, as the Mexican depor-tation program intensified, had preserved family rituals of the traditional Yaqui form, for example, the all-night *velaroa*, or leavetaking ceremony, for a dead person. Of the personal crisis rites, this was the simplest and, in the surroundings of Mexican society, the most unobtrusive. It was simpler than the Yaqui wedding or the death anniversary in that traditionally it did not require the professional Pascola dancers. In not requiring them, it did not call attention to the family as Yaquis, a matter which as we have seen was of great importance in the deportation period when they feared identification as Yaquis. It was unobtrusive also in that Mexican custom likewise included all-night wakes for the dead. Traditionally, the velaroa for the dead did require a ritual specialist, such as a Sacristan or, if pos-sible, a Maestro. Many Yaquis, however, knew fragments of the ritual for the dead and could recite these. Such fragmentary services apparently were carried out by families during the whole period of the dispersal. They were, however, felt to be imperfect, and whenever a man with Temasti training appeared, he found himself in demand. While Yaquis seem gen-erally to have accepted the Catholic marriage ceremony as a substitute for the distinctive Yaqui wedding, they clung to some form of their traditional death ceremonies. These became in Arizona the stimulus and the instru-ment for the revival of a very large part of the ceremonial aspect of Yaqui culture.

In Nogalitos we have seen that Lucas Chavez remembered his mother's vow to have him serve as a Temasti. He had come across the interna-tional line and for the first time began to feel somewhat secure. He was making good as a railroad worker and seemed to be in a position for ad-vancement, but his interests clearly, from his account, lay elsewhere, and these were determined by his early experiences in Torim. He had found a small group of other Yaquis in Nogalitos, including Teofila Lopez, the mother of Cayetano Lopez, who had some fame as a Cantora and a woman with deep knowledge of Yaqui ritual. Lucas, ostensibly in response to the memory of his manda but certainly also in response to his own desire for recognition, began to study under Teofila. He learned the chants and the ritual acts and words and found himself called on to serve as Temasti when deaths occurred in the small Yaqui settlement. This sort of revival of ritual skills seems to have occurred frequently in this and subsequent periods among the Yaqui immigrants in Arizona. The few well-trained Yaquis like Teofila and like Juana de Amarillas and others taught what they knew to individuals who were beginning to be in demand in the newly forming Yaqui settlements. Often there was an unfulfilled promise, or manda, lying back of the interest in learning, but it is clear that many learned ceremonial skills in this period who had never had mandas. There was a demand for persons who knew the rituals to manage family ceremonies. This meant recognition and distinction.

The demand for ritual specialists appears, judging from the life story data, to have rested on two facts, which were by no means unrelated. On the one hand, there was a strong sense among the immigrants that they had not been behaving like true Yaquis during their dispersal. The feeling that death ceremonies were not carried out properly in the absence of a trained Temasti or Maestro was persistent. The cultural reference point remained, as is so clearly apparent in Lucas Chavez's point of view, in the Yaqui River villages as they remembered them or had heard their parents tell of them. So long as they did not meet such standards, they were not "proper" Yaquis. This persistent feeling among the immigrants gave great prestige to persons like Teofila Lopez, the Cantora, and the well-known lame Maestro, José María García of Pascua, both of whom had had status in Yaqui River villages as ritual specialists before and just subsequent to the defeat. This prestige continued to be accorded by Arizona Yaquis to later comers from the River villages who were known to have practiced their specialties there. Even through the 1930s, Matachin Dancers, Deer Singers, and others who appeared in the Arizona villages immediately became prominent, and Arizona Yaquis sat at their feet to learn the "proper" manner of doing Yaqui things.

In the case of Lucas Chavez, it is clear enough that from the time he reached Arizona he was much concerned to see the old way of life reconstituted. The question that occurs is why his interest remained turned in that direction. He had learned Mexican ways, including the language, with much success. He was getting along well in Anglo-American economic life. For fifteen years or more he had lived, like many other Yaquis, without practicing the old customs. An understanding of his motives, and of the motives of scores of other Yaquis whose experiences had been similar, seems to emerge from consideration of his attitudes toward Mexicans and their culture. Throughout his life, hatred of the stereotype Mexican was an important value for him. Implanted in him at the time of the killing of his parents at the battle of Buatachive, this hatred remained through all subsequent friendly contacts with Mexicans. The feeling gave importance to every means for de-identifying himself with Mexicans whose ways he had had to learn. While desire for distinction among Yaquis was a motive for his learning the Temasti specialty late in life, it would appear that this was reinforced by his desire to keep himself apart from Mexicans. One of the recurrent themes of his thought, as we have seen, has been that Mexicans are degenerate in their religious life. Mexican funerals, Mexican behavior on All Souls' Day, and Mexican religious activities generally seem to him poorly carried out versions of what should be done on these occasions. He has, in other words, ever since he became acquainted with Mexican ways, regarded them as something not different in kind from Yaqui ways, but different in degree. The right and proper way is the Yaqui way and hence by learning the Yaqui way he can demonstrate the superior virtue of not only himself but of Yaquis generally. The recurrent theme of the immigrant Yaqui generation in Arizona in criticizing the younger generations as "becoming like Mexicans" is the expression of this valuation of Mexicans in relation to Yaquis. It is a valuation that many Yaquis brought with them into Arizona and must be regarded as a source of much of the activity in reviving the ceremonial aspects of Yaqui culture. It is a valuation that they kept before themselves through years of living in Arizona and one they have tried desperately to keep before their children.

As working aggregates of human beings, Yaquis carried out an adjustment to their places of early settlement, such as Nogalitos, an adjustment which made use of very little overt behavior that was in the Yaqui tradition. Aside from the language and the curtailed forms of death ceremonies, there was nothing that an outside observer might identify as Yaqui. Food, clothing, houses, family life, work habits—all that an observer might casually see—were not noticeably different from those of Mexican laborers working on the railroad and elsewhere in the vicinity of Nogales. Contemporary observers testify to that, but they also testify that on close acquaintance with Yaqui individuals, they became slowly aware of a history and a consciousness of being Yaqui, of a tribal patriotism. It was this evaluation of themselves, nourished rather than extinguished by the defeats of Cajeme and later leaders and by persecution at Mexican hands, that persisted and that increasingly found expression in Arizona.

It required symbols of some sort because the separate identity from Mexicans that they felt did not appear in the daily life and associations. The symbols that were used were supplied by the ritual specialists who turned up among the immigrants in every place of Yaqui settlement.

The Materials of the Revival

The revival in Arizona of the whole complex and closely integrated system of late nineteenth-century Sonoran Yaqui culture could not be achieved, even approximately, in the absence of Yaqui ownership of the land they were living on, an agricultural economy of small independent farmers, a sense of political independence at least at the local government level, and a sense of function and urgency in maintaining military organization. Yaqui culture as some of the immigrants had known it in Sonora was closely integrated with such economic conditions and such a framework of relationships with non-Yaquis. On the other hand, in Arizona, Yaquis were generally squatters with a keen awareness of that fact; they had long since become dependent on wage labor for a living; they were very conscious of being in Arizona on sufferance of a powerful United States government; and traditional Yaqui military organization on United States soil, so far as the data go, had meaning for no Yaqui. The aspects of Yaqui culture which were revived at the beginning of the adjustment in the United States were selected, however unconsciously, with reference to these circumstances. It was a partial revival only and yet it is clear that once a part of the system had been set in operation there was a powerful tendency to reconstitute the whole.

The revival began in the United States with the filling out of individual crisis rites according to the patterns of which only a few specialists actually knew the details, but of which most adults were conscious in a vague way. If we regard the traditional recitation in Yaqui of portions of the Mass for the Dead (taught by the Jesuits) as an innovation at funerals under these circumstances, we understand immediately why the innovation spread promptly among the Arizona immigrants. It was not at all a case of the simple persistence of well-known custom, of cultural inertia; it was rather a filling in of a pattern of which the immigrants were aware with a content which was actually new to large numbers of them.

The immediate response to the rituals presented by the trained special-ists must have taken place in some such terms. But once accepted by the people of the new Yaqui settlements as the completed rituals, the new con-tent also fulfilled the need which we have just discussed. All night wakes for the dead, which had been so little different from those of Mexican neighbors, now could be regarded as true Yaqui velaroa, a meaning which had had no existence in Yaqui River villages that were exclusively or over-whelmingly Yaqui in population. In Arizona they became an instrument for differentiating Yaquis from Mexicans. What were actually old forms of long existence in Sonora Yaqui culture assumed new meanings that had a special function in the new circumstances into which they were intro-duced. Such a conclusion seems inescapable from a review of attitudes such as Lucas Chavez's toward the content of Yaqui ritual and toward Mexican ritual behavior.

The completing of the patterns of the individual crisis rites involved the revival of more and more of the distinctive Yaqui ritual forms. This has been traced to some extent historically by Wilder[1] and Rosamond Spicer.[2] The development of the ritual patterns was accompanied by a steady growth of a sense of having nothing to fear from Mexicans in the United States or from the Anglo Americans, that is, of nothing to fear in reidentification of themselves as Yaquis. Funerals and novenas for the dead were given the new content by Maestros and Temastis from the river vil-lages and newly apprenticed Maestros and Temastis, who had never seen a river village. Maestros were taken to the public cemeteries on All Souls' Day for services over those who died in Arizona. And in addition, families slowly began to fill out the patterns of crisis rites with even more strik-ingly Yaqui customs. The funerals of children in accordance with the old pattern required the dancing of a Pascola, since the death of a child was an occasion for joy, the child being regarded as attaining heaven in inno-cence. The general Mexican pattern of the child's funeral now began to be expressed through the highly distinctive Yaqui behavior of Pascola Dance and the accompanying Pascola ritual. Death anniversaries, too, began to be celebrated in the Yaqui way with a fiesta presided over by Pascolas and enlivened by a Deer Dance to express the satisfaction of the family in re-lease from the year of mourning. A few Pascola Dancers appeared to meet the demand and immediately began to train others. There was even an occasional Deer Dancer—that relatively rarer ceremonial dance specialist —among the immigrants. Thus, as the settlements of Yaquis spread over southern Arizona from Nogalitos to the outskirts of Tucson and to the agricultural region near Phoenix, the ceremonial patterns of the crisis rites were steadily revived. There was an interest in learning the old forms, which had now spread beyond the immigrant adults to many of their sons and daughters. A new generation was growing up with the special Yaqui ritual skills.

Next in order came the revival of ceremonies, the significance of which reached beyond the household groups and the performance of which required not only the cooperation of many households but also the establishment of what in Arizona were newly organized ceremonial groups. The ceremonies of this type that were revived, beginning about 1906, were the annual Easter ceremonies. One revival took place at a ranch near Tucson, the other at Guadalupe village near Phoenix, in the two regions which had become the major centers of settlement for Yaquis. The individual who was responsible for the Tucson revival was the stepfather of Jesús García, a man who had spent a long period in Yaqui River villages but who had also lived on very intimate terms with Mexicans in Sonora, and whose household in Pascua has been characterized as mixed. García expressed his motive—and that of other men associated with him in the enterprise—in terms of the crisis rite ceremonialism which had developed in Arizona. As he says, he felt it necessary to fulfill Yaqui obligations to Jesus Christ by holding what he regards as the death anniversary (*lutupahko*) of Jesus. Again it seems to have been a filling out of patterns already partly established in Arizona.

The event is widely remembered and talked about among Arizona Yaquis, quite evidently in the same terms as its founder thought of it, as a fulfillment. It was accompanied by a sense of reestablishment of themselves as Yaquis on the part of members of the immigrant generation. There was no faltering in its annual performance from the time of its first establishment. It was accepted by large numbers of Yaquis immediately, their participation from the start indicating the immediate need that it filled. It resulted in the organization of ceremonial societies—the Fariseos as they are called in Arizona and the Matachinis—closely following the pattern of such societies in the old river culture, but with many differences connected with the specific Arizona circumstances. These societies have become the functioning framework of Yaqui community organization.

The meaning of the revival of the Easter ceremonies may be understood only in the light of knowledge of their role in older Yaqui ceremonial life. The Easter rites themselves are only a part of ceremonials extending through the whole Lenten period and until the spring ceremonial of the Finding of the Holy Cross in early May. This ceremonial season was one with many rigorous ritual taboos, and the whole period was presided over and the taboos enforced by two ceremonial societies, the Caballeros and the Fariseos, called collectively Kohtumbre Ya'ura, "our leaders of custom." The central events of Yaqui-Christian mythology were dramatized during this period; the canons of proper belief and ritual participation were made constantly explicit; civil affairs were suspended and the civil organization subordinated to the ceremonial organization; and individuals were made to feel the rigid and supernaturally sanctioned control of their lives by the dominant supernaturals—Our Mother (with manifestations as Mary) and the Lord (the great curer who wandered the Yaqui country before the coming of the Spaniards and who became known as Jesus). The Easter ceremonies were, in other words, the annual focus and climax of ceremonial life and symbolized the preeminence of the supernaturals over all Yaqui affairs.

In Arizona much of the form was lost, a fact of which Yaquis remain thoroughly conscious, and many of the meanings were different. But enough of the old meanings and associations were carried on in the form of the events to make it at once a dominant interest in Yaqui life in Arizona. And the new meaning of full identification as Yaquis and ultimate de-identification from Mexicans reinforced the surviving old meanings and quickly gave the ceremonies an important function and central place in Arizona Yaqui lives. The ceremonies have continued to command the participation of a majority of Yaquis.

The revival of Yaqui culture has consisted, then, of the reinstitution of a series of ritual patterns which are interlocked in intricate ways at many points. The ritual for proper care of the dead was linked at points with the ritual of the compadre-padrino system. It was linked also with the Pascola and the Deer-Dance ritual. The latter, in turn, is linked with a concept of the natural world and with witchcraft and diseases caused by witches or black magic. The death rituals were also linked with a set of concepts concerning Jesus and Mary and hence with the ceremonial society system devoted to serving them. This, in turn, was linked closely with another set of concepts concerning curing and diseases not caused by witchcraft. The redevelopment of the death ritual and other crisis rituals involved the Arizona Yaquis in this interlocking set of beliefs and ceremonial activities. Each reintroduced behavior and belief had its specific function for Yaqui individuals, ranging from the curing of disease to the establishment of dependable and satisfactory relations with dead and living Yaquis. But over and above such individual uses, the Yaqui customs filled the urgent need that Yaquis felt for identification of themselves as Yaquis and not as Mexicans whose culture they had had to adopt in large measure.

The reestablishment of the major features of the ceremonial system did

not constitute reestablishment of the whole Yaqui cultural system. Portions of ceremonial and belief systems were omitted in Arizona. Much of
this was connected with the village organization specifically, such as the
pahkome, or village fiesta system, and the associated ceremonials.[3] It is important to emphasize that the ritual symbols, and only an essential outline
of these as it were, were selected for revival and that these have served the
purpose—though not fully, as older Yaquis believe—of defining Yaquis as
Yaquis in their new situation.

The revivalistic tendency, once set in motion, moved steadily toward
complete revival, however. After the revival of the Easter ceremonies, there
were repeated efforts to reestablish forms of village organization approxi-
mating those on the Yaqui River. It has been possible to follow the first
of these in detail in the life story of Lucas Chavez. Certainly, Chavez regarded the Pistola government as a reestablishment of Yaqui River village organization. He interpreted it constantly in those terms. He and the
others associated in the revival made great efforts to restore the titles like
Pueblo Kobanao and even bow-chief (*Wikoi Ya'ut*) and influenced Pistola
to behave in ways that they regarded as proper for a Kobanao, since Pistola
had not experienced life in a Yaqui village firsthand. These efforts, like subsequent ones along the same line, failed. There are some data indicating the
reasons. Chief among these appear to be the facts that individual Yaquis
had already, by the time of Pistola's emergence in 1917–1918, gone far in
making the individual adjustments to job-getting and job-holding and to
making use of charity and other aid from Anglo-American sources and
that the original sanction for Pistola's office proceeded not from Yaquis
but from a group of Anglo Americans who had seen a Yaqui organization as useful in controlling the illegal movement of Yaquis back and forth
across the border. The organization, in other words, did not grow out of
Yaqui needs as they had developed, nor did it successfully meet those of
their real needs that it proposed to.

However, it may be asked, why did it not serve the need of further symbolic identification of Yaquis as Yaquis and hence gain acceptance? Chavez
and the others worked hard to make it serve that need. They obtained the
right to use a tract of land exclusively for Yaqui residence, they concocted a
"Yaqui flag," and they resurrected for a time the military society complete
with headdresses, bows and arrows, music and dances. Why did this not
supplement the identification through ritual symbols that had been already
achieved through the Easter ceremonies and so widely spread among Arizona Yaquis? Pistola's death at the crucial instant of the setting up of the
village area of Pascua undoubtedly had something to do with the non-

acceptance, but it is evident that the revival of the ceremonial system did not depend on the personality or activities of any one particular individual. There were, moreover, other Yaquis, like Francisco Matus, Tomás Alvarez, and Lucas Chavez himself who had the same ideas as Pistola and tried to further them after his death. It seems that the filling out of a pattern in the case of political organization was felt to be possible only through a return to Yaqui territory. The organization of the village, which among Yaqui River Yaquis was closely linked with land management, had meaning only in relation to Yaqui-controlled land. There is no indication in the data on individuals in Arizona that they felt the same sense of loss in connection with political life as they did in connection with ceremonial life. The incompletion here was a matter of being removed from Yaqui land, the ancestral land, and those who were remaining in Arizona had made highly conscious decisions not to return to the Yaqui country. Only the early provision by legal measures of something akin to a reservation might have resulted in the revival of the old forms of political organization. Something approaching this was done at Guadalupe, but residence there was still quite voluntary and as a result inclined to be shifting. Political organization had little more success there than it did at Pascua.

The third of the major features of Yaqui formal organization and belief, namely, the institution of the military society, also failed to be revived in Arizona, except in a curiously vestigial form. The attempt to revive it in connection with the Pistola government at Pascua resulted ultimately in the persistence of some of its ceremonial aspects, Coyote Dances at the Easter ceremonies, and some other ritual participation by individuals who had belonged to military societies in the river villages. It continued, in other words, as an adjunct of the ceremonial revival, pulled along by that in the same manner, but on a much smaller scale, as the Pascolas and the Deer Dancer.

The revival of formal patterns of behavior in Yaqui culture included, therefore, only the ceremonial patterns, and not all of those. It did not include the economic, the political, and the military aspects of the older Yaqui culture. The economic patterns, so far as subsistence activities themselves were concerned, had complete substitutions in the new situation and no opportunity for choice developed; only minor aspects of the economic life were revived—for example, food used as a medium of exchange and as payment of social obligations and the revival of techniques for making ritual paraphernalia and musical instruments, aspects which again were intimately connected with the ceremonial system.

But what of those aspects of the culture of a kind which have sometimes been called covert culture, and at other times value-attitudes or "sanctions"? Some features of Yaqui culture that may be classified under this concept are certainly present in Yaqui communities in Arizona. They are probably best described in such terms as: their concept of themselves as persons, or constellations of social personalities, rather than as unitary individuals (implicit in their identifications of other Yaquis and their use or nonuse of the impersonal name); their evaluation of ceremonial labor as not requiring justification (implicit in a large number of activities and in characteristic statements); and their classification of all bodily functions including excretion and sexual intercourse as of the same kind, that is, as simple physiological actions. None of these would seem to be formally and explicitly taught, but they are parts of a Yaqui view of life that orders considerable portions of experience in certain ways not characteristic of other peoples among whom they live, and they are therefore to be regarded as a part of Yaqui culture. Whether or not we can speak of such aspects of the culture as having been revived remains undetermined. The evaluation, for example, of ceremonial labor may not have been a result of the revival of ceremonial activities, but may have given rise to the revival of the activities. This value-attitude may conceivably have been a part of the make-up of adult Yaquis throughout the period of dispersal and have been a determining factor in the revival of the overt behavior of ceremonialism. Our data do not go far enough to enable us to say anything worthwhile about the place of these aspects of covert culture in the whole process of revival. Our analysis remains, unfortunately, at the level of overt behavior.

It should be said, finally, that the revival of Yaqui culture as symbols of Yaqui identification in Arizona has resulted in very little reinterpretation. The characteristic of the revival has not been a distortion or reworking of the old forms, but rather reestablishment of the old forms with omissions, with much loss of meaning, and with very little attribution of new meanings.

The Results of Revival

As the patterns of beliefs of Yaqui ceremonialism spread and became more and more firmly established, Yaqui population was increasing steadily in Arizona. The increase was a result of both new births and continued migration. It seems very probable that during the early 1920s the number of Sonora-born Yaquis reached a peak. Alien registration figures for 1940 indicate that the greater number of Yaqui immigrants in Pascua at that time had entered the United States after 1907 and before 1920. This period of most intensive migration began with the culmination of the Mexican deportation program for Yaquis and extended through the period of war and unrest of the Mexican Revolution. It will be noted that the major features of the cultural revival had already taken place before the new wave of migration began. It is also to be noted that most of the important innovators, or revivalists, who were still active as ceremonial leaders in 1940 among Arizona Yaquis had entered the United States some years before 1907. The revival was led by the earlier group of immigrants, although there is no doubt that much stimulus and some new leadership came from the later arrivals.

The newer immigrants had universally the same experiences of fear and flight from Mexicans in common with the old immigrants. If anything, the experiences of most of them were even more harrowing and desperate than those who preceded, for after 1900 the deportation campaign had become more ruthless than ever, and the fighting of the Yaqui guerrillas in Sonora also became more bloody as it became more desperate. The new immigrants, however, had Yaqui communities to go to in Arizona. It had been one of the accompanying conditions of the revival, in part a result of it, that Yaquis had sifted out of the general population to associate more intimately with one another. This voluntary separation of themselves resulted in little clusters of Yaqui households on the outskirts of the southern Arizona cities, groupings which have for the most part remained as the nuclei of subsequent Yaqui settlements. A territorial base, in other words, began to be established for Arizona Yaquis. Movement for Yaquis in the new extremely mobile society of Arizona became, from as early as 1905 and 1906, a movement back and forth among these new but increasingly stable points of Yaqui concentration.

As such settlements became established and the ceremonial revival continued, the attention of Anglo Americans was steadily drawn to the Yaquis. Indeed, the prompt and concrete result of the reintroduction of the old ceremonies was the Anglo-American recognition that Yaquis were different from Mexicans. This had important effects on the development of relations between Yaquis and Anglo Americans.

It resulted very soon in the establishment of an identification of Yaquis with other American Indians in the minds of a number of Anglo Americans. This, in turn, was associated with reservations, and so we see Anglo Americans attempting to develop a sort of reservation system for all Yaquis in Arizona. The establishment of Guadalupe and Pascua villages was the concrete result of this Anglo-American interest; these centers were regarded by most Anglo Americans in Arizona as containing all the Yaquis in the state. It is true that through the years these two settlements have been the most stable, both geographically and probably in terms of population as well. It is from their existence (for the majority of Anglo Americans) that Yaqui identity has been thoroughly established as unique.

We may say that the revival of Yaqui culture, therefore, had two important effects very soon after it got under way. On the one hand, it aided and accelerated the geographical separation of Yaquis from others and the consequent establishment of more or less stable centers of residence for Yaquis in Arizona. On the other hand, it contributed greatly to the identification of Yaquis as Indians distinct from the incoming Mexican immigrants, thus bringing about quite a different set of relations between Yaquis and Anglo Americans as compared with those between the latter and the Mexican immigrants.

Within the Yaqui settlements the revival of customs was establishing a social organization as the instrument for expressing the ritual beliefs and carrying out the ritual activities. The ceremonial societies, especially the Fariseo and Matachin societies, were growing in numbers and in definiteness of duties and organization. The ceremonial sponsor system was likewise developing, knitting Yaquis all over Arizona into its set of rights and obligations. Into these formal organizations, the children of the immigrants born in Arizona were being introduced one by one as they grew up in the new settlements. The values and the interests that were steadily being asserted through this organization were being taught through participation in the revived activities. The children of the immigrants were adopting ways of behavior and accepting beliefs that would prove to involve them in many conflicts as they adopted, at the same time, many of the behaviors of the non-Yaqui society, in economic as well as other aspects of life for which Yaqui customs were not presented to guide them.

CHAPTER 10
The Nature of the Contacts

Arizona Yaquis do not describe their contacts with non-Yaquis as complex or confusing. Making use of the available Yaqui stereotypes of other groups, along with their own personal experience, they appear to regard the behavior of non-Yaquis outside of Mexico as reasonable, consistent, and predictable. They frequently, however, discuss the behavior of Yaquis in Arizona in quite opposite terms, holding that it is unreasonable and inconsistent in many instances, though not in all. They describe Yaqui behavior, in other words, as complex and sometimes not easy to understand. The social world of Yaquis seems to them more complex, and the basis of this viewpoint is undoubtedly imperfect acquaintance, indicative of limited contact with the range of Anglo- and Mexican-American cultures.

It is only to the outside observer that Yaqui contacts with other groups appear to be immensely complex, and this is because the observer is in a position to view the whole variety of contacts that take place, not only in a given year, let us say, but also over the whole period of Yaqui residence in Arizona. Yaqui contacts have been numerous, as we have seen, impinging on every Yaqui in some direct way; they have involved every aspect of Anglo-American culture, from food and curing to religious belief; and many of the contacts have had far-reaching consequences on Yaqui culture.

The variety of the contacts has been indicated in great detail in earlier chapters. It will be our purpose in this chapter to consider certain general features of the contact situation for the purpose of a better understanding of the specific processes through which transfer of behaviors takes place from individuals who are not Yaqui to individuals who are Yaqui.

Directed and Undirected Contacts

From the beginning of their residence in Arizona, Yaquis have had the same sort of freedom of movement, occupational choice, and opportunities for holding religious observances that characterize the Anglos and Mexican Americans of the region. There has been no effective, organized, overall control of the contacts of Yaquis with other individuals. Although attempts were made by Anglo Americans to follow the pattern of control that they had already worked out for their relations with the native Indians of Arizona, these efforts did not go far. Directed contact in the sense of a comprehensive system of relations enforced by the political government of the state or nation, that is, a reservation, has not characterized the Yaqui situation up to 1941. We may assume that this is a result of the fact that Yaquis have not constituted in their activities a real threat to any Anglo interests; nor have Yaquis as a group appeared to any large number of Arizonans to advance any established Anglo interests.

The fact remains that various segments of the non-Yaqui population have at different times taken special interest in Yaquis and sought to control the processes of culture transfer. These efforts have arisen out of the unusual individual contacts which Anglo Americans have had with Yaquis. The United States Attorney, the schoolteacher, and various missionaries whom we have considered attempted the establishment of special relationships for Yaquis as a group. These attempts have had certain definite effects, although none of the effects have touched all Yaquis or controlled the behavior of those whom they have touched in quite the manner intended. The primary effect of all such directed contacts has been to diffuse among large numbers of Anglo Americans the idea of Yaqui distinctness which was felt by the individuals who originally gained that view and established the physical area of Pascua, the Pascua school, and the Baptist Missionary center in Pascua. We have seen how in Tucson this idea has spread from such beginnings and how it later influenced the relations of service organizations, health department, Chamber of Commerce, and other groups with the Yaquis. Certainly, in the case of the schoolteacher who was interested in Yaqui assimilation and in the case of the missionaries who were interested in the same end, Yaqui distinctness was not in line with their assimilation purposes. Distinctiveness was an effect, however, quite consistent with Yaqui desires for revival of their culture. Ironically, attempts by these Anglo institutions to overwhelm Yaqui distinctiveness resulted in Yaquis reaffirming their unique identity.

There were, however, other effects of efforts at directed contact. The Protestant missionary activities, for example, have brought about the transfer of certain ideas to Yaquis. In the conversion of Lucas Chavez we have an example of this process. He has accepted the behavior of using the term "brother" in addressing members of the Baptist church and the idea that "there is only God." These are behaviors that he maintains in addition to his Yaqui-oriented beliefs about God and his Maestro specialties. They do not seem to have replaced any Yaqui behaviors, contrary to what the missionary expected them to do. There are others who have been affected in similar ways by the missionary activities. We may say in general that the directed contacts have been effective in the transfer of behaviors in a number of instances, but not in the replacement of behaviors. The process involves learning, but it is not apparent yet that it also involves rejection of Yaqui behaviors. At the point in conversion at which a role conflicting with long-standing Yaqui behavior is demanded, the process stops, and if the efforts of the missionary are intensified, the newly learned behavior seems to be more easily rejected than the older established behavior.

On the part of the Anglo Americans, other organized contacts have been maintained for the purpose of preserving Yaqui behaviors rather than of transferring Anglo behaviors to Yaquis. The most notable example of this has been the work of the Tucson Chamber of Commerce, which has annually rewarded Yaquis in Pascua not only with food and supplies but also with prestige and attention for the performance of the ceremonies that immigrant Yaquis regard as the ultimate expression of their Yaquiness and distinctness from Mexicans. The effect of this organized contact directed toward the preservation of Yaqui customs in one of the settlements has not been confined to that settlement. It is evident, on the contrary, that the effect has been the creation of some degree of rivalry among the villages with consequent results of maintaining and invigorating the ceremonial interests.

In general, it may be said that the directed contacts have resulted in little important transfer of non-Yaqui behaviors, that their most obvious and important effects have been, on the contrary, to reinforce the tendency toward cultural revival initiated by the immigrant generation.

Outstanding characteristics of the various directed efforts have been their lack of coordination and general inconsistency. This may be taken in itself as an expression of the Anglo-American culture with which Yaquis have been in contact. On the one hand, Yaquis have been urged by missionaries to abandon their ceremonies and their beliefs. On the other hand, they have been told that they are free to worship as they please and should go on doing so. Still further, they have been assisted in very concrete ways to go on with their older types of ceremonies. They are aware of the varying attitudes toward their distinctive ceremonies by different Anglo and Mexican Americans. With few exceptions they choose to pay attention only to the approving voices and actions, but even those who do listen to the Protestant missionaries seem to find sufficient sanction in the crowds of non-Yaquis who attend ceremonies annually, as well as in Yaqui society itself, for their continuance. The external influences on Yaquis, particularly the organized ones, are thus piecemeal, inconsistent with one another, and they in no sense present a coherent set of behaviors and values. It remains for the individual Yaquis, utilizing their individual experiences, to organize these influences in accordance with certain goals.

The culture contacts of Yaquis in Arizona are thus uncontrolled, in the sense that there is no single organization within the society of the Anglo and Mexican Americans that directs the contacts of individuals and their institutions with Yaquis. There is certainly not apparent to Yaquis any overall pattern or set of values in Anglo-American culture. They continue to see their contacts as a series of ad hoc adjustments to other individuals who often do not appear to think as Yaquis do, but who do not all appear to think in the same way.

The contact situation may be classified as one of social-cultural fusion. There is participation of Yaquis in the social institutions of surrounding people, and there is participation of non-Yaquis in Yaqui social institutions. Yaquis move out of association with other Yaquis permanently or temporarily. Mexican Americans move into intimate association with Yaquis permanently or temporarily. There is fusion, therefore, of Yaquis and non-Yaquis, and this is accompanied by a certain fusion or mutual modification of beliefs and behaviors. These are processes that affect proportionately more Yaquis than non-Yaquis, but it is not wholly a one-way matter. The processes which result in this fusion are not directed. They take place between Yaquis and other people who do not have programs to push among Yaquis, in the give-and-take of daily relationships with neighbors and other members of the surrounding society whom Yaquis come to know as whole persons in the complete range of their daily activities.

It is these processes that we shall discuss in the following sections, in an effort to understand both the general nature and the effects of social cultural fusion on the Yaqui culture patterns.

Social Mobility

A pervasive circumstance of Yaqui culture contacts both before and after the revival of patterns in Arizona has been a physical mobility of individuals. The older Yaqui men and women were set in motion by war and its consequences. They moved out of Yaqui communities, mingled with Mexicans in Sonora, and sought Yaqui associates in Sonora and Arizona. Once relatively settled in Arizona, many of them continued to move about among the Yaqui settlements, and some of them moved into situations of complete isolation from other Yaquis. Their children also have moved about as they have grown up and taken jobs in the Arizona milieu. For agricultural laborers in the region, moving about from job to job is an inherent part of the occupational pattern. Yaquis have assumed that pattern even though maintaining a home base in the areas of Yaqui settlement, while moving back and forth between cotton picking or other ranch jobs and the villages. This physical mobility is a major influence on Yaqui culture, but in itself it is not a sufficient explanation of such processes as the loss or disuse of Yaqui customs or the acquisition of non-Yaqui customs. Some of the most mobile Yaqui individuals and families are some of those whose participation in Yaqui culture has remained most steady and consistent. Although it sometimes accompanies the loss of Yaqui behaviors, geographic mobility does not necessarily precipitate such loss. We must distinguish clearly between physical and social mobility if we are to understand the processes of the loss and transfer of cultural behaviors.

It is quite possible for a Yaqui in Arizona to discontinue social relationships with all other Yaquis. This has happened for extended periods to younger men like Refugio Savala and Juan Silvas. Both of them have moved away from Yaqui settlements, as members of railroad section gangs or other labor groups, and have lived for months or years at a time in contact only with Mexicans, Anglos, Negroes, or other non-Yaquis. It is true that Savala has annually renewed relations with his kin group through writing a letter and sending money back to Pascua to meet his obligation to the ancestors, but Silvas has remained completely out of touch with all Yaquis during his travels. This sort of mobility, however, results in a minimum of incorporation into the social structure of the surrounding societies. It involves, other than informal friendship relations, only participation in work groups and employer-employee relations.

The more usual procedure in withdrawal from Yaqui social relations involves a small kinship group such as an elementary family. None of the individuals whose lives have been presented herein is a member of such a family unit, but data has been gathered on a number of them, such as a daughter of Guadalupe Balthazar and her family of procreation. They have moved out of Pascua, though only a short distance away, into a Mexican section of Tucson, maintaining only a few kinship and padrino relations with Yaquis. The family has moved upward in the status scale of Mexican society and may be regarded as incorporated into the class structure of Mexican society. They visit among Yaquis occasionally, but their social life is primarily with Mexicans. There is no reason to suppose that the children of this family will not assume kinship relations with Mexicans as they grow up and become incorporated wholly into the social structure of the Mexican segment of Tucson society.

There is indeed wide knowledge in Pascua of a group of brothers named Valdenegro who many years ago chose to isolate themselves from other Yaquis at the time of the most intensive revival of Yaqui customs. They are reported to have moved up the class scale in Mexican society through successful management of a bakery. Becoming well-to-do, they are said to deny, or at least to have forgotten, their Yaqui origin. Although this group of brothers was not studied, except as reported by other Yaquis, it seems likely that what is said of them is true, for the beginnings of such complete social mobility are apparent in a number of Yaqui families. By 1941, in fact, a fringe of some families on the edges of Pascua was engaged in the withdrawal from Yaqui social relations and the upward climb in the Mexican status scale.

Yaquis have moved also into Papago society, the procedure being the marriage of a Yaqui man to a Papago woman or vice versa. But by 1941 there was only one known instance in Arizona of any Yaqui individual or family assuming kinship relations of any type other than purely economic ones with Anglo Americans. Thus, although it may be said that there are no definite limits to social mobility into Mexican society, there is a sharp limit in connection with Anglo-American society. Yaqui men may move

readily into Mexican and Papago society, assuming status in kinship and
other structures; Yaqui women, as members of Yaqui kinship groups, may
also move into Mexican society and expect their children to become members of Mexican kinship groups, as well as of other groups in Mexican
society. By 1941 a few younger Yaqui women had married or were about
to marry Mexican men and may be expected to participate in both Yaqui
and Mexican kin, ritual kin, and other groups at the same time.

The social mobility characteristic of the Arizona Yaqui situation is not
one-way. There is also mobility for Mexicans into Yaqui society. Some of
these marriages have been discussed. Mexican women for the most part
marry Yaqui men and are brought into the social life of a Yaqui settlement through kinship and ritual kinship structures. Also Mexican family
groups as units move into the orbit of Yaqui society and become participant in it chiefly through ritual kinship relations, but also to some extent
through the ceremonial organizations. Such movement of Mexicans into
Yaqui society is less frequent than Yaqui movement into Mexican society.
The latter movement absorbs a few Yaquis every year, taking them out of
participation in Yaqui society to some degree. What we mean, then, by
social mobility is the assumption by Yaquis of social relations with non-
Yaquis that result in the reduction of social relations with Yaquis or the
failure to develop such social relations. There are degrees of social mobility among Yaquis. One form removes Yaquis from social relations with
other Yaquis completely for a period but does not result in the establishment of many different forms of social relations with others. Such individuals move back and forth frequently between Yaqui and other societies.
Another form removes individuals, or more usually small family groups,
from all social relations with other Yaquis and results in the establishment
of kinship, ritual kinship, and class status relations with non-Yaquis. Still
another form, perhaps the most common, consists of the maintenance of
social relations with Yaquis in kin and ritual kin groups while at the same
time establishing ritual kin and class status relations with non-Yaquis. For
Yaquis, these forms of social mobility involve movement into only two
other of the ethnic groups of Arizona, namely, the Papagos and the Mexican Americans. The movement into these other societies appears to have
no definite limits. Persons of Yaqui origin have assumed social relations in
kinship, ritual kinship, different class status, and religious groups in the
other two societies.

There is, moreover, social mobility involving the movement of Mexican
Americans into Yaqui society. That is, Mexicans, both men and women,

have assumed relations in Yaqui kinship and ritual kinship groups. Such mobility is most usually carried out without the abandonment of all social relations with other Mexicans, but there may be, nevertheless, the maintenance of very few relations with other Mexicans. There seems to be a limit for such mobility into Yaqui society. No cases are known that involve the assumption of the traditional relations in Yaqui ceremonial societies for the mobile Mexican, although Yaqui families of which they are members are consistent participants in the societies.

For our purpose, it is of great importance to understand how these forms of social mobility have arisen. It is, of course, no answer to say that such intermingling is natural among peoples living in close geographical proximity, that it always takes place. Cultural circumstances, as we know from many cases, interfere frequently with interchange of individuals between social systems. Moreover, in the case of the Yaquis there is a specific cultural circumstance which we should expect to interfere. If it is true that the revival of Yaqui culture has depended heavily on the desire to assume a distinct status from Mexicans, how does it happen that the mobility is primarily a matter of Yaquis merging with Mexicans? Some clues emerge from a consideration of the life story data.

In the first place, the enforced learning of Mexican ways during the dispersal has established a condition which makes the assumption of relations with Mexicans relatively easy. Yaquis uniformly know Spanish. They have widely substituted Spanish for Yaqui kinship terms. Their godparent institution has many similarities to that of Mexicans. Like Lucas Chavez, many of the immigrant generation came into intimate relationships with Mexican households. There is a considerable fund of common understandings on which it is possible to build social relations. It is, however, true that this condition exists for Yaquis who have not been socially mobile in Arizona as well as for those who have. Other factors are involved.

In a number of instances the movement is clearly a result of efforts to resolve the conflict between job holding and ceremonial activity, that is, the conflict inherent between Anglo-American economic patterns and revived Yaqui ceremonial patterns.[1] In some instances, individuals holding jobs become interested in maintaining a permanent relationship with an employer, and they place this interest higher than ceremonial participation. They are influenced by approval of employers and by what they can obtain through a steady and increasing income. They, in other words, become increasingly responsive to the class status system and the emphasis on material comforts and possessions of the Anglo society. Such families and individuals frequently move away from Yaqui settlements, thus increasing the difficulties for participation in the ceremonial societies. The process is gradual and involves a steadily decreasing amount of participation rather than a sudden breaking off of relations with Yaquis. Where such a family moves is usually determined by the location of the job, and the jobs that Yaquis hold are of the type which lower-income Mexicans usually hold. The result is more intensive association with Mexicans, most of whom are oriented to the class status system. This movement into Mexican society occurs primarily among family groups whose earnings are unusually high for a period, in other words, among those whose need for the Yaqui social institutions as sources of security falls off temporarily.

It should be noted that mobile families of this sort do by no means uniformly de-identify themselves as Yaquis. It may be true, as Yaquis insist, that some of them have denied their Yaqui origin, but of those whom it is still possible to trace as Yaquis, there is an insistence still that they are Yaqui. One finds a knowledge of and interest in Yaqui history among them and often a nostalgia for earlier days when they lived among Yaquis. It is characteristic of many of them that they ascribe their declining or discontinued Yaqui participation wholly to outside circumstances—"We live too far away"; "My boss won't let me"; "We couldn't find a Pascola for the wedding"; and so on—rather than to their own desires. There is, however, at the same time, particularly among the middle-aged members of such families who have usually brought about the change of residence, a tendency to speak of Yaqui custom as "very ugly." Although identifying themselves as Yaqui, they do not regard the ceremonial activities that they have rejected as essential any longer to their Yaquiness.

This may be summed up as a process involving conflict between roles required in economic and ceremonial patterns practiced by Arizona Yaquis. The resolution of the conflict in favor of the economic role and involving the giving up of the ceremonial role leads further to a new evaluation of the ceremonial role and its associated patterns. The interest in being Yaqui is, it is true, not as great, but the identification is still as Yaqui. What happens is not only a loss of behaviors, those of the ceremonial roles, but the attribution of a new meaning to those roles and their associated symbols as "ugly," unpleasant, an association that we may consider to be a result of the remembered unpleasant experiences in the course of the conflict and the efforts to resolve it in the choice of roles. In the life story data, the case of Cayetano Lopez gives the best illustration of the retention of Yaqui identification without interest in the revived culture.

There is another aspect of social mobility which has great significance for the future of Yaqui culture in Arizona. That is the movement of Mexicans into Yaqui society through intermarriage. The usual movement is of a Mexican woman into kinship and other relations with Yaquis through marriage. Two of the case studies, those of Jesús García and Juan Silvas, involved mixed households of this type. In all the cases studied the children have remained intensive participants in Yaqui culture through childhood and early youth. This has not meant, however, that they have made use only of Yaqui culture patterns. The characteristic feature of their home life is the constant use of both the Spanish and the Yaqui languages, with Spanish usually the most frequently used. Children most often use Spanish with their mothers and Yaqui with their fathers and other older members of the household. Other members of the household, however, use Spanish with the mother and frequently with the children. There is also a blurring of lines between the languages, with usage of words not fixed. That is, sometimes the Spanish word for an object is used in the context of a Yaqui expression, sometimes not, and vice versa. The Spanish language for children in such households, then, is learned under quite different circumstances from its learning by Yaqui children in all-Yaqui households. It is acquired earlier and associated with the mother and all circumstances of early childhood in the home. Such individuals are potentially more mobile than those who learn only Yaqui in infancy. Tomás Alvarez probably represents this type of early dual language training.

The members of mixed households of the type we have just been discussing—the fathers as well as the children—are also in positions to acquire other behaviors in ways not open to Yaquis of all-Yaqui households. This operates chiefly in connection with the godparent system. The Martínez household in Pascua furnishes an example. Through the Mexican mother, the godparent relations are extended into Mexican society, and persons like Luis Martínez may find themselves in padrino groups composed wholly of Mexicans. Ceremonies in this connection have the character of Mexican celebrations with couple dancing, modern music, and food and dance customs not characteristic of Yaqui ceremonies of analogous character. The "Mexicanizing" that goes on in such cases may apparently be of a quite different sort from the Mexicanizing of isolated households discussed in the previous section. It involves, as in the case of language, no sharp de-identification with the Yaqui group. In fact, the Martínez family remains identified with Yaquis in many of the most distinctive customs. The Mexican godparent customs, like the Spanish language, are merely additional patterns in which they participate. Choice or selection of behavior is not necessary for the individual. The choices are made by associates, and the Yaqui individual participates under certain circumstances with them in one way and with Yaquis in other ways. No evidence has been found for the Martínez's that there is a higher evaluation of the Mexican ways. On the contrary, all the evidence up to this point indicates no difference in evaluation. The modes of participation merely vary for different sets of relations.

We have considered circumstances of the acquisition of non-Yaqui behaviors under conditions of mobility in which no loss of Yaqui behaviors is involved. Behaviors with similar functions but of different forms are learned and used under the social circumstances which call them forth at appropriate times. Acquisition of the non-Yaqui behaviors does not lead to loss of Yaqui behaviors. They do not require actions that are incompatible or discommoding for the individual involved. They are not alternative in the sense of both being possible under the same situation, and consequently, there is no replacement through the setting up of role conflicts. This is important in understanding the nature of the social cultural fusion that is going on in connection with Yaqui relations in Arizona. It means that individuals who have learned functionally equivalent behaviors of this type may move in either of two directions easily. Accidents of association, residence, and so forth, may be important in the gradual assumption of more roles in one or the other of the two societies involved in the contact.

The rewards of learning more than one pattern are the simple securities and satisfactions of home life. What is learned has behind it no motives of higher social status or special economic gain. So long as the family, as it often does, accepts both sets of patterns as useful and desirable, the individuals learning the non-Yaqui patterns of behavior accept them equally, and there is a simple integration of the historically different patterns in the individual life activities. The social cultural fusion most characteristic of Yaqui life in Arizona moves along these lines.

The Meanings of Being Yaqui

Being a Yaqui has many different meanings. What those meanings are for the individuals depends in large part on the kind of contacts which the individuals have had. And on these different meanings depends the future cultural participation of each individual in large part. The sense of being Yaqui is probably no less intense for the youngest children growing up and going to school in the United States than it has been for their war-scarred parents. It is immediately apparent from an examination of the life story data, however, that the associations with Yaqui identification are extremely varied.

Precisely what meaning an individual attaches to being Yaqui is rarely expressed in so many words by anyone. It is necessary to consider his statements and actions as a whole to arrive at an understanding of what associations he has with the identification. Thus, in considering the life story data we shall here and there be able to use the individual's own words, but only here and there.

There would seem to be a range of meanings within the limits of which all individual associations with the identification fall. These extremes are expressed in the life stories of Lucas Chavez and Cayetano Lopez. There is little question that we can sum up Chavez's evaluation of Yaquiness as follows: Yaquis are *righteous*. In such a summing up we are not attempting to say that Chavez believes that all individual Yaquis are righteous. We are rather saying that he believes that all Yaquis who behave as Yaquis are behaving in a righteous manner. He identifies Yaquiness in other words with not only the most desirable behavior but with the highest moral behavior. He regards "the Yaqui Law" (which he admits few Yaquis live up to), which was the guide for living on the Yaqui River, as the perfect morality. To be Yaqui in this sense is the goal of living for Chavez, and he strenuously attempts it.

On the other hand, in his godson Cayetano Lopez we find a quite different conception, insofar as there is any consistent pattern of association with the concept of Yaquiness. If we consider his behavior during the periods when he was regarded by many as spokesman for Yaquis, and also his present analysis of what happened in those periods, we see a conception which might be described as follows: Yaquis are *obstinately wrong-headed*. It is true that Cayetano is not always perfectly clear in a view of what is right behavior, but there is no doubt that he believes that an essential quality of being Yaqui is being wrong and misguided. Cayetano identifies himself as being Yaqui and in some measure regards himself as being wrongheaded, but his identification of himself would seem actually to waver between thinking of himself as Yaqui and as something else. Over and over again it is clear that he thinks of the Yaquiness of other Yaquis as being characterized by this, to him, not quite understandable obstinacy in choosing the wrong course. Yaquis stand for him not for an ultimate morality, but for an obscure recalcitrance.

Between these extremes of unquestioned excellence and befuddled obstinacy there are many meanings which Yaquiness has for individual Yaquis. Thus, insofar as we know him to differentiate Yaqui behavior from others, Rosario Escalante would seem to be near the Lucas Chavez pole of meaning. He thinks of Yaquis as normal and peaceful, as people with whom it is possible to live quietly and pleasantly. We have no evidence in our data that he thinks of Yaquis as righteous, but merely as predictable. Refugio Savala, in contrast with Chavez is not a moralist but is like him in his positive evaluation of Yaquiness; he finds some food for his imagination in Yaquiness. He might be said to think of Yaqui behavior in no moral terms at all; they are interesting and an essential feature is a connection with an interesting past, which is a challenge to know and understand. Negative evaluations nearer the Cayetano Lopez pole appear in the life story of Salamina Valenzuela and her brother Presillano who evidently feel that the essential meaning of being Yaqui is that one is poor and less educated than other people and that one has odd beliefs. These are not such sweeping viewpoints as Lopez's, but they are built on the same grounds. The youngest generation shows many youths who have begun to associate Yaquiness with illiteracy, unsanitary ways, and poverty. These associations are producing conflicts for this generation because, though they are critical of some Yaqui behaviors, they do not reject the identification as Yaquis. Dolores Martínez keeps his identification as Yaqui but insists that Yaqui does not have the meaning of "Indian," for he has learned from his schoolteacher that Indians are "savages" and he is quite sure that Yaquis are not that. Dolores Romero, too, sticks to his identification as Yaqui, as an "American Yaqui." What associations he may have in guiding him in this have not been worked out, but they are positive ones.

These meanings of being Yaqui reflect the range of cultural participation of individuals in Yaqui and in the surrounding cultures. We have gained some idea of the contacts and the movements of individuals between Yaqui and other societies. We have seen what channels are open for moving out, and how these are followed, and to some extent what happens when they are followed. It appears to be less a transfer of behaviors from others to Yaquis than a transfer of individuals from Yaqui society to other societies, where then a new learning process begins in response to certain rewards.

We have seen under what circumstances Yaquis leave Yaqui society. We have seen the kinds of stress to which the culture is subject. But we need a closer understanding of the value of Yaqui culture, not only to the relative few who have grown up in it and through childhood have known little else, but also to those who have been influenced by many different contacts but have come back to Yaqui culture in the face of these. It is these persons and what Yaqui culture means to them that we shall consider in the next chapter.

CHAPTER II

The Uses of Yaqui Culture

An outstanding common feature of the lives of the younger men and women of Pascua is fluctuation in their participation in Yaqui culture, though this fluctuation does not apply to the youngest group. It does apply to the older men and women, but for many of them the greatest fluctuation derives from a simple lack of opportunity, determined by geographical circumstances or the effects of military coercion. Most of the older men and women became regular participants in the revived ceremonial behavior once a Yaqui society had been reestablished. It is not true, however, of all of them. Tomás Alvarez, for example, constitutes an important exception. But the younger men and one woman whose life stories have been presented are characterized uniformly by great variation in their participation in the revived forms of Yaqui culture. It is not possible, moreover, to explain this variation as a result of either any simple forms of coercion or of enforced isolation from Yaqui communities. The younger men and a few of the younger women have left and returned to the Yaqui settlements at different times, have participated or not in the Yaqui ceremonial life under different circumstances, and have done this voluntarily.

The movement in and out of Yaqui communities and the acceptance and rejection of roles in Yaqui society, so characteristic of the middle age group, may be regarded as a selection of behavior on the part of the individuals concerned. Under some conditions they select Yaqui behaviors. Under others they reject them and select other behaviors available to them in the general cultural milieu. Not all Yaquis, even of this age group, may be characterized in the same terms as making frequent choices involving the acceptance or rejection of Yaqui behaviors. Some have not made these choices, but there are enough who have to make consideration of their cases important in any effort to determine the nature of the conditions under which Yaqui culture persists in the Arizona situation. That they do not uniformly reject Yaqui behaviors indicates that some of their needs are being met through participation in Yaqui culture. If we can get some insight into the bases of their choices, we shall be in a position to make statements regarding the individual needs that Yaqui culture meets for those Yaquis whose life experiences do not include the fear of and flight from Mexicans that characterizes their parents.

In the present chapter we shall consider the selection of behaviors by individuals who have been mobile, that is, who have moved in and out of situations where they were associated with other Yaquis. We shall, moreover, pay especial attention to their selection of Yaqui behaviors, since we are concerned here to discover the uses for them of Yaqui culture.

The Bases of Selection of Yaqui Behaviors

Younger Yaqui men and women are obviously not simple slaves of custom. Cayetano Lopez takes a critical attitude toward many Yaqui customs, not only in the presence of Anglo Americans, but also even in councils of Yaqui leaders. Refugio Savala passes judgment on Yaqui beliefs and considers them carefully in the light of Western literature that he has read. Salamina Valenzuela, as she returns to Pascua to care for her dying mother, scoffs at the idea of ancestral spirits returning to the village in the month of October. It is not only toward Yaqui custom and belief, however, that they assume such critical positions. Their attitudes lead them to similar judgments and criticism of Anglo-American and Mexican-American customs. Salamina Valenzuela understands, for example, that Anglos do not believe in witchcraft; she asks an Anglo, however, "How do you know that witches don't make people sick?" So strongly does she herself believe in witchcraft, that she feels Anglos should advance her some proof of their position. Cayetano Lopez, together with an older Yaqui who has gained fame as an especially able Pascola Dancer, visits different churches and considers their virtues. It is characteristic of the behavior of many of these younger persons and of some older ones that they judge and choose among customs.

If we reconsider the evidence for such choosing that has been presented in the life stories, it is possible to distinguish at least three general types of choices which appear to rest on three general types of considerations. The bases of selection may be stated as follows: security, prestige, and order. There are choices which are not easy to explain in these categories, but most of the selection of Yaqui behaviors seems to have been carried out with reference to the fulfillment of needs of these three types. Each of the categories as we shall consider them here is rather wide, and hence it will be necessary to consider examples of each in order to make as clear as possible the categories used.

Security

There are elemental and obvious securities that Yaquis, like other individuals, constantly require. Food and shelter are among these. Yaqui society, in the form which it took in Arizona during the period of the cultural revival, supplies such needs. The household, compadre-padrino, and ceremonial society groups are all organized to insure such basic needs for sick, jobless, and even shiftless Yaquis. Individuals growing up in Yaqui communities in Arizona as members of these groups learn to use and rely on the social structure for the satisfaction of such needs. Moreover, we have seen in the case of older Yaquis who became isolated during the diaspora how determinedly they sought the securities of these social units. Lucas Chavez, conditioned in his youth to the use of the compadre system, sought godparents along the whole length of Sonora. His wanderings seem to have been determined as much by the supposed location of godparents as by the opportunities for work along the line of the Southern Pacific Railroad. He, more than any other Arizona Yaqui studied, is able to state explicitly the central importance of the compadre system to individual members of the broken Yaqui society for the acquiring of the elemental securities.

The reconstituted social organization in Arizona has operated in the same way for United States–born Yaquis whose jobs or other interests have led them for a time out of association with Yaquis. Refugio Savala and Salamina Valenzuela return to Yaqui villages to reaffirm their roles in these organizations at the time of deaths of kin or compadre, and they remain dependent for months on the securities of the groups until their interests impel them out of Yaqui society again. Yaqui society figures in this simple manner as a refuge for the laid-off and the sick in a large number of cases not cited in the life stories.

One of the most striking instances of definite choice of the economic securities of Yaqui society as against those of non-Yaqui society occurs in the history of Tomás Alvarez. Moving toward moderate success and advancement in railroad work, Alvarez suddenly turned toward association with Yaquis again. A dominant motive with him was prestige, but it is apparent that he was also considering economic security. He deliberately placed himself in reliance on the ceremonial society system as a means of making his living and directed his activities in accordance with Yaqui custom to the point where he is able to spend most of his time in ceremonial labor. He is even confident now that the Yaquis of Pascua will take care of him in his old age as a result of his work in the ceremonial society of the Matachinis. He is very conscious of the economic securities that Yaqui society has to offer and prefers them to what he had been able to gain outside of Yaqui society.

There is another kind of security which has been the source of returns to participation in Yaqui society. This is the security of health. To most Yaquis growing up among other Yaquis, the use of the manda as a curing technique is a matter of course. No choice is involved, particularly for the individual who is sick and is being promised by parents or godparents. But Yaquis in the United States have many contacts with curing techniques other than the manda. They are urged to use hospitals and a few even do. Isolated entirely from Yaqui society, an individual is led by his non-Yaqui associates usually to make exclusive use of non-Yaqui curing methods. Juan Silvas, however, when he was working in Sacramento and was seriously injured, made use of both kinds of customs. Allowing himself to be treated surgically in a Sacramento hospital, he also made a vow himself (not the usual Yaqui method) to serve in the Fariseo society. Ultimately, he made good his promise and carried out his service, coming back necessarily to a Yaqui community to do so. He has continued to regard the manda curing technique as having been effective in his case. Other examples of similar use of the manda by isolated Yaquis have been observed.

Another form of security need that Yaqui customs serve and that is all too easily overlooked has to do with the use of language. One of the clearest examples of the operation of choice on this basis appears in the history of Rosario Escalante. He had no orientation whatever, it will be recalled, in Yaqui culture. His parents, in Hermosillo, however, were Mayo, who spoke the Mayo language, which is closely related to Yaqui. Escalante grew up with Mayo as his first language. It was his knowledge of that language which gave him access to Yaqui society in Arizona. He evidently derived from its use some feeling of security. He persistently characterizes Mexicans as un-understandable and unpredictable. With Yaquis he had a sense of understanding what was said to him and of being understood. He has continued to live with Yaquis, but his participation in distinctive Yaqui customs does not go beyond what his immediate Yaqui household requires of him on occasion and the use of the Yaqui language. The security that he feels in the use of the language is, of course, bound up with the social relations he has achieved in his household by means of speaking the language, but there would seem also to be a distinct and definite security involved in the simple sense of complete communication with others.

The nature of language as a source of security is also apparent in the later events of the life of Cayetano Lopez. Lopez, in a period when he has abandoned all other participation in distinctive Yaqui ways, regards his use of the language as the ultimate criterion for classifying himself as Yaqui. His social relations with other Yaquis have for the most part become tenuous and strained, but he lives in a Yaqui community, identifies himself with Yaquis, and has a strong sense of status (the only status with a traditional basis left to him) as a Yaqui. This status he thinks of as being inevitably connected with his continuing use of the language. His choice of position in the complex social world that he has known rests solidly on language.

Prestige

Yaqui society provides a functioning system for ranking individuals in relation to one another, that is, for conferring prestige. There is great variation in the sensitivity of different individuals to this aspect of the culture. For some older persons like Rosario Escalante and for some younger persons like Refugio Savala and Salamina Valenzuela it appears to have no meaning whatever. They do not choose Yaqui ways of behavior which can in any way lead to the traditional prestige statuses. For others, however, both old and young, the prestige system has much meaning and has been a stimulus to participation in the distinctive Yaqui activities. Prestige, as has been shown in detail elsewhere, depends on the nature and amount of activity in the ceremonial societies; it is not connected with occupation or income and property. Persons like Lucas Chavez and Jesús García, among those whom we have discussed, have moved in traditional fashion through increasing proficiency in ritual skills to positions of prestige as Maestro and Chapayeka leader. There are, however, others whose responses to the prestige system are much more revealing of the appeal of the system. These are individuals whose lives have been characterized by extreme mobility in and out of Yaqui society.

Tomás Alvarez is one who has chosen prestige in Yaqui society. His activities in achieving the position of a Matachin Kobanao might be described as the conquest of a role in Yaqui society. His personality, which is characterized by marked aggressiveness and interest in personal power and distinction, is poorly adapted to the achievement of status in the Yaqui ceremonial system. Moreover, his childhood and early youth were spent in isolation from Yaqui society; he had no opportunity to learn the basic dancing skills and the details of ritual of the Matachin organization until early manhood. Even during the period of his first contacts with organized Yaqui society during the first phases of the cultural revival in Arizona, his interest remained centered on work and achievement of prestige in the economic status system of the Anglo Americans. Loss of his wife upset this adjustment, and he turned to Yaqui society as a means of gaining the prestige in which he was interested. Instead of serving a long apprenticeship in the Matachin society, the usual route to its leadership, he has adopted other procedures that are consistent with Yaqui tradition in obtaining his goal. The result is a considerable measure of power over other Yaquis and an undoubted prestige and prominence among Yaquis. He has been able to use the prestige system, despite a very inadequate background in Yaqui culture.

A feeling of prestige in Anglo-American society can support, or even replace, prestige in Yaqui society. Alvarez's reimmersion in Yaqui society has resulted in his obtaining a prestige based solidly on Yaqui values, but it has not been wholly unconnected with the prestige system of the surrounding society. As Matachin leader, he is enabled to associate with officials of the Tucson government, churches, and the Chamber of Commerce as one distinguished among Yaquis. This compensates him for the failure to achieve official status in the wake of Juan Pistola, a distinction which he coveted. We may see in the life of Lucas Chavez a similar attempt to gain prestige in Anglo-American eyes through association with Yaquis in the Pistola government. Chavez himself felt that he was doing this along traditional lines. Alvarez did not care whether his role in the post-Pistola government was traditional or not. Both were ready to associate themselves with Yaquis, and both were sensitive to the prestige that might thus be gained among Anglo Americans.

The importance of prestige in the Anglo-American system as a motive for association with Yaquis is clearly illustrated in the case of Cayetano Lopez. Although in his youth Lopez was interested in acquiring the skill of a Maestro and became unusually proficient, gaining prestige throughout Yaqui society in Arizona, he lost interest in the Yaqui prestige system later in life. This did not result in his de-identification of himself with Yaquis, however. He became a leader in the political group that opposed the Guadalupe Flores program for return of Yaquis to Sonora. This group was not linked with the cultural revival in any way. It professedly followed no pattern of Yaqui village government in Sonora and was content to use such Anglo-made titles as "chief." Uncomfortable as he was under the responsibilities of leadership, Cayetano, nevertheless, valued the prestige that came to him with Anglo Americans as a result of his participation in Anglo political life through letters and conferences with state officials.

Order

We may describe this third type of the use of Yaqui culture, or aspects of it, as an idea system fulfilling an individual need for the ordering of experience. One of the notable reactions of some older, but especially of younger Yaquis to various Yaqui beliefs once they become conscious of them in relation to Anglo-American beliefs, through school or other influences, is strong and emotionally colored disbelief. Salamina Valenzuela's rejection of Yaqui beliefs concerning the dead is of this type. Cayetano Lopez's vigorous denial of the belief that wooden crosses are forms of the Virgin, which he shares with some older Yaquis, is another example. It would be possible to make a rather long catalog of such denials in the case of Cayetano Lopez. This could be supplemented by similar categorical rejections of other beliefs by many of the younger men and women. Such rejection of elements of belief is an indication of a need to construct an orderly vision of life and is one of the characteristic features of the Arizona contact situation. But not all Yaquis feel the need to purge conflicting elements of belief.

There is, however, quite a different type of attitude apparent in some of the individuals whose lives have been considered. We may illustrate with the case of Lucas Chavez, who has come into contact with a widely varying set of religious beliefs and practices. He has listened to Baptist missionaries; he has read the Spanish tracts of the Jehovah's Witnesses; he has read a variety of Catholic prayer books; and he has studied a number of versions of Biblical stories. The effect on him of awareness of these other doctrines, including the Baptist flat negation of what he was taught when younger and has since reinforced through ceremonial work among Yaquis, has not been reaction against Yaqui beliefs. His "conversion" to Baptism we have seen had nothing to do with doctrine and belief; it was a social matter, constituting an affirmation of new, warm, and friendly relationships. On the contrary, Chavez's solution has been not to reject Yaqui beliefs, but rather to reconsider some of them and attempt to make them harmonize with one another and with some of the other beliefs which appeal to him. He has not rejected one system of belief for another, but has chosen to adjust them, and, where elements have come to his attention that seem especially difficult to reconcile, to suspend belief in a somewhat scientific manner until more evidence appears one way or the other. This approach indicates, it would appear, a need for unifying the whole of his experience, for a system of ideas which included the Yaqui beliefs to which he has devoted much thought, as well as others that have come to him through non-Yaqui sources. It bespeaks, in other words, a need for ordering the whole of his experience. His continuing choice of a Yaqui-oriented religion (in terms of doctrine) rests on this need.

The other clear illustration that we have of this basis of choice of Yaqui beliefs comes from the data on Refugio Savala. Refugio's participation in overt behaviors of the Yaqui kind is at a minimum. He has a history of recognizing his kinship obligations, but he has avoided involvement in the compadre circles to a large extent, and has even allowed a manda to the Matachin society to lapse, fulfilling the three-year promise but no more. He has thus gone through life without any ceremonial participation except as a member of a kin group. The fact remains that he seeks chiefly Yaqui associates in the present period of his life. He lives among and identifies himself with Yaquis, being in this respect like Rosario Escalante of the older generation. But Refugio carries on a participation in Yaqui culture which has no counterpart whatever in Rosario Escalante. Refugio has long been interested in the details of the Pascola ritual, in Yaqui mythology, and in Yaqui historical traditions. He has observed carefully and has sought out persons who could tell him about and explain various aspects of Yaqui culture. Among Arizona Yaquis he is unusually well versed in the basic beliefs and major features of Yaqui culture. He is not ashamed of or antagonistic to Yaqui beliefs in discussion of them with Anglo Americans. On the contrary, he is interested, anxious to explain, and ready to take initiative in finding out what he does not already know.

The use to which he puts Yaqui culture might be explained as a historical one. It is quite uncertain to what extent he "believes in" the myths that he knows and the viewpoints that he is familiar with from old Yaqui culture. He believes that his parents and other older Yaquis believed in them. He accepts them as facts in that sense. He is concerned about understanding the world of his parents and other ancestral Yaquis. In his thought he has established a clear category of the past, and he is engaged constantly in filling in that category. He is evidently ordering, by means of a chronological principle, both his childhood experiences with his family and his later wide experiences of the southwestern United States. He differs markedly from Lucas Chavez in this chronological consciousness. He does not feel the need to reconcile old and new beliefs in a logical fashion, as Lucas does. Categorizing past and present seems to be more in the line of his interest. In Refugio then we have an acceptance of Yaqui customs and beliefs, an abiding interest in them, and a devotion to them for intellectual uses in the ordering of his experiences. In the case of both Chavez and Savala, an observer feels that the personality types are somewhat uncommon among Yaquis and that their type of use of the culture is relatively infrequent.

It is clear that Yaqui culture functions in such a way that it meets very specific needs of very differing types of Yaqui individuals in Arizona. It meets not only the needs of the older immigrants who have in common punishing experiences at the hands of Mexicans, it meets not only needs of younger Yaquis who have grown up in and know only the family and ritual kinship institutions that their parents have reconstructed, but it meets also at various times and under various circumstances the needs of young men and women who have grown up in the United States and have had many contacts with other peoples and cultures. It serves their needs as a security system, as a prestige system, and as an idea system.

Types of Participation in Yaqui Culture

With some understanding of the motives for choice of Yaqui behavior in particular instances, it now becomes possible to consider the manner in which Yaqui behavior may be combined by various individuals. It has become clear that the choice of a particular behavior does not necessarily lead to the choice of others and certainly not to the adoption of the whole range of distinctive Yaqui behaviors. It will be our purpose in the present section to indicate the range in individual variation in participation in Yaqui culture. In doing so, we shall shift our focus to include not only the individuals who have been spoken of as mobile, but also those characterized by constant recent association with other Yaquis.

A review of the data on individuals indicates that it is possible to distinguish five types of participation that are combinations of Yaqui behavior and belief. Although there are probably as many different combinations of specific belief and cultural behavior as there are individuals calling themselves Yaqui in Arizona, it is possible to establish a limited number of types of combinations by considering the behaviors in terms of social structure and of systems of belief. There are three systems of social relations: the kinship, the ceremonial sponsorship, and the ceremonial society systems, all of which are characteristic of Yaquis. An individual may—and there are some individuals who actually do—participate in only one of these systems. Ordinarily, however, a resident in a Yaqui community participates to some degree in all three. Again there are systems of belief, which have been touched on earlier—those of: the ancestors, the Jesus and Mary pantheon, the Pascolas and the natural world, witchcraft, and Yaqui history. These also may be participated in singly or in various combinations.

The combination of social relations and belief as we actually find them in individual organizations of the culture appear to be somewhat as follows. In the first type of participation there are individuals who have been and continue to be members of kinship groups, of godparent-godchild groups, and of ceremonial societies. These same individuals carry out their assigned roles in all the groups with great consistency. Insofar as we have data, indications are that they believe in or accept all the systems of belief and appear to have many associations with the various symbols in those systems. Examples of individuals whose lives show this sort of participation are the two older men, Lucas Chavez and Guadalupe Balthazar, the two older women Josefa Araiza and Juana de Amarillas, and the younger man, Jesús García. We might also include three members of the youngest group, but recognizing them as a subtype who have not yet developed their own families of procreation. The persons of this general type may differ a great deal from one another in the extensiveness of the meanings that any of the symbols have for them, but there is at least a common

set of meanings among them. Thus there is a great deal of difference between Chavez and Josefa Araiza in the extent to which they can "explain"
a ritual that both practice. Chavez has many associations from Yaqui tradition with which to give it meaning; Josefa Araiza knows few. Nevertheless,
they agree on one or two basic meanings. The five individuals showing
this type of participation have all, since the dispersal, been continuously
associated with Yaquis. They have not, in other words, been mobile in
their social behavior. We could, recognizing the fact that there is individual
variation among them, that each practices a specialty, and that some may
have adopted also non-Yaqui behaviors such as Lucas Chavez's conversion
to Baptism, speak of these as full participants.

A second type of participation is characterized by the assumption of
roles in kinship and ceremonial sponsor groups, but not in the ceremonial
society structure, either as members with formal roles or as observers. Such
individuals seem to fulfill faithfully their obligations as family members
and as godparents and compadres, but we do not find them participating in any of the activities that link the various households and compadre
circles in public ceremony. They remain isolated from a great deal of the
cultural expression that takes place in any Yaqui community, and an investigator finds that their familiarity with the various systems of belief is quite
limited. Although they may know by name some of the symbols, they have
very few associations with them. Their lack of participation in the ceremonial society system is evidently connected with a lack of meaning for them
of the various systems of belief. Individuals of this type are, nevertheless,
consistent in their participation in the kin and ritual systems. They are not
mobile out of Yaqui society any more than the full participants just discussed. Examples of this type of participation are to be found in Rosario
Escalante and Joaquina Martínez. We might refer to them as nonmobile
partial participants.

The other three types of participation are distinguishable among mobile Yaquis. One type is characterized by participation in the ceremonial
society system that is intermittent and when it takes place is accompanied with temporary renewals of roles in kinship and ceremonial sponsor
groups. The focus of interest is clearly in the ceremonial society system
and the objective appears to be some unitary purpose, such as fulfillment
of a manda or the seeking of prestige. The participation in other words
has a definitely instrumental character, and participation in other Yaqui
social groups is not only temporary but incidental. This type of participation is carried out by individuals whose acquaintance with the various

belief systems of Yaquis is slight or fragmentary. The clearest example of the type that has been presented is Juan Silvas, but Tomás Alvarez, despite his relatively regular participation in the Matachin society for ten years or more, is best classified also in the type. Alvarez, like Silvas, remains largely ignorant of the traditional meanings of even the Matachin ritual, despite his rather continuous recent participation, and has acquired no traditional meanings at all for other aspects of the ceremonialism. The meaning of the Matachinis is for him primarily what they do to maintain him in a position of prestige. Investigators find him able to explain little or nothing beyond the form of the Matachinis' activities. And with the exception of witchcraft, the other belief systems remain for him merely verbalisms.

Another, and the most common, type of participation among mobile Yaquis is the simple instrumental kind, characteristic of Salamina Valenzuela and of many younger men who come back to a Yaqui settlement— to family and old associates—for brief stays when they are sick, out of a job, or simply do not feel like working for a time. The participation in the social system is confined to roles in the kin groups and ceremonial sponsor groups, often only intermittently fulfilled even while in residence in the Yaqui community. Such an individual may renew an old connection with a ceremonial society by participating in its activities for a time. But the participation is casual. The individual is concerned to maintain his kinship status in order to insure his economic security as well as his emotional and supportive ties. Individuals of this kind are ordinarily found to have a vigorous disbelief in and considerable lack of knowledge of the various systems of Yaqui belief. Salamina Valenzuela might be regarded as more or less typical in her denial of the ancestor system of belief, as well as the Jesus and Mary system and the Pascola system, while maintaining a belief in the witchcraft system. Individuals showing this kind of participation are obviously highly mobile socially, and their participation is extremely intermittent.

It is doubtful whether we should discuss another form of participation as a type. It is rare, insofar as our data go, as a combination of behaviors. This is the kind of participation exemplified and discussed at some length above in Refugio Savala. The Yaqui social behavior is confined to kin group entirely, and participation here is intermittent, since the individual is mobile and moves frequently and easily out of association with Yaquis. There is no overt participation in the ceremonial sponsor or ceremonial society systems. This extremely limited and irregular social participation with Yaquis is, nevertheless, associated with wide knowledge of the belief systems and their symbols. Not only is there knowledge, but there is also interest and belief within a historical framework. In short, this type might be characterized by minimum participation in the social structures of Yaqui society coupled with a maximum number of common understandings concerning the distinctive belief systems. There is no question that such a type of participation is extremely rare, and one may suspect that a nearly unique combination of natural endowments and life experience has produced it.

Recognition of the five types of participation enables us to say that, despite the organization and system which unquestionably many older Yaquis are aware of in Yaqui culture, an individual may select, reject, and combine Yaqui behaviors and beliefs in a number of different ways. This does not mean that there is, as it were, no Yaqui culture in Arizona. There is such an organization to be found in all of those individuals discussed above as full participants. They, together with the subtype of young boys and girls who have not yet entered families of procreation, constitute a majority of the people of Pascua.

But the other organizations of the culture elements are extremely revealing of an important process, that is, the growth of new meanings for the old and revived forms. The various combinations of participation indicate that Yaqui behaviors are being practiced by the mobile individuals for quite different motives from what they are by the nonmobile individuals. This gives them different meanings, since meanings are the associations that a given behavior has for the individual practicing it. Let us take an example, that of Salamina Valenzuela returning to Pascua to live with her family for a period. Her participation is practically confined to the kinship group. She behaves pretty much as do other Yaqui daughters, but it is clear that the meaning for her of participation in the family group includes considerations that are not present for nonmobile young women of her group. She is caring for her mother because her mother is sick and her father needs help in the household. She is not living in the household because she is the eldest daughter and the most physically able woman of a line that reaches back through generations of spirits who are watching and are unhappy about the sickness and expect her to aid her mother because she has the strength. She stays on in the household after the death, not because she is the daughter of it and belongs there. On the contrary she stays because it is a chance to save a little money for her and her Mexican husband so that they can get on their feet and leave the village. The family and the household is an instrument to her individual ends and she uses it in quite a conscious manner to this end. This is the meaning which for her has replaced the meaning of the ancestral dead and the traditional status of the eldest daughter. It may be classed as an instrumental meaning for the family and household relations.

This is a type of meaning which obviously characterizes Juan Silvas's use of the Fariseo society for curing and for prestige purposes. It is also the central feature of Tomás Alvarez's use of the Matachin society. An important meaning for him of the Matachin society and its activities is that it is a means for him to personal advancement. And Cayetano Lopez even has felt in the past that the whole of Yaqui society in Arizona was an instrument usable to advance his prestige in Anglo-American society. The approval of other persons who call themselves Yaqui is not an end in connection with the adoption of Yaqui behaviors in these cases. It is a means rather than an end and in that lies a major difference as between the first two types of participation discussed and the second two types. The latter have instrumental meanings for the individual involved; the former do not. The latter lack moral meanings, in the sense of social approval of the group as an end; but the former have primarily such moral meanings for the individuals who have revived them and for those who are still growing up in them. These mobile individuals become a very important source for change in the society, because it must be remembered that they come back and live, even if only for short times, among Yaquis activated by the moral considerations and sanctions. The instrumental meanings which the mobile individuals have may and do spread by diffusion from them to other individuals, as we might say the forms of behavior diffuse from the nonmobile individuals to the mobile when they come back into association with Yaquis.

Yaqui individuals then, clearly show various degrees of belief in, understanding of, and participation in their society and culture. In some measure these variations are determined by personal experience both in and out of Yaqui culture, by need, and by attitudes. As all enduring cultures must be to continue their existence, Yaqui culture is dynamic, responding, reacting, and adapting to internal forces and external events. The carriers of a culture, on whom its survival ultimately depend, are the individuals who participate in it and carry on its belief systems, its behaviors and values, its symbols and practices. The variety of individuals makes up the whole, and the whole also affects the lives of the individuals.

Writing About the People of Pascua

Kathleen M. Sands

In Edward H. Spicer's career-long study of the cultural history of the Yaqui people both in Mexico and in Arizona, *People of Pascua* is an important contribution as an anthropological study of a specific time period at a particular place, a record of ways of seeing and coping with the world within the village and outside it, with kin, neighbors, employers, merchants, missionaries, and the myriad of racial, ethnic, social, economic, and political elements of the times and locale.

Examination of Spicer's procedures for developing and implementing the research and the writing of *People of Pascua* may give some insight into a further importance of this work in the chronology of Spicer's theoretical contributions, for it is during the period of this work that many of the areas of inquiry he was to follow and several of the theories that guide his later work were first generated.

The details of that first year in Pascua are clearly laid out in "Living in Pascua," but it should be pointed out again that this year of field research was undertaken while Ned was still a graduate student, a Ph.D. candidate at the University of Chicago. His earlier field experience, also in Arizona, had been focused on archaeology, so his 1936 study in Pascua was his first extended experience in cultural anthropology in the field. His personal correspondence suggests he was cautious and patient in going about his study of Pascua. On October 16, 1936, after several months in the field, he writes:

Since the first of September, things have been going apace with us—linguistically and ethnologically. The best policy after all was to sit tight and let things take their course. Ethnological plums have been falling into our laps steadily for six weeks just because we did wait quietly. By the last week in August I was getting desperate—even more so than when you last saw me. It seemed that I was not going to get anything at all started. The contacts that were made didn't seem to ripen into anything usable. So one morning I started out to make a break and go hire somebody. As I went out the door I ran into Lucas Chavez. Lucas said that he had been thinking that maybe he would help us learn Yaqui. I almost took him in my arms and we came in and sat down and talked the matter over. He said that he would be glad to talk with me for a couple of hours every day for awhile. And he has been doing so ever since—each morning for three or four hours. Ostensibly I am still primarily interested in learning the language, but that study has led into every aspect of the culture here. It has led us all through Lucas's considerable knowledge of the history of Pascua. And it is now leading us through his memories of his young manhood on the Rio Yaqui. He has a store of documents dating from the time of Pistola, all of which he has been glad to let me see. He has a serious interest in all the village institutions and knows a great deal about almost everything except kinship (he has no relatives here, except a wife). From him we are getting the point of view of the oldest generation here and, I believe, a good general introduction of Yaqui culture.

While this has been going on, we have still had time to carry on the sort of contacts which constituted our whole approach at first. Lately adults like Tomás Alvarez and Sixto Matus have been coming over to the house and we are beginning to feel thoroughly at home with them in Spanish. Lucas's course in "A General Introduction to Yaqui Culture" is of tremendous value for conversational purposes with them. . . .

I am sorry that I cannot go into the material that we have been collecting. It is interesting and important, but it is still mainly a formless mass that can only be organized properly after a long session with diaries and files.[1]

It is obvious from his letter that the task of studying Pascua and its inhabitants was slow going at first, but when information did begin to flow, it came in a deluge, filling diaries and notebooks that would become later the foundation of *People of Pascua*. The year in Pascua led to the fairly rapid completion of Spicer's doctoral dissertation, the manuscript for *Pascua, A Yaqui Village in Arizona*, and it provided many of the interviews with individuals that would eventually be used in *People of Pascua*. But at this point his work did not provide information Spicer saw as crucial to his growing interest in persistent peoples. He was convinced that by studying individual lives, he would be able to discover the characteristics and modes of response to change that enable a cultural group to maintain a distinct identity even in the face of pressures to be assimilated into a dominant culture. Hence, he looked to individual Yaquis and their life experiences to demonstrate the enduring nature of Yaqui culture in the face of persecution, relocation, and relations with American society.

He also wanted to know how people, both individuals and whole ethnic and racial groups, viewed Yaquis and how Yaquis reacted to the pressures exerted on them from outside their own culture. To accomplish this, he responded to a memorandum, issued by a committee of the Social Science Research Council, designed to be a guide to the study of acculturation in a systematic way.[2] In 1939, to the Social Science Research Council of New York, he submitted a request for support to continue his work with Pascua Yaquis by expanding his inquiry to Yaqui relationships with cultures surrounding the Yaqui enclaves in Arizona. In his initial request to the Council for application forms, he summarizes his rationale for continuing field research at Pascua. He says:

The original project succeeded in defining one part of the contact situation. It brought to light the specific mechanisms . . . of internal maintenance of the society. It did not take up in an adequate way the problem of the external factors which contribute to the maintenance of the cultural separateness of the Yaquis.[3]

Spicer was, it is clear, proposing his first project to explore the factors that maintain Yaquis as a distinct ethnic group within American society.

It is in the subsequent proposal that Spicer specifically articulates his intention to use life histories as a method for exploring the effects on and the affects of Yaqui individuals at Pascua. He says:

I propose to study these attitudes [of Yaquis toward themselves, Mexicans, Anglos, and others] through the medium of life histories collected from a series of selected individuals. Some of this material was gathered by the writer during a residence in one Yaqui village. These data in the form of partial autobiographies and miscellaneous biographical material stand in need of intensive analysis. Moreover, they require to be supplemented by an additional series of life histories from certain selected individuals. The procedures involved will consist in interview of various Yaquis selected with reference to their present and past mobility, and analysis of the interview material in terms of the attitudinal milieu which it discloses.[4]

This proposal, based on the fieldwork completed at Pascua in 1937 was funded beginning in the summer of 1940. After two semesters as instructor in the Department of Anthropology at the University of Arizona, Spicer returned to his research in Pascua during the summer of 1940; he came to explore an hypothesis and a fairly well-developed methodology, both of which were part of the proposal for funding. In the proposal he says:

Any conflict arising in the social relations between Yaquis and non-Yaquis results in either withdrawal into Yaqui society or out of Yaqui society, but a conflict arising in Yaqui culture need not result in any change in the society; cultural conflicts tend rather to result in the development and hence the stabilization of the culture.

The methodology for testing the hypothesis was laid out in a very specific incremental manner:

1. Preliminary classification of Yaqui individuals for the purpose of establishing a scale in terms of which degree of withdrawal and removal may be measured. This will involve a consideration of the kinds and relative amounts of participation in Yaqui culture for each individual studied. It will involve the establishment of a set of concepts concerning the types of participation by Yaquis in both Yaqui and American cultures.

2. Preliminary classification of conflict situations for the purpose of establishing concepts through which types of behavior may be analyzed. This will involve a consideration of specific behaviors of individuals involved in conflicts of any kind. It will involve a consideration of American, Mexican, and Yaqui attitudes toward each other and toward various cultural traits.

3. Preliminary classification of dynamic processes working in types of situations. This will involve a consideration of individual life experiences as wholes. It will involve the establishment of a set of concepts through which the interaction of individuals in different cultures may be analyzed.

Attached to this outline was a brief bibliography of works on culture and personality and case studies based on life history data—there were not many in existence at the time, most were lengthy autobiographies. Also attached was a list of names of twenty-five Yaquis from Pascua whom he was prepared to interview.

Spicer continued his fieldwork throughout the 1940–1941 academic year, aided by his wife Roz who also conducted extensive interviews. Field notes in the Spicer archive of the Arizona State Museum indicate that he collected far more life history data than he eventually chose to use in *People of Pascua*. They also give some indication of just how the Spicers went about gaining consent for interviews. It must be remembered that this was long before using release forms became common practice, and that the standard of ethical consent was not even commonly held. Individual field notes contain descriptions of the oral procedure used by both Spicers:

I had already explained to Joaquina that I would like to talk to her about the history of her life, that we wanted the stories of many people so that we could put them all together and get the whole picture. She willingly assented to talk and we arranged that I should go [to her house] today.[5]

Field notes also contain contextual information such as descriptions of individuals, the activities going on in the household during the interview, the outdoor location of some interviews, and other notes about the circumstances, appearance of the people, attitudes and tones of expression, even conversation about topics of mutual interest like child care or events around the village. Direct quotation from informants is a major portion of each file. Separate files for individuals, households, and topics insured that copies of notes in typed form would be categorized appropriately, the original reminder notes taken in the field having been written in notebooks in longhand. In August of 1941, research was completed, and Spicer noted in a brief preliminary report submitted to the SSRC that sixteen, not the originally planned twenty-five, individuals had been "selected for intensive study." He also included a plan for his full report which he expected to complete by the early part of 1942 and submit to the University of Arizona publications committee for publication as a Social Science bulletin.[6]

From the field notes accumulated during his two research periods at Pascua and from brief periods of research at other Arizona Yaqui villages in both the Tucson and Phoenix area, Spicer wrote a first draft of *People of Pascua*. It was not easy going. In a letter composed when he was nearing the end of his field research, he reports the struggle of evaluating and interpreting the data he had collected:

The thing is that I have got myself into deeper water than I can tread. At every turn in the delineation of some individual I need more material, more interviews, more opinions of others about him. But that is a minor trouble. Even when I have fairly adequate data, I feel that my interpretations are flimsy. They are hide-bound by over-training in the cultural approach. I don't seem to break through really into the individual. I read a little Dollard and mystify myself with Murray and gripe at Kardiner and then go back to the data—with ideas that fade in the face of it.

For instance, I can demonstrate that Lucas Chavez (let us call him A) is a little man who has sought higher status throughout his life in whatever cultural milieu (Yaqui or Mexican) he has found himself. He has always attached himself to bigger men and pulled himself up by their bootstraps. He has been equally sensitive to the status rungs in Yaqui, Mexican, and Anglo American societies. Now in his old age the particular set of rungs on which he was climbing namely, an artificial political organization of Yaquis (which was more fully recognized by Anglos than by Yaquis) has collapsed. A has been frustrated, and it is Yaquis who have frustrated him. He is as a result bitter against Yaquis and denounces them for immoral behavior. This is all clear enough. We have A pigeon-holed. But what about B? B is a little man who has never sought status, that is, he has never wanted to move up higher. He has, however, been pushed and pushed into higher status rungs because of special abilities he has, such as literacy.[7]

The analysis of the complex data he had collected was an overwhelmingly difficult task. There were really no models he could look to, and charting new territory was hard on his confidence. But he obviously worked on, meeting such ambiguities and problems as he cites above and resolving them through his narrations of individual lives and his analysis of their significance.

During that same period he was working out the historical context for the life histories, revising categories from his initial outline so that Part I had only three chapter titles: "Yaqui Society," "Yaqui Interests," and "Social Mobility and Cultural Stability." The first draft was completed early in 1942. Attached to it is a page listing four possible titles for the completed manuscript: "The People of Pascua: A Study of Individuals and a Culture," "Yaqui Americans: An Arizona Ethnic Group," and a hastily scrawled notation, "Indian Immigrants or Immigrant Indians????." "People of Pascua" appears on all subsequent drafts.[8] He did not, despite his original plans, immediately submit the manuscript for publication. Instead, he sought the advice of another scholar of Yaqui culture, Muriel Thayer Painter, giving her the manuscript to read and evaluate. She responded in a report saying,

The way it is worked out is fascinating to me and I should think would be an important contribution in the field of personality and culture. It is exciting to me to have material with which I am somewhat familiar presented in this way, and I should think that it would be useful both in the classroom and the field.

However, her praise was countered by a cautioning statement:

Ned, I cannot bear to say it but I think that if this is published we will not be able to show ourselves in Pascua again. Times have changed since you published Pascua. The book would be read by a number of young men. . . . They would feel you had betrayed them if you published this.[9]

Spicer obviously took her concern seriously. Even though he then took steps to insure the privacy of the individuals by using pseudonyms in the life history section of the study, he realized that the changed names would not disguise the identities of the individuals for Yaqui readers, since Pascua is a small village and everyone is well known by their kinship ties and roles in the village. Unable to solve the problem, he reconsidered his intention to submit the manuscript for publication. He did not, however, stop work on revision.

Subsequent drafts show evidence of restructuring of the first part, as further changes in the titles of the first three chapters indicate: "Yaqui Culture Patterns," "Yaqui Contacts with Others in Arizona," and "Arizona Ethnic Groups from the Yaqui Standpoint." What remains absolutely stable throughout the draft revisions is the use of life histories in Part II, so while Part I was rethought and revised several times, Part II was obviously the core around which the study developed. He did, however, change his focus of organization in Part II from a mixture of place of birth and age to the final organizing principle of generations.

Spicer continued to revise the manuscript for a decade, never able to resolve the problem of protecting Yaqui privacy but interested in applying new theories of culture and personality to his writing, both his own and those of others in this rapidly growing field. At one point he wrote an unfinished draft of an essay titled "Two Types of Culture Contact Among Arizona Yaquis, " which, after briefly summarizing Yaqui history, social structure, and cultural practices, focuses on the importance of Yaqui contact with other cultures in Arizona, especially Anglos.[10] The revision of the *People of Pascua* manuscript, based on developments in the theory of culture and personality, were not extensive, since his own methods had, in fact, been focused on examination of ethnic persistence, though he had not developed a cohesive theory at that time. But his notes and correspondence do show evidence of his desire to learn from advances in the discipline and the suggestions of colleagues in the field of personality and culture. It should be pointed out here that Spicer was attempting quite consciously to work within the personality and culture realm of anthropology during his revisions. While his use of personal histories was leading him gradually toward a focus on the idea of ethnicity, the study of ethnicity as a concept in anthropology had not yet been formally developed or widely recognized, so while "personality and culture" no longer has much currency in the field of anthropology, it was the terminology current during his fieldwork and early revisions, and thus is appropriate to apply to a history of his work in this period.

It is clear that Spicer was, indeed, familiar with all the major work in culture and personality research and writing. In the spring of 1949 he offered an undergraduate course titled "Culture and Personality" in the Department of Anthropology at the University of Arizona. Lecture notes in his files indicate that the course was a very comprehensive survey of the history of the field from the viewpoints of anthropology, sociology, and psychiatry. Spicer's lectures placed strong emphasis on studying both the differences and similarities between individuals and cited life history as the best method. One section of the course drew on his work at Pascua, and particularly the use of life histories collected there. The thrust of that section was that interpretation of life history was an important factor in explaining the persistence of Yaqui culture, another indication that *People of Pascua* was the soil in which the enduring peoples themes he later developed in his writing were quietly germinating. By the time he taught this course, a good number of culture and personality studies were in print, but when he began his work at Pascua in 1936, the use of life histories for the study of cultures was barely becoming recognized as a legitimate method for cultural interpretation. Perhaps the earliest statement advocating the life history method is in Paul Radin's first publication of a reminiscence of a Winnebago Indian man in 1913. In this brief history published in a folklore journal, Radin prefaces the text with a rationale for using life history to study a culture. He says:

> Realizing that here was an excellent instrument for obtaining just what was so urgently needed, an inside view of an Indian's thoughts, I approached him with the idea of relating to me—whatever he chose, in any manner he chose—something about that culture of which he had formed an integral part up to the time of my coming among the Winnebago.[11]

It is interesting to note that this first attempt at life history methodology places very firm emphasis on the use of life history for the interpretation of culture, not on the individual but on the group. This same emphasis is evident in Spicer's work, where life histories are used to interpret cultural concepts and trends.

A few other cultural studies using life history methods appeared in the years prior to Spicer's work, such as Kopper's 1924 sketches of Tierra del Fuegians and Truman Michelson's three brief narratives of Plains Indian women.[12] Longer life history works were also published, Radin's *Crashing Thunder* in 1926, marking "the beginning of truly rigorous work in the field of biography by professional anthropologists."[13] Longer works, of course, had the effect of focusing on the individual rather than the culture, an emphasis not compatible with Spicer's viewpoint. Though many life history studies began to appear, the use of life history was by no means universally greeted in positive fashion in anthropology. In some cases even getting published was difficult. Ruth M. Underhill, who published the "autobiography" of a Papago woman, Maria Chona, in 1936, had great difficulty in finding a publication outlet for her work. She was unable to find a publisher for a Walapai life history she had collected and edited, and gave up the method as a viable tool for culture interpretation.[14] Many others did not give up, however, and a growing number of publications addressed issues of methodology. In 1933 Paul Radin published a volume on life history field methodology. In various essays and publications such issues as problems of interviewing and developments in field methods were discussed, and many critiques of studies appeared between 1935 and 1944,[15] but there was much caution even by those who supported the method. For instance, Ralph Linton's forward to Abram Kardiner's *The Individual and His Society* (1939) suggests some concern for limitations of life history method: "No one individual is ever familiar with the whole of the culture in which he participates; still less does he express all its patterns in his behavior."[16] Spicer's use of multiple life histories, of course, goes far to answer this reservation.

It was not until the mid-1940s (DuBois, 1944; Kardiner, 1945; Kluckhohn 1945) that major works of theoretical importance addressed the methodology of using life history studies in anthropology, though the publication of *Sun Chief* in 1942 had generated considerable interest among professionals in the field. As its editor, Leo Simmons, clearly states, this lengthy narrative of a Hopi man was collected and edited "for the purpose of developing and checking hypotheses in the field of culture and its relation to personality development."[17]

It is quite remarkable that with little to guide him, Spicer pursued the use of life histories at all, let alone developed a hypothesis to explore during his second phase of research at Pascua. What is much more remarkable is that he was already practicing the study of life history according to theories and guidelines that would not be in print until 1945.

The work that still remains the touchstone for anthropological study of life history is Kluckhohn's (1945). It is an essay highly critical of the work published up to the time, citing problems to be overcome. His concerns are summarized as follows:

a. The vast majority are too sketchy and too limited to be objective events. They do not give even the shadow of a life, merely the partially outlined skeleton.

b. The different age and sex groups are very unevenly represented. Almost all of the subjects are fifty years of age or over at the time of giving their autobiography, and the vast majority are men.

c. With the exception of about half a dozen tribes, there is no basis for comparison of life histories within the same culture and hence of judging whether or not a particular document is a representative sample.

d. Annotation is very meager and almost exclusively of an ethnographic character. Analysis and interpretation have only begun to appear.

e. The conditions under which and the techniques by which data have been obtained are very inadequately specified.

f. Published biographical materials are, at best, only very generally and roughly comparable because conditions and techniques are either unknown or, where at least partially described, so very different.[18]

That *People of Pascua* does not suffer from the problems cited by Kluckhohn is a tribute to Spicer's professional field methods and sound judgment and instincts. Had it been published before 1945, it might well have become a model for ongoing work in the field of culture and personality, where many of the failings Kluckhohn cites still mar published works.

It might be useful to look at Spicer's work in the context of Kluckhohn's criticisms point by point:

a. Though some of the life histories in *People of Pascua* are brief and somewhat sketchy, the central biography for each generation is a well-developed life history, hardly the "shadow" or "skeleton" Kluckhohn notes prevalent in most works. While the intention of Spicer's biographies is not to develop a life story requiring the aesthetic style and symmetry required of a literary work, the life histories, especially the central ones, are charged with a sense of individuality and vitality. They are not simply flat case history outlines that concentrate solely on event, but include personal recollections of responses to important events.

b. The age and sex distribution of the life stories in *People of Pascua* are a reasonable sampling of the community. The greater number of biographies are, in fact, of individuals under the age of forty, and women are represented in every generation. Furthermore, Spicer explores degrees of adherence to and participation in Yaqui culture, so the life histories represent varying degrees of adjustment to Yaqui culture. While they are intentionally representative of types, deviance and stereotyping are not preoccupations of the study.

c. Since Spicer provides life histories for sixteen individuals representing three generations, and also several members of one household, a sound basis for internal comparison—which he develops very thoroughly in analyzing the biographies—is provided. Spicer is also very explicit in stating his purpose is exactly that of documenting a representative sample. His emphasis in culture and personality study is consistently and squarely on culture—the use of life history to interpret culture—hence representative sampling is a key criterion for his collection of data.

d. Perhaps the strongest aspect of Spicer's work in *People of Pascua* is the comprehensive interpretation of the life histories he records. In order to analyze core elements in the persistence of Yaqui culture under circumstances that might be expected to lead to disintegration, he discusses each life thoroughly. That he weaves interpretation into the presentation of each life history and reexamines each biography again in comparison to other biographies from the same generation, and finally analyzes the difference between attitudes and responses in each generation, places this work solidly in the mode of culture interpretation.

e. Though Spicer does not provide any lengthy discussion of his methods for collecting data in the actual text of *People of Pascua* his grant proposal and project report outline his methods clearly. Additionally, the text itself reveals his methods of observation and interview, since the life histories are composites of direct quotation from each individual and third person description and summary by Spicer, supplemented by comments from other villagers. The addition of an introduction by Rosamond B. Spicer who worked with her husband in collecting the data for the project provides the methodological data absent from the text.

f. Spicer can hardly be held responsible for the work of other anthropologists in the field, but perhaps his work can, even now, serve as a resource for future scholars of culture and personality, since the problems Kluckhohn addresses remain largely unresolved.

As Langness and Frank state in their study, *Lives: An Anthropological Approach to Biography* (1981), "life-centered ethnography" is a collaboration, a "negotiation," an "encounter," an "interaction," an "exchange," used for the purpose of portraying culture and aspects of culture change in a humanistic way.[19] They also point out that anthropological biographies may be used for literary purposes, but Spicer chose not to do that, reserving his literary representations of Yaquis to his writing of short stories.[20] Spicer's purpose in *People of Pascua*, as in all his works on Yaquis, is the portrayal of culture and culture change by means of close analysis of a period or periods of Yaqui culture. That he chose to use life histories in order to interpret Yaqui culture from 1880 to 1941 is distinctly innovative for the time, and the fact that his work meets the standards within the field today marks *People of Pascua* and Spicer as pioneering in the execution of personality and culture study in anthropology. *People of Pascua* is also harmonious in approach with two later important works on Yaqui culture, *A Tall Candle* (Moisés 1971) and *Yaqui Women* (Kelley 1978). *A Tall Candle*, later reissued as *A Yaqui Life* (1977), is an autobiography written by a Yaqui man who had family connections in Pascua during his lifetime, though he did not reside there on any permanent basis. In the introduction by Jane Holden Kelley, it is clear that she, as the senior editor of the text, views life history as a valid method of exploring the characteristics that define ethnic identity. Her study of four Yaqui women is clearly based on the thesis that life histories, biographies in this case, are an effective scholarly approach to the investigation of culture. Thus Spicer's work on individual life histories at Pascua village is upheld by subsequent studies by major scholars in Yaqui ethnography.

People of Pascua also marks a watershed period in the career of Spicer, for it is in this work that he first explores the concept of "enduring peoples" that directed much of his later work. From the added knowledge gained through the collection and interpretation of the Pascua life histories, Spicer began to develop and refine ideas about the values, symbols, attitudes, social units, and persistent identity systems that would eventually lead to *The Yaquis* (1980) and to a world-wide study of "enduring peoples" yet to be published.

Over a period of years, drawing upon his early research in Pascua, Spicer developed a theory of ethnic persistence and began to publish material analyzing how certain people sustain their ethnic identity despite pressures by surrounding cultures to give up the symbols and practices that set them apart. Unlike another scholar, Leo Despres, writing on ethnicity in the 1970s, Spicer chose not to focus on how ethnicity may be used in the political arena.[21] As a cultural anthropologist with early training in culture and personality scholarship, he remained inclined to look at ethnicity in terms of ethnic group members' historical, social, religious and personal relations with other groups, rather then viewing ethnicity as a factor in the competition for resources.[22] However, he does demonstrate, in agreement with theorists Anya Peterson Royce and Fredrik Barth, that ethnicity is not a result of isolation, but rather that the maintenance of separate ethnic identity often occurs in spite of, and sometimes because of, increasing contact and interaction between cultures.[23] His *People of Pascua* work, which examines both community and individual relations with neighboring Anglos, Mexican Americans, Blacks, Chinese, and O'odham (Papagos) is a foundation for views on the effects of outside influences and pressures on Yaquis and Yaqui response to threats to their ethnic persistence. His examination of Yaqui response to other groups, both at the macro and micro levels, allows the reader to examine in detail how Yaquis use their ethnicity to survive as a separate group while maintaining or being confronted with extensive and frequent interaction with the plural society surrounding them. By using individual life histories as the foundation for this study, he allows Yaquis themselves to articulate the symbols they employ in defining their identities, their goals within the village and tribe and hence the uses to which they put their ethnic characteristics, and the levels of success they achieve within and outside the community as Yaqui people. From these lives and his observations at Pascua, Spicer is able to identify certain attitudes held by Yaquis toward their own ethnic identity and toward other groups, as well as to analyze the characteristics of Yaqui culture which either accommodate or frustrate the individual personalities within the culture.

What distinguishes Spicer's theory of ethnicity from his peers' is his emphasis on particular elements shared by members of enduring ethnic groups, though, unlike some scholars, he does not rank the symbols of ethnicity by degree of importance for maintaining separate identity.[24] Rather, he demonstrates that the elements of ethnicity are cumulative in nature and that members of a group participate in them in varying degrees, a principle those early interviews at Pascua Village demonstrate in detail. Among the characteristics of persistent peoples he sees as critical to enduring ethnic identity are: a term used by the group for itself that is charged with a sense of moral superiority to the dominant group; a set of geographical locations and place names imbued with symbolic significance and meaningful even when the actual sites are no longer within the group's territory; a set of sacred laws, whether currently in use or not, which provide a foundation for institutions and the social order; dance and music unique to the group; and other cultural symbols that support the most important ethnicity factor—a sense of a shared set of historical experiences and a matrix of sentiment surrounding them that is not shared by any other peoples.[25]

For instance, in an article published in *Science* in 1971, he described identity systems that contribute to the persistence of a people, saying:

In persistent identity systems, the meanings of the symbols consist of beliefs about historical events in the experience of the people through generations. The belief that the experience is shared with and through ancestors is basic in such systems. We may think of the set of identity symbols as constituting a sort of storage mechanism for human experience, a means for organizing the accumulating experience of people. The identity concept thus takes into consideration the cumulative character of culture and encourages the search for process.[26]

Knowledge of the history and culture of the Yaqui people, and especially of those at Pascua, was important in the formulation of this theory, a theory that he would elaborate on in several other essays, as in 1975 when he wrote: "What persists is the moral image that a people maintains of itself through its interpretation of its history, not the particular symbols elected in any given phase of its history."[27] The same year, Spicer's presentation at a symposium at the annual meetings of the American Anthropological Association titled "The Yaquis: A Persistent Identity System," comments further on his theory of enduring peoples and shows clearly that the early work at Pascua made an important contribution to the climax of his career. In its conclusion, he states:

So long as a people's conception of themselves resulting from their unique human experience is not totally disrupted they will be capable of revitalization. Their "culture" may change in ways that make it impossible to describe it in the same terms over a period of years; there may be complete replacement of traits and complexes, but such cultural assimilation may not be accompanied by loss of identity.[28]

As Spicer's ideas matured and were refined over the years, they were cumulative, drawing forward his earliest research into his developing theories. Unlike some of his contemporaries in culture and personality research, he did not go into the field to validate his theories, but drew his theories from his work in the field, gradually building on his Pascua research to offer a comprehensive theory to the growing theories in the study of ethnicity. Thus Spicer's work, firmly grounded in the individual life histories which grew out of his basic community studies, remains consistent as, over a thirty-five year period, he moved steadily toward a wide theoretical view that he could apply not only to Yaqui culture, but to other enduring cultures throughout the world. The experience of Pascua remained with him, contributing to all his later work, so it is no wonder that at the end of his career he still felt confidence in this expression of it and hoped it would be made public.

NOTES TO THE CHAPTERS

Preface

1. Dr. William Willard, Director of the Department of Comparative American Cultures, Washington State University, is engaged in a broad revision of the June 1970 final report on the O.E.O. New Pascua project, *The Pascua Yaqui Development Project, 1966–69: An Office of Economic Opportunity Program in Pima County, Arizona*, by John R. Lewis, Edward H. Spicer, and William Willard. Assisted by Jane Vislocky and Mercy Martinez, the report will include a history of (Old) Pascua, events leading up to the O.E.O. project, an analysis of the Project, and developments in Yaqui history since the close of the Project.

Living in Pascua

1. Arden was established as a single tax colony in 1900 by followers of Henry George. The land was held in trust; those who wished to live on it were given ninety-nine year renewable leases for a lot, for which they paid a rental fee. This fee took care of all the taxes. This unusual system was of great interest to Ned.

Chapter 1: The Cultural Environment of Arizona Yaquis

1. Spicer 1940:133–34.
2. Drunkenness is regarded by Arizona Yaquis as one of the most desperate of their social problems. It is stressed that it interferes with both ceremonial and economic *tekipanoa*. Drinking in itself is not regarded as evil; it is only evil insofar as it interferes with other desirable activities. Drinking is a part of various ceremonies

and is a part of the ritual in weddings and even in baptisms and death anniversaries. Its ceremonial significance probably lies at the bottom of the tolerance with which it is viewed in daily life.

3. For a thorough discussion of this subject, *see* Painter 1986.

4. For a general discussion of Yaqui culture, *see* Spicer 1940, 1980.

Chapter 2: Contacts Between Anglo Americans and Yaquis in Arizona

1. Editors' note: Since the preparation of this work in 1941, occupations have changed due to mechanization and opportunities in new employment.

2. Editors' note: After World War II, machines for picking cotton replaced hand labor, causing a fundamental change in Yaqui economic life.

3. All quotations, unless otherwise noted, are from Spicer field notes, 1936–1941.

4. Editors' note: As Yaquis acquired automobiles and shopping centers were built in the vicinity of the villages, the buying patterns changed.

5. *See* Spicer 1940:25.

6. Editors' note: The status of these villages has changed considerably since 1941. Trends have been toward landownership and town incorporation.

7. Editors' note: New Pascua was founded in 1964 in southwest Tucson, and in 1978 it received reservation status from the U.S. Congress and came under the administration of the Bureau of Indian Affairs. It is now called "Pascua Pueblo."

8. Editors' note: In 1940 the federal government required the registration of all aliens.

9. Editors' note: Indians in Arizona were given the right to vote in 1948; in 1962 the Arizona law against miscegenation was rescinded.

10. *Arizona Daily Star*, August 29, 1940.

11. See, for example, the case of Ivan Williams as reported by Holden 1936:7–8. This is fairly typical of the friendly relations maintained between immigration inspectors and Arizona Yaquis.

12. Editors' note: In 1978 the U.S. Government, by act of Congress, recognized the Yaquis as an American Indian tribe.

13. *See* Spicer 1940.

14. The "army of liberation" was a small band of Yaquis caught while trying to carry guns and ammunition to the Yaquis who were fighting for their land in Sonora. See *Arizona Daily Star*, July 13, 1937.

15. Editors' note: New Pascua and Guadalupe for some time have had police and court systems based on Anglo models.

16. *Arizona Daily Star*, July 13, 1937.

17. Editors' note: Since about 1980 the City of Tucson has cooperated in constructing modern housing for the residents in Pascua Village.

18. Editors' note: Use of medical services and facilities has become common practice.

19. Editors' note: Segregation of Negroes in elementary schools in Arizona was required by law until 1948.

20. Editors' note: The Tucson school district established in 1954 a large elementary school in Pascua which is named for Miss Richey.

21. A *limosna* is a collection of food or money from households by a ceremonial society for a fiesta.

22. Bogan 1925.

23. *Arizona Daily Star*, September 12, 1940.

24. Ibid., March 25, 1934.

25. Editors' note: This law was rescinded in 1962.

Chapter 3: The Relationship of Mexican Americans and Yaquis

1. Editors' note: Considerable change for language minorities has taken place since 1941 with the introduction of the bilingual programs. The 1-C introductory class no longer exists.

Chapter 5: Older Men

1. For a detailed study of Yaqui religious concepts as held in Pascua Village, *see* Spicer 1940. For Yaqui religious concepts in general, *see* Spicer 1980.

Chapter 6: Younger Men

1. Editors' note: The Eighteenth Amendment (The National Prohibition Act or the Volstead Act) was ratified on January 16, 1919. The Twenty-first Amendment, repealing the Eighteenth, was ratified on December 5, 1933.

2. *See* Chapter 2 on contacts between Yaquis and Anglo Americans.

Chapter 9: The Revival of Yaqui Culture

1. Wilder 1963.

2. Spicer, Rosamond B., 1939.

3. *See* Spicer 1954, 1980.

Chapter 10: The Nature of the Contacts

1. *See* Spicer 1940.

Epilogue: Writing About the People of Pascua

Many of the pieces of correspondence, the proposals, reports, and drafts cited below are undated. They were placed in sequence by means of internal information, context, or information obtained from Rosamond B. Spicer, who also gave permission for use of archival materials.

1. Letter to Dr. John H. Provinse, undated, Spicer Archive, Arizona State Museum, Tucson, Arizona.

2. Preface to a draft of *People of Pascua*, Spicer Archive, Arizona State Museum, Tucson, Arizona.

3. Letter to Social Science Research Council, undated, Spicer Archive, Arizona State Museum, Tucson, Arizona.

4. Grant Proposal, undated, Spicer Archive, Arizona State Museum, Tucson, Arizona.

5. Field notes, Spicer Archive, Arizona State Museum, Tucson, Arizona.

6. Grant Report, undated, Spicer Archive, Arizona State Museum, Tucson, Arizona.

7. Letter to "Richard" (Day), July 26, 1941, Spicer Archive, Arizona State Museum, Tucson, Arizona.

8. First Draft, "People of Pascua," Spicer Archive, Arizona State Museum, Tucson, Arizona.

9. Reader Report, undated, Spicer Archive, Arizona State Museum, Tucson, Arizona.

10. Course Files, Spicer Archive, Arizona State Museum, Tucson, Arizona.

11. Radin 1913:293–94.

12. Langness 1965:7.

13. Ibid.

14. Interview with Ruth M. Underhill, November 3, 1981, Denver, Colorado.

15. Langness 1965:10.

16. Kardiner 1939:xiii.

17. Taleyesva 1942:1.

18. Kluckhohn 1945:102–3.

19. Langness and Frank 1981:1–24.

20. Spicer 1983:3–12.

21. Despres 1975:196–99.

22. McGuire 1986:x–xiii.

23. Royce 1982:40; Barth 1969:15.

24. Nadel 1957:32.

25. Spicer 1980:349–56.

26. Spicer 1971:796.

27. Spicer 1975b:49.

28. Spicer 1975a:12.

REFERENCES

Arizona Daily Star
    1934   University Library, Microfilm Archives, Tucson.
    1940   University Library, Microfilm Archives, Tucson.
    1948   University Library, Microfilm Archives, Tucson.
Barth, Fredrik
    1969   *Ethnic Groups and Boundaries*. Little, Brown and Company, Boston.
Bogan, Phebe M.
    1925   *Yaqui Indian Dances of Tucson, Arizona*. The Archeological Society of
            Tucson, Arizona.
Crapanzano, Vincent
    1972   *The Fourth World of Foster Bennett: Portrait of a Navajo*. Viking, New
            York.
    1980   *Tuhami: Portrait of a Moroccan*. University of Chicago Press, Chicago.
Despres, Leo
    1975   *Ethnicity and Resource Competition in Plural Societies*. Mouton Publish-
            ers, the Hague.
Dollard, John
    1949   *Criteria for the Life History*. Peter Smith, New York.
Dubois, Cora
    1944   *The People of Alor*. University of Minnesota Press, Minneapolis.
DuMont, Jean Paul
    1978   *The Headman and I*. University of Texas Press, Austin.
Holden, William Curry, et al.
    1936   Studies of the Yaqui Indians of Sonora, Mexico. *Texas Technological
            College Bulletin*, Vol. 12, No. 1.

Kardiner, Abram
  1939   The Concept of Basic Personality Structure as an Operation Tool in the Social Sciences, in Haring, Douglas G. (ed.) *Personal Character and Cultural Milieu*, pp. 431–448. Syracuse University, Syracuse.
  1939   *The Individual and His Society*. Columbia University Press, New York.
  1945   *The Psychological Frontiers of Society*. Columbia University Press, New York.
Kelley, Jane Holden
  1978   *Yaqui Women: Contemporary Life Histories*. University of Nebraska Press, Lincoln and London.
Kluckhohn, Clyde
  1945   The Personal Document in Anthropological Science, in Gottschalk, Lewis, Clyde Kluckhohn, Robert Angell, *The Use of Personal Documents in History, Anthropology, and Sociology*, pp. 77–173. Social Science Research Council, New York.
Koppers, Wilhelm
  1924   *Unter Feuerland Indianern*. Strecker and Schroder, Stuttgart.
Kroeber, A. L.
  1923   *Anthropology*. Harcourt, New York.
Langness, L. L.
  1965   *The Life History in Anthropological Science*. Holt, Rinehart and Winston, New York.
Langness, L. L., and Gelya Frank
  1981   *Lives: An Anthropological Approach to Biography*. Chandler and Sharp, Novato, California.
Lewis, John R., Edward H. Spicer, and William Willard
  1970   *The Pascua Yaqui Development Project, 1966–69: An Office of Equal Opportunity Program in Pima County, Arizona*. Unpublished manuscript in Arizona State Museum Archives, Tucson.
McGuire, Thomas R.
  1986   *Politics and Ethnicity on the Río Yaqui: Potam Revisited*. University of Arizona Press, Tucson.
Mandelbaum, David G.
  1973   The Study of Life History: Gandhi. *Ethos*, Vol. 14, No. 3, pp. 177–206.
Michaelson, Truman
  1925   The Autobiography of a Fox Indian Woman. *Bureau of American Ethnology Fortieth Annual Report*. Smithsonian Institution, Washington, D.C.
  1932   The Narrative of a Southern Cheyenne Woman. *Smithsonian Miscellaneous Collection 87*. Smithsonian Institution, Washington, D.C.
  1933   The Narrative of an Arapaho Woman. *American Anthropologist*, Vol. 35, pp. 595–610.
Moisés, Rosalio, Jane Holden Kelley, and William Curry Holden
  1971   *The Tall Candle, The Personal Chronicle of a Yaqui Indian*. University of Nebraska Press, Lincoln and London. (Reprinted as: *A Yaqui Life*,

the *Personal Chronicle of a Yaqui Indian*. University of Nebraska Press, Lincoln and London. 1977.)

Morgan, L. H.
1877   *Ancient Society*. Henry Holt, New York.

Nadel, S. F.
1957   *The Theory of Social Change*. Cohen and West, Ltd., London.

Painter, Muriel Thayer
1942   Reader report in Arizona State Museum Archives, Tucson.
1986   *With Good Heart*. University of Arizona Press, Tucson.

Radin, Paul
1913   Personal Reminiscences of a Winnebago Indian. *Journal of American Folklore*, Vol. 26, No. 102, pp. 293–302.

Rosaldo, Renato
1980   *Ilongot Headhunters*. University of Texas Press, Austin.

Royce, Anya Peterson
1982   *Ethnic Identity: Strategies of Diversity*. Indiana University Press, Bloomington.

Savala, Refugio
1980   *Autobiography of A Yaqui Poet*. Edited by Kathleen M. Sands. University of Arizona Press, Tucson.

Spicer, Edward H.
1936a   Correspondence in Arizona State Museum Archives, Tucson.
1936b   Field notes in Arizona State Museum Archives, Tucson.
1937   Field notes in Arizona State Museum Archives, Tucson.
1940a   Correspondence in Arizona State Museum Archives, Tucson.
1940b   Field notes in Arizona State Museum Archives, Tucson.
1940c   Grant Proposal to Social Science Research Council in Arizona State Museum Archives, Tucson.
1940d   *Pascua: A Village in Arizona*. University of Chicago Press, Chicago. Reprinted University of Arizona Press, 1984.
1941a   Correspondence in Arizona State Museum Archives, Tucson.
1941b   Field notes in Arizona State Museum Archives, Tucson.
1941c   Report to Social Science Research Council in Arizona State Museum Archives, Tucson.
1942   "The People of Pascua." Unpublished manuscript in Arizona State Museum Archives, Tucson.
1949a   "Two Types of Culture Contact among Arizona Yaquis." Unpublished paper in Arizona State Museum Archives, Tucson.
1949b   Correspondence in Arizona State Museum Archives, Tucson.
1953   "The People of Pascua." Unpublished manuscript in Arizona State Museum Archives, Tucson.
1954   Potam, A Yaqui Village in Sonora. *American Anthropological Association Memoir* No. 77. Menasha, Wisconsin.
1971   Persistent Cultural Systems. *Science*, Vol. 174 (November 19), pp. 795–800.

1975a   "The Yaquis: A Persistent Identity System." Unpublished paper read at American Anthropology Association Meeting, November 1975.

1975b   "Indian Identity Versus Assimilation." An Occasional Paper of the Weatherhead Foundation.

1980   *The Yaquis: A Cultural History.* University of Arizona Press, Tucson.

1983   Tales of Frailty and Devotion, with introduction by Rosamond B. Spicer. "Return" and "Manuel's Sickness." *Anthropology and Humanism Quarterly,* Vol. 1, No. 4 (December), pp. 1–12.

Spicer, Rosamond B.

1939   The Easter Fiesta of the Yaqui Indians of Pascua. Unpublished M.A. thesis. University of Chicago. In Arizona State Museum Archives.

Talayesva, Don

1942   *Sun Chief, the Autobiography of a Hopi Indian,* Leo Simmons, ed. Yale University Press, New Haven.

Underhill, Ruth M.

1979   *Papago Woman.* Holt, Rinehart and Winston. New York.

Wilder, Carleton S.

1963   The Yaqui Deer Dance: A Study in Cultural Change. Anthropological Papers No. 66 in *Bureau of American Ethnology Bulletin 186.* Smithsonian Institution, Washington, D.C.

ACKNOWLEDGMENTS

As is almost always the case, there are a great number of people who have been involved in one way or another through the developing phases of this book and without whom it could not have been brought to fruition. Perhaps the first of those was John H. Provinse, then professor in the Department of Archeology of the University of Arizona, who early became interested in Pascua. In 1935 he sent David J. Jones, Jr., and Philip Welles to live in Pascua and they made the way easier for the Spicers. To Davey and his cameras also goes the credit for many of the photographs. Without the help of the Department of Anthropology of the University of Chicago we could not have lived there. The direction and encouragement of that faculty, particularly that of Dr. Fay Cooper-Cole, Dr. Robert Redfield, and Mrs. Dorothy Harrington, were invaluable.

A Grant-in-Aid from the Social Science Research Council in 1940 supplied the funds which enabled the research to be completed.

During research in 1940–41 invaluable assistance was received from Helen Ascher, Wilfrid Bailey, Susan Ignacio, Refugio Savala, Albert Schroeder, and Carleton S. Wilder.

After the first draft of the book was written several people read it and gave helpful comments, including John L. Schweitzer, Luke M. Smith, Muriel Thayer Painter, and a reader whose comments were not signed. In the final preparation of the manuscript Octaviana Salazar and Ernesto Quiroga gave much help.

In 1985, when it was decided to prepare the manuscript for publication, the Word Processing Unit of Arizona State University typed it with very great care and willingly made corrections, thus relieving the editors of a long and tedious task.

Dr. Raymond H. Thompson, Director of the Arizona State Museum at the University of Arizona, was always ready with help and encouragement. The Archivists at the Arizona State Museum, Judy Ries and Jeanne Armstrong, did a great deal in making material there available.

The San Ignacio Yaqui Council and the office at Old Pascua, with its director, Lupe Sinohui, made the manuscript of the book available to all the residents of the village.

Of course Ned would most want to thank the Yaquis of Pascua, to whom this book is dedicated, and particularly those whom he selected to be the subjects of this book. He would only hope that it will prove of interest and use to them.

K.M.S.
R.B.S.

INDEX

Orientation
of children, 222–23
in two worlds, 243–50
See also Identity; Participation
Orthography, Yaqui
new, by Yaquis, xix
as used, xix

Pahkome, 262
See also *Fiestero*
Painter, Muriel Thayer, xiv
comment on *People of Pascua*, 300
Papago
attitude toward Yaquis, 97–98
contact with, 33, 77, 96–98, 167–68,
175, 196
and food custom, 182
Papago-Chinese marriage, 94
pascolas to Papago Reservation, 97, 243
Yaqui movement to Papago society,
272–73
Yaqui-Papago marriage, 96
Yaqui views of, 98–99, 103, 215, 242
Yaquis living with, 1
Yaquis at San Xavier, 96, 97, 164, 182,
241
Participation
in Anglo-American world, 198–201, 243
instrumental, 290–93
Yaqui lack of participation in Yaqui
culture, 161–62, 167, 186–87, 192,
220–21, 234
types of participation, 161–62, 288–93,
298
Yaqui participation in Yaqui world, 197,
201, 205, 215–17, 237–38, 241, 249,
279–80
See also Adjustment
Pascola
arts, 32
dancer, 82
humor, xxxix, 160, 223
and natural world, 28–29
and Papagos, 97, 243
ramada, xxix, *xxx*
and sex, 24
Yaqui attitude toward, 181, 194, 234–35
Pascua, A Yaqui Village in Arizona, xv,
296
Pascua Pueblo, xvi, 309n. 1, 310n. 7

Pascua, establishment of village of, 47, 63
Pastores, 121, 205
People of Pascua
delay in publication of, xiii–xiv, 299
drafts of, xiii, xviii, xx, 299–301
editing of, xiv, xv
period of, xiv, 295
pseudonyms in drafts, xviii, 300–301
Pérez de Ribas, Antonio, 4
Persistent peoples, xiv, 3, 293, 296–97,
301–2, 306–8.
See also Ethnicity; Identity
Photographing, xix, xxxvi
at Easter, 103, 242
Pilato, dedicated as, 82–83
Pimas
contact with, 33, 96–98
living with, 1
Piskanyaut (head church official), 122
Pistola, Juan
as "chief," xxxvii, 46–47, 55, 63
in *El Tucsonense*, 77
opinion of, 182
political organization and Lucas Chavez,
109, 110, 115–16, 123–26
political organization and Tomás Alvarez,
147–49, 158, 166, 189, 262–63,
285–86
and status, 143–44
wife of, 193
See also History of Yaquis, in Arizona
Placera mine, Sonora, 212–13, 215
Political organization of Yaquis in Arizona.
See History of Yaquis, in Arizona;
Pistola, Juan
Political status of Yaquis. See Immigration
and Naturalization Service, U.S.;
Citizenship
Population, Yaqui, in Arizona, 1, 264–65
Potam
community study, xlv
connections with, 155, 199, 205
Presbyterian, 57, 179, 184
Prestige, 284–86
See also Status, social
Protestant churches. See Baptist; Jehovah's
Witnesses; Methodist; Presbyterian
Provinse, John H., xxv, xlii
theoretical interest in Yaquis, xxvii, xxviii
Pseudonyms. See Names; *People of Pascua*

Women, 237–38
  insulation of older, 237–38
  withdrawal from Yaqui culture of
    younger, 238
  See also Family; Marriage; and *under* case
    studies
Wright, Dolores, 87

Yaquis, The, A Cultural History, xiv
Yaqui culture
  enduring nature of, xv, 3, 108, 293
  omissions in Arizona, 262
  negative attitude toward, 180–83,
    222–24, 244–45
  revival of. *See* Easter; Revival
  selection of behaviors and beliefs, 292–93
  uses of, 281. *See also* Order; Prestige;
    Security
  See also Individuals; Values
Yaqui culture, recent changes in, xv–xvii
  cotton picking, xvi, 310n. 2
  dress, 208, 209
  education, 311n. 20, n. 1
  economics, xvi, 310n. 1, n. 4

employment, xvi
health, 310n. 18
housing, xvi, 310n. 17
New Pascua (Pascua Pueblo), 310n. 7
new paths, 239
reservation (federal status), 310n. 12
status of Arizona villages, 310n. 6
Yaquiness
  "American Yaqui," 279
  feeling about, 244
  inferior, 279
  not "Indian," 279
  poles of, 237–38
  predictable, 279
  righteous, 278
Yaqui River. *See* Eight Pueblos
Yocupicio, Roman, Governor of Sonora,
  45, 137
Yoemem, term, xxxviii, 12, 99
Yucatán, 157, 187, 205
Yuku, Juliana (aunt of Cayetano Lopéz),
  170
Yuma, 37, 39, 194

ABOUT THE AUTHOR
AND EDITORS

EDWARD H. SPICER (1906–1983) and ROSAMOND B. SPICER first came to Tucson, Arizona, in the early 1930s, to make a community study of immigrant Yaqui Indians at Pascua Village. For the next fifty years they were in close contact with the Yaquis, including involvement with the founding of a new village of Pascua Pueblo and the attainment of tribal status and a reservation. Other books on the Yaquis written by Edward H. Spicer include *The Yaquis: A Cultural History* (1980) and *Pascua: A Yaqui Village in Arizona* (reissued in 1984), both published by the University of Arizona Press, and *Potam: A Yaqui Village in Sonora* (1954).

The Spicers also worked with many other Southwestern Indian tribes, and Rosamond Spicer conducted a community study of the Papago. Edward Spicer joined the faculty of the University of Arizona first in 1939 and again in 1946. Both the Spicers received post-graduate degrees in anthropology from the University of Chicago.

KATHLEEN M. SANDS, who is co-editor with Rosamond B. Spicer of *People of Pascua*, has been a professor at Arizona State University since 1977 where she teaches courses in American Indian literature, folklore, and Western American literature. She is the editor of *Autobiography of a Yaqui Poet* (University of Arizona Press, 1980) and co-author of *American Indian Women Telling Their Lives* (1984). She is currently editing an anthology of contemporary American Indian literature.